Marketing Management for Nonprofit Organizations

Marketing Management for Nonprofit Organizations

SECOND EDITION

Adrian Sargeant

OXFORD
UNIVERSITY PRESS

OXFORD

UNIVERSITY PRESS

Great Clarendon Street, Oxford OX2 6DP

Oxford University Press is a department of the University of Oxford.
It furthers the University's objective of excellence in research, scholarship,
and education by publishing worldwide in

Oxford New York

Auckland Bangkok Buenos Aires Cape Town Chennai
Dar es Salaam Delhi Hong Kong Istanbul Karachi Kolkata
Kuala Lumpur Madrid Melbourne Mexico City Mumbai
Nairobi São Paulo Shanghai Taipei Tokyo Toronto

Oxford is a registered trade mark of Oxford University Press
in the UK and in certain other countries

Published in the United States
by Oxford University Press Inc., New York

British Library Cataloguing in Publication Data
Data available

Library of Congress Cataloging in Publication Data
Data available

ISBN 0–19–927182–8

Typeset by Newgen Imaging Systems (P) Ltd., Chennai, India
Printed in Great Britain
on acid-free paper by Antony Rowe Ltd, Chippenham

■ PREFACE

Nonprofit marketing has finally come of age. Rising from its status as a relatively obscure variant in the early 1970s, it is now widely accepted that marketing has much to offer a variety of different categories of organization. This is a considerable feat of recognition for it was only a few years ago that one would have been severely chastised in many nonprofit circles for even daring to mention the 'M' word in public.

Perhaps part of the reason for marketing's increasing acceptance in the sector is due to the broadening and softening of its definition. Marketing is no longer defined as the provision of required goods and services at a profit. The focus has switched to the satisfaction of consumer wants and, more generally, to sensitively serving the needs of a particular society. Thus marketing has begun to lose something of its association with the relentless pursuit of profit and has evolved into a philosophical approach to the management of an organization that has just as much relevance for 'profit' and 'nonprofit' alike.

In recognition of this somewhat wider definition of marketing there are now a variety of texts on the market which address its specific application to one or more nonprofit sub-sectors. Broadly speaking, this literature can be divided into two categories – highly theoretical texts written for an academic audience and 'how to do it' books written by practitioners for the benefit of their peers. Both categories of approach have a valuable role to play, but the development of this dichotomy is perhaps unfortunate as both categories of author/audience could have much to offer one another. The approach taken in this text is therefore to combine the experience of practitioners working in each nonprofit subsector with the available academic research. As the reader will later appreciate, the amount of research in some areas of nonprofit marketing is often sadly lacking, but where it is available, it can prove a valuable aid to shaping the approach a particular organization might take to its market.

The text has been written primarily for use by undergraduate and post-graduate students, taking nonprofit marketing as an optional part of their studies. It has thus been structured to reflect the usual content of such course modules – namely, an introduction to marketing, the development of a marketing plan and the complexities of marketing in a number of specific nonprofit contexts. It will however, also be of interest to practitioners seeking to learn from the activities of marketers/researchers working in other parts of the nonprofit sector. A broad range of issues will be addressed and sufficient marketing concepts and frameworks introduced to allow the reader to approach the development of a marketing plan for their own organization with confidence.

The general approach adopted in this text has thus been to divide the subject into three sections. In the first of these sections the scale and scope of the nonprofit sector will be explored. We will endeavour to disentangle the complex web of terminology that is used to describe the sector and shed light on the mnemonics used to refer to different categories of organization. The ICNPO (International Classification of Nonprofit Organizations) will be introduced as a means of conceptualising the great diversity of organizations that can be considered as nonprofit in nature. Clearly the exact categories of organizations that will be nonprofit in a given society will vary, depending on the historical development of that society, its relative degree of economic sophistication, the relative degree of state involvement and the existence of appropriate infrastructure supports. Nevertheless the ICNPO constitutes an effective framework through which to analyze the work of nonprofits. In the first section of this text, therefore, marketing's relevance to a variety of these categories of nonprofit will be established and a number of the typically expressed reservations towards the concept explored.

While we are on the topic of reservations, I was criticized in the first edition of this text for using the word 'nonprofit' to define the audience and focus for my work. Many prefer the term 'not-for-profit' or 'not-for-gain', while others prefer to use a range of terminology defining different sectors by what they are, rather than by what they are not. My own perspective on this is that it would be desperately irritating to have to use a combination of different words to describe what is admittedly a very diverse sector. Clarification after clarification is not easy on the eye and from a pragmatic perspective in a global text such as this, it is undoubtedly easier to focus on one word, acknowledge its limitations and move on. Of the available choices I admit a preference for nonprofit because while this does define organizations by a negative I believe it can be a badge of considerable pride. Here we need not be slaves to the market. Nor do we need to ride roughshod over the needs of our fellow human beings in the pursuit of personal gain. Rather we are concerned with the general betterment of society and of facilitating groups of individuals of all races and creeds coming together to make that a reality. What is genuinely distinctive about this activity is that no-one is concerned for their own financial betterment. It is the welfare of others, or the welfare of society that is at issue. Nonprofit therefore works well for me!

In the second section of the text, the implementation of marketing will be discussed at both philosophical and functional levels. With regard to the former, Chapter 2 will examine how a nonprofit might attain a market orientation, the benefits that this might bring and the specific actions that might be required to bring this about. Chapters 3-7 will then move on to consider the subject of marketing planning and guide the reader through the necessary steps that will facilitate the development of a marketing plan for a given organization. Thus, the intention of this section of the text is to facilitate a discussion of how marketing should typically be managed in a nonprofit context. The reader will be introduced to a series of concepts and frameworks that have a general relevance to all nonprofit organizations.

In the third and final section of the text marketing's specific application to social ideas, fundraising, arts organizations, educational institutions, healthcare organizations, volunteer management and the public sector will be explored. These chapters have been designed to build on the general framework for marketing planning provided earlier. The reader will be appraised of the key influences on the marketing function in each case and a number of the specific nuances of marketing in each particular nonprofit sub-sector. Whilst this section has been designed for the reader to 'dip in and out of', a number of the issues discussed in each chapter have relevance for all nonprofit organizations. These 'application' chapters have been carefully structured so as to minimize any overlap of coverage and the reader will hence find that each chapter deals with a different mix of nonprofit marketing issues such as direct/database marketing, the achievement of a marketing orientation, the management of service quality and the development of a marketing communications campaign.

Of course the latter section of this text could be criticized on the grounds of scope. Whilst it is now almost universally accepted that fundraising, arts and social marketing can now be legitimately regarded as nonprofit marketing activity, a number of readers may question the inclusion of chapters relating to healthcare, education and the public sector. These latter chapters have been included because such activities are most definitely nonprofit in nature in a number of different countries. Even in the USA, where much healthcare marketing is for-profit in nature, for example, there remain a number of nonprofit hospitals that could stand to benefit from marketing at both conceptual and practical levels. Moreover in the UK, where perhaps a more hybrid system of healthcare is beginning to develop, the marketing of healthcare will benefit much from the concepts and frameworks introduced in this text than it would from a standard for-profit approach. This is simply because the healthcare environment exhibits many of the same characteristics as other categories of nonprofit – that is, there is a distinction between the markets for resource attraction and resource allocation, there is a need to achieve a balance between the satisfaction of individual customer requirements and the longer-term satisfaction of society as a whole – and there are also a greater number of different publics that each institution must address, even if no exchange (in the economic sense of the term) actually takes place between them and the institution concerned. Such complexities are characteristic of the majority of nonprofit marketing and the content of this text will hence be of particular relevance.

In this second edition I have included a number of new chapters. The section on marketing planning has been extended with a detailed and explicit consideration of topics such as branding now included. I have also added to the final section of the text including chapters on the recruitment/retention of volunteers and a final and broader chapter on the relevance of marketing to the public sector. I therefore believe the text provides much greater coverage than the first edition while retaining its fundamental structure.

I hope it meets your needs.

■ ACKNOWLEDGMENTS

With sincere thanks to Elaine Jay and John Grounds for their help in compiling this second edition.

■ CONTENTS

■ LIST OF FIGURES

◼ LIST OF TABLES

1 Scope, Challenges, and Development of the Nonprofit Sector

OBJECTIVES

By the end of this chapter you should be able to:

(1) distinguish between the public, private, and voluntary sectors;

(2) define and describe the extent of the nonprofit sector;

(3) understand the development of the nonprofit sector in both the UK and USA;

(4) understand the contribution of the nonprofit and voluntary sectors to society;

(5) describe a range of the current issues facing nonprofit and voluntary sector managers.

Introduction

A recent search on the Internet bookseller Amazon revealed there are presently 22 570 textbooks on marketing currently available for purchase. A further search on nonprofit marketing revealed rather fewer examples—a mere 80, many of which appear to be out of print or available only through special order. In the 30 years since Kotler and Levy (1969) first mooted the possibility that the tools and techniques of marketing might have something to offer nonprofit organizations one might have expected interest in the topic to grow—yet relatively few scholars and practitioners have as yet given the subject serious consideration. While a number of universities now offer courses on nonprofit marketing and two scholarly journals have emerged on the topic (*Journal of Nonprofit and Public Sector Marketing, International Journal of Nonprofit and Voluntary Sector Marketing*), our knowledge of this field remains very much in its infancy.

Of course, one could argue that marketing need or societal issues require identical skills and thought processes to the marketing of cars, perfume and other consumer products. The requirement to consider nonprofit marketing as a distinct discipline in its own right is thereby greatly diminished. But is it? Is it really possible to adopt commercial marketing practice in order to make a potential donor aware of a starving baby or encourage a committed smoker to quit? To paraphrase Michael Rothschild, can one really promote brotherhood like soap (Rothschild 1979)?

In this text it will be argued that the answer to this question is no. Although many of the tools and techniques commonly used in commercial marketing practice are indeed equally applicable to the nonprofit realm, the ethos that drives their application can be radically different. Indeed, the underlying marketing philosophy that should guide an organization's approach to its markets must be conceptualized and applied rather differently in relation to nonprofits—a theme we shall return to in detail in Chapter 2.

We are also at the point where we are able to adapt existing theory or develop our own about how nonprofit markets operate and the manner in which nonprofit resources should best be marshalled to deliver the maximum possible value to the various stakeholder and interest groups they serve. Many crass decisions have been taken by managers seeking to apply blindly marketing tools and concepts developed in a very different environment directly to the nonprofit sector. As we shall see in later chapters, some considerable adaptation may often be required.

In structuring this text I have sought to provide three distinct components. The first of these is concerned with introductions—an introduction to the nonprofit sector and an introduction both to the tools of marketing and to marketing philosophy itself. The second stage of the text addresses the marketing planning process and illustrates how marketing planning has equal relevance to the nonprofit context. A range of existing theoretical models will be adapted and extended and a variety of new theories expounded.

The final section of the text is designed to deal with sector-specific issues. As we shall shortly see, the nonprofit sector comprises a broad range of often very diverse organizations. The approach to arts marketing is a little different from the approach to healthcare marketing, which in turn is very different from fund-raising. We will thus explore issues specific to each of these contexts and, in addition, also discuss education marketing, public sector marketing, social marketing, and finally volunteer recruitment and retention.

We begin, however, with a discussion of what we mean by the term 'nonprofit', deal with definitional issues and trace the development of the nonprofit sector in both the USA and the UK. We will conclude the chapter with an exploration of the key issues presently faced by the sector in both countries.

Defining the Nonprofit Sector

Given that it is our intention to examine the application of marketing to the nonprofit or not-for-profit (NFP) sector, it is important to begin by defining what we mean by this term. Over the years, many authors have developed widely differing terminology for what is ostensibly the same cohort of organizations. Labels such as the third sector, independent sector, not-for-profit sector, nonprofit sector, charitable sector, and voluntary sector are used with varying frequency in many different countries. Unfortunately they are all too often used interchangeably and with rather different emphasis of meaning, making it impossible to be sure with any degree of certainty that any two writers are addressing the same facet of society. Salamon and Anheier (1997: 3) argue that this complexity develops because of the great range of organizations that are included in these umbrella

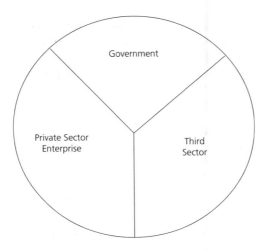

Figure 1.1 The role of nonprofits in society

headings 'ranging from tiny soup kitchens to symphony orchestras, from garden clubs to environmental groups'. Unfortunately the range of organizations embraced by each term also tends to vary, country by country.

Our first task in this text must therefore be to begin to navigate a way through this complexity. The logical starting place is the term 'third sector' which is now in common usage on both sides of the Atlantic and reflects the distinctive role the sector has in society. The notion of a third sector is illustrated in Figure 1.1. The third sector is distinguished by being somehow different from both government and the private sector. All three sectors are important facets of human society and all three have a role to play in the satisfaction of human need.

The private sector or 'market' caters for the majority of human need, certainly in the developed world, matching the supply of producers with consumer demand for goods and services. This market ensures that people can obtain much of what they want and need from others at a reasonable price—or at least that those with money are facilitated in doing so! Economists argue that the market works since suppliers are prevented from charging excessive prices by the knowledge that others will enter the market to cater for the need if they do so. Similarly, the market ensures that a multitude of different needs are met, by ensuring that a reasonable profit will be available to suppliers in each case. There is no philanthropy at work here! The market works purely on the notion of self-interest. As Adam Smith (1776: 119) noted: 'It is not from the benevolence of the butcher, the brewer, or the baker that we expect our dinner, but from their regard to their own self-interest. We address ourselves, not to their humanity but to their self-love, and never talk to them of our own necessities but of their own advantages.'

There are instances, however, where this market mechanism fails and where governments may be compelled to intervene to ensure that certain minimum standards of consumption are met for all individuals in a given society. During and immediately after the Second World War many governments had to introduce food rationing to ensure that those on low incomes were not priced out of the market and starved as a consequence. Equally, the National Health Service (NHS) established in the UK in the immediate post-war period had as its goal the provision of healthcare to all, irrespective of the ability to pay. The term 'public sector' is typically used to refer collectively to those institutions a society considers necessary for the basic well-being of its members. Adam Smith (1776: 122) defined the public sector as:

... those public institutions and those public works, which though they may be in the highest degree advantageous to a great society, are, however, of such a nature that the profit could never repay the expense to any individual, or small number of individuals; and which it, therefore, cannot be expected that any individual, or small number of individuals, should erect or maintain.

Such institutions are both founded and funded by the State, both with its own interests in mind (to prevent civil unrest and to facilitate re-election) and those of its citizens. The funds to provide these institutions and works are derived from taxation (either local or national) and the funding each will receive is a function of allocation, rather than the level of use per se. Thus in state-provided healthcare, it may be appropriate to allocate considerable funding to highly experimental and innovative forms of treatment that, if successful, will benefit only a very small number of people.

In the public sector, the State takes legal responsibility for institutions and the work they undertake. Indeed, as Chapman and Cowdell (1998: 2) note, 'it is one of the characteristics of public sector organizations that they are bounded by and operate within extensive legislation which creates an often creaking bureaucracy, much of which is concerned with the "proper" use of public monies.'

This notion of 'proper' use warrants elaboration. In a democracy, what may be deemed proper use will be subject to change. As various parties stand for election, they map out in their manifestos the role that government should play in all aspects of social life, but in particular in balancing the needs of society for the provision of public services, against the burden of the additional taxes that would be needed to pay for them. While it would be ideal for governments to meet every basic human need, it is probably unrealistic to expect that wage-earners in a given society would be willing to fund such comprehensive social provision through taxation and in practice a balance is therefore created with only the most widespread, popular and/or fundamental needs being met in this way. Other facets of need are simply neglected.

It is within this neglected space, where neither government nor private sector enterprise is willing to engage, that the so-called third sector has a critical role to play. The third sector is distinctive since it comprises individuals or groups of individuals coming together to take 'voluntary' action. In other words, the sector comprises people electing to help other people to resolve issues or concerns. 'The essence of voluntary action is that it is not directed or controlled by the State and that in the main it is financed by private, in contradistinction to public, funds. It embodies the sense of responsibility of private persons towards the welfare of their fellows; it is the meeting by private enterprise of a public need' (Nathan 1952: 12).

It is the notion that the sector is not controlled by the State or by business that leads to the description of the sector in the USA as the 'independent sector'. While organizations in this sector may indeed be free of direct control, the difficulty with this terminology is that in financial terms they can often be far from independent, drawing financial support from a plethora of government departments and/or private businesses. This has been a particular issue in the past 30 years as government has sought to withdraw progressively from many facets of social life, leaving the third sector to shoulder the burden (albeit with support from, often large, government grants). This has particularly been the case in the USA as Tempel and Mortimer (2001: vii) note:

Philanthropy and the nonprofit sector occupy a position in the American institutional landscape unlike that in any other developed country. Undertaking functions typically assigned to government in other countries and also accorded unparalleled tax advantages for so doing, these American institutions are thought to be central to furthering democracy and the search for social justice.

The fact that the sector occupies this third space means that the activities it undertakes can be unique. Third sector or 'voluntary sector' organizations often deal with local issues, politically unpopular issues, or with facets of life that attract little interest from politicians, all too often because few votes hang on the issue. Nevertheless these can be critical issues for a society to address and the need is no less pressing simply because the state or private sector enterprise fails to take an interest.

The characteristic of voluntarism can give rise to what Lord Dahrendorf refers to as the 'creative chaos' of the voluntary sector. Most voluntary organizations are small and involve only a handful of people in trying to solve a particular problem. The individuals involved frequently believe passionately in the work they are undertaking and can apply the kind of constructive energy that can lead to highly innovative and creative solutions to social problems. It is important to realize, however, that the chaos that Dahrendorf refers to can also be a negative since there is a danger that organizations can proliferate and there can be considerable duplication of effort as a number of organizations independently seek to tackle the same issue. There are not the market or political pressures to achieve the merger of similar interests that would exist in either of the other two sectors.

The term 'civil society' has been used interchangeably with that of 'voluntary sector' by many authors. This too has been taken to refer to the formal and informal associations, organizations and networks that are separate from, albeit deeply interactive with, the state and business sector. Authors such as Putnam (1993) argue that these organizations produce 'social capital' which he defines as the norms of trust and cooperation that permit societies to function. The voluntary sector thus plays a critical role in deepening the levels of trust that exist between individuals in a society. This the author believes is essential if a given country's economy is to expand and develop. In the absence of trust, trade will flounder.

The World Bank (2001) has highlighted what it regards as the other defining characteristics of the voluntary sector, outlining a number of key strengths and weaknesses of voluntary organizations. These include the following.

Strengths
- *Strong grassroots links.* Voluntary organizations comprise groups of individuals directly involved with the social issues or problems.

- *Field-based development expertise.* Many international organizations possess real expertise, gained over many years in dealing with the problems of the developing world and are thus better placed than government to deliver aid and ultimately development.

- *The ability to innovate and adapt.* Voluntary organizations are frequently, because of their small size and/or grassroots links, able to adapt and innovate faster than commercial organizations or government.

- *Participatory methodologies and tools.* Many organizations are democratic and inclusive, being driven by a mission rather than the pursuit of profit or votes. As such, they are well placed to seek the views of minorities whose voices may not otherwise be heard.

- *Long-term commitment and emphasis on sustainability.* Since voluntary bodies are established to deal with specific issues, they tend to do so until such issues are eradicated. Freed from the pressure of generating ever-greater profit or votes, they do not pick and choose the issues they will address on the basis of how fruitful they might be for the organization.

- *Cost-effectiveness.* Many voluntary bodies are staffed by professional managers and many employ large numbers of staff. The overwhelming majority of voluntary organizations are, however, very small and rely in no small measure on the time and resources of the volunteers or founders that hold them together. From a government's perspective, they can thus be a very cost-effective way of making a difference to a social issue. This aside, voluntary organizations can also be 'cost-effective' because the individuals comprising them have a genuine and detailed understanding of the issue and how resources can best be applied to effecting change.

Weaknesses

- *Limited financial and management expertise.* The voluntary nature of these organizations often encourages the involvement of those with a great knowledge of, or passion for, the particular issue they are designed to address. They may thus have great 'subject' expertise, but lack financial or management expertise. This must frequently be bought in and/or takes time to develop.

- *Limited institutional capacity.* The small size of voluntary bodies may limit their ability to cope if the issue or cause suddenly becomes more pressing. While international development charities are continually planning for the worst to happen and have well developed plans to cope for most eventualities, they are the exception rather than the norm.

- *Low levels of self-sustainability.* While those individuals who found voluntary bodies may lack little by way of enthusiasm for the work they will undertake, these individuals may frequently lack the resources they need to achieve the mission of the organization. Funding must frequently be sought from government, corporates and individual donors and in the absence of this the organization will fail.

- *Small-scale interventions.* Frequently the small size of these organizations can be a further drawback. The impact that individual organizations might have on a cause can be minimal.

- *Lack of understanding of the broader social or economic context.* Finally, those that comprise voluntary organizations, as we have noted above, can be highly focused on the cause or issue itself. They can thus fail to grasp the 'bigger picture' and fail to see the wider role that they may play in bettering society were they to amend their approach or actions in some way. Some writers have referred to this as the 'blinkered' vision of many voluntary sector bodies.

Of course in this text we are concerned with what Figure 1.1 refers to as the third or nonprofit sector, rather than the voluntary sector, per se. Combining the public and voluntary sectors in this text makes intuitive sense since neither are concerned with profit and many nonprofit marketing tools and frameworks are applied in an identical way in each. Here, however, the similarity ends: the public sector is a highly distinctive and complex entity in its own right and the history of its development warrants separate elaboration. For this reason, although we use the generic term 'nonprofit' throughout, we shall focus on public-sector marketing issues, in particular, in Chapter 14.

In the meantime, it is appropriate to settle on terminology that can comfortably embrace both third sector and public sector organizations. The term 'nonprofit organization' will be used for this purpose, which we define as one that exists to provide for the general betterment of society, through the marshalling of appropriate resources and/or the provision of physical goods and services. Such organizations do not exist to provide for personal profit or gain and do not, as a result, distribute profits or surpluses to shareholders or members. They may however, employ staff and engage in revenue-generating activities designed to assist them in fulfilling their mission.

This definition correlates strongly with the use of the term in the USA and comfortably embraces all the specific contexts of nonprofit marketing that will be considered in this text.

The Development of the Voluntary Sector

All of the great cultures of the world have proud traditions of individuals coming together to help others in their community. This is often enshrined in the doctrine of a particular religion, but it can arise purely as a consequence of historical tradition. The voluntary sector has also been shaped in no small measure by government, with particular pockets of activity being encouraged by the often-arbitrary award of 'tax exempt' or 'charitable status'. Over the years this has come to be defined somewhat differently from one country to another. In many countries, such as the UK, a charity is a distinctive legal form of organization that has a series of tax advantages enshrined in law. A charity is thus a particular type of voluntary organization.

One of the oldest surviving charities in England is Week's charity, an organization originally set up in the fifteenth century to provide faggots (bundles of sticks) for burning heretics, an activity supported by the government of the day. The State has therefore long had a vested interest in controlling what should, or should not, be considered charitable in nature. In Tudor times, those seeking to raise funds for the poor were well advised to stay within the law or risk fines, flogging, or worse. Even the donors themselves had to be mindful of this legislation, at one stage risking the punishment of having their ears forcibly pierced for giving to the unworthy.

Barbaric though this might sound, Tudor England was much concerned with public order and vagrancy, two concepts which governments of this time saw as inextricably linked. It was thus felt that giving should be strictly controlled to encourage the channelling of alms only to those who were referred to as the impotent poor (i.e. those who were prevented by their age, health or other circumstances from earning their own living). The able-bodied poor were to be encouraged to take responsibility for the amelioration of their own condition. In short, they should be compelled to find work or starve. Such a preoccupation would, it was felt, preclude the possibility of their finding time to pose a threat to the State. As a consequence, all legitimate beggars were licensed and private persons were forbidden to give to anyone not in possession of such a document.

Aside from giving of this very individual and personal nature, there were many great 'general' causes that the public could support at this time. Indeed, many of these are very similar to those we are encouraged to support today. In probably the earliest reference to 'appropriate' charitable causes, William Langland's fourteenth century work, *The Vision of Piers Plowman*, encourages rich and troubled merchants to gain full remission of their sins and thus a happy death by the fruitful use of their fortunes:

> And therewith repair hospitals,
> help sick people,
> mend bad roads,
> build up bridges that had been broken down,
> help maidens to marry or to make them nuns,
> find food for prisoners and poor people,
> put scholars to school or to some other craft,
> help religious orders and
> ameliorate rents or taxes.

It was not until 1601, however, that English law officially recognized those causes that might be considered as charitable for the first time. The preamble to the Elizabethan Charitable Uses Act of that year appears to have much in common with the fourteenth-century work alluded to above, delineating as it did the legitimate objects of charity:

Some for the Relief of aged, impotent and poore people, some for Maintenance of sicke and maymed Souldiers and Marriners, Schooles of Learninge, Free Schooles and Schollers in Universities, some for Repair or Bridges, Ports, Havens, Causewaies, Churches, Seabanks and Highwaies, some for Educacion and prefermente of Orphans, some for or towards Reliefe Stocke or Maintenance of Howses of Correccion, some for Mariages of poore Maides, some for Supportacion, Ayde and Help of younge tradesmen, Handicraftesmen and persons decayed, and others for releife or redemption of Prisoners or Captives, and for the aide or ease of any poore inhabitanta concerninge paymente of Fifteens, setting out of Souldiers and other Taxes.

The Act was significant, not only because it outlined these objects, but also because it acknowledged that trustees and officials of charitable institutions sometimes misused the assets under their care and hence created a means by which they would be made accountable to the public. The law empowered the Lord Chancellor to appoint Charity Commissioners whose responsibility it was to investigate abuses of these charitable uses and thereby to protect the interests of those that had chosen to endow charitable organizations. It perhaps bears testimony to the quality of work undertaken by these early charity legislators that this Elizabethan Act was only repealed in the latter half of the twentieth century. Even today its influence is felt, as the preamble to the Act is still influential in determining those causes that might properly be regarded as being charitable in nature.

Of course charities only comprise a very small proportion of voluntary-sector organizations—certainly today. In the UK alone there are estimated to be well over 500 000 voluntary organizations currently in existence, of which only a small percentage are registered charities. The history of such voluntary organizations is a relatively recent one. Prior to the seventeenth century, voluntary activity had largely been confined to charitable trusts and endowments and thus expressed the interests of particular individuals. As the very first joint stock companies emerged in the commercial sector, so too did collaborative philanthropy where groups of individuals got together to achieve social change. One of the most noteworthy developments here was the school movement, with over 1400 voluntary schools being formed by 1729 catering for over 22 000 pupils (Davis-Smith 1995). Other great causes addressed in the eighteenth century included child welfare, moral reform and discipline, reflecting the need to boost the labouring population while minimizing the likelihood of civil unrest. Not all the voluntary organizations formed at this time were philanthropic. Debating societies such as the Kit Kat Club and the Athenaeum were also created, as were early equivalents of our modern Neighbourhood Watch schemes.

The real growth in the number and influence of voluntary sector bodies took place in the nineteenth century, almost certainly as a consequence of the explosion of human need brought about by the population growth of the time and rapid industrialization and urbanization. Between 1837 and 1880 there were 9154 new charities known to the Charity Commissioners, and between 1880 and 1900 the number rose sharply to 22 607 (Williams 1989). Working people also developed mutual groups for self-help and formed pressure groups to campaign on issues as diverse as factory legislation, sanitary improvements, slavery and the observation of the Sabbath.

In the USA, the Elizabethan Charitable Uses Act was highly influential in shaping the development of the voluntary sector, although the term 'charity' is not applied in the same way and does not in this country define a distinct legal entity. In the USA the term has come to mean simply serving the poor and needy (Gurin and Van Til 1990).

Historically the revolution of 1777 led to the creation of many nonprofits as the public was 'swept up in waves of civic enthusiasm and religious fervor' (Hammack 1998: 116) with many churches, clinics, schools, orphanages, libraries, colleges and hospitals being built as a consequence. Indeed, the founding fathers had been careful in drafting the US constitution to ensure that it was difficult for their government to levy taxes, take vigorous action or grant wealth and power to a privileged few. In the absence of strong taxation, religion, education, healthcare, and social services had to be funded by alternative means. State legislators responded by making it easier to create nonprofit organizations and began shaping them to fit the needs of society in a variety of ways, notably excluding a number of them from property tax, which at the time was the most significant source of government revenue. States also granted 'appropriate' nonprofits land and began regulating their ability to create endowments.

It is important to note that this tradition of private philanthropy has continued and become what Marts (1966) regards as one of the most durable factors of American life. When Alexis de Tocqueville wrote in 1835 of his travels in America he was impressed by the willingness of the people to give freely of their own funds for social improvements (Probst 1962). He observed that when a community of citizens recognized a need for a church, school or hospital, they came together to form a committee, appoint leaders and donate funds to support it.

Today the Internal Revenue Code permits 20 categories of organization to be exempt from federal income tax and the majority of those that are able to receive tax-deductible contributions also fall into one specific category of the code: Section 501(c)(3). To qualify for this additional benefit, organizations must operate to fulfil one of the following broad purposes: charitable, religious, scientific, literary, or educational. A number of narrower purposes are also included: testing for public safety, and prevention of cruelty to children or animals. The code also requires that no substantial part of an organization's activity should be focused on attempts to influence government, either directly or through participation in political campaigns.

These tax incentives have largely been held to be successful. In the USA 51 per cent of hospitals are nonprofit—58 per cent of all social service providers, 46 per cent of all colleges and universities and 86 per cent of all museums, botanical, and zoological gardens. The country boasts 1.2 million registered nonprofits and 341 000 religious congregations eligible for tax concessions but not required to register.

Factors Driving the Development of the Voluntary Sector

In the brief history of the voluntary sector outlined above we have deliberately focused on the UK and the USA, both countries with relatively well-developed provision. This isn't always the case, and many Eastern European countries with a rather different historical tradition are only just beginning to experience growth in this dimension of their society. The crumbling of often oppressive regimes, lack of formal welfare provision and strong sense of social identity are leading to an explosion of voluntary activity. Indeed, Salamon and Anheier (1992) suggest that there are six sets of factors which are important in explaining the scope and scale of the nonprofit sector in any one given country.

(1) *Heterogeneity.* The more diverse a given population, the larger the nonprofit sector is likely to be. This factor seems to derive from the needs of various ethnic communities to preserve and protect their own unique cultures and identities. In most cases, this task can best be accomplished through the formation of a variety of nonprofit organizations, which are by definition less susceptible to influence from both government and the private sector.

(2) *Scope of the welfare state.* The scope of a nonprofit sector will vary widely depending on the scope of government involvement in social welfare. The sector will usually expand to fill the most important gaps left by the state.

(3) *Level of development.* Less developed countries may have more traditions of mutual aid and collaboration, but they lack the 'middle class' base which has proved important in the development of the nonprofit sector in the developed world. The middle classes have traditionally, by virtue of their position within society, been quick to recognize the needs of the poorest, or most under-privileged, segments of their population and been among the first to invest both their time and capital in the relief thereof. As economies make the transition from developing to developed, therefore, the number of nonprofit organizations is likely to increase substantially.

(4) *Legal framework.* Interestingly, common-law systems are found to be more conducive to the growth of the nonprofit sector than civil law systems.

(5) *Historical traditions.* Historical and religious traditions can act either to encourage or discourage the voluntary sector. Each society thus evolves its own pattern of societal supports.

(6) *Freedom.* Voluntary activity was actively suppressed in many Eastern European countries. For the voluntary sector to flourish, people must be permitted the freedom to associate, deliberate and act together in the public sphere (see Clotfelter and Ehrlich 2001).

A Classification of Nonprofits

As will already be apparent, the voluntary sector is characterized by its diversity. While this is certainly a key strength, it is also an active hindrance to those looking to study the sector and evaluate the significance and scope of its economic contribution. To achieve this, there needs to be an effective system of categorizing nonprofit organizations and a number of organizations and academic writers have attempted to get to grips with this issue. Hansmann (1980), for example, suggests that nonprofits should be distinguished according to their source of income and the way in which they are controlled. Nonprofits that receive a substantial portion of their income from donations are termed 'donative' nonprofits, while those whose income derives primarily from the sale of goods and services are termed 'commercial' nonprofits. The RSPCA (Royal Society for the Prevention of Cruelty to Animals) is an example of the former, while an organization such as the Eden Project (a biodiversity project) in the UK derives the majority of its income from the entrance fees it charges visitors to the site. Hansmann uses the term 'patron' to identify those individuals who supply the organization's funding. These may be donors, customers, or some combination of the same.

The notion of patron is important since this is the key to the second of Hansmann's categorizing criteria—control. Those nonprofits in which ultimate control rests with the patrons are termed 'mutual', while those in which control is vested in a board of directors are termed entrepreneurial. Figure 1.2 illustrates the intersections between

	Mutual	Entrepreneurial
Donative	Common Cause National Audoban Society Political clubs	CARE March of Dimes Art museums
Commercial	American Automobile Association Consumers Union Country clubs	National Geographic Society Hospitals Nursing homes

Figure 1.2 Hansmann's classification of nonprofits

Source: Hansmann (1980). Reprinted by permission of the Yale Law Journal Company and William S. Hein Company from *The Yale Law Journal*, Vol. 89, 835–901.

Table 1.1 Common mnemonics

Mnemonic	Description
NFP	Not For Profit Organization
NFGO	Not For Gain Organization
PVO	Private Voluntary Organization
NGO	Non Governmental Organization
GONGO	Government Organized Non Governmental Organization
QUANGOs	Quasi Autonomous Non Governmental Organizations
BONGOs	Business Organized Non Governmental Organizations
FONGOs	Funder Organized Non Governmental Organizations
PONGOs	Political Non Governmental Organizations

these criteria—donative mutual, donative entrepreneurial, commercial mutual, and commercial entrepreneurial.

Hansmann argues that this classification of nonprofits is helpful managerially since the category into which an organization might fall will impact on the nature of the strategies it might adopt and the difficulties it might encounter in implementation. He does, however, acknowledge that a number of organizations might simultaneously exhibit the characteristics of two or more groupings and that as a consequence the categories should not be regarded as mutually exclusive, merely as a guide.

Developing the theme of using ownership as the basis for classification, a number of organizations have begun to adopt a complex pattern of mnemonics to define often subtle differences in nonprofit categories. Texts may therefore be found which refer to NFPs, NGOs, NFGOs, and PVOs. Dig a little deeper and you may even find texts referring to subgroups of organizations such as QUANGOs, BONGOs, GONGOs, FONGOs, and my personal favourite, PONGOs. Table 1.1 provides enlightenment.

There are also a number of more detailed classification systems in existence. In North America, for example, the National Taxonomy of Exempt Entities (NTEE) assigns a

Group 1: Culture and Recreation

Organizations and activities in general and specialized fields of culture and recreation

1 100 Culture
Media and Communications
Visual Arts, Architecture, Ceramic Art
Performing Arts
Historical, Literary and Humanistic Societies
Museums
Zoos and Aquaria

1 200 Recreation
Sports Clubs
Recreation and Social Clubs

1 300 Service Clubs

Group 2: Education and Research

Organizations and activities administering, providing, promoting, conducting, supporting, and serving education and research

2 100 Primary and Secondary Education
Elementary, Primary, and Secondary Education

2 200 Higher Education Fundraising Organizations
Higher Education

2 300 Other Education
Vocational/Technical Schools
Adult/Continuing Education

2 400 Research
Medical Research
Science and Technology
Social Sciences, Policy Studies

Group 3: Health

Organizations that engage in health-related activities, providing healthcare, both general and specialized services, administration of healthcare services, and health support services

3 100 Hospitals and Rehabilitation
Hospitals
Rehabilitation

3 200 Nursing Homes
Nursing Homes

3 300 Mental Health and Crisis Intervention
Psychiatric Hospitals
Mental Health Treatment
Crisis Intervention

3 400 Other Health Services
Public Health and Wellness Education
Health Treatment, Primarily Outpatient
Rehabilitative Medical Services
Emergency Medical Services

Group 4: Social Services

Organizations and institutions providing human and social services to a community or target population

4 100 Social Services
Child Welfare, Child Services, Day-care
Youth Services and Youth Welfare
Family Services
Services for the Handicapped
Services for the Elderly
Self Help and other Personal Social Services

4 200 Emergency and Relief
Disaster/Emergency Prevention and Control
Temporary Shelters
Refugee Assistance

4 300 Income Support and Maintenance
Income Support and Maintenance
Material Assistance

Group 5: Environment

Organizations promoting and providing services in environmental conservation, pollution control and prevention, environmental education and health, and animal protection

5 100 Environment
Pollution Abatement and Control
Natural Resources Conservation and Protection
Environmental Beautification and Open Spaces

5 200 Animals
Animal Protection and Welfare
Wildlife Preservation and Protection
Veterinary Services

Group 6: Development and Housing

Organizations promoting programmes and providing services to help improve communities and the economic and social well-being of society

6 100 Economic, Community, and Social Development
Community and Neighbourhood Organizations
Economic Development
Social Development

6 200 Housing
Housing Associations
Housing Assistance

6 300 Employment and Training
Job Training Programmes
Vocational Counselling and Guidance
Vocational Rehabilitation and Sheltered Workshops

Group 7: Law Advocacy and Politics

Organizations and groups that work to protect and

Figure 1.3 The international classification of nonprofit organizations

promote civil rights, or advocate the social and political interests of general or specific constituencies, offer legal services, and promote public safety

7 100 Civic and Advocacy Organizations
Advocacy Organizations
Civil Rights Associations
Ethnic Associations
Civic Associations

7 200 Law and Legal Services
Legal Services
Crime Prevention and Public Safety
Rehabilitation of Offenders Victim Support
Consumer Protection Associations

7 300 Political Organizations

Group 8: Philanthropic Intermediaries and Volunteerism Promotion
Philanthropic organizations and organizations promoting charity or charitable activities

8 100 Philanthropic Intermediaries and Volunteerism Promotion
Grantmaking Foundations
Volunteerism Promotion and Support
Fundraising Organizations

Group 9: International Activities
Organizations promoting greater inter-cultural understanding between peoples of different countries and historical backgrounds and also those providing

relief during emergencies and promoting development and welfare abroad

9 100 International Activities
Exchange/Friendship/Cultural Programmes
Development Assistance Associations
International Disaster and Relief Organizations
International Human Rights and Peace Organizations

Group 10: Religion
Organizations promoting religious beliefs and administering religious services and rituals; includes churches, mosques, synagogues, temples, shrines, seminaries, monasteries, and other similar institutions, in addition to related associations and auxiliaries of such organizations

10 100 Religious Congregations and Associations
Congregations
Associations of Congregations

Group 11: Business, Professional Associations, and Unions
Organizations promoting, regulating, and safeguarding business, professional, and labour interests

11 100 Business, Professional Associations, and Unions
Business Associations
Professional Labour Unions

Group 12: Not Elsewhere Classified
12 100 N.E.C.

Figure 1.3 (*Continued*)

four-digit code to each distinct category of nonprofit, non-governmental organization in the USA. The first digit defines the purpose of the organisation. The second and third digits define the major focus of the organization's programmes, while the fourth defines the nature of the primary beneficiary group.

A similar system has now been developed for the purposes of international comparison. The ICNPO (International Classification of Non Profit Organisations) is illustrated in Figure 1.3. While the ICNPO system has enormous advantages in that we may now compare the performance of the nonprofit sector across international boundaries, it is sometimes difficult to apply. The reader will appreciate that the work of many nonprofits still cuts across the neatly defined categories listed in Figure 1.3. A charity such as the International Red Cross, for example, is engaged in projects that could be classified under many of the headings provided. All such classification systems should thus be applied and interpreted with great care, as a truly definitive classification of such organizations has yet to be developed.

Current Developments in the Nonprofit Sector

The nonprofit sector is currently undergoing a period of radical change. On a global scale, there has been an explosion in the number of nonprofit organizations over the past 30 years, almost certainly in response to rapidly changing environmental, social, and economic conditions. These conditions have recently included the impact of climatic changes, increasing national debt, the emergence of new diseases, the breakdown of some traditional political structures and an ongoing succession of armed conflicts. Aside from this sheer growth there are a number of other key trends that warrant consideration. These include the following.

Globalization

Many nonprofits are now truly global in scope. The funding and dissemination of international aid is one notable global project, as are the recent efforts to eradicate (in various ways) the AIDS epidemic now sweeping the developing world. Organizations such as the World Bank and the International Monetary Fund have begun to impact on the strategy adopted by some nonprofits through their capacity to exert influence over the policies adopted by individual governments in a general trend towards standardization of approach. While some may welcome these moves, it is undeniable that moves towards globalization are gradually leading to the erosion of national traditions and cultures. There is also a danger that the uniquely tailored and innovative approach that characterizes so much of voluntary activity will be lost as people seek global solutions to what might better be regarded as national or even local issues.

It is important to note that it is not only the organization of nonprofit programmes that is experiencing pressure to globalize, but the same may be said of the funding side of their operations. Large corporate donors, for example, may be global corporations in their own right and may require that the nonprofits they support offer a package of benefits in return in a number of the countries in which they operate. UNICEF, for example, has a number of large corporate donors who, in return for support, expect that the organization will work with them to provide recognition and benefits in each of the countries in which they operate.

Individual giving has been similarly impacted with the Internet creating a truly global market for the funding of nonprofits. It is now possible for individuals irrespective of their country of residence to identify and fund what they regard as worthy projects in countries all over the globe. Indeed, it is also possible for the provision of immediate feedback both to acknowledge the donor for the impact their gift will have and to seek other ways in which they could potentially engage with the cause (e.g. lobbying, campaigning, fundraising).

The Rise of a Contract Culture

Aside from the changing patterns of nonprofit provision worldwide, there are also considerable changes taking place in the way in which the sector operates within individual national boundaries. In the UK, for example, many nonprofits are increasingly coming to resemble business organizations in the manner in which they are operated or managed. Legislation such as the Community Care Act (1992) has encouraged charities to bid for funding contracts to provide services on behalf of local authorities. For many charities, this has proved to be one of the most significant changes in their history. Hard-nosed contractual negotiations and business deals now sit alongside the more traditional collecting tins and flag days. Charities are no longer competing just with one another for funds; they are now competing with private companies (and other bodies) for the right to provide the services their mission suggests they should.

The growth in contract culture has encouraged a concomitant rise in the professionalism of voluntary sector management and with it the adoption of an increasing number of business practices. Market forces are increasingly in the ascendancy, which creates a very real danger that decisions will be taken for 'business' reasons (e.g. growing market share, income, or the profitability of a particular service) rather than because the impact on the beneficiary group will be optimal. In the current environment, nonprofits are under increasing pressure to put aside the primacy of their missions and accountability to the communities they serve. If they succumb to such temptations there is a very real risk that they will begin to lose their distinctive identity (Boris 2001).

Public Trust and Confidence

There has been increasing interest over the past ten years in the role of trust in the voluntary sector. Governments in both the UK and the USA believe that trust is essential if the levels of public support of the voluntary sector are to be maintained and developed. Prime Minister Tony Blair has indicated, 'it is crucially important that public trust and confidence in the charitable and not-for-profit sector should be maintained and if possible increased' (Strategy Unit 2002: 6). Greater trust (the government feels), equates to greater giving and engagement in general with the voluntary sector. The maintenance of 'public goodwill' necessary to support both giving and volunteering activity is consistently tied to the presence of trust as the enduring and central relationship that sustains the sector as a whole (Strategy Unit 2002; Charity Commission 2001, 2002). Trust is also regarded as important in this context, since it is trust that defines both the credibility and legitimacy of the sector and affords it a 'higher' moral tone than the private or public sector.

Regrettably, the reason for the increasing interest of government in this issue has been the concern expressed in various national media about the activities of a number of nonprofit organizations. The press, in particular, has not been slow to criticize the sector for what it regards as inappropriate behaviour. Trust and confidence slipped, for example, after the events of 9/11 when nonprofits were seen as slow to respond, and in 2003 alone the news media have focused on improper payments, conflicts of interest and the sacking of at least one controversial nonprofit CEO. Such events, it has been argued, damage trust in the sector and giving/volunteering as a consequence.

Accountability

In a bid to bolster public trust, initiatives have been launched in both the UK and USA to improve the accountability of the nonprofit and voluntary sectors. The public, it has been argued, have a right to know how their donated monies have been applied, what has been achieved and whether organizations spend too high a proportion of their income on fund-raising and administration. In the past, information about the performance of voluntary organizations has been scant, with considerable scope for interpretation existing in the rules governing what must be reported and how this should be presented.

This has been allowed to occur because historically the accountancy profession has been more concerned with the measurement and control of for-profit enterprise. As Henke (1972: 51) notes, 'the profession has never really faced up to the problem of trying to convey to the constituent groups of (nonprofit) organizations the data which would disclose the operational stewardship of the management of these entities'. This is partly due to the fact that there is seldom any real measure of operational efficiency for these organizations. While in the for-profit sector, loss-making organizations are soon forced out of existence, in the case of nonprofits, an operating deficit could easily indicate to donors an organization worthy of additional support. Inefficient organizations can potentially survive as the donor has no way of distinguishing those that are efficiently meeting the needs of their recipient group(s) from those that expend needless sums of money on administration and management.

In a bid to plug this gap, a variety of bodies now stipulate 'acceptable' benchmarks of performance, with the Council of Better Business Bureaus and the Philanthropic Advisory Service in the USA currently specifying a 35 per cent limit, for example, on fund-raising costs. Standards developed by the National Charities Bureau (NCIB) specify that a minimum of 60 per cent of annual expenses should be spent on direct programmes while Hind (1995) recommends 70–90 per cent. In all cases, the recommendations appear somewhat arbitrary and little justification is offered.

At the time of writing, the UK government is encouraging a new initiative to promote the accountability of UK charities. Each year registered charities will be required to complete a Standard Information Return (SIR), which must then be returned to the Charity Commission (the body that regulates charities in the UK). The Commission then intend to share this data with the Guidestar organization which will then allow members of the public access to the information through a new web portal **www.guidestar.org.uk**. It is anticipated that users will be able to compare the performance of charities they are interested in supporting and read data in respect of the outcomes achieved for each organization together with some measures of operational efficiency.

It is already possible to access some of this information on US nonprofits through Guidestar's US website. It should, however, be noted that the information hosted in the USA is based on annual returns to the IRS on what is known as a Form 990 and the data these contain is very limited. Indeed, the categories of reporting are open to widespread abuse, with many organizations actually lying on their returns (Tempel 2002). A large number of nonprofits, for example, show substantial sums of fund-raised income, yet show absolutely no costs of fund-raising. Such creative accounting does the sector no favours, suggesting it may have something to hide and attracting the interest of legislators as a consequence.

Changing Definitions

In the UK, as was explained earlier, the legal definition of charity has changed little since the Charitable Uses Act of 1601. Those facets of society that are regarded as so important as to warrant special attention and in particular distinctive tax advantages have been laid down for some time. This has historically prevented many nonprofit causes, particularly those involved in campaigning/lobbying against government policy, from achieving charitable status. Many seemingly worthy causes have been excluded from registration.

At the time of writing, the UK government is wrestling with these and other issues as it undertakes a complete review of charitable status and the classes of organization that may presently exist. It seems likely that the government will revise the definition of charity and allow a greater diversity of organizational forms, many of which will benefit from tax concessions to a greater or lesser extent.

Growth in Community Foundations

It is worth noting that one of the most popular forms of nonprofit organization to emerge in recent history is the community foundation. Such organizations have experienced rapid growth in the USA, where the number almost doubled in the 1990s, but they are also becoming increasingly popular in other countries (Boris 2001). Community foundations have a strong local base and are typically created to fund initiatives that matter to local people. In the USA they tend to deal with issues such as crime, drugs, and the failure of public schools. In essence, groups of local people get together to deal with issues they feel strongly about. Fostering and encouraging this sense of community has appealed to many large grant-making trusts such as the W.K. Kellogg Foundation and the Charles Stewart Mott Foundation, and a succession of large grants have been made to communities who have been prepared to organize in this way. Community foundations have also appealed to corporate donors who see them as a good way of supporting the communities in which they are based and also of investing in the health and general welfare of their workforce.

Civic Disengagement

One of the biggest challenges the nonprofit sector will face in the coming decade is that of civic disengagement. In many Western countries the gap in income between the very wealthy and the very poor continues to grow. While this is a serious issue in itself, for the nonprofit sector it creates a particular problem. It raises the need for programmes to support the poor, yet reduces the number of individuals who might be prepared to undertake this work. Research tells us that participation in voluntary activity increases with education and income—so the widening disparity between the rich and the poor is becoming a real problem for societies to address (Guterbock and Fries 1997; Hodgkinson 1996).

Of particular concern is the level of engagement in voluntarism we are presently able to achieve among the young. While the under-30s have always been the least engaged with the voluntary sector it appears that a smaller percentage elect to participate with every passing year. The young are increasingly hedonistic and less concerned with the welfare of the society in which they live (Yankelovich 1981; Verba et al. 1995; Pharoah and Tanner 1997; Boris 2001). Re-engaging with this significant demographic will be an increasingly important goal for nonprofit organizations in the coming years.

■ SUMMARY

In this chapter I have introduced the terminology that will be used throughout this text. While a number of different words have been used to describe what is ostensibly the same category of organization, I prefer here to use the generic term 'nonprofit'. This is particularly appropriate given that it is our intention to focus on marketing in both the public and voluntary sectors. It is sufficiently broad in scope to embrace both these dimensions of society and has the further advantage that it is now in everyday usage, being preferred by most practitioners to the arguably more accurate terminology of 'not-for-profit'.

In this chapter we have focused largely on the development of the third or voluntary sectors and indicated the size and significance of each in modern society. We shall return to the development of the public sector in the final chapter of this text. In discussing the development of the voluntary sector in both the UK and the USA I have also highlighted a number of schema that may be employed to categorize nonprofits and thus to define the focus of a particular activity. Finally, we discussed a number of key marketing-related issues that are currently impinging on the sector and/or are likely to in future. In Chapter 2 we will move on from this broad consideration of sector issues to introduce the topic of marketing and in particular how the marketing philosophy could be adopted by a nonprofit organization.

■ DISCUSSION QUESTIONS

1. Explain, for a country of your choice, the role that the voluntary sector plays in society. How does this role differ from that of government or the private sector?

2. Why are there so many different terms employed to define what is ostensibly the same sector in society? Explain how these terms are applied in your own country. Does this differ from their application in the UK or the USA? If so, why might this be?

3. What is meant by the term 'charity'? In the context of the UK what is the rationale for offering a distinctive legal charitable status?

4. What do you regard as the biggest challenges or issues that must be addressed by the nonprofit sector in your own country? How might these be addressed, both by the sector itself and by government?

■ **REFERENCES**

Boris, E.T. (2001) 'The Nonprofit Sector in the 1990s' in Clotfelter, C.T. and Ehrlich, T. (eds.) *Philanthropy and the Nonprofit Sector in a Changing America*, Indianapolis, Indiana University Press, 1–33.

Chapman, D. and Cowdell, T. (1998) *New Public Sector Marketing*, London, Financial Times Publishing.

Charity Commission (2001) *Fundraising Through Partnerships With Companies*, Charity Commission Guidance Note, London, HMSO.

Charity Commission (2002) *Charities and Fundraising*, Charity Commission Guidance Note, London, HMSO.

Charity Commission (2003) *Facts and Figures*, Charity Commission Website, Accessed 20 February.

Clotfelter, C.T. and Ehrlich, T. (2001) *Philanthropy and the Nonprofit Sector in a Changing America*, Indianapolis, IN, Indiana University Press.

Davis-Smith, J. (1995) 'The Voluntary Tradition: Philanthropy and Self-Help in Britain 1500–1945', in Davis-Smith, J., Rochester, C. and Hedley, R. (eds.) *An Introduction To The Voluntary Sector*, London, Routledge.

Gurin, M.G. and Van Til, J. (1990) 'Philanthropy in its Historical Context', in Jon van Til and Associates (eds.) *Critical Issues in American Philanthropy*, San Francisco, Jossey Bass, 3–18.

Guterbock, T.M. and Fries, J.C. (1997) *Maintaining America's Social Fabric: The AARP Survey of Civic Involvement*, Report Prepared for the American Association of Retired Persons, Washington, DC.

Hammack, D.C. (1998) *Making of The Nonprofit Sector in the United States*, Indianapolis, IN, Indiana University Press.

Hansmann, H. (1980) 'The Role of the Nonprofit Enterprise', *Yale Law Review*, 89 (April), 835–99.

Henke, E.O. (1972) 'Performance Evaluation for Not-For-Profit Organizations', *Journal of Accountancy*, Vol. 133, No. 6, 51–5.

Hind, A. (1995) *The Governance and Management of Charities*, London, The Voluntary Sector Press.

Hodgkinson, V. (1996) *Volunteering and Giving Among Teenagers 12–17 Years of Age*, Washington, DC, Independent Sector

Marts, A.C. (1966) *The Generosity of Americans: Its Source, Its Achievements*, Englewood Cliffs, NJ, Prentice Hall.

Nathan, L. (1952) *Report to the Committee on Law and Practice Relating to Charitable Trusts*, London, HMSO.

Pharoah, C. and Tanner, S. (1997) Trends In Charitable Giving, *Fiscal Studies*, Vol. 18, No. 4, 427–43.

Probst, G.E. (1962) 'The Happy Republic: A Reader,' in de Tocqueville, A. (eds.) *America*, New York: Harper and Brothers.

Putnam, R. (1993) *Making Democracy Work*, Princeton, Princeton University Press.

Rothschild, M.L. (1979) 'Marketing Education in Nonbusiness Situations or Why It's So Hard To Sell Brotherhood Like Soap', *Journal of Marketing*, Vol. 43 (Spring), 1–20.

Salamon, L.M. and Anheier, H.K. (1992) *In Search of the Non-Profit Sector II: The Problem of Classification*, Johns Hopkins Comparative Non-Profit Sector Project, Baltimore, Johns Hopkins Institute for Policy Studies.

Salamon, L.M. and Anheier, H.K. (1997) *Defining The Nonprofit Sector*, Manchester, Manchester University Press.

Smith, A. (1776) *The Wealth of Nations*, Letchworth, Dent and Sons Ltd.

Strategy Unit (2002) *Private Action, Public Benefit: A Review of Charities and the Wider Not-For-Profit Sector*, Strategy Unit, HM Government Cabinet Office, September.

Tempel, E. (2002) 'Nonprofit Trends and Challenges', Presentation to the Charities Aid Foundation Conference—*A Lot of Give*, July, London.

Tempel, E.R. and Mortimer, D.H. (2001) Preface to Clotfelter, C.T. and Ehrlich, T. (eds.) *Philanthropy and the Nonprofit Sector in a Changing America*, Indianapolis, Indiana University Press.

Verba, S., Schlozman, K.L. and Brady, H.E. (1995) *Voice and Equality: Civic Voluntarism in American Politics*, Cambridge, MA, Harvard University Press.

Williams, I. (1989) *The Alms Trade: Charities, Past Present and Future*, London, Unwin Hyman.

World Bank (2001) 'Nongovernmental Organizations and Civil Society/Overview'. See **http://wbln0018.worldbank.org/essd/essd.nsf/NGOs/home**. Accessed 8 June 2001.

Yankelovich, D. (1981) *New Rule: Searching For Self-Fulfilment In A World Turned Upside Down*, New York, Random House.

2 Introduction to Marketing: Developing a Societal and Market Orientation

OBJECTIVES

By the end of this chapter you should be able to:

(1) define the role of marketing as it applies to a nonprofit organization;

(2) respond to typically encountered objections to marketing in the nonprofit context;

(3) operationalize the marketing concept in a nonprofit organization;

(4) distinguish between product, sales, market, and societal orientations;

(5) understand the key requirements for achieving a societal orientation.

What is Marketing?

Many definitions of marketing exist, and with each new textbook that is published another definition is added to the list. Resisting the temptation to add my own, it is useful to begin by examining in detail some of the best known and widely accepted. In the UK the most popular definition is that offered by the Chartered Institute of Marketing: 'Marketing is the management process responsible for identifying, anticipating and satisfying customer requirements profitably.' Ignoring for a moment the unfortunate emphasis on profit, there are two very striking components to this definition, which are central to understanding marketing's role in any organization. In short, marketing is both a concept and a function. At a conceptual level, marketing represents a philosophy or approach to management that places the customer right at the centre of everything that an organization does. At a functional level it may be regarded as that part of the organization which gathers research, helps design new services, prices them, distributes them and ultimately promotes them to the consumer. It is important, though, that a wider perspective on marketing be retained. In too many organizations, marketing is regarded only as this latter, somewhat narrow functional field of endeavour and the conceptual level is ignored altogether. Marketing should not be seen as the preserve of a few personnel in the marketing department, but rather as a global approach to an organization's operations that should be adopted by all, irrespective of their position in the organization.

The concept of 'process' is also an important one since the 'process' of marketing in a genuinely marketing-led organization should start by determining customer needs and using these to form the basis of the products or services that the organization will supply. Indeed, an understanding of customer requirements can offer an organization much more than the mere design of its market offering. Value can be created at every contact the customer has with an organization. If one understands what creates this value, it is possible to enhance the design of all an organization's systems with the simple goal of delivering the maximum possible value to the customer. The definition of marketing developed by Kotler and Fox (1985: 5) says far more about the mechanics of how this might be achieved: 'Marketing is the analysis, planning, implementation and control of carefully formulated programs designed to bring about voluntary exchanges of values with target markets for the purpose of achieving organizational objectives. It relies heavily on designing the organization's offerings in terms of the target market's needs and desires and on using effective pricing, communication and distribution to inform, motivate and service the markets.'

It is clear from both definitions that marketing is primarily concerned with identifying and satisfying the needs of an organization's customers and it is equally clear that the actual personnel responsible for fulfilling this role will not be exclusively those located in the marketing department. In the case of universities, for example, while the marketing department may well produce the prospectus and its associated advertising, the contact a student has with the admissions office, an academic in her selected department, the accommodation office, etc. will all be likely to have rather more impact on that student's ultimate decision about whether or not to study there. There is therefore a need for marketing to be embraced as a management philosophy which permeates all departments and all levels within an organization.

Regrettably, however, in some organizations the creation of a marketing department is simply a knee-jerk response to falling sales. The purpose of the marketing department in such organizations is not to ensure the satisfaction of the organization's customers, but rather to hard-sell failing products and services. It is no coincidence that many traditional universities have now created marketing roles and even whole marketing departments as they find themselves competing for students with the new universities from the ex-polytechnic sector. Rather than embrace the marketing concept and design new courses and services around the preferences of the market, many established organizations have simply looked to find better ways of selling their existing services. This is not what good marketing is all about. These two contrasting views of marketing are illustrated in Figure 2.1.

In the first figure (2.1a) marketing is regarded purely as a functional role that can be 'bolted on' to an organization, as and when circumstances require it. Nonprofits adopting this approach would tend to produce the services that the members of their board, often in isolation, decide are appropriate for the target group. Little or no effort would typically be made to ascertain the genuine needs of their users, and failing demand would usually be met with increasingly aggressive attempts to convince them of the desirability of the provision. The marketing function would therefore lack resources for activities other than promotion and would fail to have any real input to the strategic direction the organization might take. It is therefore with good reason that Malcolm MacDonald,

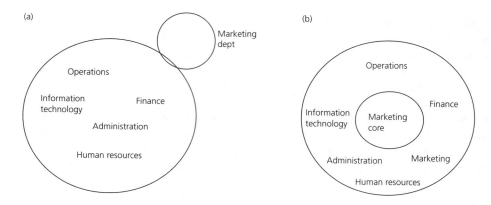

Figure 2.1 (a) Marketing as a 'bolt-on' discipline; (b) Marketing as a management philosophy

one of the UK's leading authorities on marketing, refers to such departments as the 'Corporate Zit'.

By contrast, an organization such as the one in Figure 2.1b would regard marketing as the guiding philosophy which drives the whole approach to the management of the nonprofit. Such organizations plan their service provision in close consultation with users and ensure that they are structured/designed so as to provide the maximum possible benefit and value. Moreover, each of the organization's systems are structured to enhance this value and every employee or volunteer is specifically encouraged to regard marketing as his/her responsibility. The marketing function would be expected to engage in a wide range of activities, including market research, new service development, pricing, etc., and would have representation at the most senior level in the organization concerned. The details of how a change in emphasis from that depicted in Figure 2.1a to that in Figure 2.1b might be achieved is a subject that we shall return to later in this chapter.

Certainly all organizations will want to consider and carefully manage the functional aspects of marketing in order to secure take-up of their service, but a focus solely on such activities will never actually involve the organization in genuine marketing. Indeed it is such narrow views of 'what marketing is' that have specifically contributed to earning the subject a bad name, particularly in some nonprofit quarters. Many arts organizations have until recently rejected the marketing concept because they saw it as being synonymous with selling, which by definition lowered the perceived quality of the service they were trying to provide. Indeed, when the author recently approached a senior member of staff in a neighbouring faculty to canvass views about arts marketing he was told quite categorically that the whole idea of marketing the arts was quite 'reprehensible'. While such one-word definitions of marketing have the merit of being easier to remember than those offered previously in this text, they represent a crass misunderstanding of what marketing is, and what it is trying to achieve. Genuine marketing both begins and ends with a thorough understanding of the needs of the 'customers' that a particular organization exists to serve. The concept therefore has a clear relevance to *all* types of organization, whether they are motivated by profit or not.

What can Marketing Offer?

Having examined what marketing is, we are now in a position to explore the extent to which it can be of value to a nonprofit organization. There has been considerable debate over the years concerning whether the marketing concept can legitimately be applied to the management of such organizations.

In the late 1960s, Kotler and Levy (1969) were the first to open the debate on the relevance of the marketing concept to nonprofit organizations. In their view, marketing had the capacity to grow beyond its role as a narrow business activity and to take on a broader societal meaning. The authors defined marketing as 'sensitively serving and satisfying human need'. While this definition is somewhat broader than those introduced earlier, it does draw attention to what good marketing can achieve. It also has the merit of removing the emphasis on profit that was developed earlier in the CIM definition. Most nonprofits are, after all, by their definition less concerned with profit than they are with meeting some particular need in society. Marketing in this context is therefore concerned with facilitating an exchange process between an organization and its public, so that a societal need can be fulfilled. The question therefore remains—whose need? Dare we refer to customers? The term has already been used in this text and Kotler and Levy are in no doubt on this issue. The authors feel that all organizations have customers whether they choose to refer to them as such or not. A list of typical customers for a variety of nonprofit organizations is given in Table 2.1.

Viewing those groups in society that a nonprofit is designed to serve as customers is a very powerful notion because it forces those responsible for the marketing of

Table 2.1 Nonprofits and key customer groups

Category of organization	Key customer groups
Charities	Volunteers Individual donors Corporate donors Charitable trusts Recipients of goods/services
Arts organizations	Visitors Audiences Corporate sponsors Arts funding bodies
Healthcare trusts	Patients Visitors/relatives of patients General practitioners Insurance companies Government funders
Education	Students Alumni Industry Research funders Local communities Local/national government

such organizations to begin their planning processes by defining precisely the requirements of those customers. Think, for example, of those wonderfully boring museums we all encountered as children. Row after row of neat glass cases each displaying their sterile collection of antiquities. At least if you were physically fit you could drag yourself from one end of an exhibition to another, but what about those with some form of disability? Until comparatively recently few facilities were provided for the disabled and museums were therefore largely perceived as unwelcoming by such groups. Fortunately there has now been a sea change in the sector. The Albert Memorial Museum in Exeter, for example, has completely redesigned its displays. Market research revealed (not surprisingly) that visitors actually did not like to see everything behind glass. Sets were therefore created which now give an impression of walking through a particular age in history. There are also a few animated displays and children can touch and feel some of the less fragile exhibits. Moreover the whole collection has been designed so that those with a visual impairment can still read the written commentaries and those who are confined to a wheelchair can still get a good view of the exhibits and not feel constricted.

What this example clearly illustrates is the difference between a product and a marketing orientation in the arts sector. At one extreme we have a picture of a museum which views its collection as the primary or even sole reason for its existence. At the other end of the spectrum we see a museum that is so proud of its collection that it desires to encourage as many people as it can to come and enjoy it. Moreover, such museums want the visitor to be enthused about their collections and to go away believing that they have had an educational, yet entertaining visit. In short, one form of museum is attempting to satisfy its customers while the other is not. Which of these should be regarded as performing the greatest service to society?

There are many clues in this simple example to what marketing can offer a nonprofit. Specifically the following benefits are worthy of note:

• Marketing can improve the levels of customer satisfaction attained—in the simple example outlined above, the Albert Memorial Museum has been able to substantially improve levels of visitor satisfaction without compromising the integrity of the collection.

• Marketing can also assist in the attraction of resources to a nonprofit organization. Many nonprofits need to raise funds to support their work. Marketing tools and techniques can offer fund-raisers substantial utility and afford them greater opportunities to fulfil an organization's mission.

• The adoption of a professional approach to marketing may help an organization to define its distinctive competencies. In other words, marketing can define what an organization can offer society that others cannot. This may be manifested in an ability to work with particular categories of people in society, or it may be manifested in the way in which such work is conducted. Whatever the case, if an organization can identify those areas where it can add value, over and above that which can be offered by 'competitors', it can refine those competencies and use them to enhance both fund-raising and service delivery as a result.

• A professional approach to marketing also offers organizations a framework within which to work. A systematic approach to researching needs, setting objectives, planning to meet those objectives, and the instigation of formal control activities to ensure that they will actually be achieved should minimize the wastage of valuable marketing resources.

Despite the obvious benefits that marketing can offer a nonprofit, there are a number of important differences between the application of marketing in a for-profit and a nonprofit context. Various authors have discussed these differences and there is considerable debate about whether the differences are as real as they might at first appear. Nevertheless, the following list developed by Lovelock and Weinberg (1990) may help to explain some of the complexities the marketing functions in a typical nonprofit may encounter.

Multiple Constituencies

In a for-profit context the marketing function is concerned with developing goods and services which will then be sold to customers. This, it is hoped, will generate revenue which can then be used to purchase the raw materials necessary to produce the next generation of goods and services, and so on. In short, there is only one constituency that needs to be addressed by the marketing function. In many charities, however, there are two constituencies, since the individuals who donate funds are rarely those who will actually be able to benefit from the services that the charity provides. In other words, there is a clear distinction between resource attraction and resource allocation.

From this simple description you can probably already see why the idea that multiple constituencies might be something unique to the nonprofit sector has been criticized by some writers. It has been argued, for example, that many business organizations draw income from a variety of sources, not necessarily just their primary customer group. Some may attract significant government funding or occasionally seek to raise funds from a new issue of shares. Thus marketers in business organizations can also find themselves dealing with multiple constituencies. It does seem safe to conclude however that the division between resource attraction and resource allocation is unlikely to be as clear-cut as it is in many nonprofit organizations.

Non-financial Objectives

As Drucker (1990: 107) notes, 'performance is the ultimate test of any institution. Every non-profit institution exists for the sake of performance in changing people and society. Yet, performance is also one of the truly difficult areas for the executive in the non-profit institution.'

Setting objectives which can then be used to monitor performance is a particular problem for nonprofit organizations because of the intangible nature of much of the service provided. It is also a problem because, as Drucker goes on to note, 'the results of a non-profit institution are always outside the organization, not inside'. Their results are therefore inherently more difficult to measure. This is not to suggest, however, that nonprofit organizations should not at least try to set targets, although the question then remains, to what should these relate?

It is fair to dispense with profit maximization theories in this sector. Most nonprofits are, by definition, little concerned with profit. They may, however, still be concerned with the concept of maximization, in the sense that they may have objectives that are concerned with input or output maximization. In the case of the latter, many nonprofits appear perpetually to find that demand always outstrips their capacity to supply. The charity for the homeless, Shelter, for example, would undoubtedly view its primary objective as being to help as many homeless people as possible. In the case of the former, some charities have as their goal resource attraction, on the basis that there will always be needs for them to meet. The charity Guide Dogs for the Blind is arguably one such organization as it has been criticized for generating substantial reserves in recent years. The charity would argue however that it is very necessary for them to continue fund-raising as, some day, all the guide dogs they have already supplied will need replacing.

It is also clear that the subject matter of any objectives set will differ from the for-profit sector. Nonprofits cover a very wide range of human interests and behaviours and this is reflected in the broad diversity of objectives they possess. This author has encountered objectives written in terms of the numbers of people aided, an individual's quality of life, changes in public attitudes, and even mortality rates!

Services and Social Behaviours rather than Physical Goods

The majority of nonprofits produce services rather than physical goods. Indeed, many organizations do not even produce a service that one could clearly define. Some organizations exist simply to attempt to alter some form of social behaviour through either direct communication with the target group, or indirectly through the lobbying of government. Nevertheless, the distinction between services and products is an important one since many charities do market services and doing so is an inherently more complex process than the marketing of physical goods. As Zeithaml (1985) notes, there are four key differences which should be taken account of, namely:

(1) *Intangibility.* When a customer purchases a physical item or service he/she can assess it by its appearance, taste, smell, etc. They can therefore 'confirm' their expectations about the properties of the product they are going to receive. With a service, however, the consumer has no way of verifying the claims of the producer until the service has actually been purchased.

(2) *Inseparability.* Physical goods are produced and then purchased by the customer. With services, the process is the other way around. Services are sold first and then produced at the time of consumption by the customer. (In this sense production and consumption are said to be inseparable.) This means that producer and consumer have to interact to produce the service. Marketing a service therefore involves not

only facilitating an exchange process, but also facilitating an often quite complex producer/consumer interaction.

(3) *Heterogeneity.* Allied to the previous point, since production and consumption are inseparable there are few chances for a service supplier to carry out pre-inspection or quality control in the same way that one can with physical goods. Indeed monitoring and control processes are necessarily considerably more complex in the context of services.

(4) *Perishability.* Services cannot be stored in the same way that one can store food or electrical items in a retail outlet. If a theatrical performance begins with a half-empty house, or there are last-minute cancellations of a physician's appointments, those services have been lost forever. Marketers, therefore have a more complex balancing operation to perform to ensure that their services remain as optimally utilized as possible

These differences are summarized in Table 2.2.

Where nonprofits are concerned with physical behaviours rather than services, additional complications arise. Attempting to influence social behaviours will never be a non-controversial task, no matter how much benefit may ultimately accrue to society as a result of such endeavours. Organizations such as ASH, the anti-smoking campaign, for example, continually face pressure from organizations with diametrically opposed views, such as nonprofits set up by smokers' rights activists. This is not competition in the way that one may define it in the for-profit context, but rather an attempt by one nonprofit to deride the work of another.

Table 2.2 Services are different

Goods	Services	Resulting implications
Tangible	Intangible	Services cannot be inventoried Services cannot be patented Services cannot be readily displayed or communicated
Standardized	Heterogeneous	Service delivery and customer satisfaction depend on employee actions Service quality depends on many uncontrollable factors There is no sure knowledge that the service delivered matches what was planned and expected
Production separate from consumption	Simultaneous production and consumption	Customer participates in and affects the transaction Customers affect each other Decentralization may be essential Mass production is difficult
Non-perishable	Perishable	It is difficult to synchronize supply and demand with services Services cannot be returned or resold

Source: Zeithaml et al. (1996), *Services Marketing*, McGraw Hill, New York. Reproduced with the kind permission of McGraw Hill.

Public Scrutiny/Non-market Pressures

Certain categories of organization within the nonprofit sector are open to intense levels of public scrutiny. The emergency services, local authorities, hospitals, and even universities are subject to regular public scrutiny. UK universities, for example, are subject to a comprehensive audit of the quality of their teaching and research every four years. In the healthcare sector, the government White Paper 'Working For Patients' introduced an independent body, the Audit Commission, into the UK healthcare framework. The commission (which has been performing a similar function for local authorities for some years) now has responsibility for ensuring that the National Health Service continues to provide 'value for money'. Such public scrutiny simply does not occur on the same scale in a for-profit business context.

Nonprofits also have to contend with a variety of other non-market pressures. While no-one would claim for a moment that it is easy for a business organization to be able to forecast demand for its products, demand for the services of a nonprofit can fall away to nothing or literally double overnight. The nature of Oxfam's work overseas with Third World countries can change radically from year to year depending on political, economic, and climatic conditions. The very nature of their focus on the disadvantaged makes it almost impossible to know where future priorities might lie.

The instability of the environment in which many nonprofits operate thus contributes to the fact that such organizations often have less control over their own destiny than their counterparts in the for-profit sector. Marketers in nonprofits therefore have a much more complex role to perform.

Tension between Mission and Customer Satisfaction

The final key difference that may be encountered in the nonprofit sector relates to the nature of some nonprofit missions. Many such organizations are compelled by their mission to take a long-term view of their relationships with their target markets. Health and welfare groups in the Third World, for example, may be promoting the use of contraception in direct conflict with the established patterns of local belief and culture. Similarly many theatres and arts centres have a mission to explore a wide range of art forms, not just to provide those forms of entertainment that they know will be well patronized by their local community. There is therefore a tension between the satisfaction of current customer needs and the fulfilment of a particular organization's mission. Short-term customer satisfaction may often have to be sacrificed by nonprofits as they take a longer-term view of the benefit they can offer to society.

The idea that organizations should take this longer-term view of the welfare of their 'customer' groups is a notion that one would rarely encounter in the for-profit sector. Business organizations make their money by satisfying the immediate needs of their customers today, and need therefore to devote the maximum effort to the achievement of this goal. One of the key advantages of a strong nonprofit sector is that the division between resource attraction and resource allocation affords a greater opportunity for a longer-term perspective to be adopted. While the needs of the current customer group are important (and will be ignored completely at the organization's peril), nonprofits do have the luxury of being able to strike a balance between the short- and long-term needs of their key customer groups. Hence the role of marketing in this context genuinely becomes one of 'sensitively serving the needs of society'.

Typical Objections to Marketing

Despite the benefits that marketing can provide, there have been a number of objections raised over the years when writers have mooted the possibility of its application to the nonprofit sector. The most common of such objections, usually raised by managers working in the sector, are dealt with below.

'Marketing is not Necessary'

This objection stems from a belief that the nonprofit is doing worthwhile work and is therefore worthy of support for its own sake. In the UK this idea has been particularly prevalent in the education sector where established universities have traditionally not felt the need to market their services, as they have expected students to research the quality of various institutions and to seek them out to study a particular subject. The idea that academics are somehow intellectual monks to whom people will turn for an education because of the perceived quality of an institution is now hopelessly outdated. Students have a much wider choice of courses than they had even ten years ago and because of this can pick and choose the institutions at which they want to study. Given that a much larger percentage of young people are being encouraged to enter higher education, the profile of the student body has also changed. As a result, all but the Oxbridge universities are now finding themselves having to compete hard to attract the brightest students.

'Marketing Invades an Individual's Privacy'

Marketing is viewed by some as intrusive as it is seen as invading an individual's right to privacy. This criticism is perhaps a little more difficult to answer since at some point marketers will undoubtedly conduct research in an attempt to identify consumer needs. As Kotler and Clarke (1987: 22) point out, 'Market research in any consumer industry is invasive; market researchers may enter people's homes to ask about likes and dislikes, beliefs and attitudes, income and other personal characteristics. Moreover in (the nonprofit sector), the research is more likely to cover sensitive areas individuals would prefer not to reveal to strangers.'

Of course, if organizations are to get close to their market and understand what requirements customers might have, a certain amount of marketing research will always be necessary. This is particularly so in the context of the nonprofit sector since, as we have already seen, the concern is often with services and social behaviours which are by definition more difficult for an organization to monitor. However, if one considers that the ultimate aim of this research should be to benefit society as a whole, perhaps an occasional 'invasion of privacy' could be forgiven.

Of course, market research is simply one way in which an individual's privacy can be compromised. Many forms of promotion are judged to be unwelcome and invasive. Advertising, direct mail, telemarketing, etc., have all attracted a bad reputation at one point or another for entering someone's home with unwelcome messages about an equally unwanted product or service. This is not however a criticism of marketing per se, but rather a criticism of the way that marketing tools have been employed by particular organizations. Poorly planned and executed campaigns may often target individuals who have no interest in the service being promoted, and this gives the marketing profession a bad name. Neither does it make sense for nonprofits to engage in such activities as they waste valuable marketing resources. Instead organizations should look to refine their targeting and to develop a more focused campaign to promote their services only to those who would stand to benefit.

'Marketing Lowers Perceived Quality'

The author was recently approached by a university admissions officer who felt aggrieved that his university was going to begin actively marketing its undergraduate courses. This, he felt, would lower the perceived quality of those courses in the minds of potential students. In his words, his 'university will appear desperate' to attract students. On further enquiry what he was actually objecting to was the proposed advertising of his undergraduate courses. He may indeed have had a point since until recently the advertising of undergraduate courses was taboo in the UK. The existence of a gentlemen's agreement between universities to avoid unseemly competition precluded the use of advertising (except during clearing). It would therefore be relatively unusual for a university to advertise and it may yet prove to have a detrimental effect on recruitment.

However, the reader will by now appreciate that marketing is much more than mere advertising alone and this criticism is therefore based on a false premise. The idea that the attainment of a customer focus would somehow result in a drop in the quality of service provision is frankly obtuse. There are regrettably, however, still a significant number of organizations that have failed to grasp the value of marketing as a concept and this objection is thus still one that is commonly encountered.

'Marketing is Immoral'

This objection also stems from a fundamental misunderstanding of the marketing concept. It is often raised because marketing is seen as manipulating consumers into purchasing goods and services that they don't really need. The origins of this objection are rooted in a failure to grasp the difference between marketing and sales. It is certainly true that a sales-oriented organization continually strives to persuade customers to buy as much of their product or service as possible. Such organizations are little concerned with the genuine needs of customers. Market-oriented organizations, on the other hand, have realized that such an emphasis is ultimately self-defeating. Instead they focus on supplying customers with the services they actually need and make it clear who their target groups actually are, in an attempt to avoid unnecessary purchases by those who would be better served by another organization. If this sounds a little trite, it is worth remembering that this is simply good business practice. Dissatisfied customers are estimated to discuss their experiences with an average of seven close friends, relatives, and colleagues. Making a sale at any cost can hence result in a significant amount of negative word-of-mouth 'advertising' and is ultimately self-defeating.

'Marketing will Stifle Innovation'

This criticism is a little more subtle. It is raised by those who argue that a marketing-oriented organization will attempt to serve studiously the needs of its target markets. It will concentrate harder on trying to exactly match its products/services with the profile of those demanded by its customers. In doing so, however, it will be unlikely to devote much time and effort to the development of radical new initiatives which could ultimately benefit society as a whole. Consumers do not generally enjoy change and are hence unlikely to suggest it to market researchers if asked.

Clearly there is a danger that marketing could force an organization unwittingly into a form of management myopia, but this pitfall is perhaps more relevant to a business organization where profit is the prime consideration. Since new product development is an inherently risky strategy, a business organization will tend to demand considerable evidence that an investment in a new product/service is likely to pay off. In the nonprofit context, however, one could legitimately argue that managers have considerably more latitude in terms of how they choose to fulfil an organization's mission, particularly where there is a separation of resource attraction and resource allocation. While one still has to be conscious that funders have their own agenda and would not wish to see a nonprofit engage in unnecessary risk, it is certainly true that some funders may actually encourage the organization they are supporting to be innovative. This is the case with much arts funding; indeed, evidence of the ability to innovate may well be one criterion to be awarded such funding in the first place.

In essence these are the typical objections that are raised to marketing in a nonprofit context. Those readers who are interested in learning more about specific objections raised in the context of healthcare or education are advised to consult Kotler and Clarke (1987) or Kotler and Fox (1985).

The Development of the Marketing Concept: Products, Sales, and Marketing Orientations

Marketing ideas and concepts are not new—the underlying concepts have been around for centuries. As long ago as 1776, Adam Smith, widely regarded as the father of modern economics, remarked that:

Consumption is the sole end and purpose of all production; and the interest of the producer ought to be attended to, only so far as it may be necessary for promoting that of the consumer. The maxim is so perfectly self-evident that it would be absurd to attempt to prove it. But in the mercantile system, the interest of the consumer is almost constantly sacrificed to that of the producer; and it seems to consider production, not consumption, as the ultimate end and object of all industry and commerce.

'Perfectly self evident' this concept may be, but in some quarters little appears to have changed over the past 220 years! Indeed it was not until comparatively recently that the idea of focusing on the needs and wants of consumers has come to the fore. Up to the beginning of the twentieth century much of British industry could be criticized for concentrating excessively on the economics of production. With an almost insatiable demand worldwide for the goods and services it could produce, there was little need to focus on consumer needs, as someone somewhere would undoubtedly want the product. It is therefore no surprise to find that management theorists of the time were concerned with concepts such as efficiency and regarded management as a pure science which could be explored and developed in an attempt to find 'the one best way of doing things'. Organizations from around this time could therefore be regarded as being production-oriented. A typical structure for such an organization is given in Figure 2.2.

With the recession of the 1920s and 1930s, however, producers suddenly found themselves facing a considerable slump in demand. Being an efficient producer was no longer enough to guarantee survival. The efficient production of inventory which could not be sold was a sure route to disaster. In recognition of this, a change in emphasis evolved. The sales function within the organization began to take on a new significance. A typical organization structure for what might be termed a sales-oriented organization is shown in Figure 2.3.

Once again, organizations of the time were little concerned with the actual needs and wants of consumers. The focus was largely on how best to sell what the company could produce. It is worth noting in Figure 2.3 how the sales function has risen to a more dominant position and appears to embrace all forms of contact with the customer, including the provision of customer service. The division between sales and the advertising and PR function is also worthy of note, particularly as the latter function was perceived as being of far less significance. This is a division typical of the

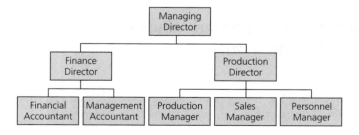

Figure 2.2 Structure of a typical production-oriented organization

Figure 2.3 Structure of a typical sales-oriented organization

time and it reflects the dominant paradigm—the fervent desire to sell product to the customers.

It is interesting to note that while few genuinely production-oriented organizations remain in business today, there are a large number of sales-oriented organizations still in existence. Those organizations that have retained a sales orientation tend to be those that provide a product/service that will only ever have to be purchased once. It could therefore be argued that the concept of customer satisfaction is less important since the organization will not be looking to solicit a repurchase. Such a philosophy ignores the fact that consumers talk to one another, and organizations can very quickly obtain a poor reputation for customer service. If you would like some proof of this, compile your own list of organizations that you consider to be sales-oriented and ask a colleague to do likewise. My guess is that a comparison of both lists will reveal considerable similarity.

After the Second World War, the pattern of world trade was changed irrevocably. By the early 1950s, companies in the UK, for example, suddenly found themselves competing with organizations in America, Japan, and a revitalized Europe. Consumers were faced with a considerable choice of producer from whom to purchase. Moreover, the mushrooming of the mass media made consumers more generally aware of the range of purchase options open to them. Faced with this choice, consumers were finally able to exercise considerable power over producers and to elect to purchase only from those that they felt would adequately service their needs.

To be truly successful in these newly competitive markets, organizations needed to focus on customer needs and ensure that they met those needs better than any of the competition. Organizations therefore finally began to recognize the importance of developing a customer or market focus, and a new type of organization began to emerge. Figure 2.4 illustrates a structure typical of a market-oriented organization.

This new type of organization placed a high emphasis on the collection of marketing research and its use to identify customer needs. This information would then be used to inform new product development, to develop appropriate pricing strategies, to make the product accessible to the market, and, finally, to promote the advantages that it could offer the consumer and reassure them that it could meet their needs. As a result, the sales function is no longer of such importance. Indeed, if the marketing is handled correctly there may be no need to 'sell' the product at all—it should 'sell' itself. It is interesting to note, therefore, that the sales function in this example has now been

Figure 2.4 Structure of a typical market-oriented organization

subordinated to marketing in recognition that selling is simply one component of an overall marketing mix.

Operationalizing the Marketing Concept

In the brief history of marketing described above, the term 'market orientation' was introduced for the first time. A market-oriented organization is in essence one that has embraced the marketing concept and successfully operationalized it. Kotler and Clarke (1987) define marketing orientation as follows: 'A marketing orientation holds that the main task of the organization is to determine the needs and wants of target markets and to satisfy them through the design, communication, pricing and delivery of appropriate and competitively viable products and services.' While this definition makes it clear what market orientation is, it offers little insight into how it might be achieved. Kohli and Jaworski (1990) thus prefer to define it as: 'The generation of appropriate market intelligence pertaining to current and future customer needs, and the relative abilities of competitive entities to satisfy these needs; the integration and dissemination of such intelligence across departments; and the coordinated design and execution of the organization's strategic response to market opportunities.'

Narver and Slater (1990) have usefully distilled the definition given above into three behavioural strands, namely customer orientation, competitor orientation, and interfunctional coordination, and argue that all three should be regarded as being of equal importance. These are illustrated in Figure 2.5.

Customer orientation involves the organization in achieving a sufficient understanding of its target markets to be able to create superior value for them. Since in a service environment the creation of value is often highly dependent on the quality of customer interactions with staff, the achievement of a market orientation thus involves the development of an appropriate set of cultural attitudes that should ultimately permeate the whole organization (Deshpande and Webster 1989).

The concept of a competitor orientation involves the organization in understanding the short-term strengths/weaknesses and long-term capabilities/strategies of both its current and future competitors. This is essential if the organization is to avoid being overtaken by competitive innovation (see, for example, Porter (1985)).

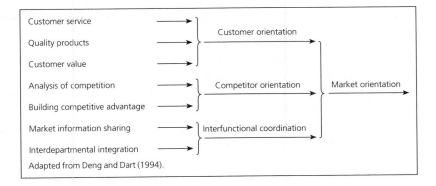

Figure 2.5 The components of market orientation
Source: Adapted from Deng and Dart (1994).

Interfunctional coordination refers to how the organization utilizes its internal resources in the creation of superior value for target consumers. It is important, for example, for opportunities for synergy to be exploited across traditional departmental boundaries and for customer and competitive intelligence to be shared constructively between all those who stand to benefit. Kohli and Jaworski (1990) expand on the concept of interfunctional coordination in a detailed study of a number of market-oriented organizations. The authors suggest that such organizations can be characterized as having:

- a close integration of the marketing function into the organizational structure and strategic planning process;
- a primary identification with the organization as a whole rather than individual departments;
- inter-departmental relations based on cooperation rather than rivalry.

It is important to recognize that the preceding discussion is of more than simply theoretical interest. A succession of studies have now demonstrated links between the extent to which an organization has successfully operationalized the marketing concept (i.e. its degree of market orientation) and its performance relative to others operating in the same sector. It is also important to note that while the majority of these have been conducted in the for-profit context, there is now an emerging body of literature that suggests it is equally well related to many facets of the performance of nonprofit organizations.

For this reason in the next section we shall examine each of Narver and Slater's behavioural strands in more detail, and suggest how each of these behaviours might be inculcated.

Achieving a Customer Focus

The achievement of a customer focus, particularly among recipient groups, has traditionally been harder for many nonprofits to accomplish because staff and even volunteers have historically failed to value them. While this sounds a little counter-intuitive given the ethos of many voluntary organizations, Bruce (1995) suggests that there are a number of reasons why this should be so, including the following.

- *Monopolistic position.* The position of many nonprofits in the market is one of a monopoly supplier. There can therefore be a danger that customers are so reliant on their services that such organizations may adopt a 'take it or leave it' attitude and fail to take the time to adapt their offerings to individual needs.

- *Demand far exceeds supply.* Often even where competition does exist, the demand in many nonprofit markets for the services the organization can supply is so great that they can never hope to meet even a fraction of it. The temptation here for nonprofits is to tackle the most homogenous categories of need, since these are usually easier to serve in volume with an undifferentiated service. There may be occasions, however, when such categories of need are not the most pressing and smaller groups of customers with more acute levels of need may find themselves ill-served by the standard services available.

- *Patronizing attitude of 'haves' to 'have nots'.* There is a particular danger of this phenomenon in markets where the demand is high for the service provided. Service delivery staff may take the view that recipients are lucky to be among the 'chosen few' and should by implication feel only gratitude towards the supplying organization. The idea that recipients have the right to express any form of negative comment or criticism remains anathema to many.

- *Professional training encourages the view that 'I know what's best for you'.* Many nonprofit service providers are highly trained professionals, who possess expert knowledge in their field. They may therefore feel that they have a complete understanding of the needs of the recipient and thereby not be sensitive to signs of differing individual need.

- *Motivation of belief-based organizations.* Nonprofits whose mission is to promote certain behaviours because of religious beliefs may fail to take a true account of the needs of their recipients. Service providers may strive to inculcate behaviour patterns that directly conflict with what the recipients perceive to be their needs. There is of course, nothing inherently wrong with this approach, as it may cut to the heart of the reason for the nonprofit's existence, but even the most zealous of religiously oriented organizations may find their path somewhat easier if they begin by understanding current customer requirements. It is so much easier to plan a strategy if one understands where one is starting from.

- *Action-oriented approach.* Historically one of the greatest strengths of the voluntary sector has been its ability to respond rapidly to changing patterns of need. Unconstrained by government bureaucracy or the profit needs of shareholders, voluntary organizations have been able to take immediate action, specifically tailored at a local level to alleviate the distress and/or suffering of those in need. While the speed of response may legitimately be regarded as a very real strength, there are also key difficulties that can be encountered with this approach. Principal among these is the fact that fundamental *a priori* customer research is not widespread throughout the sector. This in turn can create a situation where the solutions proposed by voluntary organizations are sub-optimal from a customer's perspective because their real needs have not been fully understood.

Bruce is clearly not optimistic about the ability of nonprofits to achieve a genuine customer focus among their beneficiary groups. In many cases there remain very real difficulties to be overcome. Nevertheless, the culture within the nonprofit sector is changing and it is fair to say that a great many organizations are now becoming increasingly focused on the task of satisfying their customers.

Developing a Competitor Orientation

The first step in developing a competitor orientation is once again research. Organizations with strong competitor orientations continually evaluate their positions in respect of each of their key competitors, in order to discover areas of strength and weakness and to find ways of strengthening their own competitive advantage (see for example Bennett (2003)). The only way that this can be achieved is through the creation of an effective competitor monitoring system, which generates benchmarking data in respect of each key aspect of competitor operations and alerts the organization to actual and potential competitive innovations. This benchmarking data allows a nonprofit organization to compare factors such as those listed below.

- Its own portfolio of provision against other actual or potential providers. While an often insatiable demand for nonprofit services ensures that most adequately managed organizations will continue to have the capability to provide some form of service to their client groups, some organizations may be guilty of providing services which might be more effectively provided by others in the market. Nonprofits, perhaps more than any other category of organization (by virtue of their use of third-party funds) have a duty to ensure that they provide the most appropriate range of services to their recipient groups. They can only achieve this by monitoring competitive strengths and concentrating only on those areas where they have a comparative advantage. This may take the form of specialist expertise most closely suited to one form of need, or it may, for example, be the ease of access to one category of recipient group. A competitor orientation can hence optimize the use of resources across the sector as a whole and maximize the potential benefit to society as a result.

- The costs of providing goods and services to their recipient groups. The level of need that a nonprofit is able to cater for compared to other service providers will not only be of concern to management but also to potential funders. Most will want to ensure that their funding is directed to the organization that is likely to have the most impact on the target beneficiary group. It is thus no surprise to learn that most charitable trusts require quite detailed information about the category and level of need that will be serviced before their trustees will reach a decision in respect of whether an application for funding will be granted.

- The costs of fund-raising. All nonprofits that have to fund-raise to conduct their primary activity should be concerned with the relative efficiency of each form of fund-raising activity. They will want, for example, to ascertain from which sources major competitors derive their income and the fund-raising techniques (such as direct mail, telemarketing, etc.) used to solicit it. A comparison of both the sources of funding utilized and the expenditures on each fund-raising technique relative to income generated will aid management in targeting future scarce fund-raising resources more effectively (see for example Sargeant et al. 2003).

The design of a competitive information system and the gathering of competitive and benchmarking data are but the first stages in developing a competitor orientation. Having gathered information about other providers in the market, or key competitors for funding, the next stage is to use it to the organization's own advantage. Profiling competitor strengths and weaknesses can allow an organization to see where its performance lags behind the competition, but it can also highlight areas where it either outperforms the competition, *or has the capacity to do so*. These areas are key, because they could represent a major source of competitive advantage that an organization has over its rivals. This can then form the basis of extremely powerful communications with all the categories of customer with whom the organization has contact. For example, if an organization by virtue of its extensive network of volunteers has the potential to be the lowest-cost provider in a given market, this fact needs to be communicated strongly to all potential funders who will undoubtedly be looking for the organization that can make the most effective use of their resources. Similarly, if an organization has the leading researchers working in a particular field on its payroll, this fact should be emphasized to both recipients and funders alike because it has the capacity clearly to identify the organization as a market leader and therefore position it as being the most worthy of support/patronage.

There are a number of bases that can be used to develop a competitive advantage. These include:

- *Low cost.* The key to the competitive advantage here is the fact that the organization can provide goods/services at a lower cost than their major competitors.

- *Service quality/content.* Some organizations may elect to differentiate the standard of care they provide to donors and/or their recipient groups. They may strive to make the service in some way unique in areas *that are important* to their customers. To be truly sustainable, however, these distinctions in service quality/content should be difficult for competitors to emulate.

- *Access to resources.* As in the example quoted above, many nonprofits possess specialist expertise. This expertise in itself can serve to differentiate the organization from potential competitors in the minds of funders and recipients.

- *Access to recipients.* The channels used to deliver some services may be long and complex. Many Third World charities, for example, have developed complex infrastructures which enable them to reach the most needy societies at comparatively short notice if disaster strikes. This flexibility of response can in itself form the basis of a competitive advantage, as speed may be of primary importance to funders and recipients alike.

Of course this list is not exhaustive but it does serve to illustrate one key point. If an organization is not clear about why it is distinctive, neither will its potential funders or the recipients of the goods and services provided. In the case of the former, this will lead to cash shortages as funds are diverted to other organizations that are perceived as being more deserving. In the case of the latter, those most in need of the support of the organization may be reluctant to come forward to seek the help that could be available, because they fail to understand what is unique about the provision and hence why it might match their need.

Enhancing Inter-functional Coordination: Internal Marketing

Over the years much has been written about how enhancements could be made to the level of cooperation taking place between different departments within an organization. In recent years however a small body of literature has been building up which suggests that the key to achieving this enhancement might lie in applying the same marketing tools and concepts *within* an organization that have traditionally only been employed *outside* the organization, in its dealings with external customers. Not surprisingly, this paradigm has come to be known as 'internal marketing'.

The concept of internal marketing is based on one simple premise:

satisfied employees = satisfied customers

If one is able to recruit and maintain a motivated workforce and inculcate within them an understanding of the organization's mission and the needs and wants of its external customers, the argument runs that positive improvements in the quality of service provided by those employees to their customers should result. Moreover, if employees can be encouraged to view *other employees* in the service chain as their customers and treat them with the standards of care normally reserved for external customers, overall levels of morale should begin to rise as everyone within the organization begins to notice an improvement in the quality of service provided to them by other members of staff. The resultant 'customer' driven culture, it is argued, should have a knock-on effect into dealings with external customers, who should also notice a difference in the quality of service provided.

The reader will doubtless be relieved to discover that there is now a sizeable body of evidence to suggest that this is indeed the case (see for example Berry 1987; Bowen and Schneider 1985; Grönroos 1981*a*; Tansuhaj et al. 1988). The quality of employee interaction *is* strongly correlated with perceived (external) service quality. Indeed, the quality of the delivered service will be strongly correlated with the extent to which:

- employees feed back information to management in respect of customer requirements;
- management and staff pool their expertise to match service specifications to the needs of the target customer groups;
- staff are encouraged to deliver to the service standards set and, moreover, receive the support of their colleagues, where necessary, to do so;
- staff are kept regularly informed of the content of external communications and have the opportunity to feed back their views on the same to management.

Internal marketing activity can help facilitate each of these processes. So what exactly does the term 'internal marketing' mean? It has been variously described as 'viewing employees as internal customers, viewing jobs as internal products that satisfy the wants of these internal customers while addressing the objectives of the organization' (Berry 1981); 'a philosophy for managing the organization's human resources based on a marketing perspective' (George and Grönroos 1989); 'the spreading of the responsibility for all marketing activity across all functions of the organization and the proactive application of marketing principles to "selling the staff" on their role in providing customer satisfaction within a supportive organizational environment' (Gilmore and Carson 1995); and '(describing) the work done by the company to train and motivate its internal customers, namely its customer contact employees and supporting service personnel to work as a team to provide customer satisfaction' (Kotler 1997).

At the heart of these various definitions lie two basic principles. First, internal marketing is seen as a mechanism for spreading the responsibility for marketing across the whole organization, while the second key idea is that to achieve this effectively each employee should be encouraged to regard their successor in the service chain as an internal customer, not merely as a colleague.

Other authors such as George (1990) have chosen to focus on the two roles that internal marketing can perform in an organization. First, it may be viewed as a tool help individuals understand the significance of their roles and to create an awareness of how these roles relate to others within the organization. The aim of this approach is to improve cross-functional coordination and cooperation. Second, it can help to promote, develop, and sustain the ethos of customer service for internal as well as external customers. Piercy and Morgan (1994: 5) meanwhile, propose a rather more elaborate set of internal marketing 'goals':

- gaining the support of key decision makers for organizational plans;
- changing the attitudes and behaviours of employees and managers who are working at key interfaces with customers and distributors;
- gaining commitment to making the marketing plan work;
- managing incremental changes in the culture from 'the way we always do things' to 'the way we need to do things to be successful'.

Internal marketing thus has a variety of benefits to offer a nonprofit organization. Of course, identifying goals and benefits is one thing—making them a reality quite another. To aid in this, there are a variety of techniques that could legitimately be regarded as components of internal marketing. Helpfully Grönroos (1981a) draws a distinction between what he sees as the strategic and tactical levels of internal marketing. While these levels should not be viewed as being carved in stone, because what are strategic issues for some will only be tactical concerns for others (and vice versa), it does constitute a useful framework within which to group the essential ideas. The next sections discuss Gronroos's idea.

Strategic Internal Marketing

Gronroos argues that each of the following dimensions of organizational management can be regarded as strategic internal marketing activity.

Adoption of Supportive Management Styles

If an internal marketing programme is to be developed and implemented, it must have the complete support and backing of senior management. Encouraging staff to view colleagues and volunteers as customers requires a major change in organizational thinking and without top-level support the change is unlikely to occur. Staff need to be given the necessary time to develop internal service standards and plan ways in which performance could be monitored against them. This will only occur if senior staff are seen to support the initiative.

Supportive Personnel Policies

One of the fundamental ideas underlying internal marketing is that individuals should be matched with the job(s) to which they are most suited. This requires careful recruitment, job, and career planning for all individuals within an organization. Many nonprofits have always put effort into attracting personnel with the right skills and attitudes for customer-facing roles, but perhaps rather less effort is typically applied to matching the right 'type' of person to the right job role internally, even if skill sets can be seen to match.

Customer Service Training

Critical to the achievement of a market orientation is customer service training. Staff need to understand the importance of both internal and external customers and how they should be treated. It is helpful if staff are developed from the outset with this form of training as they can then be involved in the setting of appropriate service standards and the monitoring thereof. In short, they should be allowed to 'own' the process and hence not fear the results that might accrue. One of the key mistakes made by many organizations initiating a customer focus for the first time is that the systems that should be used to monitor and enhance service standards are used only as a stick to beat staff with who are seen to be 'underperforming'. This is one way of guaranteeing considerable resistance to change.

Customer-Focused Planning Procedures

The author was introduced some years ago to a model known as the 'Iceberg of Ignorance'. Based on research, it posits the simple idea that the higher up an individual might be in their organizational heirarchy, the more 'ignorant' they are likely to be of the requirements of their customers. It's an interesting idea since taken to its logical conclusion it would suggest that to get on in this life, one should aspire to ignorance! Perhaps more constructively, however, the iceberg provides a very graphic illustration of a concept, an understanding of which still manages to elude many organizations. The idea is presented visually in Figure 2.6.

At the bottom of the iceberg are positioned the front line staff who, as a consequence of their job role, have a good understanding of the customer's requirements and problems. In the case of most service providers, these individuals are interacting with customers on a daily basis and if problems are encountered they will be the first to be aware of them. The

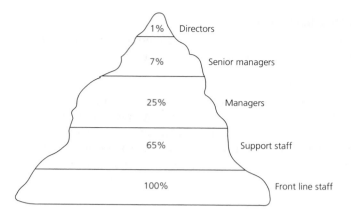

Figure 2.6 The iceberg of ignorance

higher up the iceberg you climb, the less in touch personnel become. A typical charity director will only be acquainted with around 1 per cent of the problems experienced by recipients of his/her goods/services. Even the lowest levels of managerial staff may get to learn of only 25 per cent of the problems/difficulties experienced by their customers.

It is therefore perverse that many organizations continue to plan the future of their organizations from the top down. In reality those who have the most responsibility for strategic planning often have the least understanding of the key issues at stake. For this reason, the adoption of an internal marketing perspective should facilitate the involvement of staff at all levels within an organization in the planning process. While it may be physically impossible (and probably not very desirable!) for all staff to be present when strategy is decided upon, there is absolutely no excuse for not seeking input and/or suggestions from those staff most frequently interacting with customers, as one of the first steps in the planning process.

Tactical Internal Marketing

Tactical internal marketing considerations include the following.

Training

While a commitment to customer service training should often be considered a strategic issue, as it will concern all individuals within an organization, there is also a case for investment in informal and ongoing training, the requirements of which will be specific to particular divisions or functions. Periodic training of volunteer fund-raisers, would for example, fall under this general heading.

Encouragement of Informal and Interactive Communication

Staff from different functional areas within the organization should be encouraged to communicate with each other informally, as well as formally, in the course of performing their job role. Any form of communication that gets away from the traditional 'memo' would be desirable. Inter-disciplinary meetings, social events, and the informal monitoring of internal service levels should facilitate this goal. One voluntary sector organization recently built the factor 'delivery against internal service standards' into its criteria for the award of performance-related pay. This encouraged staff from all departments to develop informal links and communicate more effectively with each other, thereby maximizing the likelihood of improving overall performance in this key area.

Formal Internal Communications

Formal internal communications include newsletters, updates, intranets, briefing documents, etc. These serve a useful purpose in that they can convey developments to staff economically and explain often complex changes to the nature of service provision. The better of these communications also serve to promote a feeling of organizational identity rather than a series of departmental identities, which can often lead to internal conflict and competition.

Internal Market Research

A prerequisite to the attainment of internal customer satisfaction is understanding those elements of the service that are perceived as being most important and concentrating efforts accordingly. While this might sound a little obvious, many nonprofit organizations have been slow to recognize that volunteers in particular usually come to an organization with a series of expectations and requirements, which if not met (at least in part), will lead to the high attrition rates among volunteers currently experienced by many within the sector. Internal market research should therefore be regarded as essential.

Cross-disciplinary Teams

This is a further technique that can be used to promote greater cooperation between departments. Teams are brought together of staff working in often quite disparate sections of the organization. These teams work together to solve quality and/or other organizational problems and report back their suggestions to management. Staff thereby have the opportunity to work with others and to understand a variety of different organizational perspectives.

Staff Secondments

Some organizations approach the problem of inter-functional coordination in a rather different way. They allow staff to experience what it might be like to work in another department with which they will ultimately have much contact, by seconding them there for a period of several weeks or months. This allows them to experience first-hand problems of internal service quality and to see these difficulties from the perspective of their internal customer.

Suggestion Schemes

The question of staff input to the strategic planning process has been dealt with above. In most organizations, however, the planning process (if it happens at all) will tend to happen only once, or at most twice, a year. In such circumstances a mechanism for communicating good ideas to senior managers quickly and efficiently may well be called for. Ideas are often collected centrally in a box, or a hotline is provided to staff so that they can speak directly to a senior executive. Staff suggestion schemes sometimes, but not always, reward the best of the ideas presented.

Once again this list is in no way exhaustive, but it should serve to provide an appreciation of the many techniques that can be used to promote inter-functional coordination and thereby enhance the overall level of market orientation attained.

Market versus Societal Orientation

As we noted above, a number of authors have studied the difference that achieving a market orientation can make to the performance of nonprofit organizations. The education sector appears to have attracted the most attention, and various authors have identified links between market orientation and the degree to which an institution can attract and retain students (see, for example, Caruana et al. 1998). Bennett (1998) has also explored the issue in the context of fund-raising and identified a link between market orientation and fund-raising performance in small/medium-sized UK charities.

It should be noted, however, that these and other studies begin from the fundamental assumption that it is appropriate to seek to achieve a market orientation in a nonprofit context. While I have elaborated on this in some depth there are a number of reasons why the notion of a nonprofit market orientation might be questioned.

First, the market orientation construct was an attempt to operationalize for-profit definitions of marketing that were developed in large commercial organizations in the mid-1960s. Very different definitions of marketing have been developed in the non-profit context and attempting to operationalize Kotler and Levy's 'sensitively serving and satisfying human need', for example, is likely to have a very different outcome from operationalizing the definition of marketing provided by the Chartered Institute of Marketing.

Similarly, some of the terminology used in the for-profit context does not transfer well to the nonprofit arena. The very term 'market orientation' implies an orientation towards markets. Even though one could argue that nonprofits have a market for resource acquisition and a market for resource allocation, these are often not markets in the economic sense of the term. In fact, as Hansmann (1980) notes, nonprofits can often be seen as a response to a very particular form of market failure.

The second key argument for revising the terminology in this context is that the notion of 'market' implies that some form of exchange will take place between the supplier and the recipient of goods and services. There are a plethora of occasions when nonprofit organizations do exchange monetary value with the recipients of their goods or services (or even a warm feeling in return for donations), however there are also many occasions when the notion of exchange has little meaning. The recipients of international aid exchange nothing except their need and gratitude with their supplying organization.

The components of market orientation are also problematic in the nonprofit context. While a focus on customers is still important, in the nonprofit context (as was explained earlier) organizations are often less concerned with customer satisfaction per se than they are with the notion of longer-term benefit to society. It is thus necessary to broaden the focus on customers to address the needs of a wider range of stakeholders and perhaps even society as a whole.

Competition is also different in the nonprofit arena. Demand for nonprofit goods and services is often so insatiable that to regard other organizations as direct competitors would be ludicrous (Bruce 1995). Naturally there are occasions when competition is of significance—when, for example, organizations compete for funds—but it is often the case in relation to service delivery that potential collaboration between organizations is more of an issue than competition per se.

It has also been argued that to serve sensitively the needs of society, nonprofits must be responsive to such needs. While businesses too must be responsive, in the nonprofit context it is the rapidity of this response that defines many organizations. This is accomplished because there is no requirement to consider either the political consequences of action or the financial returns that might accrue to shareholders. Nonprofits have the necessary freedom, flexibility, and moral imperative to respond quickly to the dictates of social need and must ensure that they do so if the maximum benefit to society is to accrue (Jordan 1964; Dahrendorf 1997).

In recognition of these difficulties, Sargeant et al. (2002) propose the alternative framework of 'societal orientation' illustrated in Figure 2.7. The model is offered as an attempt to operationalize the Kotler and Levy definition of marketing referred to earlier. In this case the authors have delineated the societal orientation construct itself and included what they regarded as the antecedents of a societal orientation and the benefits and consequences thereof.

Considering first the antecedents, the authors argue that nonprofits will only be able to achieve a societal orientation if they have a strong, clear mission that reflects the goals of the organization's key stakeholder groups. Similarly, these goals should be common (i.e. shared) across all the stakeholder groups and the nonprofit must have established appropriate systems and structures in place to ensure that they are in a position to be achieved.

In respect of benefits, the authors posit that societally oriented organizations will achieve significantly higher performance than those without such an orientation. In the

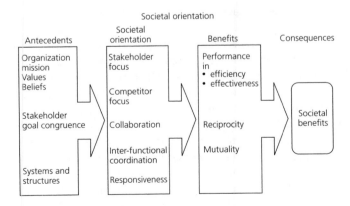

Figure 2.7 Model of societal orientation

Source: Sargeant et al. (2002). *Journal of Nonprofit and Public Sector Marketing*, Vol. 10, No. 2, 41–65.

nonprofit context, this means that nonprofits would be (a) more effective in achieving their mission and (b) make more efficient use of resources in doing so.

According to the authors, however, these should not be viewed as the only out-comes from the successful attainment of a societal orientation. An additional dimension derives from the division between resource acquisition and resource allocation; a defin-ing characteristic for many nonprofit organizations. Those individuals who supply an organization's funding are not necessarily those who will derive the primary benefit therefrom. One of the primary outcomes from the attainment of a societal orientation can therefore be the bringing together of these two groups, resulting in a mutual exchange of values, ideas, and a sense of identity. The authors refer to this as reciprocity and mutuality.

■ SUMMARY

In this chapter we have introduced the topic of marketing and explained its relevance to nonprofit organizations. We have drawn a distinction between the functional aspects of marketing, which we shall deal with in subsequent chapters, and the philosophical aspects of marketing, namely the marketing concept itself. In relation to the latter we have explored how a nonprofit organization might seek to operationalize the marketing concept and to achieve what is known as a market orientation.

We stated that a market orientation might be thought of as having three dimensions, namely cus-tomer orientation, competitor orientation, and inter-functional coordination. A customer orientation involved developing an understanding of the dimensions of the service that were perceived as of greatest importance by customers, and engineering value in these key areas. The achievement of a competitor orientation was shown to deliver a number of strategic benefits to a nonprofit organiz-ation and involved the creation of an effective competitor monitoring system. This, it was argued, could provide valuable data against which to benchmark performance and suggest key areas to management that could be used as the basis for a sustainable competitive advantage. The issue of inter-functional coordination was also explored and the concept of internal marketing introduced as one route to the attainment thereof. A variety of both strategic and tactical applications were described.

We concluded the chapter by examining a competing view on how the marketing concept should be operationalized and explored some of the criticisms of nonprofit market orientation. The notion of societal orientation was discussed, and a variety of antecedents and consequences suggested. It is important to recognize that although this latter model is persuasive it has yet to be empirically validated and may thus itself be open to criticism.

The achievement of a market or societal orientation involves an equal focus on each of its dimen-sions and can potentially offer a number of benefits to an organization in terms of both its use of resources and the pattern of market responses it develops. The reader will appreciate that if equal weight and emphasis is given to each of the dimensions alluded to above, the organization will evolve a new 'way of doing business' which focuses far more on the markets (or the soci-ety) that the organization serves and the needs thereof. Chapter 3 goes on to examine in greater detail the functional components of marketing, in particular discussing the first stage of a typical marketing plan.

▒ DISCUSSION QUESTIONS

1. Using examples from your own experience, list some nonprofit organizations that have a product, sales, or a market orientation. How do these differ?

2. What are the key benefits that marketing can offer a nonprofit organization?

3. What typical objections may be encountered in attempting to introduce marketing to a nonprofit organization for the first time? How might these be countered?

4. What is internal marketing? To what extent do you believe it is a valid context?

5. With reference to your own organization, or one with which you are familiar, describe how you might set about enhancing the level of market orientation it has attained.

6. How does market orientation differ from societal orientation? Which of these alternative perspectives do you find to be the most convincing? Why?

▒ REFERENCES

Bennett, R. (1998) 'Market Orientation among Small to Medium Sized UK Charitable Organizations: Implications For Fund-raising Performance', *Journal of Nonprofit and Public Sector Marketing*, Vol. 6, No. 1, 31–45.

Bennett, R. (2003) 'Competitor Analysis Practices of British Charities', *Marketing Intelligence and Planning*, Vol. 21, No. 6, 335–45.

Berry, L.L. (1981) 'The Employee as Customer', *Journal of Retail Banking*, Vol. 3, March, 33–40.

Berry, L.L. (1987) 'Service Marketing is Different', *Business*, Vol. 30, No. 2, 24–9.

Bowen, D.E. and Schneider, B. (1985) 'Boundary Spanning Role Employees and the Service Encounter: Some Guidelines for Management and Research', in Czepiel, J., Solomon, M. and Suprenant, C. (eds.) *The Service Encounter*, Lexington, Lexington Books, 127–45.

Bruce, I. (1995) 'Do Not-For-Profits Value their Customers and their Needs?' *International Marketing Review*, Vol. 12, No. 4, 77–84.

Caruana, A., Ramaseshan, B. and Ewing, M.T. (1988) 'The Marketing Orientation—Performance Link: Some Evidence from the Public Sector and Universities', *Journal of Nonprofit and Public Sector Marketing*, Vol. 6, No. 1, 63–82.

Dahrendorf, R. (1997) Keynote Address to Charities Aid Foundation Conference, QEII Conference Centre, October, London.

Deshpande, R. and Webster, F.E. (1989) 'Organization Culture and Marketing: Defining The Research Agenda', *Journal of Marketing*, Vol. 53, No. 1, 3–15.

Drucker, P. (1990) *Managing The Non-Profit Organization*, Oxford, Butterworth Heinemann.

George, W. (1990) 'Internal Marketing and Organizational Behavior: A Partnership In Developing Customer Conscious Employees at every Level', *Journal of Business Research*, Vol. 20, No. 1, 63–70.

George, W.R. and Grönroos, C. (1989) 'Developing Customer Conscious Employees at every Level—Internal Marketing', in Congram, C.A. and Friedman, M.L. (eds.) *Handbook of Services Marketing*, AMACOM.

Gilmore, J. and Carson, C. (1995) 'Managing and Marketing to Internal Customers', in Glynn, W.J. and Barnes, J.G. (eds.) *Understanding Service Management*, Chichester, John Wiley, & Sons.

Grönroos, C. (1981*a*) 'Internal Marketing—An Integral Part of Marketing Theory', Proceedings, *AMA Services Marketing Conference*, 236–8.

Grönroos, C. (1981*b*) 'Internal Marketing—Theory and Practice', Proceedings, *AMA Service Marketing Conference*, 41–7.

Hansmann, H.B. (1980) 'The Role of the Nonprofit Enterprise', *Yale Law Journal*, Vol. 89 (April), 835–98.

Jordan, W.K. (1964) *Philanthropy in England 1480–1660*, London, George Allen and Unwin.

Kohli, A.K. and Jaworski, B.J. (1990) 'Market Orientation: The Construct, Research Propositions and Managerial Implications' *Journal of Marketing*, Vol. 54 (April), 1–18.

Kotler, P. (1997) *Marketing Management: Analysis, Planning and Control*, 9th edn, Englewood Cliffs, NJ, Prentice Hall.

Kotler, P. and Clarke, R.N. (1987) *Marketing for Health Care Organizations*, Englewood Cliffs, NJ, Prentice Hall.

Kotler, P. and Fox, K.F.A. (1985) *Strategic Marketing for Educational Institutions*, Englewood Cliffs, NJ, Prentice Hall.

Kotler, P. and Levy, S. (1969) 'Broadening the Concept of Marketing', *Journal of Marketing*, Vol. 33 (Jan.), 10–15.

Lovelock, C.H. and Weinberg, C.B. (1990) *Public and Nonprofit Marketing*, 2nd edn, San Francisco, The Scientific Press.

Narver, J.C. and Slater, S.F. (1990) 'The Effect of a Market Orientation on Business Profitability', *Journal of Marketing*, Oct., 20–35.

Piercy, N. and Morgan, N.A. (1994) 'The Marketing Planning Process: Behavioural Problems compared to Analytical Techniques in Explaining Marketing Plan Credibility', *Journal of Business Research*, Vol. 29, No. 3, 167–78.

Porter, M. (1985) *Competitive Advantage*, New York, Free Press.

Sargeant, A. and Kaehler, J. (1998) *Benchmarking Charity Costs*, West Malling, Charities Aid Foundation.

Sargeant, A., Foreman, S. and Liao, M. (2002) 'Operationalizing the Marketing Concept in the Nonprofit Sector', *Journal of Nonprofit and Public Sector Marketing*, Vol. 10, No. 2, 41–65.

Sargeant, A., Jay, E. and Lee, S. (2003) 'Benchmarking Charity Performance: Returns from Direct Marketing in Fundraising', *Journal of Nonprofit and Public Sector Marketing*, forthcoming.

Smith, A. (1776) *The Wealth of Nations*, Letchworth, Dent and Sons Ltd.

Tansuhaj, P., Randall, D. and McCullough, J. (1988) 'A Service Marketing Management Model: Integrating Internal and External Marketing Functions', *Journal of Service Marketing*, 2, Winter, 31–8.

Zeithaml, V.A. (1985) 'How Consumer Evaluation Processes differ between Goods and Services', *Journal of Marketing*, Fall, 186–90.

3 Marketing Planning: The Operating Environment and Marketing Audit

OBJECTIVES

By the end of this chapter you should be able to:

(1) outline a structure for a marketing plan;

(2) explain the purpose of a marketing audit as the first part of the plan;

(3) discuss the key information requirements of a marketing audit;

(4) understand the categories of information gathered in the audit, why this data is important, and how it can be used in planning;

(5) utilize key tools commonly employed in the audit process such as PEEST, SWOT, and portfolio analyses.

Introduction

In this chapter it is my intention to outline a process that may be employed by nonprofits in planning their marketing activities. While the format may differ slightly from one organization to another, at its core a marketing plan has three common dimensions:

(1) *Where are we now*? A complete review of the organization's environment and the past performance of the marketing function. Only when the marketing department has a detailed understanding of the organization's current strategic position in relation to each of the audiences it serves can it hope to develop meaningful objectives for the future.

(2) *Where do we want to be*? In this section of the plan the organization will map out what the marketing department is expected to achieve over the duration of the plan. Typically, there may be income generation targets as well as objectives for awareness, attitudes towards the organization, and the take-up of service provision.

(3) *How are we going to get there*? This stage of the plan contains the strategy and tactics the organization will adopt to achieve its targets. The strategy, as we shall see in Chapter 5, specifies in general terms what the broad approach to marketing will be, while the tactics supply the minutiae of exactly how each form of marketing will be undertaken.

In this chapter we will provide a generic framework for marketing planning and concentrate our attention on the first of the above three components of a marketing plan. We will consider the information requirements of an organization when it commences the planning process, the sources that this information can be gathered from, and a range of analytical tools that can be used to help marketers interpret the data.

A Planning Framework

A simple marketing planning process is illustrated in Figure 3.1. It should be noted that there is no one right way in which to write a marketing plan and the style and format will hence vary considerably from one organization to another. There are almost as many different formats as there are authors of marketing texts! Nevertheless, the process outlined in Figure 3.1 includes the key ingredients of a typical marketing plan, namely an analysis of where the organization is at present, where it would wish to be in the future, and the detail of how it proposes to get there.

Mission Statement
Organizational Objectives
Marketing Audit

(a)   *PEEST Analysis*
■   Political
■   Economic
■   Environmental
■   Socio-cultural
■   Technological
(b)   *Market Analysis*
(c)   *Competitor Analysis*
(d)   *Analysis of Publics*
(e)   *Analysis of own Organization*

SWOT Analysis
Marketing Objectives
Key Marketing Strategies
Tactical Marketing Mix
■   Product/Service
■   Price
■   Place
■   Promotion
■   People
■   Process
■   Physical Evidence

Budget
Scheduling
Monitoring and Control

Figure 3.1 Marketing planning framework

Many organizations find it helpful to begin the development of their marketing plan by restating their mission and organizational objectives. This helps to focus the minds of those responsible for marketing on the issues which are considered to be of paramount importance for the organization as a whole. It also assists them in delineating those aspects of the organization's role which warrant further investigation in the detailed marketing audit which follows. If an arts centre, for example, has the mission of supporting new forms of art and encouraging local talent, it will not only have to spend time and resources in identifying these in the first place, it will also have to examine the nature of potential audiences for these new art forms as they emerge. A good mission therefore has the capacity to guide the direction that the organization will take and ensure the best use of valuable marketing resources.

A number of nonprofit organizations have to date resisted the temptation to develop a mission statement, feeling, perhaps, that to do so would be to adopt yet another business practice which many such organizations still actively resent. They believe that mission statements serve as little more than promotional hype and serve no useful managerial purpose. Such views are, however, short-sighted as good mission statements can act as a reference point from which it is possible to derive appropriate and clear organizational objectives. To facilitate this, the more useful mission statements address in general terms the reasons for the organization's existence and contain reference to most, if not all, of the following ingredients:

- the customer groups that will be served
- the customer needs that will be met
- the technology that will be employed in satisfying these needs (Abell 1980).

A glance through a selection of nonprofit publicity material reveals that many nonprofits have been intuitively writing mission statements for years, even if they prefer to use alternative terminology such as 'aims', 'purpose', or 'philosophy'. In truth, the terminology is unimportant. What matters is that the organization can summarize in a few words its raison d'etre. Not only does this aid planners in the manner described above, but it can become a remarkably useful reference point for potential donors, or those who might stand to benefit from the goods/services being provided. Supporters and potential beneficiaries can see at a glance what the organization is trying to achieve and confidently initiate some form of relationship if they feel it will be appropriate.

A selection of 'missions' are given below.

In 1978, the World Wildlife Fund (WWF) decided that its 'purpose' was 'to raise the maximum funds possible from UK sources and to ensure that the funds are used wisely for the benefit of conservation of the natural environment and renewable natural resources with emphasis on endangered species and habitats'.

The Elizabeth Svendsen Trust For Children and Donkeys has as its stated 'aim' 'to bring enjoyment and pleasure into the lives of children with special needs and disabilities and the satisfaction that comes with the achievement of learning riding skills'.

The Horder Centre for Arthritis describes its 'philosophy' as follows:

'The Horder Centre exists to improve the quality of life primarily to people stricken with arthritis. The mainsprings of our philosophy are:

- to provide professional help by all available methods for people suffering the pain and disabling effects of all forms of arthritis;
- to restore maximum independence and alleviate pain wherever possible;
- to remain at the forefront of the battle against arthritis as a Centre of Excellence.

The mission of Planned Parenthood is:

- to provide comprehensive reproductive and complementary healthcare services in settings which preserve and protect the essential privacy and rights of each individual;
- to advocate public policies which guarantee these rights and ensure access to such services;
- to provide educational programmes which enhance understanding of individual and societal implications of human sexuality;
- to promote research and the advancement of technology in reproductive healthcare and encourage understanding of their inherent bioethical, behavioural, and social implications.

The reader will appreciate that in all these examples there is a noticeable absence of figures. Mission statements should address what the organization wishes to achieve, but in such a way as the mission can be adopted consistently for a reasonable period of time. It should not be necessary to re-address the mission on an annual basis, since it should serve only to provide the most general of signposts.

The specific detail of what an organization seeks to accomplish within each planning period would normally form part of the content of the organizational objectives. Drucker (1955) isolated eight aspects of operations where organizational objectives could be developed and maintained. These have been modified slightly below to relate them more specifically to the context of nonprofit organizations:

- market standing
- innovation
- productivity
- financial and physical resources
- manager performance and development
- worker/volunteer performance and attitude
- societal needs to be served
- public responsibility.

Clearly, each of these areas has some relevance for marketers even if many of them do not specifically relate to the marketing function. It is important, however, to realize that these objectives are stated for the organization as a whole to work towards. Their achievement will require a coordination of effort across all divisions/departments within the organization. Managers with responsibility for finance, human resources, service delivery, etc. will all have a part to play in ensuring that the organization delivers what it says it is going to deliver. It is for this reason that it is common practice to re-state such objectives at the beginning of a typical marketing plan. Marketers should then be able to isolate what they as individuals need to be able to achieve over the planning period to facilitate the achievement of these wider objectives. There would be little point, for example, in the marketing department raising vast sums of money for causes that are not perceived as congruent with the organization's goals, while failing to raise sufficient sums for those that are. A re-statement of the corporate objectives can therefore serve as an important focus for the marketing plan which follows.

The Marketing Audit

The marketing planning process can be conceptualized as having three main components:

1. Where are we now?
2. Where do we want to be?
3. How will we get there?

The marketing audit specifically addresses the first of these issues. As such, it is arguably the most crucial stage of the whole planning process since without a thorough under-standing of the organization's current position it will be impossible for planners to develop any kind of vision of what they wish to accomplish in the future. The marketing audit is essentially a detailed review of any factors likely to impinge on the organiza-tion, taking into account both those generated internally and those emanating from the external environment. The marketing audit is thus a systematic attempt to gather as much information as possible about the organization and its environment and, import-antly, how these might both be expected to change and develop in the medium- and long-term future. A typical framework for a marketing audit is given in Figure 3.2.

Figure 3.2 Marketing audit framework

PEEST Analysis

It is usual to begin the process by examining the wider or 'macro' environmental influences that might impact on an organization. Often these may be factors over which the organization itself has little control, but which will nevertheless affect the organization at some stage during the period of the plan. The framework utilized for this analysis is typically referred to as a PEEST analysis, and comprises the following elements:

- political
- economic
- environmental
- socio-cultural
- technological.

In each case the aim is to accumulate a list of all the pertinent factors and how these are expected to change over the planning period. It is best at this point in the process not to spend too much time deliberating about the impact that these factors might have on the nonprofit organization, but rather to note them, detail how they might change, and move on. The danger of precipitating a discussion at this stage, as the author has found to his cost, is that other clues as to the impact these PEEST factors might have will tend to emerge as the audit process progresses. It is therefore better to consider potential impacts en masse when the audit is complete. A sample PEEST analysis for a nonprofit concerned

Political factors	Economic factors
Attitudes of government	Employment
Legal framework	GNP trends
Fiscal framework	Interest rates
Government contracts	Inflation
Activities of pressure groups	Business cycles
Environmental factors	**Technological factors**
Environment protection legislation	Government investment in research
Levels of deterioration	Development of new materials
Sustainable practices	Sources of technology transfer
Activities of major polluters	Manufacturing practices
Location/development of major polluters	
Socio-cultural factors	
Attitudes to recycling	
Awareness of environmental decay	
Consumer lifestyles	
Demographic patterns	
Content of school education	
Major influences on consumer behaviour	
Patterns of consumption	

Figure 3.3 Sample PEEST analysis

with raising public awareness of the impact of modern industrial practices on the quality of the environment is presented in Figure 3.3.

In researching these macro trends, the main challenge lies in the selection of accurate and pertinent information, and in the production of summaries succinctly setting out the main points for the reader. Data for PEEST analyses is gathered through secondary sources via desk research, i.e. information is found through existing publications rather than being sourced through the commissioning of new (or primary) research. In gathering information for a PEEST analysis one would look at practitioner and academic journals, books and reports, often via online information databases such as ProQuest available through libraries and academic institutions, or by searching the web more generally. Reports and publications published by trade bodies would also be utilized. Many nonprofits find that much of the necessary information for the production of PEEST analyses is already held internally in the form of publications and reports, or that staff have knowledge of where such information can be sourced internally or externally. The role of the 'auditor' is often therefore to interview staff, find out what information they have on file or can help with, and manage the gathering of that data. In this scenario the auditor would then seek to update the data where appropriate, and fill in any gaps through further research.

It is important to note that simply identifying the key factors is not enough, and it is vital that as much data as possible is gathered against each factor to ensure that decision makers are fully informed. For example, most nonprofits would identify 'increasing use of the Internet' as a key technological trend. Having identified this, the auditor would need to relate this factor to the context of the specific organization. They might hence collate information on the likely growth in users over the duration of the plan, new features, and developments, and on the current use of the Internet in raising awareness or service provision. Likewise, predicted falls in disposable income levels among members of the public might be identified as an important economic factor, but this would mean little if data on the recorded impact of a fall in disposable income on fund-raising and nonprofit performance was not included in the PEEST.

Analysis of Competitors

There are three categories of competitors who are worthy of investigation at this stage in the audit. They are:

1. *Competitors for resources.* Other nonprofit organizations seek to attract resources from the same sources as the nonprofit in question.

2. *Competitors for provision of nonprofit services.* Nonprofits may also encounter competition from other organizations which seek to provide the same services. Increasingly this competition may come from for-profit organizations which may decide to compete, for example, for government service contracts.

3. *Organizations with competing missions.* Many nonprofits now exist whose primary goal is to persuade society to adopt new forms of purchasing, smoking, or sexual behaviours. Such nonprofits typically encounter opposition from other

organizations which exist to further exactly the opposite forms of behaviour. In such circumstances these organizations should be regarded as competitors and be subject to an equally detailed level of analysis.

To be able to compete successfully in their chosen markets nonprofits need to have a sound understanding of the behaviours of organizations that might be regarded as competitors and attempt to determine what their future strategies might be. It is also helpful to understand something of the capabilities of each major player and to define clearly their individual strengths and weaknesses. The following checklist could therefore be used as the starting point for analysis, although it should be noted that the specific factors an organization will need to examine are likely to vary considerably from case to case:

- contact details of each competitor
- size and geographic location(s)
- financial performance
- resource capabilities
- past strategies
- tactical marketing mixes employed
- key alliances formed.

When information has been gathered the auditor will need to present and summarize it in a suitable format. This might involve a comparative study, or an exercise plotting the position of competitors against various axes. One useful tool is to run an analysis of the apparent strengths and weaknesses of each competitor, and an assessment of how their activities might impact on the focal organization in the future.

Collaborative Review

Competition is a key strategic issue for many nonprofits, but collaboration is an equally important facet of their relationship with other organizations. Many Third World agencies, for example, will share transportation channels to maximize the distribution and impact of aid, while minimizing cost. In addition to other similar organizations, nonprofits may be able to identify suitable opportunities for collaboration with both public and private sector bodies (Andreasen and Kotler 2003). It is also common for nonprofits to share lists of lower-value donors with other organizations, in the hope that every participant in the exchange will benefit from the sharing of these resources (Sargeant and Jay 2004).

Thus in conducting a fund-raising audit it will be instructive to consider examples of where organizations have collaborated successfully in the past and the factors that led to that success. The nonprofit should look to see what it could learn from these collaborations and whether there might be any way in which it could work in partnership with others. If this is felt to be desirable, it will be useful to conduct background research into potential partners and to explore how such relationships might develop. An approach to one or more partners could then be included in the marketing strategy/tactics.

Market Analysis

The next stage of the audit involves conducting a thorough analysis of the markets in which the nonprofit perceives itself and, importantly, is perceived by its stakeholders, as operating. Chapter 2 detailed the dangers of developing too myopic a view of the market to be analysed, and it is important therefore that this is developed from the customer's perspective.

The other complexity associated with this stage of the analysis derives from the fact that nonprofits often have two or more markets in which they may be considered as operating. At a very minimum the marketer is likely to have to deal with the distinction between the market for the goods and services of the organization (resource allocation) and the market for the acquisition of those resources (resource attraction). This section of the audit should therefore be structured to consider in detail the factors relevant to each. The precise content of this section of the audit will clearly vary from one organization to another, but Figure 3.4 contains a number of suggestions in respect of each of the categories of data that might be found useful at this stage.

Analysis of Publics

Kotler and Andreasen (1991: 89) use the term 'publics' to refer to 'a distinct group of people, organizations, or both, whose actual or potential needs must in some sense be served'. The term 'public' is therefore more general in its meaning than the concept of 'customer' and embraces every group whose needs must be taken account of by the focal organization. For a registered charity, this might include individual donors, funding

Resource allocation	Resource acquisition
Size, growth, and trends (by both value and volume)	Size, growth, and trends (by value, volume, and category of support)
Principal needs to be met—characteristics	Needs of prospective supporters
Patterns of need	Patterns of giving/donor behaviour
Geographic concentration of need	Ability to segment donor market
Physical resources available in market to meet need	Current/anticipated fundraising practices
Relevant trade bodies—Associations—public/private/voluntary	Principal channels of communication
Trade practices/behaviour of other bodies	
Ability to pay within overall market	
Common methods of distribution	
Principal methods of communication	

Figure 3.4 Nonprofit market analysis

bodies, the local community, the general public, media, recipients of goods and services, the organization's own staff, volunteers, etc. It is therefore important that the focal organization understands the needs and behaviours of these target groups, so that they might be taken account of in the subsequent development of strategy. The following information could prove useful:

- identification of each key public
- requirements/needs/wants of each group
- basis (if any) for market segmentation
- buying/giving behaviours
- attitudes
- media exposure
- patterns of change in any of the above.

The Internal Environment

Having now summarized the key external influences on the organization it is possible to move on to consider an audit of the organization's own marketing activity. The aim here is to scrutinize past marketing performance and to appraise carefully what has worked well in the past and what has not. Current marketing activities, trends in performance, and the current structure and support systems that underpin marketing activity will all be considered. The following checklist is indicative of the categories of information that might typically be regarded as relevant, but it should not be regarded as exhaustive.

Resource Attraction Activities

- fund-raising income (sub-divided by source, e.g. individual, corporate, and trust donations);
- fund-raising income (sub-divided by method of fund-raising employed, e.g. direct mail, telemarketing, etc.);
- income from contracts;
- sales (subdivided by channel) and margins achieved;
- attractiveness of service provision to potential funders;
- marketing procedures;
- marketing organization;
- marketing intelligence systems;
- marketing mix.

Resource Allocation Activities

- sales/service take-up rates (sub-divided by location, market segment, and service category);
- market share analysis;
- cost-effectiveness of services being provided;

- marketing procedures;
- marketing organization;
- marketing intelligence systems;
- marketing mix.

Clearly, conducting a marketing audit can be a very time-consuming process and given that it is good practice to conduct an audit each year, it can place considerable demands on organizational resources. Nevertheless, the benefits that an audit can offer in terms of enhanced management decision-making far outweigh the costs that might be incurred. If the auditing process is instituted on an annual basis, most of the necessary mechanisms for the gathering of data will have been put in place in the first year, and hence the costs in both time and effort should subsequently fall substantially.

Regrettably, however, many organizations continue to take the trouble to complete this exercise only when they are facing a crisis. Faced with decreased demand for their services, or a dramatic reduction in funding, organizations begin to panic and only then seek reasons for these occurrences. Had a systematic approach to environmental scanning been adopted, not only would they have been less likely to have been taken by surprise, but the development of suitable strategies to counter the problems might already be well underway.

Data for the internal audit is usually gathered through a mixture of desk research, meetings, and interviews with staff. Directors and senior staff will be able to provide information on past strategy, tactics, and performance, and will also provide the necessary data on financial performance, human resource strategy, and issues concerning governance, and the general direction of the organization. It is often necessary to interview non-marketing senior staff at his stage, such as the finance director and the CEO, to paint a full background picture of the nonprofit and to establish the positioning and importance of marketing within the organization.

As with the external audit, the internal data gathering should be an iterative process, with checks being performed throughout to ensure that full and accurate information is being gathered and expressed. The financial, structural, and performance information gathered can be used to provide benchmarking data for comparison against other organizations.

Analytical Tools

The audit of internal factors allows the auditor to capture a wealth of data on the performance of existing products or services. In essence, each product or service that the organization provides can be scrutinized to see whether it is worth continuing, what future performance might look like, and how it compares with other similar products or services being provided by other organizations. While it may be perfectly plausible to draw out a series of such conclusions from raw audit data, it may be preferable to use one of a number of analytical models which can assist the auditor in interpreting the mass of data accumulated. A number of the most commonly employed are outlined below.

Product/Service Life Cycle

One of the most fundamental concepts in marketing is the idea that a product or service will pass through several distinctive stages from the moment it is first introduced until it is finally withdrawn from the market. An understanding of these stages can greatly aid a marketer as the appropriate tactics for the successful management of the product/service will often vary greatly between each stage of its life cycle. From the perspective of the marketing audit, it can thus be a useful tool to assess whether the organization's existing marketing activity is appropriate given the product or service's position in its life cycle. Wilson et al. (1994: 274) summarize the implications of the life cycle concept thus:

- Services have a finite life.
- During this life they pass through a series of different stages, each of which poses different challenges to the seller.
- Virtually all elements of the organization's strategy/tactics need to change as the service moves from one stage to another.
- The profit potential of services varies considerably from one stage to another.
- The demands upon management and the appropriateness of managerial styles also vary from stage to stage.

This idea is illustrated in Figure 3.5.

During the introductory stage of the life cycle the service will take time to gain acceptance in the market and sales will hence be relatively low. At this stage the organization will be unlikely to have recouped its initial set-up and development costs and profitability remains negative. Over time, as the service begins to gain acceptability in the market, sales will experience a period of sustained growth and provision of the service should at this stage become profitable. With the passage of time, the level of sales will eventually begin to level off as the market becomes saturated, until ultimately the service becomes

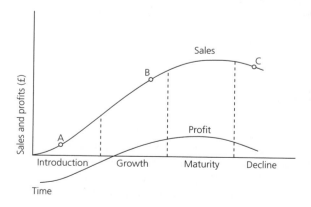

Figure 3.5 Product/service life cycle

obsolete and sales begin to decline. At this stage the organization may wish to consider discontinuing the service, since with a lower volume of sales, the costs of provision may prove prohibitive.

The life cycle concept has been much criticized over the years but it is still useful to marketers in that it can help to define the form that the marketing mix might take at each stage. As an illustration of this point, consider the role of advertising in the marketing mix. At point (A) in Figure 3.5 the role of advertising would almost certainly be to inform the potential market that the service exists and the potential benefits that it might offer. Raising awareness would hence be a key objective at this stage. As the service moves to point (B) in the life cycle, however, the nature of the market has changed. If the new service has been particularly innovative it will be unlikely that competitors have stood idly around watching developments. Instead they will probably have entered the market with their own version of the service at this stage and the objectives of the advertising will thus need to change. A continual emphasis on raising awareness would be inappropriate since it would only serve to increase the overall level of demand in the market and thus benefit both the advertiser and its competition. Instead, a more useful objective might be to differentiate the service offered from those provided by the competition. The emphasis would change to identifying a clear positioning in the minds of target consumers. By the time that the service moves to point (C) in its life cycle, advertising support may be withdrawn altogether to reduce costs, or additional monies may be spent to 'prop up' ailing demand in the market.

While I have focused here solely on how the model can assist the planning of advertising, it is clear that equal utility could be offered to any other ingredient of the marketing mix. In most cases, pricing, distribution, and even the characteristics of the service itself will be modified as the life cycle progresses. Indeed, the model can also be used to help charities think about the nature of their provision. In such cases it is often helpful to move away from the concept of a service and to attempt to visualize the life cycle of a need. Bryce (1992), for example, makes the point that many nonprofits are addressing fairly specific needs within society. These may remain very stable from one generation to the next or they may change fairly rapidly. The need to deal with the design of a vaccine for polio has now been dispensed with, but the arrival of the AIDS virus poses a new threat. Disasters and emergencies create a more transient need, hence the likely life cycle of a need can have important planning implications, particularly when you consider that some needs are perceived by donors as being more immediate and worthwhile than others.

As with their counterparts in the for-profit sector, however, nonprofits normally have more than one service available at any one time and the life cycle concept has the significant drawback that it tends to focus management attention on each service individually without viewing the organization's portfolio as a coherent whole. A nonprofit organization may be viewed as a set of activities or projects to which new ones are intermittently added and from which older ones may be withdrawn. These activities and projects will make differential demands on, and contributions to, the organization as a whole. Hence some form of portfolio analysis might prove a useful tool in deciding how the service mix might be improved given the resource constraints that are valid at any one time.

Portfolio Analysis

While there are a variety of portfolio models that have been employed over the years, these have largely been developed in the business context and are thus difficult to apply to the context of nonprofit marketing. In particular, nonprofit marketers should studiously avoid any portfolio model which has as its base the concept of market share (e.g. the Boston Box), since this notion cannot be meaningfully applied to this context. This is the case for three reasons:

1. The sheer scale of the nonprofit sector and the fact that service and/or fund-raising performance is usually reported in aggregate terms only means that it would be impossible to quantify meaningfully market share for most organizations.

2. Portfolio models employing market share assume that the performance of a product or service is related to market share (i.e. that there are economies of scale). This is simply not the case in many nonprofit contexts.

3. Finally, market share is employed in many portfolio models because it indicates the position of each competitor in a given market. Since many nonprofits do not compete, the use of such models is again problematic.

For these reasons the portfolio model shown in Figure 3.6 is to be preferred.

To utilize the model it is necessary to begin by examining in detail the components of the two axes, namely external attractiveness and internal appropriateness. If we consider first the question of external attractiveness, this relates to a particular organization's ability to attract resources. Not all an organization's services will be equally attractive to potential funders and while most charities would not exclude the provision of a service, simply because it was perceived by donors as unsavoury, few would argue that the ability to raise funds was not an issue. While the specific factors will undoubtedly vary from one organization to another, the degree of support donors are willing to give a particular activity is likely to depend on the level of general public concern, likely trends in public concern, the numbers of people aided, and the immediacy of impact on the beneficiary group.

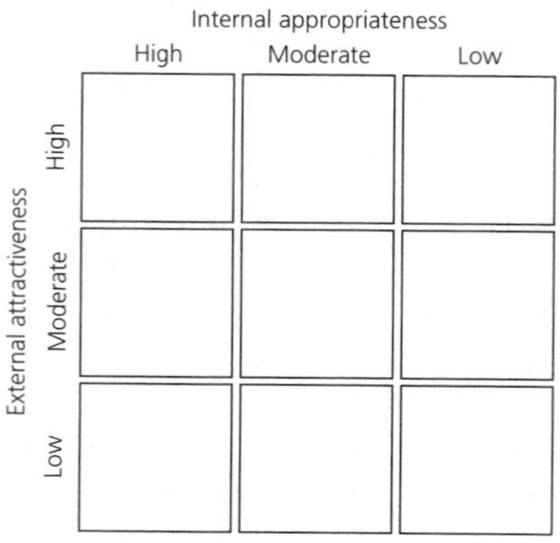

Figure 3.6 Nonprofit portfolio matrix

It is important to recognize that this list is not exhaustive and the beauty of this model is that organizations can utilize whatever factors they perceive as being relevant to their own environment and circumstances.

Turning now to the question of internal appropriateness, this relates to the extent to which the service 'fits' the profile of the organization providing it. In other words, is provision appropriate given the skills, expertise, and resources available within the organization? Relevant factors here might include the level of previous experience with the activity; the perceived importance of the activity; the extent to which the activity is compatible with the organization's mission; and the extent to which the organization has unique expertise to offer.

Once again, this list can be expected to vary from context to context and an organization should try to identify those factors which are most pertinent to its particular circumstances.

Having now defined the components of both internal appropriateness and external attractiveness, the reader will appreciate that not all the factors identified may be seen as having equal importance to a given organization. For this reason it is important to weight the factors according to their relative importance. This is illustrated in Table 3.1. The reader will note that the weights for the components of each axis should all add up to 1. In the example given, the numbers of people the organization can aid is seen as being a more important determinant of external attractiveness than how immediately the assistance can be provided. Donors to this organization do not appear to have any difficulty in taking a long-term view of the impact of their support.

The next step is to take each activity in which the organization is engaged and give it a score from 1 (very poor) to 10 (excellent) in terms of how it measures up against each of the components listed. To make this process clear, a fictional example (let us call it Activity A) has been worked through in Tables 3.1 and 3.2. Considering first the question of how externally attractive this activity might be, it is clear that public support for it looks set to decline in the future and it is for this reason that a relatively low rating of 3 has been awarded against this factor. The activity does have the merit, however, of having an immediate and beneficial impact on a large number of people and somewhat higher ratings are therefore awarded for these factors. Multiplying the weights by the ratings

Table 3.1 Calculation of external attractiveness

Vertical axis	Weight	Rating	Value
External attractiveness			
Level of public concern	0.2	5	1.0
Likely trends in public concern	0.3	3	0.9
Numbers of people aided	0.4	8	3.2
Immediacy of impact on beneficiary group	0.1	7	0.7
TOTAL	1.0		5.8

Table 3.2 Calculation of internal appropriateness

Horizontal axis	Weight	Rating	Value
Internal appropriateness			
Level of previous experience	0.1	5	0.5
Perceived importance of the activity	0.2	2	0.4
Compatibility with mission	0.5	6	3.0
Possession of unique expertise	0.2	7	1.4
TOTAL	1.0		5.3

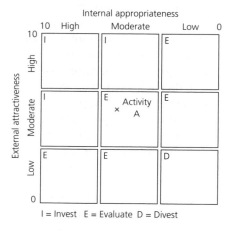

I = Invest E = Evaluate D = Divest

Figure 3.7 Utilizing the portfolio model

assigned produces a value for each factor. Summing these values gives an overall score for (in this case) the external attractiveness axis of 5.8.

Similarly in the case of the internal attractiveness axis, each factor is assigned a weight. Each activity in which the organization is engaged is given a rating according to its performance in respect of each factor. Once again 1 = very poor and 10 = excellent. Returning to our analysis of Activity A, Table 3.2 makes it clear that the charity has only moderate experience to offer and does not view its provision as being particularly important (even though it would appear to come within the organization's mission). The charity does however have unique areas of expertise which it could offer to recipients. The result is an aggregate score of 5.3 on the internal appropriateness axis.

These figures can now be plotted on the matrix in Figure 3.7, where the position of Activity A has been clearly indicated. If it is conceptually useful, some organizations choose to progress the analysis one stage further and draw a circle around the plotted position, the diameter of which is directly proportional to the percentage of overall expenditure allocated to each activity. In this way managers can see at a glance how funds are allocated between each of the services in the portfolio. Of course, for this to happen, all the services that a particular organization provides would be plotted in this way and then an analysis undertaken of the health (and balance) of the portfolio as a whole. Depending on the location of each activity within the matrix, the organization can then either look to invest further in its development, divest the activity and use the resources elsewhere, or subject the activity to further evaluation if the position still remains unclear.

Activities falling in the top left-hand corner of the matrix are clearly those which are perceived as fulfilling an important need in society, and the attraction of funding is unproblematic. The organization also appears well placed to provide these services as it has the necessary expertise and/or experience in-house. The activities are also more likely to be seen as compatible with the organization's mission and are hence excellent candidates for continuing investment.

Activities falling in the bottom right-hand corner, however, are activities which could be causing an unnecessary drain on resources. They are not seen as being important by society and are not compatible with the organization's mission. Indeed, there may be other potential providers who could provide a much higher quality of service. Activities in this area of the matrix should then be scrutinized with a view to divestment. After all, if the activity is difficult to raise funds for, and the organization is not good at providing the service anyway, what could be the rationale for continuing? Of course, this is only a model and the activity would have to be scrutinized very carefully before a divestment decision was taken, but the analysis has at least yielded considerable insight into the potential for valuable resources to be conserved and perhaps put to other, more appropriate use.

This leaves the question of activities falling within the central diagonal, such as the one in our example. These should be carefully evaluated as they are only moderately

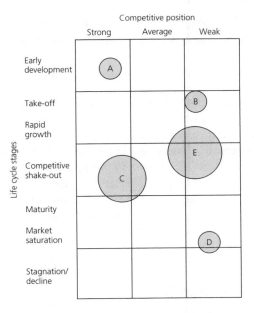

Figure 3.8 Life cycle matrix

Source: Hofer and Schendal (1978).

appropriate for the organization to provide and they have only limited external attractiveness. It may be that here are very good strategic reasons for continuing to offer these services, or it may also be that they could comfortably be left to another better qualified organization to supply. Further analysis is clearly warranted.

The Life Cycle Matrix

In examining the health of a portfolio it is also possible to employ an adapted version of a matrix originally developed by consultants at Arthur D Little Inc (see Hofer and Schendel 1978). The matrix is illustrated in Figure 3.8. In this matrix the user plots competitive position against life cycle stages. The diameters of the circles around each activity are once again proportional to the revenue they generate. The goal of using this matrix, as with that detailed above, is to guide investment decisions in nonprofit services. In Figure 3.8, Activity A could be labelled a developing winner, Activity B a potential loser, Activity C an established winner, and Activity D a loser. The power of this matrix is that it illustrates graphically how the services are positioned in respect of various stages of evolution. This may be important in deciding when to create new services and divest those at the end of their life cycle lacking a clear rationale for their continuing existence.

The decision over where to place an activity on the competitive position axis depends on how that activity rates against a variety of factors. These typically include:

- how well the organization's strengths match the success factors in the particular market;
- the profitability associated with an activity;
- the extent to which the organization has the requisite marketing skills;
- the extent to which the organization has developed a reputation for delivering that activity; and
- the perceived costs/benefits to the user of engaging with the activity.

A combination of these factors determines how strongly positioned a particular product or service might be in its market. In employing the matrix, nonprofits can either take an entirely subjective view of the score on this access, or they may construct a weighted axis just as with the previous matrix to impose a little more rigour on the analytical process.

In interpreting this matrix, it is possible to infer a number of conclusions in respect of how the performance of particular products/services might change over the duration of the plan. Similarly, the matrix can be used to guide investment decisions and in particular to highlight those products that should be divested. Those products/services towards the end of their life cycle where the organization does not have a strong competitive position are clear candidates for this.

Drawbacks of Portfolio Models

In electing to employ a portfolio model, it is essential that the user be aware of some of the disadvantages of such models.

- *Definition of market.* It is not always clear how the market should be defined when drawing conclusions about the position of a product/service on a given axis. When examining corporate fund-raising products, for example, is the market the whole corporate marketplace, only those corporations that presently give to nonprofits, only those companies in particular sectors, or only those companies of a particular size? It is essential in using a portfolio model that the market is clearly defined and that the implications of this definition are fully understood.

- *Innovation.* The difficulty with some models is that they can understate the significance of an innovative new product. When such products first appear on a matrix, they are characterized by low profitability/revenues and a weak market position as they fight to get established. Thus a cursory glance at a portfolio model might suggest that such products are struggling and that divestment is warranted. This is clearly not the case and care is required in interpretation.

- *Divesting unwanted products.* It should be recognized that while a number of products may be highlighted as candidates for divestment, this may frequently not be desirable. While it makes little financial sense to continue with a particular product, there may be a number of good human reasons why it should be continued. Perhaps volunteers have a long and proud tradition of managing the product and there are strong emotional attachments to its continuation. It may also be the case that some products gain the organization very welcome publicity that assists in the fulfilment of the mission, even though the performance of the activity itself is poor. Nonprofits thus need to subject the recommendations to emerge from a portfolio analysis to greater scrutiny before divestment decisions are taken.

- *The desirability of growth.* Finally, most portfolio models assume that an organization is looking to achieve growth in usage or revenue and the prescriptions offered by such models may therefore not be appropriate to the circumstances facing every organization.

SWOT Analysis

Clearly at this stage the output from the fund-raising audit may be regarded as little more than a collection of data, and in this format it is of limited value for planning purposes. What is required is a form of analysis which allows the marketer to examine the opportunities and threats presented by the environment in a relatively structured way. It should be recognized here that opportunities and threats are seldom absolute. An opportunity may only be regarded as an opportunity, for example, if the organization has the necessary strengths to support its development. For this reason, it is usual to conduct a SWOT (Strengths, Weaknesses, Opportunities and Threats) analysis on the data gathered during the audit. This is simply a matter of selecting key information from the audit, analysing its implications and presenting it under one of the four headings. The important word here is 'key'. It is important that some filtering of the data gathered at this stage is undertaken so that the analysis is ultimately limited to the factors of most relevance for the subsequent development of strategy. SWOT analysis addresses the following issues.

- What are the strengths of the organization? What is the organization good at? Is it at the forefront of particular developments? Does it have access to users/donors that are not reached by competitors? Does it have a strong database system/great support agencies/high local awareness?

- What are its weaknesses? In what ways do competitors typically outperform the organization? Are there weaknesses in terms of internal support or structures? Are there barriers to future development in some areas?

- What are the main opportunities facing the organization over the duration of the plan? Are there new ideas to test, new audiences to attract? Are new developments within the organization likely to present extra opportunities for either service provision or income generation?

- What are the major threats facing the organization? Is a major competitor likely to launch a new service or fund-raising appeal? Will economic changes impact on certain core funders and leave them with less to give? Are planned changes to legislation likely to curtail service activity?

Good SWOT analyses have a number of distinctive characteristics.

- They are relatively concise summaries of the audit data and are typically no more than four or five pages of commentary focusing on key factors only.

- They recognize that strengths and weaknesses are differential in nature. This means that a strength is only a strength if the organization is better at this particular activity or dimension than its competitors. Similarly, weaknesses should be examined from the perspective of where the organization lags behind its competition.

- They are clear and easy to read. Quality suffers if items are over-abbreviated and the writer concentrates on micro rather than macro issues. As MacDonald (1995: 406) notes, 'If a SWOT analysis is well done, someone else should be able to draft the objectives which logically flow from it. The SWOT should contain clear indicators as to the key determinants of success in the department'.

A separate SWOT should be completed for each segment of stakeholders critical to the organization's future. What may be perceived as a strength in relation to individual donors may well be a weakness when communicating with service users. Thus, the global SWOT analyses that are so frequently conducted by marketing departments can often tend towards the meaningless. For all but the smallest and simplest organizations, a series of highly focused SWOTs will be necessary.

■ SUMMARY

In this chapter we have examined the structure of a typical nonprofit marketing plan. While there are many such frameworks in existence, they all have the common core of 'Where are we now?', 'Where do we want to be?' and 'How will we get there?' The marketing audit comprises the first of these stages and it is therefore here that the marketer summarizes all the available data on the key factors that are likely to impinge on the organization over the duration of the plan and beyond.

A framework for a marketing audit was provided and a series of information requirements delineated under each heading.

In the next chapter we will move on to look at how all this information might be gathered, at typical sources of nonprofit information, and at a variety of primary research methods. We will also examine how primary research data is typically presented.

DISCUSSION QUESTIONS

1. Why should a nonprofit organization consider developing a mission statement? What advantages might this confer?

2. What is the purpose of a fund-raising audit? For an organization of your choice, develop a list of key information requirements utilizing the standard audit headings as a guide.

3. What is meant by the term 'publics'? For an organization of your choice, identify who the key publics might be and the demands they might place on the organization.

4. How might the portfolio models outlined in this text be amended to be suitable to the fund-raising context?

REFERENCES

Abell, D.F. (1980) *Defining The Business: The Starting Point of Strategic Planning*, Englewood Cliffs, NJ, Prentice Hall.

Andreasen, A. and Kotler, P. (2003) *Strategic Marketing for Nonprofit Organizations*, Englewood Cliffs, NJ, Prentice Hall.

Bruce, H.J. (1992) *Financial and Strategic Management for Nonprofit Organizations*, Englewood Cliffs, NJ, Prentice Hall.

Drucker, P.F. (1955) *The Practice of Management*, London, Heinemann.

Hofer, C.W. and Schendel, D. (1978) *Strategy Formulation: Analytical Concepts*, St Paul, MN, West Publishing.

Kotler, P. and Andreasen, A. (1991) *Strategic Marketing for Nonprofit Organizations*, Englewood Cliffs, NJ, Prentice Hall.

Sargeant, A. and Jay, E. (2004) *Fundraising Management*, Routledge, London.

Wilson, R.M.S., Gilligan, C. and Pearson, D.J. (1994) *Strategic Marketing Management*, Oxford, Butterworth Heinemann.

Marketing Research

OBJECTIVES

By the end of this chapter you should be able to:

(1) explain the relevance of research to marketing planning;

(2) distinguish between primary and secondary research;

(3) distinguish between qualitative and quantitative data;

(4) utilize a wide range of secondary sources of data;

(5) identify and employ relevant primary research methods;

(6) present marketing research data.

Introduction

In Chapter 3 we explored a range of information needs typically encountered by a nonprofit in writing a strategic marketing plan. While this list seems extensive, it must be remembered that good information can be used to great effect in guiding the decisions and policies an organization might adopt, and is therefore invaluable.

Of course market research should not be seen as a substitute for good managerial decision-making. The role of market research is not to usurp executive experience or judgement; rather, market research provides the basic data that managers can use to help *inform* the decision-making process. It thus reinforces good decision-making rather than replacing it.

It is important to note that there is an element of risk associated with every management decision and that decision-making in the absence of research data simply exposes an organization to unnecessary additional risk. In the nonprofit sector, this risk is all the more acute because of the agency role that nonprofits play in stewarding the resources supplied by donors. If, for example, a fund-raising campaign goes badly wrong and loses money, it will effectively be wasting the resources donated by previous donors to the organization and will put the organization in breach of their trust. Similarly, if an organization designs a new service that fails to meet the key requirements of its beneficiary groups, a considerable amount of resources will be wasted and the organization's cause will be no further advanced.

There are thus a number of advantages to be gained by an organization in conducting thorough research in relation to each of the issues highlighted in Chapter 3. Given the plethora of information needs and the equal plethora of potential information sources, there is no shortage of data to be had about the marketing function or the environment in which it operates. Sadly, this is frequently irrelevant, incompatible with the specific information need, or excessive in terms of volume. Problems can also arise when managers fail to understand the nature of the information presented: then, even in the presence of high-quality data, the wrong decisions can be taken.

In this chapter we will navigate some of the pitfalls associated with conducting marketing research, outline a process that may be used to manage the activity, and explain the research tools and techniques available that might be employed to assist an organization capture data.

A Definition of Marketing Research

Before beginning with this process it is important to clarify exactly what we mean by marketing research. Over the years there has been considerable confusion between the terms 'marketing' and 'market research'. Although market research has tended to be used as a synonym for marketing research, there was originally a distinction drawn between these two terms by virtue of their scope. Market research was regarded as research into markets (e.g. in the case of fund-raising; individual donors, corporate supporters, and foundations) whereas marketing research applies more broadly to every aspect of marketing. This would thus include researching the activities of competitors, trends in the external environment, the performance of an organization's own marketing activity, etc.

The American Marketing Association (AMA) (1961) defined marketing research as 'the systematic gathering, recording and analyzing of data about problems relating to the marketing of goods and services'.

More recently, Kotler (1967) preferred to emphasize the goals of marketing research and defined it as 'systematic problem analysis, model building and fact finding for the purposes of improved decision making and control in the marketing of goods and services'.

Thus marketing research is concerned with the disciplined collection and evaluation of data in order to help managers understand the needs of their target audiences more fully. It can be used to reduce risk in decision-making and to control (to some extent) the risks surrounding each aspect of marketing.

While perspectives on the research process frequently differ from one organization to another, the approach adopted will always share a number of common features, as outlined in Figure 4.1.

The marketing research process is typically initiated by an organization realizing that it has a problem or issue to resolve. To operationalize this for the purposes of research it must first be expressed as a series of specific research objectives. These are then addressed through initial desk research of existing data. In some cases this may yield all the answers

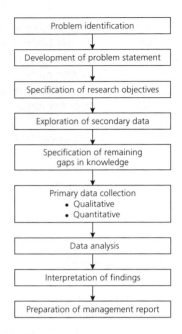

Figure 4.1 Marketing research process

an organization needs, in which case an appropriate analysis of this material can result in the preparation of the requisite report for management. It is frequently the case, however, that not all of the information needs can be met in this way and that new or *primary* data may have to be collected and analysed for this purpose.

The sections below discuss each element of this process beginning, with the specification of the research problem.

Specifying the Research Problem and Research Objectives

The first stage of the research process involves a clear specification of the marketing problem on which the research is expected to focus. This is essential if the organization is to achieve a satisfactory outcome from the research process, particularly if external agencies are to be employed for the purposes of data collection.

Where it is intended that the organization will work with an agency, it is important that both management and the research team should work closely together in this crucial task of developing a problem statement. Unless the agency thoroughly understands the issues facing the client, it is quite possible that the research objectives designed to provide information to resolve these problems will be irrelevant or possibly even counter-productive.

Having defined the problem, it is then possible to design the research objectives. This requires the organization and/or agency to turn the problem into a series of information needs. Thus, for example, if the problem facing the organization is a decrease in the demand for its service, the research objectives might be as follows:

- to profile existing and past users of the service;
- to identify user motives for utilizing the service;
- to identify user perceptions both of the service itself and of those provided by key competitors;
- to determine why previous users have terminated their use of the service;
- to determine why non-users are not trialling the service.

This list is by no means exhaustive and, depending on the circumstances facing a particular organization, the actual content of this list will vary considerably. The point is that the problem must be broken down into a series of research objectives that will address each of the likely causes for the decline, providing enough information for managers to take remedial action. Again, if an agency is to be employed for the purposes of data collection, it must also be involved in selecting research objectives since they may well have insight into the issues which could help shape these objectives, and also because they need to understand the rationale underlying each information need and how it pertains to the problem as a whole.

Secondary versus Primary Data

The next stage in the research process is to conduct desk research of existing information sources. Typically, many of the organization's information needs can be adequately and cheaply met by simply reading through the trade press, research reports, or specialist journals. Collectively, this is known as secondary data.

Secondary data is data that has already been collected for some purpose in the past. It has thus *not* been collected specifically to address the issues at hand. Such data can typically be found within the nonprofit organization in management/consultancy reports or an analysis of database records, but more frequently it will be found outside the organization in government publications, syndicated research, trade/professional reports, electronic databases, professional/academic journals, etc.

Secondary data is always the starting point in seeking to satisfy research objectives since it has the advantage of being cheap to collect and will typically be a fraction of the cost of the collection of new market research (e.g. surveys, focus groups, etc.). It does, however, have a number of distinct disadvantages, in that (a) it has been collected for another purpose that may not meet the exact information needs of the organization; (b) it is often out-of-date, having been collected a year or more prior to the current investigation; and (c) it can be of dubious quality and thus a careful consideration of the source and the methodology adopted will be necessary to ensure that the data offers appropriate validity and reliability.

Having exhausted the sources of secondary data, the organization may then return to the research objectives and determine those that have not been fully addressed with this extant data. Where information gaps remain, it will be necessary to commission primary research to supply the missing information. Primary research involves collecting new data specifically for the purpose of answering the questions posed by the current research objectives. This is typically an expensive exercise and will not be undertaken lightly by the commissioning organization. Primary research may be either qualitative or quantitative.

Qualitative Research

Nonprofit marketers are frequently concerned with issues such as how donors view the organization, what motivates them to support it, what they like and don't like about the communications they receive, etc. If the organization lacks an understanding of the factors likely to be at work in each case, it would be advised to begin by conducting what is known as *qualitative* research. This form of research is designed to provide such an insight and is a good way of gathering data about people's attitudes, feelings, and motives. It is impressionistic in style rather than conclusive, and it probes for data rather than counting responses. The most common qualitative research methods include focus groups (group discussions), detailed 'depth' interviews, and projective techniques.

Depth Interviews

The use of this technique involves the researcher in a free-flowing discussion with members of the group whose opinions are being sought. They are conducted on a one-to-one basis, so that there is no need for the interviewee to feel under any pressure to respond in a socially acceptable way, or to worry what other participants in the research process might think of their views. It is thus a very open and non-threatening research setting and interviewers are trained to put their subjects at ease. Such interviews can be either unstructured or semi-structured depending on the level of knowledge the researcher has about the factors likely to be of interest. Where detailed knowledge is lacking, the interviewer will find an unstructured approach of most value as this will facilitate a general discussion of the research question and allow the conversation to focus on whatever factors emerge.

Focus Groups/Group Discussions

This technique requires the researcher to assemble a group of six to ten respondents who agree to take part in (typically) a one- to two-hour discussion that addresses the research objective(s). This discussion may be held at the organization's premises or at a centrally located venue that is easy for the respondents to access. The researcher carefully facilitates a discussion of the topic and ensures that the views of each member of the group are elicited. He/she may also have to deal with 'difficult' personalities that attempt either to dominate the discussion, or fail to express a point of view. It is important that the views of every participant are considered equally and the process of facilitation is thus a highly skilled task. Focus group proceedings are typically either audio- or video-taped, so that they can subsequently be analysed by the research team. The biggest drawback of this technique is the cost, with a typical focus group costing between £800–£1000 and between six and eight groups typically being necessary to address a given research task. Basing decisions on a smaller number of groups can be risky since focus group participants may prove to be highly unrepresentative of the donor/user (or other) population and thus the results will be misleading. The insights gained from focus groups can be of considerable value, but this is frequently gained at substantial cost.

Projective Techniques

The use of projective techniques has moved in and out of fashion over the past 50 years. They are said to generate considerable insight into feelings, beliefs, and attitudes that individuals find it difficult to articulate by other means. A number of techniques are in existence, where research subjects can express their views by 'projecting' those views onto objects, pictures, or third parties.

An organization interested in the perception of its brand might thus provide a group of eight to ten individuals with a set of cards and crayons and ask them to create an image that for them embodies the brand. This can also be achieved through the use of clay, where subjects create a physical representation of the brand in question. The shapes and pictures created will then be subject to expert analysis to identify the common themes to emerge.

A further common technique would involve asking subjects to create a personality for an organization or brand. Thus, 'If this organization were a well known celebrity, who would it be?' The description and subsequent rationale can then form the basis for discussion.

Projective techniques have also been used in the context of cartoons, where research subjects are presented with a cartoon illustration of a social situation embodying the research objective(s). Blank dialogue boxes (or speech bubbles) are provided and the subject asked to supply appropriate speech. The technique works because subjects may find it easier to address some topics by projecting their own values and beliefs onto these cartoon characters thereby expressing views they would feel uncomfortable expressing in a traditional interview. Again, this speech can be subject to a content analysis at the end of the research process and common themes elicited.

A Caveat

It should be noted that qualitative techniques are rarely used in isolation. The samples are inadequate, the method of questioning inconsistent, and the means of interpretation subjective. Two or three people (or agencies) doing the same piece of qualitative research can often come up with very different results. This is simply because the use of eight to ten individuals in a focus group is rarely representative of the 'population' as a whole and the results will therefore always have a high degree of bias. To take a fund-raising example, one might commission a series of focus groups to determine the reasons why donors support the organization. Such a group would likely generate an excellent list of reasons, but it could never tell you what proportion of the donor base might be motivated by each rationale for support. It is thus only half a story. The real strength of the technique lies in its ability to generate *hypotheses* about how the user population as a whole *might* feel or *might* behave. To be used to inform marketing strategy an organization might typically test these hypotheses with quantitative techniques and a larger, more representative sample of the target population.

Quantitative Research Techniques

Quantitative research typically involves the gathering of numerical information about the market or particular audience the researcher is concerned with. Unlike qualitative research the goal is to quantify the number of members of a particular group that hold certain views, donate in particular ways, are motivated by particular factors, etc. Quantitative research techniques include:

- *Personal interviews.* These may be conducted by a trained researcher in the home, an office or a central location/street. Both qualitative and quantitative data could be gathered, although cost and time restraints frequently confine data collection to quantitative data. The interviewer follows a set script and simply poses a range of questions, noting down the replies he/she receives for subsequent analysis.

- *Telephone interviews.* Increasingly, marketing research is being conducted by phone. Researchers from the organization or agency ring a sample of individuals and again follow a set script, posing each question in turn. Modern technology now facilitates a process known as CATI (Computer Assisted Telephone Interviewing) where the questions appear on a screen in front of the interviewer and when each response is given it is typed into the database (or the appropriate box clicked on). Depending on the nature of the response the interviewer is then prompted by the system to ask the next appropriate question.

- *Postal questionnaires.* Here the contact with the research sample is impersonal. A series of questions are developed, printed onto a questionnaire and dispatched to members of the target audience whose opinion is sought. Often the response is incentivized in some way and facilitated through the inclusion of a reply paid or freepost envelope.

- *E-mail questionnaires.* The recent rise in computer ownership and access to the Internet has now made the acquisition of market research data much more affordable. Sudman and Blair (1999) argue that electronic surveys will replace telephone surveys over the next 25 years as more and more individuals become comfortable with the medium. Surveys can easily be e-mailed to service users, donors, or other categories of supporter. Alternatively, if the questionnaire is lengthy, it is possible to post the questionnaire on an organization's website and then to e-mail respondents asking them to visit the site and complete it. Sudman and Blair (1999) recommend locating the questionnaire in a password-protected part of the site, so that responses from members of the sample do not become confused with those of other site users who decide to complete the questionnaire during their visit.

- *Fax questionnaires.* In the USA the fax is a medium now commonly employed for advertising and other forms of marketing solicitation. Its use is more common in the context of business-to-business (B2B) marketing, although home faxes are growing in number and significance. In some instances, if involved in research with corporate organizations it may thus be appropriate to consider employing a fax survey, which respondents may complete and fax back to the nonprofit. Such forms of research are unlikely to work in the UK at present, where unsolicited faxes are regarded as highly intrusive.

Taking a Sample

In undertaking quantitative research it may be possible to solicit the opinions of everyone in the whole group or *population* of interest. Under these circumstances the researcher is effectively conducting a *census* since everyone of interest can be contacted and asked for their views. More frequently, however, it is not practical to pose questions of everyone in a target population, by virtue of the sheer number of contacts involved, the costs of soliciting their views, or the difficulty of contacting them, perhaps because of their geographic spread. In such circumstances, researchers take a sample of the members of the population and calculate statistics about that sample, which allow them to make statements and estimates about the population as a whole, without the need to contact everyone.

There are four main methods for sampling of relevance to marketers: random sampling, systematic random sampling, stratified random sampling, and quota sampling. Random sampling is referred to as *probability sampling*, while quota sampling is referred to as *non-probability sampling*. This difference matters because it impacts on the way we may interpret the results of the research undertaken.

Under random sampling each member of a population has an equal chance of being selected in the sample. Because of this it is possible to calculate a *level of confidence* and limit of accuracy from the results of such a sample. A level of confidence is a statement about how confident we can be about the results from the sample holding good across the population as a whole. At the 95 per cent level of confidence, for example, there is only a 5 per cent (or 1 in 20) chance that the sample results do not hold good for the whole population. Confidence levels can be set higher than this to offer greater accuracy, but this would add substantially to the cost since it would require the extraction of a larger sample.

It is important to note that probability samples are not necessarily more representative than non-probability samples. Indeed, the converse can often be true. The point is that probability samples allow for the calculation of *sample error* or the extent to which errors in the results occur because a sample was used rather than asking the whole population for their views. You cannot do this with non-probability samples since no objective method is used in the first place to gather the sample.

We now consider each form of sampling in turn.

Random Sampling

To generate a random sample, as noted above, every member of the population must have an equal chance of selection. To take a random sample it is thus necessary to begin by defining or assembling a *sampling frame*. This is simply a complete list of all the individuals in the target population. This may, for example, be a list of names on a database, a directory of organizations, or a list of contacts. Each name on this list would then be assigned a number and all the numbers entered into a hat. If a 10 per cent sample of individuals is required, 10 per cent of those numbers and associated names would then be drawn at random out of the hat.

Of course, modern technology now makes this process much less cumbersome and many modern software programs generate numbers at random which can be used to generate a random sample for the researcher. Indeed, in many cases the researcher will be oblivious to the process since it is necessary only to request this kind of sample from the database software.

Systematic Sampling

There are occasions, however, when a truly random sample is not practical, perhaps because the sampling frame is supplied in a list format and where the number of contacts on that list is large. Assigning numbers and then selecting numbers at random from the list would then be time-consuming and potentially costly. Under these circumstances it may be more practical to take a *systematic random sample*. Suppose we wish to take a 10 per cent sample from a list of 1000 names. We could then proceed by selecting a random start point and thus selecting at random a number between 1 and 10. Suppose we select the number 4. We would then work down through our list taking the 4th name, the 14th name, the 24th name, the 34th name, etc. until we had completed the list and extracted the 10 per cent of contacts required. This is a systematic random sample.

Stratified Random Samples

To illustrate the need for this form of sampling let's consider the example of a local authority wishing to explore views on facilities that will be made available in a new community sports complex. To investigate this issue, it has been proposed that a 10 per cent sample of the local population be sent a questionnaire to ascertain their views. Intuitively the marketing team feels that these reasons might vary by the age of the individual. Now suppose that the age profile of the local population is as depicted in Table 4.1.

Table 4.1 Stratified random sample

Age profile	% of population
Under 20	10
21–40	20
41–60	40
61–80	20
81+	10

By taking a purely random sample of 10 per cent of these individuals it is possible, however unlikely, that a sample could be generated where the individuals contacted are over 80. This could greatly bias the results, particularly in the context of a sports centre! Instead, researchers would better proceed by deciding in advance that of their sample 10 per cent will be under 20, 20 per cent will be aged 21–40, 40 per cent will be aged 41–60, 20 per cent will be aged 61–80 and 10 per cent will be aged 80+. In other words, the composition of the sample mirrors that of the population to ensure that each category or *strata* is properly represented.

Non-probability Sampling

With non-probability sampling the chances of selection are not known therefore the ability to generalize about a population, based on the results of a sample, are much reduced. Kumar *et al.* (1999) argue that the results of non-probability sampling may contain biases and uncertainties that make them worse than no information at all. Not all writers are as pessimistic, however, and the decision of whether or not to use probability-based sampling will be a function of the degree of accuracy required, the likely costs of error, the population variability, and the type of information needed (Tull and Hawkins 1996).

Non-probability sampling does not require the use of a sampling frame and thus the project's costs might be reduced. The sample is chosen at the convenience of the researcher to fit the needs of the particular project. Samples can be created by convenience sampling (simply selecting individuals convenient to the research project), purposive sampling (where individuals are selected who are felt to be appropriate to the project objectives), or quota sampling.

In quota sampling, the researcher makes a clear effort to ensure that the sample he constructs mirrors the characteristics of the sample as a whole. Thus if a nonprofit were looking to assess the awareness of their organization/brand among members of the local population, the researchers could proceed by identifying the demographic profile of that population. They might do this by age and gender, for example. They would then create a quota such as that depicted in Table 4.2 to ensure that the balance of people whose opinions they solicit reflects that of the population as a whole.

It is important not to confuse quota sampling with stratified sampling. The major difference is that in the former the interviewer/researcher selects the individual respondent, while in the latter the selection process is carried out by random selection.

Sample Size

The question of how big a sample to use for research is not an easy one to answer as it depends on a number of factors. Much depends on the type of sample, the statistics that will be calculated, the homogeneity of the population, and the resources (time, people and money) available. It is impossible in this chapter to cover all the pertinent factors, but it is worth noting that there are now a number of tables, calculator functions, and software programs that will prompt the user with the relevant questions and generate an appropriate sample size. There are also many websites hosted by research agencies that

Table 4.2 Quota sample of 50 individuals

Characteristic	% of population	Quota sample
Male		
Aged under 30	10	5
Aged 31–60	10	5
Aged over 60	30	15
Female		
Aged under 30	20	10
Aged 31–60	10	5
Aged over 60	20	10
TOTAL	100	50

have sponsored online tools to help the inexperienced researcher. An often surprising point to consider when calculating the sample size is that it has little to do with the size of the population. The reason for this is quite straightforward. Rather than the size of the population being the key, it is the extent to which all the members of the population have the same value or response. If you had 20 000 people in a population who all responded in exactly the same way to an advertisement appeal to stop smoking, then obviously you would only need a sample of one of them to ascertain the behaviour of the others. Not a very likely scenario. Not everyone who sees the ad will smoke and individuals who do will respond in very different ways. Thus what affects the sample size that will be necessary is the variability of the population. Obviously the greater the variability, the larger will be the sample required to estimate aggregate behaviour with any precision.

Questionnaire Design

General Advice

In designing a research questionnaire, there are a number of points to bear in mind.

Overall Length

People quickly get bored with completing surveys, particularly in face-to-face or telephone situations. In these circumstances the length of the questionnaire should be held to an absolute minimum with the questions posed tightly integrated with the overall research problem. Postal questionnaires can be longer since respondents may complete them at their leisure, but researchers employing questionnaires of over four pages will note a sharp drop-off rate in the achieved response rate.

Questions should be Clear and Unambiguous

Questions should be written in the language of the target audience. It should be remembered that while a marketer may be highly conversant with the language employed by the cause, members of the public may not understand much of the specialist terminology and even fewer of the mnemonics. These must be avoided or explained.

Each question should also be written and checked for clarity. The question should also avoid ambiguity and the notorious 'and' word. Consider the following example.

Please indicate the extent to which you agree with the following statement, employing the following scale:
1=Strongly Disagree
2=Strongly Agree
3=No Opinion
4=Agree
5=Strongly Agree

Donating money to this charity gives me a sense of real pride and I enjoy receiving the communications they send me.

_1   2   3   4   5_

If this question seems appropriate at first glance, consider how a donor might answer if donating to the organization gives them a sense of pride, but they hate the communications they receive. Each question in a questionnaire should address one dimension only.

Use Closed Questions Wherever Possible

It is important when designing a questionnaire to consider how the data will be analysed. Closed questions are much easier to analyse since they only allow respondents a range of options in respect of their response. The example below is thus a closed question.

Please indicate your age category:
[ ]   Under 20
[ ]   21–40
[ ]   41–60
[ ]   61–80
[ ]   81+

Open questions, by contrast, invite the respondent to offer an answer which then has to be coded into categories (or interpreted) post hoc by the researcher, e.g. please tell us what you think of the communications you receive from us. It is this latter dimension that makes the inclusion of open questions undesirable since they can substantially slow down the analysis undertaken and greatly increase the costs of analysis as a consequence. It should be noted, however, that the use of closed questions requires the researcher to have a firm grasp of the subject area in advance, since they must ensure that the options available to respondents are comprehensive. Where doubt remains, some researchers add a final category, namely 'other—please specify'.

Classifications should be Carefully Designed

Where closed questions are employed, researchers should take great care to design the categories appropriately. Each option should be discrete, unlike the example below where it is possible to tick two boxes if one is aged 20, 40, 60, or 80.

Please indicate your age category:
[ ]   20 and under
[ ]   20–40
[ ]   40–60
[ ]   60–80
[ ]   80+

Similarly, confusion can arise of the meaning of some categories. In the author's experience, asking a person's occupation can be a particular problem since in one instance an individual chose to describe his occupation as 'bank director' when in reality his role involved greeting customers at the door and directing them to the correct counter!

Avoid Leading Questions

Leading questions are those that direct the respondent to give a specific answer, thus, 'Did the recent financial scandal affect your giving?' is doomed to failure from the outset. Less obviously asking a donor whether they have read a particular magazine or communication may simply prompt them to say 'yes'. If a researcher is interested in recall of specific communications or the media exposure of a particular individual s/he will be advised to generate a list of communications and to ask the respondent which of them he/she can recall or has read, respectively. Respondents are then less likely to answer in an 'ego-defensive' manner.

Order Questions in a Logical Sequence

In designing a questionnaire it is also important to group together questions that pertain to a particular issue to avoid confusing the respondent as to what specifically is being asked. Similarly it is appropriate to seek to 'funnel' responses down from general questions about the issue as a whole down to the specifics of exactly what data is being sought. In other words, questionnaires should be constructed in a logical order that guides the respondent in an orderly manner through the topic.

Keep Personal Questions until the End

If it is necessary to ask any sensitive questions of respondents, perhaps their ethnic background, income level, religion, or attitudes to tough social issues, it is better to ask these at the end of the questionnaire rather than at the beginning. Asking these questions up front is likely to put off the respondent, as he/she is likely to assume that all of the questionnaire will probe for such personal data. Asking for this at the end of a questionnaire, when a respondent has already invested considerable time in the process, and when some form of relationship has been established, is far less likely to result in non-completion.

Pilot Test

It is absolutely essential that any questionnaire be piloted before rolling it out to a particular audience. While all the questions posed might seem entirely logical and appropriate to the researcher, there are inevitably a few that create confusion, fail to be understood, or attract answers that the research team were not expecting. A pilot test can be undertaken at low cost with a small percentage of the sample and any necessary changes can be made before the time and expense of the full survey rollout are incurred.

Scaling Techniques for Surveys

There are two important scaling techniques that are typically used by researchers in surveys, Likert scales and semantic differential scales. There are others, but these are the most commonly employed.

Likert Scales

A Likert scale is a list of statements with five (or sometimes seven) possible choices such as strongly agree, agree, neutral (or no opinion), disagree and strongly disagree. The scale is used against a battery of questions that are given to respondents. The researcher is then able to measure the attitudes of respondents. Typically the items included in the battery will have been generated from prior qualitative research or secondary sources. An example battery of questions is provided below.

To what extent do you trust the Nature Conservancy to undertake each of the activities listed?

STATEMENT	Strongly disagree		Strongly agree		
Always to act in the best interest of the cause	1	2	3	4	5
To conduct their operations ethically	1	2	3	4	5
To use donated funds appropriately	1	2	3	4	5
Not to exploit their donors	1	2	3	4	5
To use fund-raising techniques that are appropriate and sensitive	1	2	3	4	5

In presenting the results from questions designed in this format it is now common practice to present the mean and/or median scores calculated from all the respondents who answered each question. Thus the higher the average score, the greater the degree of agreement with each of the statements listed.

Semantic Differential Scales

These scales are designed to measure differences between words. As previously, qualitative work may have identified a series of constructs or ways in which people think about the organization and its services. An attitude battery consisting of bipolar constructs can then be developed. A five- or seven-point rating scale is frequently used. As an example, the name of a particular organization could appear at the top of a page on a questionnaire. Respondents could then be asked to rate this organization using each of the scales in

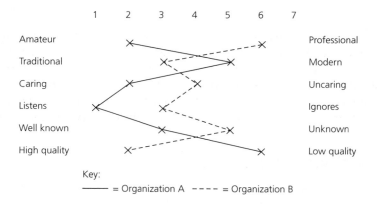

Figure 4.2 Profile of two nonprofits

the battery. Computed results could then allow the researcher to compile an attitude profile, perhaps comparing perceptions of their own organization with those of a key competitor.

In this example the bipolar constructs could include the following:

Amateur	Professional
Traditional	Modern
Caring	Uncaring
Listens	Ignores
Well known	Unknown
High quality	Low quality

The profile of two organizations could then be compared, as indicated in Figure 4.2.

Data Analysis

Qualitative Data

The process of data analysis differs greatly between qualitative and quantitative data. Qualitative data from interviews and focus groups is typically transcribed from recordings of the original research. The resultant text is then input into a software package such as NUD*IST or NVIVO which allows the researcher to examine and code each aspect of the content.

The majority of qualitative software packages operate in a similar way and allow a researcher to highlight a line or lines of text that contain a particular idea. This idea is then assigned a code. Subsequent text containing similar ideas will also be assigned this particular code. In a typical analysis of focus group data there may be 100 or more codes that reflect different facets of the discussion and responses. Text can also be coded according to who is speaking and reflect gender, income, age, etc.

In writing up the results, researchers can then request that the software groups the text of the discussions by code—and thus the themes to emerge from each facet of the discussion can easily be written up and peppered with direct quotations from respondents to illustrate why a particular conclusion has been drawn. One might also explore, again using the codes, whether the views of participants varied by categories such as age, gender, income, etc.

An example of this form of analysis and how it is written up is provided below. In this example the researchers were interested to explore the factors that might lead individuals to offer a legacy (or bequest) to charity. A series of focus groups was conducted with individuals who had pledged a legacy gift, and a range of motives for support of this nature were identified. The researchers subsequently grouped these into one of two categories, namely organizational factors and individual factors. In the brief extract reproduced below, the researchers report their findings in respect of the organizational issues. Notice how each idea expressed in the interviews is expressed in turn, described, and, where appropriate, illustrated with a direct quotation. This is typical of the format of many qualitative research reports.

Organizational Factors

Performance

The performance achieved by a particular organization was a key factor in determining whether a legacy gift would be offered. This was a theme that was addressed at many points through all the focus groups conducted. It appeared to be more of an issue than was the case in conventional giving because of the relative size of the gift that would be offered. As one participant noted, 'A legacy is a bigger decision. I thought long and hard about which charity to leave it to. I wanted to be sure they wouldn't squander it.' Others indicated that they had conducted a more thorough information search than had been the case for other types of giving they had engaged in. Again this occurred because of the likely size of the gift, but also because the individuals realized it would be the final contribution they would make to charity. 'I looked carefully at what they'd achieved and how they used their money. I had to be sure it would get to where it was needed. I had to be sure this gift would count.'

Professionalism

The quality of an organization's management was also very much an issue. Many participants felt that they needed to be sure that the organizations they were supporting in this way were well managed. As one participant noted, 'I'd never support organizations that were poorly managed—not with a legacy. I might send them a small donation if I really liked the cause, but not a legacy.' Many pledgers had sought information and advice from the charity before changing or making their will. This personal contact had caused many to form a view about the professionalism of the charity and in a number of cases deterred a donor from making a bequest. 'You can forgive a lot from charities. After all, they're

continues

---

focused on their work, aren't they? But there's a limit, you know. If I'm making such a major decision I expect them to behave professionally.'

Responsiveness

Participants stressed the uniquely personal nature of the legacy gift. For most it would be the single largest gift they would ever be able to offer a charity. There was thus a strong sense that this gift was in some way 'special' and that in offering it they were strengthening the bond between themselves and the organization. The financial and moral significance of the gift appeared to generate higher expectations of how the organization might deal with them in future. As one participant noted 'It was a really big thing for me. I'd had to discuss it with my family and go along to the solicitors. I think the least they can do in return is answer my letters and be prepared to call me if I have any queries or concerns.' Others indicated that the notion of responsiveness could also be a factor for them in deciding which charities to support with a legacy. 'I knew I couldn't support all eight of my favourites and I really wanted there to be a big gift, not lots of small ones. So I thought back about how I'd been treated and who seemed genuinely interested in me, who cared enough to send a personal letter and thank me properly.' Many respondents felt that a legacy was such a substantial gift that those who wanted recognition (perhaps a mention in a book of remembrance) should be afforded this.

Communications

Participants were generally satisfied with the quality of communications they received from the non-profits they support. They enjoyed being kept informed about how their gifts had been used and the issues/challenges facing those organizations. While they recognized this was true of all the organizations they supported, legacy pledgers were found to be particularly concerned with the quality of communications received from the organizations they had elected to support in this way. 'When I was giving just a few pounds a month I didn't really pay much attention to what they sent me. When I changed my will I guess I needed reassurance I'd made the right decision and I read everything they send me now.' Others indicated that communications were particularly important because they cared passionately about the cause. It was felt that anyone leaving a legacy to a charity by definition cared particularly about its work and that as a consequence they would be particularly interested to keep up to date with that work. As one participant noted, 'I don't read half of the charity solicitations I receive, but I lost my wife to cancer and (their work) really matters, you know—that's why I'll remember them in my will.' The quality of these communications was felt to be important, and pledgers were highly focused on being kept regularly up to date with information about what was being achieved.

Quantitative Data

Software packages are also available to analyse quantitative data and these vary in terms of sophistication and cost. Among the most commonly employed are SNAP (which also aids in questionnaire design) and SPSS (Statistical Package for the Social Sciences). There are a range of statistics that may be calculated to assist the researcher in summarizing and interpreting the results they have achieved. Such analysis is beyond the scope of this text, but interested readers may wish to consult Hair et al. (1995).

The most common forms of summary used to represent this form of data include tables, bar charts, histograms, and simple numerical summaries such as the mean, median, and standard deviation.

Charts

Bar charts or frequency diagrams are probably the most common forms of graphical representation of statistical data. They consist of a series of bars, the height of which is either proportional to the frequency with which a particular outcome occurs, or to the probability that this outcome will occur.

A simple bar chart is presented in Figure 4.3. In this example, the seat utilization rate (i.e. the percentage of seats occupied) in each of the performances on offer at a local theatre is presented for the period shown. While the same information could be presented in tabular form, the reader will appreciate the greater degree of impact that can be achieved with a graphic presentation. It is immediately obvious to the eye which of the performances has attracted the largest audience.

A second type of chart commonly employed for the presentation of data is the histogram (see Figure 4.4). In this case it is not only the height of the bars that is significant, but also the dimensions of the base. In this example the dolphin sanctuary has plotted the response rates that it has historically received to one of its most popular donor recruitment mailings. It seems clear that a common outcome for this particular mailing would be to achieve a response rate of circa 1–1.5 per cent.

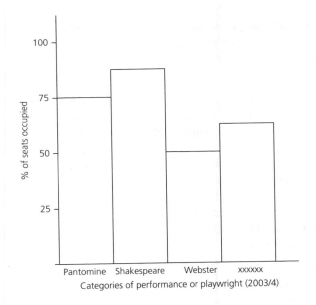

Figure 4.3 Bar chart of seat utilization rate

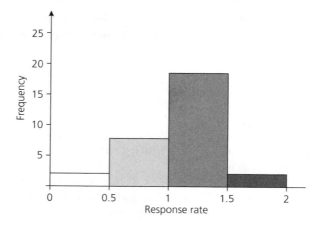

Figure 4.4 Histogram of mailing response rates

Descriptive Statistics

Mean

One of the most commonly encountered descriptive statistics is the mean, denoted by $\bar{x}$. It is also one of the simplest to calculate. You simply add up the results of a given set of measurements and then divide by the number of measurements. This is shown in mathematical notation below:

$$\bar{x} = \frac{\sum_{i=1}^{} x_i}{n}$$

In this case the formula simply indicates that to calculate the mean one has to calculate the sum of the values of x from the first observation to the last and then divide by the number of observations (denoted by n).

Median

A second commonly used descriptor is the median. This is simply the measurement that falls in the middle of a given set of observations or 'distribution'. There are many occasions when it is preferable to quote the median rather than the mean. The median is preferable where there are a number of outliers in the distribution that would bias the mean and thus give a misleading picture of the nature of the distribution. Suppose, for example, we were interested in reporting the 'average' salaries earned by service users. We take a small sample of the salaries earned for five individuals and obtain £20K, £22K, £23K, £24K and £70K. In this case the median value would be £23K while the mean distorted by the outlier would be £31.8K. The median would thus be a more reasonable representation of this distribution than the mean.

Standard Deviation

Both the mean and the median give the researcher some idea of where the centre of a distribution is located. While this is clearly useful, information researchers are usually also interested to know how spread around this distribution might be. One possible way that this measure might be derived would be to take the difference between each measurement and the mean and then to calculate the average of this deviation. The problem with this approach, however, is that the deviations will be both positive and negative. Consider a distribution containing the measurements 1, 2, and 3. In this case the mean would be 2 and the deviation −1, 0 and +1. The mean deviation in this case would be zero and we would therefore be no further forward in attempting to find a measure of spread. The way around this difficulty is to calculate the deviations from the mean as previously and then to square these numbers (which removes any negative signs), add these squared numbers together, divide by the number of measurements, and then take the square root of the answer. In our previous example, the square deviations would be 1, 0, and 1 and their sum would be 2. If we then divide this by 3 to get the mean of the squared deviations and take the square root of the answer we obtain a result of circa 0.8. This somewhat wordy description is represented in mathematical notation below:

$$s = \sqrt{\frac{\sum_{i=1}(x - \bar{x})^2}{n}}$$

The more spread out a given distribution might be, the greater will be its standard deviation.

Range

In cases where the median has been used to describe the 'average' point on a distribution, a good measure of spread to accompany this value is the range. The range is simply the highest value observed minus the lowest value. While this is a useful figure, it is helpful to recognize that this too can be strongly influenced by outliers. For this reason some researchers prefer to quote the inter-quartile range. This is simply the difference between two points. The lower of these corresponds to a point below which one-quarter of the observations lie (the lower quartile) and the second to the point above which one-quarter of the points lie (the upper quartile).

In the example provided below, we reproduce an extract from a quantitative research report. Here the researchers have chosen to present the data in tabular form and to cite many of the statistics listed above. The objective of this research was to compare the demographic profile and attitudes of individuals who have pledged a legacy (or bequest) to a nonprofit with members of the standard (i.e. non-pledger) supporter base. In this extract the researchers provide the details of their demographic comparison. It is interesting to note that alongside their comparison they have also performed a number of statistical tests to determine whether differences they note between pledgers and supporters are 'significant' differences, represented in the population as a whole, or not significant since they might well be due to sampling errors and the operation of random chance. Comparisons of this type are common in market research and the exact statistical tests that may be employed are a function of the categories of data being examined. This is beyond the scope of this text, but the illustration shows just how useful this additional form of analysis can be.

EXAMPLE

Profile of Respondents

Tables 4.3–4.8 present the details of the demographic profile of respondents. The results are presented for both legacy pledgers and supporters. The results in Table 4.3 illustrate the slight female bias present on many charity databases. There is no significant difference, however, in the balance of gender between the supporter and pledger groups.

Table 4.3 Gender of respondents

Gender	Supporter %	Pledger %
Male	40.2	35.1
Female	59.8	64.9

Table 4.4 Past/present occupation of respondents

Occupation	Supporter %	Pledger %
Director	5.4	4.2
Housewife/husband	8.5	6.4
Manager	6.9	7.8
Manual/factory	0.9	1.4
Office/clerical	12.6	16.9
Professional	27.0	23.7
Self-employed	6.6	8.0
Shop assistant	0.9	0.8
Skilled tradesman	2.1	2.0
Supervisor	0.7	1.6
Teacher/lecturer	17.0	18.1
Other	11.4	9.0

The occupation of each group is depicted in Table 4.4. It may be noted that both the supporter and pledger groups have a high concentration of office/clerical and professional individuals, reflecting the bias towards socio-economic groups B and C1 in giving. The high concentration of teachers/lecturers is also noteworthy and again typical of the profile of many charitable databases. No significant differences between pledgers and supporters could be identified.

continues

EXAMPLE continued

The income profile of respondents is reported in Table 4.5. In this case it can be seen that pledgers report a significantly lower annual income than supporters ($X^2 = 46.98$, significance level 0.000).

Table 4.5 Current income profile of respondents

Category	Supporter %	Pledger %
Up to £4,999	3.6	4.6
£5,000–£9,999	8.4	17.5
£10,000–£14,999	13.8	17.3
£15,000–£19,999	11.1	14.2
£20,000–£24,999	12.1	14.4
£25,000–£29,999	8.4	7.0
£30,000–£39,999	13.6	10.1
£40,000+	29.0	14.9

Significant differences between the two groups were also reported when examining the marital status of respondents. Pledgers are significantly more likely to be living alone, either because they are single or because they have been widowed (Table 4.6) (Goodman and Kuskal Tau value 0.061, significance level 0.000). This difference is also supported in Table 4.7 where it can be seen that pledgers are significantly less likely to have children ($X^2 = 107.55$, significance level 0.000).

Table 4.6 Marital status

Status	Supporter %	Pledger %
Single	18.7	34.9
Married	55.1	33.3
Separated	0.3	1.8
Divorced	5.4	5.7
Living with partner	6.2	5.0
Widowed	14.3	19.4

Table 4.7 Presence of children

Children	Supporter %	Pledger %
No	31.1	61.3
Yes	68.9	38.7

continues

EXAMPLE continued

Table 4.8 presents the remaining demographic data captured in the survey and in addition presents the total amount donated by each group to the charity sector in the past year. As the results indicate, the mean age at which both pledgers and supporters completed their full-time education is very similar, suggesting that many individuals were educated to degree level. No significant difference between the two groups was reported. It can be seen that pledgers are significantly older than supporters, having a mean age of 68.4 years.

Table 4.8 Demographic and behavioural characteristics

Variable	Supporter mean	Pledger mean	F	Sig
Age at which full-time education completed	20.9	19.0	1.27	0.26
Age	59.2	68.4	53.06	0.00
Amount given to charity each year	£600.64	£701.26	2.41	0.12

No differences could be discerned between the two groups in relation to the total amount given to charity each year, with supporters offering £601 per annum and pledgers £701. It should be noted that the distributions in each case were highly skewed and that as a consequence a better measure of the typical amount given per annum is the median. The median amount donated per annum by both supporters and pledgers was found to be £300.

■ DISCUSSION QUESTIONS

1. Distinguish, with examples, between qualitative and quantitative marketing research.

2. As the fund-raising manager of a small children's charity looking to explore the motives for legacy giving, explain and justify a programme of marketing research you would propose to adopt to explore this issue.

3. In your role as the marketing director of a medium-sized arts charity you have been asked by your chief executive to prepare a marketing research plan to explore why audience numbers are in decline. Explain what primary and secondary research you would recommend the organization undertake.

4. As the marketing director of a local (government) council you have been asked to determine how satisfied local residents are with the refuse collection service and recycling facilities the organization provides. Suggest a programme of primary research that could be adopted to provide this information.

■ REFERENCES

AMA (American Marketing Association) (1961) *Report of the Definitions Committee*, Chicago, American Marketing Association.

Hair, J.F., Anderson, R.E., Tatham, R.L. and Black, W.C. (1995) *Multivariate Data Analysis with Readings*, 4th edn, Englewood Cliffs, NJ, Prentice Hall.

Kotler, P. (1967) *Marketing Management: Analysis, Planning and Control*, Englewood Cliffs, NJ, Prentice Hall.

Kumar, V., Aaker, D.A. and Day, C.S. (1999) *Essentials of Marketing Research*, New York, John Wiley & Sons.

Sudman, S. and Blair, E. (1999) *Sampling in the Twenty-First Century*, Greenvale, Academy of Marketing Sciences.

Tull, D.S. and Hawkins, D.I. (1996) *Marketing Research: Measurement and Method*, 6th edn, New York, Macmillan.

Marketing Objectives and Strategy

By the end of this chapter you should be able to:

(1) write SMART marketing objectives;

(2) develop strategic direction and collaborative/competitive strategy for a nonprofit organization;

(3) segment a range of nonprofit markets;

(4) Develop positioning strategy for a nonprofit organization.

Introduction

Having now examined the first stage of the marketing plan (i.e., Where are we now?) and identified the research tools that may be used to supply this information, we are now in a position to address the second stage, i.e., Where do we want to be?

The marketing audit provides a concise summary of where the organization stands in relation to its environment and, as such, should provide a sound basis on which to decide what is going to be achievable over the duration of the plan. When this has been decided, the nonprofit is in a position to develop marketing objectives for the planning horizon in question. Once set, the nonprofit can then address how exactly these objectives are going to be met through its marketing strategies and tactics. In this chapter we will focus on marketing objectives and key marketing strategies. Tactics will be dealt with in Chapter 7.

Setting Marketing Objectives

The importance of setting objectives in a not-for-profit context has long been under-rated. As Drucker (1990: 107) notes:

In a non-profit organisation there is no such [thing as a] bottom line. But there is also a temptation to downplay results. There is the temptation to say: 'We are serving a good cause. We are doing the Lord's work. Or we are doing something to make life a little better for people and that's a result in itself.' That is not enough. If a business wastes its resources on non-results, by and large it loses its own money. In a non-profit institution though, it's somebody else's money—the donor's money. Service organisations are accountable to donors, accountable for putting the money where the results are, and for performance. So, this is an area that needs special emphasis for non-profit executives. Good intentions only pave the way to Hell!

Objectives are an important part of the plan as they are the only mechanism by which its success can be measured. If a plan achieves its stated objectives we might reasonably conclude that it has been a success. Without them, one can only speculate as to the planner's original intent and the effectiveness of the activities undertaken have no benchmark against which to be assessed. Valuable resource could be being wasted, but the organization would have no mechanism for identifying that this was in fact the case. As a minimum therefore, marketing objectives for nonprofits should address the following two issues:

1. The match between the services produced and the markets that those services are intended to serve. Thus objectives should specify the services that will be provided and for whom.

2. The level of resource that it is intended to attract to support the services identified above.

It is also important to realize that the style in which the objectives are written is also a significant issue. Objectives are only of value if it is possible to use them as an aid to managing the organization's resource; hence vague terms and needless ambiguity should be avoided.

Vague objectives, however emotionally appealing, are counter-productive to sensible planning and are usually the result of the human propensity for wishful thinking which often smacks more of cheerleading than serious marketing leadership. What this means is that while it is arguable whether directional terms such as decrease, optimise, minimise should be used as objectives, it seems logical that unless there is some measure, or yardstick, against which to measure a sense of locomotion towards achieving them, they do not serve any useful purpose. MacDonald (1984: 88)

Hence, to be managerially useful, good objectives should be:

- *Specific*. Objectives should be related to one particular aspect of marketing activity. Objectives which relate simultaneously to diverse aspects of marketing activity are difficult to assess since they may require the organization to use different techniques of measurement and to look across different planning horizons. Attempting to combine activities might therefore lead to confusion, or at best a lack of focus.

- *Measurable*. Adjectives such as 'maximize' or 'increase' are not particularly helpful when it later becomes necessary to assess the effectiveness of marketing activity. To be useful, objectives should avoid these terms and be capable of measurement. They should hence, specify quantifiable values whenever possible, e.g. 'to achieve a 20 per cent market share', or 'to produce a 5 per cent reduction in smoking nationwide'.

- *Achievable*. Marketing objectives should be derived from a thorough analysis of the content of the marketing audit and not creative thinking on the part of managers. Objectives which have no possibility of accomplishment will only serve to demoralize those responsible for their achievement and serve to deplete resources that could have had a greater potential impact elsewhere.

- *Relevant.* Marketing objectives should be consistent with the objectives of the organization as a whole. They should merely supply a greater level of detail—identifying specifically what the marketing function will have to achieve to move the nonprofit in the desired direction.

- *Timescaled.* Good objectives should clearly specify the duration over which they are to be achieved. Not only does this help to plan the strategies and tactics by which they will be accomplished, but it also assists in permitting the organization to set in place control procedures to ensure that the stated targets will indeed be met. Thus monthly 'sub-targets' for each form of fund-raising could be set and corrective action initiated early in the duration of a plan, as soon as a variance is detected.

Thus good marketing objectives should be SMART!

Having now outlined the 'rules', it might be helpful to demonstrate what a typical non-profit marketing objective might look like. In the context of arts marketing, an objective for a theatre might take the form: 'To achieve a 20 per cent increase in student attendance at all performances between 15 October and 10 December 2005.'

In a fund-raising context the objectives might read: 'To attract £200 000 in voluntary income from individual donors by the end of the calendar year' and 'To attract £50 000 of (cash) corporate support by the end of November 2005'.

Having specified the objectives it is intended that the plan will achieve, it is then possible to address the means by which these will be accomplished. The overall approach to their attainment is termed 'marketing strategy'. Strategy deals with the major issues that will impact on the whole organization's approach to its markets (or subject). They differ from tactics since tactics supply the minutiae of exactly what will be done, when, and by whom. Thus it may be a strategy to continue to build the organization's brand through awareness-raising advertising, but the specifics of where the advertising will take place, how frequently it will appear, the nature of the copy or design, etc. will be left to the tactical component of the plan to follow.

What comprises the general approach to meeting an organization's objectives will clearly vary from one situation to another, and it is thus impossible to develop a definitive list of what might be regarded as strategic marketing issues. As a broad guide, however, the following issues are typical of those that need to be addressed:

- overall direction
- merger/collaborative strategy
- competitive strategy
- segmentation strategy
- positioning strategy
- branding strategy.

We will now consider the first line of these in turn. Branding will be the focus of Chapter 6.

Overall Direction

There are four key strategic directions that an organization could follow if it wants to achieve growth. These are illustrated in Figure 5.1. All the options involve making decisions about the range of services that will be provided and the markets into which they will be delivered. Each strategic option will now be considered in turn.

Market Penetration

This option involves the organization in attempting to gain a greater impact in its existing markets. The existing range of services continues to be marketed to the existing market segments and no changes are planned to either. There are many ways in which a non-profit could look to penetrate the market, including finding some way to reduce the price charged for the service, enhancing promotional activity, improving distribution facilities, or more likely, maximizing output. Many charities, for example, face almost unlimited demand for the services they currently supply and could hence gain greater penetration simply by looking for ways to maximize the output from their own organization.

In cases where demand is less buoyant, however, or where the charity has a comparatively low level of awareness among its target audience, the organization may have to resort to intensifying its marketing activity to stimulate the additional demand it requires. If there are competitors in the market, this may prove to be no easy task, as additional 'sales' may have to be gained at their expense. This is perhaps less of a problem in an expanding market as there may be sufficient increases in demand per annum to allow all competing organizations to realize their growth objectives without having to compete directly with others in the sector. In static or declining markets, however, the reverse is true and additional sales will only be generated by stealing them from others competing within the same market.

Service Development

Service development will normally be an attractive option where the organization does not perceive sufficient opportunities for growth by continuing merely to deliver its

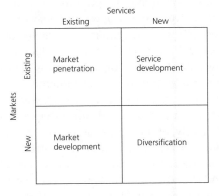

Figure 5.1 Ansoff's matrix

Source: Adapted from Ansoff (1968).

existing services. The demand for service development may also be driven by demands from customers, as many local authorities have discovered in recent years. Faced with such a situation an organization may decide that it is appropriate to develop other services, which the members of its existing markets may utilize. Indeed, for some organizations a continuing strategy of service development may be the sole reason for their existence. Those, for example, that provide care to patients suffering from terminal illness will continually seek to develop their services as levels of medical and technical knowledge are expanded.

It should be noted that service development is inherently more risky than market penetration since substantial investment is often required to develop new services and there is no guarantee that once developed they will be favoured by the organization's current customer groups.

Market Development

Market development involves the organization in continuing to provide its current range of services, but extending the range of markets into which they will be delivered. The nonprofit can hence elect to target additional market segments, to exploit new uses for the service, or both. A strategy of market development may be most appropriate where a given organization has distinctive expertise to offer. In such cases it may make more sense to target other segments rather than dilute the available expertise by attempting to broaden the range of services available.

A number of nonprofit organizations may be forced into a strategy of market development even in circumstances where they have yet to completely satisfy demand in their existing markets. The housing charity Shelter, for example, has found it necessary to support the homeless in an increasingly larger percentage of Britain's towns and cities, whereas only a few years ago it could have concentrated solely on a small number of these, secure in the knowledge that it was addressing the needs of the majority of individuals at risk.

Diversification

This is perhaps the most risky of all the four potential growth strategies. It involves the nonprofit in beginning to deliver services of which it has no experience and supplying these to completely new groups of customers. The degree of risk the organization is subjecting itself to will depend on whether the diversification is related or unrelated. In the case of related diversification, the organization is continuing to operate within broadly the same sector but is attempting to do something new for the first time. The rush to create retail outlets for charities in the 1980s would have constituted related diversification for the organizations involved, since they had long experience of fundraising, but perhaps little, if any, of running a successful retail enterprise.

Unrelated diversification is perhaps less common since this would involve an organization in a radical departure from its existing services/markets. This may be necessary for some nonprofits who find that their raison d'être has ceased to exist as, for example, a cure is found for a disease, the relief of whose sufferers they exist to serve. Government legislation can also force organizations into unrelated diversification. Many of the oldest charity trusts in the UK were originally formed with the express purpose of maintaining bridges, highways, etc. Now that local authorities have statutory obligations to look after the transport networks within their boundaries, the objects of these trusts have changed over time to allow them to support other worthwhile causes, many of which, on the face of it, bear no resemblance whatsoever to the original reasons for the trust's creation. It should be noted, though, that for the sub-group of nonprofits—charities—unrelated diversification is a relatively rare strategy. In many countries the reason for this is a legal one. Charities in the UK are obligated to pursue their 'objects', which are specified at the time of the charity's formation, and they require formal permission from the Charity Commission if these are to be extended or adapted in some way.

Are there other Strategic Directions?

For the sake of completeness it is worth noting that not every organization may wish to achieve growth. Ansoff's matrix as depicted in Figure 5.1 assumes that this is the case and ignores the other strategic options available, which include:

- *do nothing*—where the organization takes a conscious decision not to alter current strategy;
- *withdraw*—where the organization decides to sever its links with a particular service/market;
- *consolidate*—which involves the nonprofit in seeking strategies that will allow it to maintain its current market position. This should not be confused with the 'do nothing' option since the strategies necessary to support a current strategic position are unlikely to be identical to those that allowed an organization to create it in the first place.

Merger/Collaborative Strategy

The incidence of nonprofit merger activity in both the USA and the UK remains relatively low. Of the more high-profile mergers to take place in the UK in recent years, the Jewish Blind Society merged with the Jewish Welfare Board in 1990 to become Jewish Care, and the National Council for Carers and Elderly Dependants merged with the Association of Carers to form the Carers National Association. The Terrence Higgins Trust has also undertaken a series of mergers with six other AIDS charities (McCurry 1999) and the country's two biggest cancer charities, the Imperial Cancer Research Fund and the Cancer Research Campaign, merged in 2001 to form Cancer Research UK.

We have already noted a number of reasons for the possible reticence of nonprofit organizations to consider a merger as a strategic option, even where this would be the best way of achieving the objectives of the organization. They are not subject to the same market pressures as business organizations and their founders often have such a passion for the cause that they are simply blinded to the activities of organizations undertaking related work. This is a great shame as there may be a variety of benefits that could accrue from either outright merger or some form of collaboration.

In their ground-breaking work, Singer and Yankey (1991) identify three potential motives for collaboration and merger; the lure of efficiency gains, the ability to build a monopoly position (based on a shared vision), and empire-building on the part of non-profit managers. In their later study, Cowin and Moore (1996) confirmed these findings, and added the additional dimension that those mergers that had been enforced by funders (which can often be the case) appeared to be less successful than those undertaken willingly and based on a shared vision.

In his study of motives for merger in the nonprofit housing sector, Mullins (1989) identifies additional motives such as the potential to spread overheads, the achievement of scale economies, opportunities to increase the asset base/borrowing capacity, geographical and sectoral expansion, the elimination of competition, and responses to tax changes. Schmid (1995) further suggests that the need to control the operating environment and reduce uncertainty can be additional motives. Not surprisingly, in the nonprofit context, the needs of beneficiary groups can, in addition, precipitate merger or collaborative activity. Authors such as Singer and Yankey (1991) have noted the ability of a newly merged organization to increase the quality and range of services it provides to clients.

There is also evidence that organizations look to merge when a crisis threatens their future survival. The merger between RADAR (Royal Association for Disability and Rehabilitation) with the Enham Trust occurred when RADAR was on the verge of insolvency and the Enham Trust acted as a 'white knight' in offering a merger. The service provision of both organizations was of course complementary, so there was a good strategic fit between them but the final impetus was undoubtedly the crisis facing RADAR. This is an idea also supported by Singer and Yankey (1991: 361) who note that mergers are 'often depicted as a last resort for survival in the face of intense competition for resources' (see also Golensky 1999).

The role of funders in precipitating merger or collaborative activity is also receiving increasing attention and there is now considerable anecdotal evidence of the direct or indirect role that funders can have in precipitating a merger or collaborative decision. Cowin and Moore (1996) have provided empirical evidence that pressure from funders is a key factor in 38 per cent of all mergers (both planned and actual). Funders are quoted as wanting value for money, wanting evidence that their money makes a real difference, and wanting their funds to be professionally and honestly accounted for. Many funders (especially the better informed trusts and foundations) therefore encourage collaboration and joint working, and are critical of what they regard as needless duplication.

In respect of the direct influence of funders, the rationalization of HIV/AIDS charities has been described as a forced development; the result of improvements in drug therapy and treatment, and pressure from health service funders for more cost-effective services. The merger in the UK undertaken in 1999 between Parentline and the National Stepfamilies Association was also, reportedly, undertaken because of pressure from a corporate funder (British Telecom). Even in the nonprofit housing sector, where traditionally a considerable degree of autonomy has existed, the 'best value' agenda of the government is putting increasing pressure on organizations to rationalize and cut costs by stripping out duplicate layers of management.

Funders may also impact indirectly on a decision to merge. A recent opinion poll in the UK conducted by MORI concluded that over 82 per cent of the British public believe that there are too many charities (Wethered 1999). Similarly more recent work undertaken in the commercial sector concludes that 75 per cent of businesses believe that charities should merge if conducting similar work. Mather (2000) notes that the opinion of donors and potential donors is now often cited as a reason that charities should consider merger as an option: 'There is a danger that the patience and support of funders and the general public is growing thinner as the number of charities and their calls for help escalate. There is a real need to show that the sector is behaving responsibly for charitable causes and beneficiaries and not for the vested interests of paid and unpaid charity workers' (2000: 12).

In reviewing their marketing objectives, it is therefore important that nonprofits identify appropriate partners with whom they might collaborate, either in respect of income generation or, more likely, service delivery. It may be that a number of partnerships may be developed across a range of different services and at the strategic level of the marketing plan, it will be important to outline who these partners might be and how ongoing relationships may be inculcated. As these relationships develop it will thereafter be important to specify how each partnership will operate and the relative strengths of each partner that it is intended to utilize.

Competitive Strategy

There may also be instances where a nonprofit finds itself faced with competition. This may take the form of competition for funds, or it might be competition to provide specific services to a beneficiary group. Here, just as in the commercial sector, the organization needs to decide on what basis it will compete. Authors such as Porter (1980) have argued that organizations may either compete on the basis of being the lowest cost provider, or on the basis of being differentiated in some way. The mistake organizations make, at least according to Porter, is in being unclear as to what the basis for competition will actually be and thus creating a strategic fudge lying somewhere between these two options. Porter argues that successful strategy is predicated on the selection of one of these alternatives.

Choosing to compete on the basis of cost is only a viable strategy where economies of scale or other cost advantages are genuinely achievable (or have already been achieved) by the nonprofit in question. It must also be difficult, or ideally impossible, for a competitor to match this performance. Assuming this is the case, a cost leadership strategy will flourish where:

- price competition is especially vigorous;
- the product or service is essentially standardized and readily available from a range of suppliers (which encourages buyers to select on the basis of price);
- there are few ways to differentiate the service;

- buyers incur low switching costs in changing from one supplier to another, thus giving them the flexibility to switch readily to lower priced sellers having equally good products/services; and

- buyers are large and have significant power to bargain down prices.

It is interesting to note that a number of charities are now beginning to compete for donations on the basis of cost leadership. Some charities now advertise the fact that 'all donated monies will be employed directly on the cause' or 'no donated monies will be spent on management overheads'. Others specify the exact percentage of the gift that will be applied to the cause and use this as the primary basis for competing with other similar organizations. Putting aside the legitimacy of such claims (administration never comes entirely for free!) it is interesting that such strategies appear to be on the increase and that the criteria listed above all now appear to be met in the fund-raising context.

Differentiation strategies become an attractive competitive approach whenever buyers' needs and preferences are too diverse to be fully satisfied by a standardized product/service. To succeed with a differentiation strategy, an organization has to study buyers' needs and behaviour carefully to understand what they regard as being important, what they think has particular value, and what they are willing to pay for.

Differentiation can be achieved by:

- *Physical differentiation of the market entity*. The design of the product/service may be enhanced in some way to distinguish it from the competition.

- *Psychological differentiation of the market entity*. The imagery associated with the product/service may be formulated to be in some way unique.

- *Differences in purchasing environment*. The outlets through which the product/service is marketed or delivered may offer features which differentiate it from the competition.

- *Difference by virtue of physical distribution capability*. Thus customers may find that the products/services are delivered more efficiently or on a more timely basis than would be available from another supplier.

- *Difference in after-purchase assurance of satisfaction in use*. After-sales service can also be used for the purposes of differentiation, perhaps through the provision of a higher-quality service than that offered by competitors. This may be of particular relevance to fund-raisers who could seek to reassure donors that their monies have been used to good effect.

Segmentation Strategy

Having decided on overall direction and the basis for competition it will be important to define the customers or users whose needs will be addressed in the marketing plan. This process is known as market segmentation, which Kotler (1991: 66) defines as 'the task of breaking the total market (which is typically too large to serve) into segments that share common properties'. In a similar vein, Simpson (1994: 564) defines it as 'the process of dividing up a market into two or more parts, each having unique needs and then developing products and related marketing programmes to meet the needs of one or more of these segments'.

A number of different methods may be used to segment the market. Green (1977) suggested that these methods could be categorized as being either *a priori* and cluster-based or post hoc. An *a priori* approach is based on the notion that the marketer decides in advance of any research which basis for segmentation he/she intends to use. Typically this might involve categorizing customers according to their projected usage pattern (e.g. heavy, medium, or light user), demographic, and/or psychographic characteristics. The marketer would then carry out research to identify the attractiveness of each segment and make a decision on the basis of the results as to which segment or segments to pursue. Post hoc segmentation involves the marketer in carrying out an amount of initial research into the marketplace. This research might highlight attributes, attitudes, or benefits which relate to particular groups of customers—information which may then be used to decide how best to divide the market. In practice, whether *a priori* or *post hoc* segmentation is undertaken will depend on the relative degree of experience a marketer has within a given market. In cases where the marketer is close to the market and has considerable experience of it an *a priori* approach may best suit the company's needs. Alternatively, where the marketer has little knowledge, a *post hoc* method of segmentation may be most appropriate.

Criteria for Segmenting Consumer Markets

Over the years a plethora of different variables have been used as the basis for market segmentation. Fortunately the majority of these can now be grouped as follows:

- demographic
- geographic and geodemographic
- behavioural
- psychographic.

Each of these classes of variables will now be considered in turn.

Demographic Variables

It may be possible to segment a market on the basis of variables such as age, gender, socio-economic group, family size, family life cycle, income, religion, race, nationality, occupation, or education. These are collectively known as *demographic variables*. This method of market segmentation is particularly popular in consumer markets since consumer wants, needs, and preferences are often highly correlated with these characteristics. The other reason for the popularity of demographic segmentation is a historical one. Such data have been collected over a great many years and hence much is known about the consumer behaviour of each target group. One may purchase, for instance, data relating to the media exposure of each individual demographic category.

It should be noted that it is now rare for an organization to use one demographic variable in isolation and they now tend to use some combination of the same (Stanton 1978). Despite their popularity, they are seen by many as offering only a low utility primarily because they are based on descriptive rather than causal factors and hence cannot be relied upon as accurate predictors of future behaviour. Despite these reservations, their use is still widespread. A selection of such variables will therefore now be considered in turn.

Age

Age has frequently been used as the basis for segmentation since purchasing patterns are clearly related to an individual's age. One interesting reason for this observation may have been revealed by a study carried out by Philips and Sternthal (1977) who concluded that age differences result in changes to the sources of information a particular individual will use. Age was also shown to affect the ability to learn and the susceptibility to social influence. Clearly these are all factors which could influence purchasing behaviour and all three have a relevance to the nonprofit sector.

Gender

Kotler (1991) notes that an individual's gender has proved to be a good indicator of a propensity to buy a particular product or brand. In particular he cites cosmetics, clothing, magazines, and toiletries. Gender has proved to be a useful criterion in the nonprofit sector too, as it seems that charity donors are more likely to be female. Females have also been shown to respond differently to different forms of appeal. In seeking to raise funds for cancer research, for example, one major nonprofit identified, through testing a variety of messages, that females responded best to case studies of successful treatments for the disease, while males responded best to specific sets of scientific data (e.g. research results). Much social marketing may also have to be designed on the basis of a segmented approach by gender. Attitudes, for example, to safe sex, abortion, and healthcare screening have all been found to vary significantly by gender, and communications messages must be tailored to reflect this.

Family Life Cycle

Segmentation conducted on this basis, is based on the premise that demand for goods/services will vary depending on the stage that customers have reached in terms of the development of their family. Segmentation can hence be based on whether individuals are single, married, married with children, etc. The idea is certainly not new. Rowntree first suggested it at the beginning of the twentieth century. However, the model now in most common usage is that first presented by Wells and Gubar (1966), and illustrated in Figure 5.2.

As a composite model (made up of age, number of years married, ages of children, and working status), the concept of the family life cycle has proved to be more useful than simple segmentation based on age alone (Lansing and Kish 1957). It is however not without its critics since it is based on the conventional nuclear family. When one views the current pattern of family life in many countries, this model is clearly no longer completely valid. The model, for example, takes no account of the high divorce rate and subsequent increase in one-person households and has a somewhat outdated view of women. Women are now able to work a larger proportion of their lives and are able to continue working even during the early years of their children's lives. Despite the criticisms, however, the model is still in wide usage and has been proven to be a good indicator of a propensity to purchase certain categories of services (see, for example, Dominguez and Page (1984)).

Stages in the family life cycle	Buying patterns
1. Bachelor stage: young single people living at home	Few financial commitments—recreation and fashion oriented
2. Newly married couples: young, no children	High purchase rate of consumer durables—buy white goods, cars, furniture
3. Full nest 1: youngest child under six	House buying is at a peak. Liquid assets are low—buy medicines, toys, baby food, white goods
4. Full nest 2: youngest child six or over	Financial position is improving—buy a wider variety of foods, bicycles, pianos
5. Full nest 3: older married couples with dependent children	Financial position is improving still further. Some children now have jobs and wives are working. Increasing purchase of desirables—buy furniture and luxury goods
6. Empty nest 1: older married couples, no children at home, head of household still in workforce	Home ownership is at a peak—savings have increased and financial position improved. Interested in travel, recreation, and self-education. Not interested in new products—buy luxuries and home improvements
7. Empty nest 2: older married, no children living at home, head of household retired	Substantial reduction in income. Buy medical products and appliances that aid health, sleep, and digestion
8. Solitary survivor in the workforce	Income still high but may sell home
9. Solitary survivor, retired	Same medical and product needs as group 7. Substantial cut in income. Need for attention and security

Figure 5.2 The family life cycle

Source: Wilson et al. (1994). Reproduced with the kind permission of Butterworth-Heinemann, Oxford.

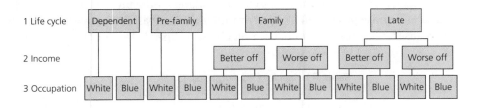

Figure 5.3 The sagacity model

Source: Reproduced with kind permission.

In recent years a new version of the family life cycle has emerged which also takes account of an individual's aspirations and behaviour patterns as they progress through the phases of the life cycle model. Four main stages of the life cycle are defined and these are then subdivided by income and occupation. The resultant model, known as Sagacity, is shown in Figure 5.3.

This model improves on the earlier family life cycle since an individual's needs will clearly be related not only to his/her position in their life cycle but also to their occupation and relative income level. The definition of a typical segment would hence involve all three variables and on the basis of these one would then be in a position to identify the purchasing patterns of the individuals concerned.

A further variation on this theme was supplied by Levy (1992) who suggested that the demographic variable career phase could be used as the basis for segmentation, particularly in the market for continuing education. This has clear implications for both colleges and universities, which could closely monitor the needs of a variety of career phase segments and determine on the basis of such intelligence which were likely to be the most appropriate to serve with their particular educational programmes.

Income/Occupation

Income has also been proven to be a further useful base for segmentation and despite difficulties in identifying a true picture of income for a particular group of consumers (i.e. taking account of the black economy and traditional reluctance to disclose such data), has been shown to be a good indicator of a propensity to purchase certain categories of products or services, or even to give to certain categories of cause.

A more common method of segmentation, however, is to be found by combining income and occupation into a single model. Since its conception in the UK, the NRS (National Readership Survey) has classified readers of press/magazines into one of six categories according to social grade. Buyers of magazine/press advertising space may then use this data to select media that provide a high concentration of readers belonging to one or more of their target groups. The NRS classification is shown in Table 5.1.

It should be noted, however, that the system is now almost fifty years old and therefore based on a time when society was considerably more stable than it is at present. As Chisnall (1992: 210) notes, 'originally the grading system was intended to reflect the impact of lifestyle, income, and status; but society has been in a state of flux for (many) years'. Social strata no longer exist in the way that they once did. Educational opportunities are now spread through all societal levels and many women are now providing a primary or second income for their households, making it difficult to identify a 'head of household' on whose profession a categorization could be based. The system is further flawed because it takes no account of customer lifestyles, needs, or aspirations—in short,

Table 5.1 Socio-economic groupings

Social grade	Example occupation
A	Senior professional/managerial
B	Middle professional/managerial
C1	Supervisory management—clerical
C2	Skilled manual labour—e.g. electrician
D	Unskilled manual—e.g. labourer
E	Unemployed, students, etc.

it says nothing about consumers as people. All of these characteristics clearly have the capacity to influence one's choice of product or service and since the social grading system was based on the fundamental premise that people's propensity to purchase certain categories of products would depend primarily on their level of income, its use must surely be called into question.

Geographic Segmentation

It has been argued that in terms of historic development, segmentation on the grounds of geographic location was the first to develop. Until quite recently, transportation systems would have limited the access that organizations had to more distant geographical markets. They therefore had little choice but to set up their businesses in close proximity to a key concentration of potential buyers. Given that many nonprofits are set up with the objective of supplying services to a particular geographic community this may be a very effective (and necessary!) method of segmenting the potential market for a wide variety of such organizations. However, segmentation on the basis of geography represents a very broadbrush approach to segmentation and can supply little in the way of fine detail, particularly when one is investigating consumer markets. By contrast, 'geo-demographics' is an attempt to improve significantly on some of the limitations of the simple geographic model.

Geo-demographics

The study of geo-demographics arose from work carried out by Webber in 1973. He was originally interested in studying urban deprivation in Liverpool, and classified neighbourhoods using techniques of cluster analysis to produce a system containing 25 separate neighbourhood types. Each exhibited different mixes of problems and required a different type of social policy. Each neighbourhood was also defined in terms of its population, housing, and socio-economic characteristics. With the collaboration of the Census Office, he was later able to extend this analysis and derive 38 separate neighbourhood types with which he was able to classify the UK as a whole.

The next significant development came when Baker (1982) of the British Market Research Bureau was able to identify that Webber's system had considerable potential for controlling the activities of the TGI (Target Group Index). He was able to identify that certain neighbourhood groups displayed a particular type of purchasing pattern. In short, similar neighbourhoods tended to buy similar types of products. The techniques of geo-demographics have recently been refined and a variety of commercial systems are now in existence. In the UK the most well-known of these is undoubtedly a system produced by CACI called ACORN (A Classification Of Residential Neighbourhoods). The full classification system is shown in Table 5.2.

Users of the ACORN system can take an individual's postcode and identify the type of housing that that individual lives in, approximately what income they have, whether they are house owners or tenants and approximately what stage they have reached in their family life cycle. They can also identify details of those product categories most likely to be of interest to the individual in question. This is a powerful marketing tool since an organization can request that its database be profiled and if certain ACORN categories are found to predominate, the information can then be employed to good

Table 5.2 The ACORN classification system

Acorn Groups 1991	% of population
Wealthy Achievers, Suburban Areas	14.0
Affluent Greys—Rural Communities	2.2
Prosperous Pensioners, Retirement Areas	2.8
Affluent Executives, Family Areas	3.4
Well Off Workers, Family Areas	7.0
Affluent Urbanities, Town and City Areas	2.5
Prosperous Professionals, Metropolitan Areas	2.5
Better Off Executives, Inner City Areas	4.0
Comfortable Middle Ages, Mature Home Owning Areas	13.7
Skills Workers, Home Owning Areas	10.8
New Home Owners, Mature Communities	9.9
White Collar Workers, Better Off Multi-ethnic Areas	4.0
Older People, Less Prosperous Areas	4.4
Council Estate Residents, Better Off Homes	10.9
Council Estate Residents, High Unemployment	3.6
Council Estate Residents, Great Hardship	2.4
People In Multi-ethnic Areas, Low Income	2.8

Source: © CACI Limited, 1998. All Rights Reserved. ACORN and CACI are registered trademarks of CACI Ltd.

effect by targeting other households which have a similar profile. This would ensure that only individuals who are more likely to have an interest in (or need for) an organization's services will be selected for contact. The ACORN system can hence help save valuable marketing resources, particularly when one considers that the subsequent purchase of lists of prospects is relatively inexpensive.

It should be noted that a number of other companies are now offering geo-demographic systems on a commercial basis. These systems include MOSAIC and PINPOINT.

Behavioural Segmentation

Kotler (1991: 272) defines behavioural segmentation as dividing buyers 'on the basis of their knowledge, attitude, use, or response to a product'. He goes on to say that 'many marketers believe that behavioural variables are the best starting point for constructing market segments'. There are many bases for segmentation under this general category, among them benefit segmentation, brand loyalty, user rate, user status, and usage situation.

Benefit Segmentation

Almost certainly the best-known writer concerning benefit segmentation was Haley (1968). His research related to the toothpaste market and he identified four benefit segments; seeking economy, protection, cosmetic, and taste benefits. In Haley's view, the benefits identified in each case are the primary reason for the existence of true market segments. Interestingly, his analysis showed that each benefit group was associated with distinct sets of demographic, behavioural, and psychographic characteristics. For example, the category seeking decay prevention were found to have large families, use consequently large amounts of toothpaste, and be conservative in nature. All this information is clearly valuable to toothpaste manufacturers, who can use it to buy space in media channels which reach the target group cost effectively and, more importantly, design promotional straplines (or unique selling propositions) that will appeal to the target market. A single product or brand may even be dedicated specifically to the needs of that target audience.

The concept of benefit segmentation has also been explored in the nonprofit sector. Cermak et al. (1994) for example, have attempted to derive a benefit segmentation of potential donors. Their study was based however not on the behaviour of members of the 'donor market' but rather on an analysis of the reasons why decision makers in charitable trusts choose to make donations to a particular cause. The authors identified four distinct benefit segments, namely:

1. *affiliators*—donors who benefit through social affiliation and the opportunity to exercise humanitarian impulses;
2. *pragmatists*—donors who are primarily motivated by the tax advantages that might accrue from a donation;
3. *dynasts*—donors who give because there is a family tradition of giving;
4. *repayers*—donors who seem to give because of a need to reciprocate—perhaps because someone close to them has benefited from the cause.

An understanding of the key benefits sought by such donors could hence be of immense value to fundraisers in facilitating the design of appropriate marketing communications.

Benefit segmentation may be particularly useful where a particular product/service category already exists. It will then be somewhat easier to encourage individuals to list the benefits sought and subsequently use this as the basis for segmentation. As an example of this, Brown (1992) carried out a benefit analysis of the fitness market. He identified that while considerable attention had been paid to the fitness and wellness needs of people by healthcare and related marketing organizations, little research had been carried out directed at identifying the market segments for fitness based upon consumer's perceived benefits of fitness. His study resulted in the definition of three distinct segments of fitness customers, namely:

1. *winners*—those who tend to do whatever it takes to get ahead in life and have realized the importance of becoming and remaining physically fit;
2. *dieters*—those who are mainly interested in weight control and physical appearance using exercise to obtain these goals;
3. *self-improvers*—those who see exercise as a way to feel better.

From the perspective of a GP looking to encourage his/her patients to adopt better standards of fitness, it would hence appear that there are three distinct sets of benefits that patients could view as directly resulting from an exercise regime. By implication, promotional material could be produced which would be likely to strike a chord with each segment.

Brand Loyalty Status

The second technique encompassed by behavioural segmentation is that of brand loyalty status. This is an attempt to segment consumers on the basis of their purchase/usage patterns. Wilson et al. (1994) identify the following four segments.

1. *Hard-core loyals*—consumers who buy one brand all the time. Hence a buying pattern of AAAAA may be used to represent the consistent purchasing pattern of brand A.
2. *Soft-core loyals*—consumers who buy from a limited set of brands on a regular basis. Their purchasing pattern may be represented by AABABB.
3. *Shifting loyals*—consumers who switch loyalty on a regular basis. Their purchasing pattern may be represented by AABBCC.
4. *Switchers*—consumers who show no loyalty to any one brand. This group may be considered especially susceptible to special offers or be attracted by variety. Their purchasing pattern may be represented by ABBCACB.

If, however, one is considering the use of loyalty as the criterion for segmentation one should also consider the difficulties that might be encountered in the measurement thereof. What appear to be brand loyal purchase patterns might in reality reflect habit, indifference, a low price, or the non-availability of other brands. There is therefore a need to probe what lies behind the purchase patterns observed. Even when various degrees of loyalty in the marketplace have been identified, it is not always a straightforward exercise to take advantage of this information. While one can clearly identify one's own 'hard-core loyals' etc. it may not be easy to identify those of other organizations. The utility of the concept will hence depend on the extent to which each segment also exhibits a unique set of demographic or lifestyle characteristics. Knowledge of these details may lead to the development of a strategy designed to influence traditional patterns of loyalty, specifically targeted at those groups of consumers most likely to respond. Soft-core loyals purchasing competing services may, for example, be a particularly worthwhile segment to address.

User Status

A further popular method for segmenting the market is to utilize data relating to product/service usage rate. Customers may be classified according to whether they are heavy, medium, or light users of the product and treated accordingly. This method may be particularly useful since it is often a relatively small percentage of the market that accounts for a large percentage of consumption. Twedt (1964) argued that in many markets 20 per cent of the customers account for 80 per cent of the consumption. Thus there would be considerable utility in profiling those consumers who exhibit high usage rates. Not only can existing heavy users then be treated with an appropriate level of care, but other individuals in society who have a similar profile can be targeted in an attempt to get them to sample the organization's services. This method does however have the drawback that not all heavy consumers are usually available to the same provider because they are seeking a different set of benefits. For example, regular theatre attenders may be subdivided by a preference for different categories of performance.

Lifestyle Segmentation

Lifestyle or psychographic segmentation is an attempt to move away from earlier views of people expressed mainly in behavioural, demographic, and socio-economic terms. In this case, individuals are grouped in terms of their hobbies/interests, feelings, aspirations, etc. In modern times this represents one of the most powerful criteria which can be used for market segmentation since a mass of lifestyle data now exists in respect of the readership of a whole variety of different publications, making it possible to target individuals on this basis very cost-effectively.

Kotler (1991: 171) defines lifestyle as a 'person's pattern of living in the world as expressed in the person's activities, interests and opinions. Lifestyle (therefore) portrays the whole individual interacting with his/her environment.' It may therefore be considered as distinct from personality. Personality variables describe the pattern of psychological characteristics that an individual might posses, but say nothing of that individual's hobbies, interests, opinions, or activities. Lifestyle data can supply these missing variables. Boyd and Levy (1967: 38) assessed the implications of the lifestyle concept and drew the following conclusions:

Marketing is a process of providing customers with parts of a potential mosaic from which they, as artists of their own lifestyles, can pick and choose to develop the composition that for the time seems the best. The marketer who thinks about his products in this way will seek to understand their potential settings and relationships to other parts of consumer lifestyles and thereby to increase the number of ways they fit meaningfully into the pattern.

A number of early lifestyle classification systems are to be found in the literature; among them Wells (1975: 201) who questioned some 4000 male respondents and, using the technique of factor analysis, was able to derive the simple classification system as shown in Table 5.3.

Wells was also able to define the media and product usage of each group described above. The utility of this very simple classification lies in its ability to suggest effective promotional strategies that can be used with each segment. Group 4, for example, may well be deemed an appropriate target for arts marketers promoting a series of live classical music concerts. If so, price may be less of an issue for this group and rather than trying to compete with other arts events on this basis, marketers may instead try to emphasize the quality of their events and price them to reflect this. However, as the reader will no doubt appreciate, classifications such as this are very vague and it should hence be no surprise to learn that writers such as Young (1971) warn us that this form of general societal segmentation system can never have the same degree of accuracy as that produced by a product-specific approach. As a result Young argues that the only way to utilize psychographic variables to their best effect is to analyse them in the context of a particular product/service—a view shared by Wells (1975). This is an important argument because it suggests that organizations would be well advised to look to those lifestyle variables that are most closely associated with their organization and explore first the potential for segmentation on these grounds. Indeed, many examples are to be found in the literature

Table 5.3 Wells's psychographic classification system

Group 1. The Quiet Family Man—8% of total males

He is a self-sufficient man who wants to be left alone and is basically shy. Tends to be as little involved with community life as possible. His life revolves around the family, simple work, and television viewing, has a marked fantasy life. As a shopper he is practical, less drawn to consumer goods and pleasures than other men. Low education and economic status, he tends to be older then average.

Group 2. The Traditionalist—16% of all males

The man who feels secure, has self-esteem, follows conventional rules. He is proper and respectable, regards himself as altruistic and interested in the welfare of others. As a shopper he is conservative, likes popular brands and well-known manufacturers. Low education and low or middle socio-economic status. The oldest age group.

Group 3. The Discontented Man—13% of all males

He is a man who is likely to be dissatisfied with his work. He feels passed by life, dreams of better jobs, more money, and more security. He tends to be distrusting and socially aloof. As a buyer he is risk conscious. Lowest education and lowest socio-economic group, mostly older than average.

Group 4. The Ethical Highbrow—14% of all males

This is a very concerned man, sensitive to people needs. Basically a puritan, content with family life, friends and work, interest in culture, religion, and social reform. As a consumer he is interested in quality, which may at times justify greater expenditure.

Group 5. The Pleasure Oriented Man—9% of all males

He tends to emphasize his masculinity and rejects whatever appears to be soft or feminine. He views himself as a leader among men. Self-centred, dislikes his work. Seeks immediate gratification for his needs. He is an impulsive buyer, likely to buy products with a masculine image. Low education, lower socio-economic class, middle aged or younger.

Group 6. The Achiever—11% of all males

This is likely to be a hard-working man, dedicated to success and all that it implies, social prestige, power, and money. Is in favour of diversity, is adventurous about leisure time pursuits. Is stylish, likes good food, music, etc. As a consumer he is status conscious, a thoughtful and discriminating buyer. Good education, high socio-economic group, young.

Group 7. The He Man—19% of all males

He is gregarious, likes action, seeks an exciting and dramatic life. Thinks of himself as capable and dominant. Tends to be more of a bachelor than a family man, even after marriage. Products he buys and brands preferred are likely to have self-expressive value, especially a man-of-action dimension. Well educated, mainly middle socio-economic status, the youngest of the male groups.

Group 8. The Sophisticated Man—10% of all males

He is likely to be intellectual, concerned about social issues, admires men with artistic and intellectual achievements. Socially cosmopolitan, broad interests. Wants to be dominant and a leader. As a consumer he is attracted to the unique and fashionable. Best educated and highest status of all groups, younger than average.

Source: Reprinted with permission from *Journal of Marketing Research*, published by the American Marketing Association, Wells W. D. (1975) Vol. 12, no. (2), 196–213.

of researchers who have adopted this product-specific approach. In a general study of healthcare Rubinger (1987) has identified 9 psychographic segments which define how consumers view the provision thereof. The segments are given below:

1. *quality-minded users*—the largest group nationwide; they look for the best healthcare at any cost;

2. *ready users*—the second largest group; they represent a very receptive market for healthcare and will readily accept whatever is available;

3. *independently healthy*—participate in sports, are concerned about nutrition, and pay more for healthcare;

4. *avoiders*—stay away from healthcare;

5. *naturalists*—seek alternatives to traditional healthcare;

6. *family-oriented users*—believe their children's health to be paramount, interested in nutrition, wellness, and family;

7. *clinic cynics*—sceptical about all forms of organized health care;

8. *generics*—see no difference between healthcare provision from one institution to another;

9. *loyalists*—find one institution and stay with it.

There are many implications for marketing strategy that come out of this research since certain segments can clearly be targeted with campaigns either to address their specific needs or to facilitate a change in attitude. A great number of studies may be found in the literature which make exactly this point and demonstrate how an understanding of customer lifestyles makes it possible to select media which reach those customers cost-effectively and to select promotional messages which a particular group will find intuitively more appealing.

Given the enthusiasm in the literature for the use of psychographic variables, it is not surprising to learn that most national/international advertising agencies now have their own classification system to assist in campaign planning. There are also a number of commercially available systems. Among these is a system known as VALS (Values and Lifestyles Segmentation) which attempts to measure and segment people based on their goals, motivations, and values. People in a large number of different countries have now been categorized. Developed in the USA by Arnold Mitchell of the Stanford Research Institute, the system categorizes people into one of nine lifestyle groups, namely:

1. *survivors*—who are generally disadvantaged and who tend to be depressed, withdrawn, and despairing;

2. *sustainers*—who are disadvantaged but who are fighting hard to escape poverty;

3. *belongers*—who tend to be conventional, nostalgic, conservative, and generally reluctant to experiment with new products or ideas;

4. *emulators*—who are status-conscious, ambitious, and upwardly mobile;

5. *achievers*—who make things happen and enjoy life;

6. *I-am-me*—who are self-engrossed, respond to whims, and are generally young;

7. *experientials*—who want to experience a wide variety of what life can offer;

8. *socially conscious*—people with a marked sense of social responsibility who want to improve the conditions of society;

9. *integrateds*—who are psychologically fully mature and who combine the best elements of inner and outer directedness.

The designers of VALS believe that individuals can be seen to pass through a number of development phases, with the integrated stage being seen as the ultimate. In terms of marketing, each segment can be seen to have very different needs and hence products and services could be designed to focus specifically on a particular group of people. Helpfully, it is possible to purchase lists of individuals who can be categorized as belonging to one or either of these segments, so targeting can now be greatly enhanced.

There are many other systems available commercially, most of which work on a similar principle although the variables tested in each case are slightly different. It would therefore be advantageous prior to utilizing one of these systems to have carried out some initial market research to identify specifically which lifestyle variables are significant in a given market. Other commercially available systems include Young and Rubicam's 4Cs and Taylor Nelson's Monitor.

A Cautionary Note

Having extolled the virtues of lifestyle segmentation, it is important to be clear about their use in a not-for-profit setting. Many of the systems now available were designed with the commercial sector in mind. They may therefore not offer the same degree of utility to the nonprofit sector, particularly given the observation of Young (1971) who suggested that to use lifestyle data effectively, only those variables of direct relevance to the work of a particular organization should be selected. Having sounded this word of caution, however, many of the largest lifestyle houses in the UK *do* now gather data in respect of nonprofit products and services. As a result it is now possible to buy lists of individuals who have a propensity to give to particular charitable causes and, moreover, to profile these individuals to ascertain whether they exhibit any other lifestyle characteristics which might suggest appropriate promotional messages and acceptable modes of contact. It is also possible to buy lists of individuals with an interest in specific categories of the arts, further/higher education, and aspects of healthcare. At the time of writing, this service is relatively inexpensive, costing typically only around £80–£150 per thousand names and addresses, depending on the degree of refinement (i.e. number of criteria) required. It should be noted, however, that for smaller nonprofits, even this cost may be prohibitive as most lifestyle houses have a minimum order quantity of between five and ten thousand names.

Criteria for Segmentation of Industrial Markets

Many nonprofits will be concerned not only with individuals in society but also with corporate organizations, particularly those that have the potential to act as sponsors of certain nonprofit activity. Indeed the support of corporate donors remains an important source of income for the voluntary sector. As a result it is worth briefly examining the criteria that can be used as the basis for segmentation in industrial markets.

Fortunately, the consensus to emerge from the literature is that it is possible to use many of the same criteria in industrial markets as one would typically use in consumer markets (see, for example, Nicosia and Wind (1977)). Wind and Cordozo (1974) suggest that industrial segmentation should however be considered in two stages. The first stage involves defining the segments in terms of industry demographics, size, industrial sector, SIC (Standard Industrial Classification) code, and product usage. The second stage they advocate is to define the segments in terms of the behavioural characteristics of their decision-making units or buying centres. The result is a hybrid segmentation system that

Table 5.4 Criteria for segmentation of industrial markets

Demographic

Industry type—Which industries that buy the product should be focused on?

Company size—What size companies should be focused on?

Location—What geographical areas should we focus on?

Operating variables

Technology—What customer technologies should we focus on?

User status (i.e. heavy, medium, light)—Which type of user should we concentrate on?

Customer capabilities—Should customers having many or few needs be concentrated on?

Purchasing approaches

Buying criteria—Should customers be targeted that are looking for price, quality, or service, etc.?

Buying policies—Should customers requiring leasing facilities, for example, be targeted?

Current relationships—Should the company focus only on those customers with whom a relationship already exists?

Situational factors

Urgency—Should customers requiring immediate delivery be targeted?

Size of order—Should customers requiring large or small orders be targeted?

Applications—Should customers requiring only a certain application of the product be targeted?

Personal characteristics

Loyalty—Should only companies exhibiting high degrees of loyalty to their suppliers be targeted?

Attitudes to risk—Should risk taking or risk avoiding customers be targeted?

Buyer–seller similarity—Should companies with similar characteristics to the seller be targeted?

Source: Bonoma and Shapiro (1983).

reflects not only the type of business, but also the manner in which it operates. To help illustrate the variety of criteria that are available it is worth briefly reviewing the work of Bonoma and Shapiro (1983) who developed one of the most comprehensive reviews of industrial segmentation currently available. The criteria that the authors identify are given in Table 5.4.

The authors originally suggested that these criteria are arranged in descending levels of importance. In the specific context of the nonprofit sector, however, many of the criteria towards the bottom of the list can actually offer considerably more utility than those towards the top. As an example, charities will look particularly to solicit support from corporate organizations that have a track record of loyalty to their suppliers. It takes time to establish relationships and a charity can invest considerable amounts of time and money securing appropriate corporate partnerships. They clearly have a vested interest in ensuring that, once established, these relationships prove to be as enduring as possible and to a certain extent this can be researched up-front.

Similarly the purchasing approaches adopted might also form the basis for appropriate market segmentation. Those organizations that are looking for a genuine degree of commercial gain to accrue from their involvement with a nonprofit organization should be approached rather differently from those that are likely to view their association purely as a philanthropic activity.

Since criteria such as company size and location will clearly determine the likelihood and amounts of funding to be supplied, it would seem that charities should give the greatest consideration to a mix of demographic, purchasing approach, and personal characteristic variables when designing an appropriate commercial segmentation system.

Criteria for Evaluating the Viability of Market Segments

The reader will now appreciate the diversity of variables that could potentially be used as the basis for market segmentation. While there are many potential segments that an organization could look to pursue, it is likely that only a few of them will actually be worth exploiting. The difficulty facing marketers is just how to evaluate the possibilities.

In practice, there are seven criteria that can be used to evaluate the potential offered by each segment proposed. Only if the analysis is favourable in each case should the segment be pursued. The segment must be:

1. *Measurable.* The market should be easily measurable and information should therefore either exist or be obtainable cost-effectively about the segment and its characteristics.

2. *Accessible.* It should be possible to design a distinct marketing mix to target the segment cost-effectively. One would therefore need to look, for example, at appropriate channels of distribution and media opportunities which could be used to target customers cost-effectively with the minimum of wastage.

3. *Substantial.* It should be cost-effective to market to the segment. Clearly the segment should be large enough in terms of sales volume (or small with sufficiently high margins) to warrant separate exploitation.

4. *Stable.* The segment's behaviour should be relatively stable over time to ensure that its future development may be predicted with a degree of accuracy for planning purposes.

5. *Appropriate.* It should be appropriate to exploit a particular segment given the organization's mission resources, objectives, etc.

6. *Unique.* The segment should be unique in terms of its response (to marketing activity) so that it can be distinguished from other segments.

7. *Sustainable.* Sustainability is an issue that is rapidly gaining in importance. It refers to the extent to which particular categories of customer can be sustained by the organization. The National Trust, for example, would hope to attract only conscientious walkers to their coastal paths; those that will treat the countryside with respect, stick to the signposted paths, take home their litter, etc. Not every segment of society will thus be sustainable, and marketing activity must hence be carefully targeted.

Point six warrants further elaboration. A segment may meet all of the other criteria but may behave identically to other segments in terms of its response to different types

(a)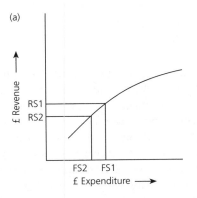

(b)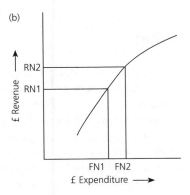

Figure 5.4 Hypothetical responses of two markets to fundraising activities

Source: Kotler and Andreasen (1991) *Strategic Marketing for Nonprofit Organisations*, 5th edn, © 1996. Adapted by permission of Prentice Hall Inc. Upper Saddle River, NJ.

and timing of strategy. If this is the case, Kotler and Andreasen (1991: 170) identify that 'although it may be conceptually useful to develop separate segments in this way, managerially it is not useful'. As an example, if two segments of attenders at arts events both enjoy the same category of performance, both expect the same level of service at the venue and both exhibit the same sensitivity to price, it is not manageri-ally useful to continue to regard them as unique, even if they differ in demographic or lifestyle terms, since the organization will treat both these segments of customers alike. Differential treatment is only appropriate where there is some form of differential response.

As a further example, Figures 5.4a and b show the allocation of a fundraising budget between two geographically separate markets, North and South. It can be seen from the slope of the two graphs that the North is more fundraising elastic (i.e. more sensitive to fundraising expenditure) than the South.

The points FS1 and FN1 represent equal fundraising expenditures in the two mar-kets. This allocation strategy yields total response results of (RS1 + RN1). However, if the expenditure is shifted around between the two regions and £2000 is moved from the South to the North, then the total amount raised will rise (RS2 + RN2) even though total expenditures are unchanged. Clearly, fundraisers should continue shift-ing their fundraising budget to the North until such time as the incremental gain in one market just equals the incremental loss in the other. One would normally take advantage of any differential responsiveness until there is no variation in total responsiveness given any small changes that might be instigated. It should also be remembered that in this simple example the only variable under consideration is fund-raising expenditure. In reality, segments may exhibit differential responsiveness to a wide range of differing criteria and these data can be utilized to great effect in market-ing planning. Clearly, if no differential responsiveness is exhibited one might question the value of segmenting the market on that basis since no managerial advantages accrue.

Positioning

Once the organization has decided appropriate targets for the marketing plan to address, it will be necessary to develop a strategy that will shape the image that the nonprofit wishes to project in the minds of those targets. This is in essence what marketers refer to as positioning and it may be defined as the act of defining in the minds of the target market what a particular organization's services can offer in relation to the others on the market. It is therefore essential that the organization understands how its various customer groups perceive it in relation to the other 'suppliers' in the market. For example, imagine that a university (let's call it Bloomsville) wanted to identify how it was perceived by prospective undergraduate students. It understands that students are attracted to it for a number of reasons, and decides to investigate how it is positioned in relation to other institutions in respect of just two of these—its academic reputation and the quality of life it offers to its students. The process would begin by some exploratory research to determine how the university and each of its competitors was rated on these two dimensions. A perceptual map could then be developed like the one depicted in Figure 5.5.

Bloomsville administrators could then see at a glance how their university was perceived in relation to others. It seems quite clear from the figure, for example, that although the quality of life offered by the university is perceived as being quite reasonable, the university has a relatively poor academic reputation. This may be a reputation that is entirely deserved and felt by the management to be a reasonable perception, in which case no further action might be necessary. If, however, Bloomsville academic research is actually well respected in the academic community and/or the university has recently figured well in the latest Research Assessment Exercise (RAE), management might take the view that this perception is unacceptable and initiate action to improve it. A communication plan could thus be implemented which would highlight recent Bloomsville research success in an attempt to shift its relative positioning, in the manner indicated in Figure 5.6. Further research would then be necessary to track the implementation of the communications plan, to ensure that it was having the desired effect in the market.

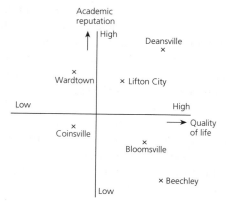

Figure 5.5 Initial positioning of Bloomsville University

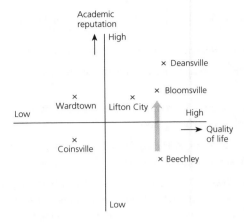

Figure 5.6 Final positioning of Bloomsville University

EXAMPLE

In 2003 St Luke's Medical Center in Milwaukee ran an advertising campaign implying that a general hospital with a full roster of specialists was safer for patients who might suffer complications during surgery. The campaign included print advertisements in local newspapers and a series of 60-second TV commercials aimed at countering competition from two newly opened specialized heart facilities in the metropolitan area. The commercials clearly define the positioning of the institution, suggesting that competitors cannot provide the kind of comprehensive service available in a full-service hospital. The commercials featured appearances from several specialists at the hospital, including an emergency physician who tells the camera, 'Many patients that come to St Luke's with symptoms of heart attacks are not having a heart attack at all. These patients' lives depend on our ability to treat more than heart problems.'

■ **SUMMARY**

In this chapter we explored how organizations can develop marketing objectives to identify exactly what will be achieved over the duration of a plan. We have argued that to be truly effective, such objectives should be SMART. We then focused on how these objectives might be achieved, drawing a distinction between strategy (i.e. the overall approach to the achievement of the objectives) and tactics (the minutiae of exactly what actions will be taken, when, and by whom). It is important to recognize that in the case of very small nonprofits, this division is unlikely to be so clear-cut and as a consequence, while a consideration of all these issues will remain important, tactics may be considered alongside strategy.

It is impossible to be definitive about the issues that will be strategic for a particular nonprofit to address, but I have suggested five layers of strategy that might typically be considered: overall direction, competitive/collaborative strategy, market segmentation, positioning, and branding. This list should not be regarded as exhaustive, merely indicative of the headings that might be considered. In this chapter we have dealt with the majority of these topics. We will explore branding in Chapter 6.

■ DISCUSSION QUESTIONS

1. Explain the relationship between corporate objectives and marketing objectives.

2. Under what circumstances should a nonprofit consider merger or collaboration as a strategic alternative?

3. What factors might a nonprofit organization take into account when deciding on an appropriate partner for a strategic collaboration?

4. How might a charity such as the RNLI (Royal National Lifeboat Institution) proceed to segment the market for potential donors to its organization? What issues would it need to consider?

5. With reference to your own organization, or one with which you are familiar, identify the basis that is currently used for market segmentation among potential funders and/or users of the nonprofit products/services. How might this be improved/refined?

6. Selecting a nonprofit sector you are personally familiar with, identify the criteria that are typically used for the purposes of positioning. Produce a series of perceptual maps that illustrate how each organization in this sector is presently positioned against these criteria. What conclusions might you draw from this analysis?

■ REFERENCES

Baker, K. (1982) quoted in Clark, E. (1982) 'Acorn finds new Friends', *Marketing*, 16 Dec., 13.

Bonoma, T.V. and Shapiro, B.P. (1983) *Segmenting The Industrial Market*, Lexington, Lexington Books.

Boyd, H.W. and Levy, S.J. (1967) *Promotion: A Behavioural View*, Englewood Cliffs, NJ, Prentice Hall.

Brown, J.D. (1992) 'Benefit Segmentation of the Fitness Market', *Health Marketing Quarterly*, Vol. 9, No. 3, 19–28.

Cermak, D.S.P., File, K.M. and Prince, R.A. (1994) 'A Benefit Segmentation of the Major Donor Market', *Journal of Business Research*, Vol. 29, No. 2, 121–30.

Chisnall, P. (1992) *Marketing Research*, Maidenhead, McGraw-Hill.

Cowin, K. and Moore, G. (1996) 'Critical Success Factors for Merger in the UK Voluntary Sector', *Voluntas*, Vol. 7, No. 1, 66–86.

Dominguez, L.V. and Page, A. (1984) 'Formulating a Strategic Portfolio of Profitable Retail Segments for Commercial Banks', *Journal of Economics and Business*, Vol. 36, No. 3, 43–57.

Golensky, M. (1999) 'Merger as a Strategic Response to Government Contracting Pressures: A Case Study', *Nonprofit Management and Leadership*, Vol. 10, No. 2, 137–52.

Green, P.E. (1977) 'A new Approach to Market Segmentation', *Business Horizons*, Vol. 20, No. 1, 61–73.

Haley, A.T. (1968) 'Benefit Segmentation: A Decision-oriented Research Tool', *Journal of Marketing*, Vol. 32, No. 3, 30–5.

Kotler, P. (1991) *Marketing Management: Analysis, Planning, Implementation and Control*, 8th edn, Englewood Cliffs, NJ, Prentice Hall.

Kotler, P. and Andreasen, A. (1991) *Strategic Marketing for Nonprofit Organizations*, Englewood Cliffs, NJ, Prentice Hall.

Lansing, J.B. and Kish, L. (1957) 'Family Life Cycle as an Independent Variable', *American Sociological Review*, Vol. 22, No. 5, 512–19.

Levy, D.R. (1992) 'Segment your Markets', *Association Management*, Vol. 44, No. 8, 111–15.

MacDonald, M.H.B. (1984) *Marketing Plans: How To Prepare Them, How To Use Them*, London, Heinemann.

Mather, B. (2000) *Merging Interests*, London, The Baring Foundation.

McCurry, P. (1999) 'Society Finance', *The Guardian*, 27 October, 45.

Mullins, D.W. (1999) Managing Ambiguity: Merger Activity in the Non-Profit Housing Sector, *International Journal of Non-Profit and Voluntary Sector Marketing*, Vol. 414, 349–64.

Nicosia, F. and Wind, Y. (1977) 'Behavioural Models of Organizational Buying Processes', in Nicosia, F. and Wind, Y. (eds.) *Behavioral Models of Market Analysis: Foundations for Marketing Action*, Hinsdale, IL, Dryden Press, 96–120.

Philips, L.W. and Sternthal, B. (1977) 'Age Differences in Information Processing: A Perspective on the Aged Consumer', *Journal of Marketing Research*, Vol. 14, No. 4, 444–57.

Porter, M.E. (1980) *Competitive Strategy: Techniques for Analysing Industries and Competitors*, New York, Free Press.

Rubinger, M. (1987) 'Psychographics help Health Care Marketers Find and Serve New Market Segments', *Marketing News*, Vol. 21, No. 9, 4–5.

Schmid, H. (1995) 'Merging Nonprofit Organisations: Analysis of a Case Study', *Nonprofit Management and Leadership*, Vol. 5, 377–91.

Simpson, J.A. (1994) 'Market Segmentation for Appraisal Firms', *Appraisal Journal*, Vol. 60, No. 4, 564–7.

Singer, M. and Yankey, J. (1991) 'Organizational Metamorphosis: A Study of Eighteen Nonprofit Mergers, Acquisitions and Consolidations', *Nonprofit Management and Leadership*, Vol. 1, No. 4, 357–69.

Stanton W.J. (1978) *Fundamentals of Marketing*, 5th edn, New York, McGraw-Hill.

Twedt, D.W. (1964) 'How Important to Marketing Strategy is the Heavy User?' *Journal of Marketing*, Vol. 28, No. 1, 301–35

Wells, W.D. (1975) 'Psychographics: A Critical Review', *Journal of Marketing Research*, Vol. 12, No. 2, 196–213.

Wells, W.D. and Gubar, G. (1966) 'Lifecycle Concept I Marketing Research', *Journal of Marketing Research*, Vol. 3, No. 4, 355–63.

Wethered, J. (1999) 'Public say there are too many Charities', *Third Sector*, 20 October, 7.

Wilson, R.M.S., Gilligan, C. and Pearson, D.J. (1994) *Strategic Marketing Management*, Oxford, Butterworth Heinemann.

Wind, Y. and Cordozo, R. (1974) 'Industrial Market Segmentation', *Industrial Marketing Management*, Vol. 3, No. 1, 153–65.

Young, S. (1971) 'Psychographics Research and Marketing Relevancy', in King, C.W. and Tigert, D.J. (eds.) *Attitude Research Reaches New Heights*, Chicago, American Marketing Association, 220–2.

6 Branding

OBJECTIVES

By the end of this chapter you should be able to:

(1) define branding and describe a number of models of 'brand';

(2) describe why an organization might elect to develop brands;

(3) explain the various approaches to brand management an organization may adopt;

(4) develop a brand strategy for a nonprofit organization.

Introduction

In the previous chapter we concluded by examining positioning strategy—in other words, how an organization communicates why it is in some way distinctive from other providers in the market. In this chapter, it is my intention to focus on a closely related topic; brand strategy. Both positioning and branding are closely intertwined, since as we shall see, if a nonprofit develops a brand for the organization as a whole (e.g. the United Way, or the NSPCC—National Society for the Prevention of Cruelty to Children) a positioning statement is one way in which this overall brand can be expressed. As we shall also see, however, brand strategy can have many more facets than mere positioning. In order to deal with this complexity we will focus exclusively on brand strategy in this chapter.

This separate consideration is also warranted because the topic of branding has recently generated significantly more interest in nonprofit circles. It is increasingly recognized that organizational brands, in particular, can convey significant advantages in terms of a nonprofit's ability to fundraise, campaign, and even deliver mission related goals through service provision, education, and lobbying.

It is interesting to reflect on how times have changed. Branding was until recently regarded as something of a 'dirty' word by nonprofit managers afraid of being seen to grasp at some of the most 'disreputable' elements of for-profit marketing practice. There was a fear that in giving active consideration to branding, nonprofit organizations would somehow lose a sense of what made them distinctive (Ritchie and Swami 1989).

In reality, nothing could be further from the truth; attempts to manage an organization's brand should actually enhance the character of the nonprofit, emphasizing its strengths and achievements alongside its *modus operandi*. Saxton (1995) suggests that the practice of branding in this context should differ from commercial approaches in so far as it should both draw on, and project, the beliefs and values of a nonprofit's various stakeholders. This leads to what Hankinson (2000) regards as the greater complexity associated with managing charity brands. She argues that charity brands require a different approach that distinguishes between the 'functional attributes of the brands—their causes—and the symbolic values of the brand—their beliefs' (Hankinson 2001: 233). She cites the example of the RSPCA whose cause is preventing cruelty to animals, while its values are 'caring', 'responsible', 'authoritative', and 'effective.' Both dimensions pervade its communications.

In this chapter we examine the concept of 'brand' and explore what it can offer a nonprofit. We will also discuss a number of models of brand and discuss the implications for brand strategy and the development of integrated communications.

What is a Brand?

The American Marketing Association (AMA) defines a brand as follows: 'A brand is a name, term, sign, symbol, or design, or a combination of them, intended to identify the goods or services of one seller or group of sellers and to differentiate them from those of competitors.'

In the nonprofit context, a brand is thus a device to allow members of the public to recognize a particular nonprofit that may take the form of a name, trademark, or logo. Legislation in Northern Europe and North America provides protection to the owners of these devices that ensures that no other organization can impinge on their intellectual property. Brands may not be borrowed or copied without permission. This degree of protection is important since brands are in essence a promise to the public that an organization possesses certain features, or will behave in certain ways. Aaker (1997) argues that in fact brands can convey up to six distinct levels of meaning to a consumer:

(1) *Attributes*. Brands can suggest certain attributes the organization might possess. These attributes may include the size of the nonprofit, the scope of its activities, the nature of the work undertaken, etc. In short, the brand can act as a vehicle for summarizing what the organization does and how it does it. While there is much more to a brand than a mere logo, these can play a critical role in a brand strategy, in suggesting the characteristics a nonprofit organization might possess. Figure 6.1 depicts four distinctive brand logos. The UNICEF brand (United Nations Children's Fund) makes clear both the nature of the organization's work and the truly global nature of its coverage. The US nonprofit, Mothers Against Drunk Driving (MADD), is similarly expressive, indicating both the nature of the organization's work and making a statement about those who do choose to drink and drive. Arts organizations too are making increasing use of brands to convey the nature of what they do, London's Science Museum offering a particularly inventive example. Finally, even the public sector has recognized the utility of branding, as the e-Plymouth logo clearly demonstrates. The brand logo designed by the city council

© 2004. Plymouth City Council
Reproduced With Kind Permission

® MADD 2004: Reproduced With
Kind Permission

© 2004 UNICEF. Reproduced
With Kind Permission

© The Science Museum (2004)
Reproduced With Kind Permission

Figure 6.1 Nonprofit brand logos

immediately conveys the maritime history of the city together with one of its major landmarks, Smeatons Tower.

(2) *Benefits*. Brands also offer a series of functional and emotional benefits. From a donor's perspective, when they elect to associate themselves with a particular brand by offering their support they are buying a distinct set of functional benefits either for themselves, or more likely the beneficiary group. Donors to the US nonprofit Planned Parenthood, for example, know that when they support that organization the monies will be used for the purposes of education, but also to campaign for a woman's 'right to choose'. By electing to support a branded organization, donors are able to circumvent the usual search for information (about what the organization stands for and what it does) that would have to take place if they were approached by an organization that they were not already familiar with. A well-developed brand can provide this sense of familiarity.

Benefits can also accrue to the donor and these again could be functional in nature. Some donors may be motivated to give because of the status their association with the organization will confer. They may also wish to attract the awards on offer through a donor recognition programme. However, donors may also gain emotional benefits from their association with a brand. Wearing the logo or symbol of a nonprofit organization might confer an identity to the donor, just as in the commercial world wearing a brand such as Nike conveys an identity to the young people who sport its shoes. Of course in the nonprofit context this process may be a little more thoughtful and can often involve a desire to express a sense of solidarity with the cause. A powerful UK example of this would be the Royal British Legion's Poppy Appeal, where many millions of small gifts are solicited in return for the token of a poppy that may then be worn in public from the time of purchase until Remembrance Sunday when the nation acknowledges the sacrifice of its armed forces. It is interesting to note how many public figures elect to wear their poppy in the run-up to the commemoration, and that over 33 million poppies are produced in total.

The concept of functional and emotional benefits can also apply in many other non-fundraising contexts. Arts organizations, for example, can use their brands to remind individuals of the enjoyment they experienced when they attended a particular event or exhibition. Branded merchandise is often the most frequently purchased of items in the retail outlets associated with these organizations and they serve as pleasurable reminders of the experience each time a coffee mug is used or a T-shirt worn, etc.

Increasingly, healthcare providers are also recognizing the utility of brands to provide reassurance to patients, potential patients, and their relatives that the service provided will be professional and that they can be trusted to do all they can to bring about a satisfactory outcome. Brands might convey a particular specialism of the organization or say something of the caring nature of the staff that comprise it.

(3) *Values.* The brand can also convey something of the organization's values, not only what it stands for, but also the way in which it will approach key issues related to the cause. A nonprofit for example may have the values, bold, authoritative, and challenging, while another might be helpful, sympathetic, and caring. The values of an organization will often be derived from the passion of the founders of the organization, from religious associations, or from the nature of the work undertaken. What is actually happening here is that the values of the various stakeholders to the organization are being projected into how the organization communicates with the outside world.

(4) *Culture.* In the nonprofit context this element is tough to differentiate from values. In the commercial sector an individual brand may have distinctive values, but it will also communicate something of the corporate culture of the parent organization (i.e. the way it does business). For nonprofits, the culture of the organization will be driven in large measure by the values of the various stakeholder groups. A nonprofit organization is often a melting pot of such values, which in turn drive the organization's behaviour. Greenpeace's culture, for example, has historically been very confrontational as the nonprofit seeks to put pressure on commercial organizations it sees as damaging the environment. On 14 June 2003, Greenpeace volunteers from the Forest Crime Unit visited twenty-four Travis Perkins stores across the UK. At the Dalston store in East London, a crew of eight people from the unit cordoned off what they claimed to be illegally logged Indonesian timber. They found nineteen crates of Barito Pacific ply in one section and branded it a 'forest crime scene'. The volunteers then hung a banner which read 'Stop Rainforest Destruction'.

(5) *Personality.* Aaker argues that some brands can convey a personality. In the case of commercial sector marketing, the Fosters lager brand drew heavily on the character of the Australian comic Paul Hogan in the late 1980s. Nonprofit brands can also convey a distinctive personality and there are often personal characteristics that can accrue to the image of an organization. This may occur because of the activities of a particularly flamboyant founder whose own personality becomes indelibly stamped on the organization's brand, but equally it can simply develop over time as the public come to view the nonprofit more as a personality than an organization. The charity Comic Relief is an excellent example of this.

(6) *User.* Many brands also convey a sense of the nature of the user. Charity brands can suggest the kind of individual who will either donate to the cause, benefit from the work it undertakes, or some combination of the two. Age Concern, for example, has built a brand that is regarded as responding to the needs of the elderly, tackling the issues that are of concern to this group, and attracting funding both from this age category, but also from caregivers (carers) in the preceding generation, who will be facing these issues themselves

in ten or twenty years' time. Similarly the charity ENABLE uses its brand to good effect. It is the largest membership organization in Scotland for people with learning disabilities and family caregivers. It was formed in 1954 by a small group of parents because many families with a child with learning disabilities felt alone and isolated. They wanted better services for their sons and daughters and better support for parents. The brand they have now built over the years conveys a strong sense of what the group is really looking for from supporters. The message is not one of sympathy or pity, but rather that the organization seeks to empower its beneficiaries to make a real change in their lives. The brand conveys to donors that this is what they are 'buying' by making a donation.

Of course, there is more to branding than the mere selection of an appropriate name. All the communications the organization creates, both in character and style, should reinforce the brand image the nonprofit is trying to project. The focus should thus be not only on what is said, but how it is said, and this should pervade all the communications channels employed. Thus all direct mail, press, TV, radio, Internet, and outdoor advertising should reflect the brand, but so too should the manner in which the organization responds to telephone enquiries, interacts with all its beneficiary groups, and even presents required statutory data such as annual accounts.

This complexity is illustrated in Figure 6.2. As the figure makes clear, a nonprofit's purpose or mission is the starting point for the development of a branding strategy. The reason for the nonprofit's existence will be likely to drive what is distinctive about the nature of the organization's work and why therefore it might deserve our attention. There

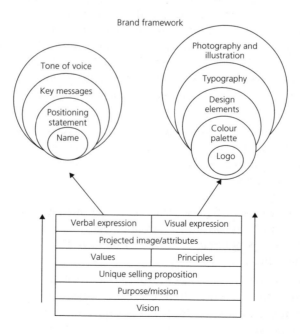

Figure 6.2 A brand framework

Source: © NSPCC 2004. Reproduced with kind permission.

is little point in developing a brand that follows a 'me-too' strategy merely emulating the activities and values of another organization. Indeed, in the nonprofit context, one would have to question the rationale for the existence of such an organization. If an alternative is already undertaking identical work in an identical way, there would seem little point in a duplicate being developed.

Fortunately, most nonprofits do make a genuine contribution to society and may lay claim to some aspect of their work, or the way it is conducted, that is genuinely distinctive. It is important in developing a brand strategy that this is recognized from the outset. What makes an organization distinctive may be a function of its values (as discussed above), the actions it will take, or the manner in which these actions will be undertaken (i.e. the organization's principles). Indeed, it may well be some combination of these three. The values and principles espoused by the NSPCC, for example, are illustrated in Figure 6.3.

Having delineated the values, actions, and principles that define the organization, it is then possible to construct the brand image or attributes that the organization wishes to convey. When the WWF went through a rebranding exercise they determined that the brand should convey the following dimensions that, in their case, they elected to classify as functional, comparative, and emotional.

- *Functional*: 'We influence attitudes and behaviour through education, fieldwork, advocacy, and partnerships.'
- *Comparative*: 'We bring practical experience, knowledge and credibility to build towards long-term solutions, locally and globally.'
- *Emotional*: 'Improving the quality of life on earth.'

The next step in developing a brand strategy is to decide on how these attributes will be expressed to the target stakeholder groups, both verbally and non-verbally. If an organizational brand is being developed, it will be important to begin by deciding on an appropriate name. The previous example of MADD (Mothers Against Drunk Driving) is a particularly effective case study of how a name can convey a variety of different meanings and simultaneously be an effective aid to recall.

Verbal expression can also be accomplished through an effective positioning statement. As we discussed in Chapter 5, this will map out how exactly the organization is different from its competitors and/or the stance on a social issue that the organization will take. The organization will also wish to consider the key messages that will be conveyed. These may be:

- *campaign related*—encouraging specific behaviours on the part of the target audience (e.g. recycling, stopping smoking, preventing child abuse, etc.);
- *funding related*—specifying why the work of the organization is important, why it warrants support, and stressing how the funds will be used;
- *education related*—deepening stakeholder understanding of some aspect of the organization's work.

Finally, the tone of voice that the nonprofit chooses to use in its communications will also convey dimensions of the organization's brand. All written communications have

Courage
Trust
Respect
Protect

We also uphold the values of the UN Convention on the Rights of the Child:

The Convention on the Rights of the Child consists of 54 articles. A 'child' is defined as every human being below the age of 18. The key principles of the Convention are: That all rights apply to all children without exception or discrimination of any kind (article 2); that the best interests of the child must be a primary consideration in all actions concerning children (article 3); that States have an obligation to ensure as much as possible every child's survival and development (article 6); and that children's views must be taken into account in all matters affecting them (article 12). The key provisions covered by the Convention can be summarised within four broad categories:

Survival rights, from the child's right to life through the most basic needs, including food, shelter, and access to health care.

Development rights, or all those things that children require in order to reach their fullest potential, from education and play to freedom of thought, conscience and religion.

Protection rights, requiring that children be safeguarded against all forms of abuse, neglect and exploitation.

Participation rights, including the right to free expression, which allow children to take an active role in their communities and nations.

The UN Convention on the Rights of the Child
- UNICEF - February 2000

NSPCC Principles

1. We will pursue our objectives with courage. We are ready to challenge and lead change for children through our service provision, campaigning, public and professional education, fundraising and communications.

2. We are open and transparent with all those who seek our assistance, fellow professionals, employees, volunteers, the media and the public.

3. We will not compromise the principle that everyone, every individual, every organisation, every community, has responsibility for the care and protection of children, to safeguard them and take action to end abuse. Every child should have someone to turn to.

4. We challenge inequalities for children and young people. In all our activities, including our employment practice, we seek to demonstrate respect, inclusion and appreciation for the value of diversity including ethnicity, nationality, gender, belief, ability, sexuality, age or status.

5. We strive to be a learning organisation. Our collective knowledge, understanding and information must be shared, and this is enabled by the most effective use of information systems infrastructure. We learn from people, research, external changes and experience, and use this to inform our future programme of work.

6. We seek to support and fulfil the potential of the children and young people with whom we work, and that of employees and volunteers. We listen to their views with respect and respond to them, giving due weight to what we are told.

7. We recognise our employees as our most important resource. We will treat them with fairness and respect, involve them in decisions affecting their own jobs, help them fulfil their potential and support them in their own efforts to help children.

8. We seek to co-operate and forge partnerships with others to share learning and ensure safeguarding support is accessible to all children. Most abuse of children is avoidable but we cannot end it on our own.

9. We will work in partnership with donors to achieve our objectives.

10. We will use our independence, our experience and our partnerships with many organisations and individuals to influence changes in the law to the benefit of children.

11. We will be open and honest in all our communication. We will use all channels of communication ethically, with a sense of responsibility and with respect for the children on whose behalf we are speaking out.

12. We work directly in England, Wales, Northern Ireland and the Channel Islands. We collaborate closely with child protection charities in Scotland and Ireland and nongovernmental organisations for children in Europe.

13. We are accountable to all our stakeholders, including those who use our services, partners, donors and other funders, employees, volunteers, those who campaign on our behalf, those who publicly support us and the wider public.

14. Everything we do must contribute towards ending cruelty to children and have a clear and assessable objective. There must be evidence of effectiveness and a balance between long- and shortterm impact and commitment to continuous improvement.

15. We will be effective and efficient in raising and allocating our resources, communicating with others and securing sustainability.

Figure 6.3 NSPCC values and principles

Source: © NSPCC 2004. Reproduced with kind permission.

the potential to influence how an organization is regarded and it is all too easy for an organization that wishes to be seen as 'confident' to be perceived as 'arrogant' or 'smug' through a poor choice of language. It is important to note that all communications an organization sends out have the potential to influence this dimension, not just those that are deliberately created by the marketing and/or fundraising departments. All external (and ideally internal) communications must reflect the organization's brand.

The visual expression of the brand in communications is similarly important. The most obvious facet of visual expression is an organization's logo, which as we noted earlier should be designed in such a way as to convey as much meaning as possible to the target group. It is interesting to note how much time and effort is applied to the design of a logo. Once decided upon, organizations tend to retain their logo for a considerable period of time. This reflects the obvious investment of resources that has been made in the design and subsequent promotion of the logo, but it also reflects the need for continuity. Where a symbol or image has been successfully linked to a brand, or where it successfully evokes it, change can seriously impede an organization's ability to communicate, as individuals become confused as to whether they are still being addressed by the same organization or not. When the National Canine Defence League became the Dogs Trust in 2003 the organization was careful to maintain some continuity in identity so as not to confuse its various stakeholders. While the name changed, the logo was only slightly modified and the espoused organizational values continued unaltered. Thus, if change should be necessary the favoured strategy for many organizations is simply to update their logo, and for the design to evolve with the passage of time, reflecting subtle changes in the organization or its approach. The WWF logo in Figure 6.4 provides a good example of how this evolution can take place.

Colours can also convey meaning, even at a subconscious level. Some colours are rich and welcoming, while others are stark and cold. Organizations thus expend equal amounts of energy on deciding what colour palette will be right, both for the logo, and also for all the brand-building communications the organization will produce. Figure 6.5 contains a selection of brand-building ads designed by UK charities. The WWF example uses subtle tones of blue and green to convey the medical nature of the ad, while the NSPCC uses the pink of a child's wallpaper to evoke a sense of innocence in this 'still' from a recent television campaign. Clearly other design elements, such as the content and layout, have a critical role to play, as does the choice of photography and even typography (e.g. Times New Roman, Arial, etc.).

Figure 6.4 Evolution of WWF brand logo

Source: © 2004 WWF. Reproduced with kind permission.

Why Brand?

It is important to recognize that the issue of whether to brand or not may not be something that a nonprofit organization has much control over. Even where the management do not believe the development of a brand strategy will be worthwhile, there may still be instances where the organization develops a brand 'by default'. Members of the public may come to ascribe differing attitudes and behaviours to the organization with the passage of time and may use the name or title of the organization to group these associations. The organization may thus develop a brand in the absence of a conscious generation of strategy. For many organizations the choice of whether to brand or not is illusory—instead it becomes a question of whether it will be proactively managed or not.

Where a genuine choice does exist, organizations may find that developing a brand strategy conveys a number of benefits.

• *Differentiation.* As we established earlier, a brand can communicate what is distinctive about the range of activities undertaken, or the manner in which these are approached. This is important since it can convey to service users what they might expect to receive from the organization and allow them to 'self-select' whether they wish to use the organization's services or not. On the income generation side it can also aid recognition of the organization and ensure that it does not become confused with others in the minds of the public. Extant fundraising research has shown that organizations with similar brand names, values, or personalities can quickly become confused to the point where a regular payment is offered to one organization, while the donor believes they are supporting another (Sargeant and Jay 2003).

EXAMPLE

In 2003 the University of Ottawa conducted awareness research among high school students in Ontario and Quebec. It discovered that only one in twenty was 'very familiar' with the institution. In response, the university recently launched a major branding campaign repositioning itself as 'Canada's University', a national, bilingual institution offering unique opportunities. At the core of the campaign was a promise that the university was determined to 'live' its brand. In this case living the brand entailed a considerable investment in a wide range of student services specifically designed to meet the needs of current and future students. As an example, the university purchased a 16-storey hotel with the intention of increasing both the quanity and quality of its first-year accommodation.

• *Enhanced performance.* Effective brands encourage the take-up of nonprofit goods and services. Brands that are effectively and consistently communicated over time begin to engender trust, which encourages individuals who might not otherwise have used the service to turn to the organization. Extant research also tells us that organizations that develop brands are more successful at fundraising than those that do not. Frumkin and Kim (2001) found that nonprofit organizations that spent more money on marketing themselves and branding their organization to the general public did better at raising contributed income. Regardless of the field that nonprofit organizations serve in, positioning around mission and using this to drive the brand positively influenced the flow of contributions.

• *Reputation insurance.* Branding can also offer a form of reputation insurance to a non-profit. Having built up a consistent image over time that becomes trusted and increasingly well understood by donors and other stakeholders, short-term crises can be survived. The Aramony scandal rocked the United Way in the USA when the chief executive was accused of wasting donated funds by building up expenses such as unnecessary flights on Concorde. This had a dramatic impact on donations in the short term; however, the reputation of the organization was such that in the medium term the organization was able to regain its share of gifts and relative position in the market. Thus while one would hope that scandals as acrimonious as the Aramony affair would be relatively rare, nonprofits will inevitably find that on occasion they will make mistakes. A strong brand makes it considerably more likely that such mistakes will be forgiven or even overlooked.

• *Enhanced loyalty.* As we discussed earlier, individuals choosing to associate with a particular brand may derive functional or emotional benefits from so doing. In the non-profit context this frequently accrues from the pleasure of associating with a particular campaign or cause. In such cases, the personality of the brand can actually add value or deepen the emotional benefits that the supporter derives. Polonsky and Macdonald (2000) thus argue that organizations with an established brand can leverage this to build donor loyalty and protect themselves from competitive pressures.

• *Additional partnerships.* Successful branding can open up opportunities to offer the brand to appropriate third parties, as is the case with *cause-related marketing* (see Chapter 9). In the USA a number of large charities have even introduced their own branded products, earning substantial sums of revenue as a consequence. The Children's Television Workshop has been highly successful in its licensing arrangements for some 1600 Sesame Street products, ranging from a Big Bird battery-operated toothbrush to a Cookie Monster Bulldozer, to 30 companies, including J.C. Penney and Hasbro (Meyers 1985).

There are thus a number of benefits that can accrue from the development of a brand strategy. These primarily arise for one of two reasons. First, brands are an aid to learning. If branding has been used as a tool to educate members of the public over time there is then no need for a marketer to begin from a 'zero base' in communicating with them. There will be a baseline of understanding about the work the organization undertakes and its values in the minds of potential supporters. This makes the marketing task a lot easier, as brand communications drip-feed information to the market over an extended period of time. In effect brands serve as a 'hook' in memory on which subsequently received messages can be hung.

Second, brands also serve to reduce risk for individuals looking to have contact with the organization. This is particularly the case where individuals might be having contact with a particular category of organization or service for the first time. In such circumstances individuals look to reduce the risk to them in selecting an appropriate 'supplier'. If they are already familiar with a particular brand name they will be significantly more likely to trust this particular supplier than those of which they have no knowledge or awareness. In the context of fundraising this also holds true. Brands provide assurance that an organization is worthy of trust and that funds donated will be used in a manner consistent with standards that have been established over time (Ritchie and Swami 1998).

Branding—A Caveat

Despite the numerous advantages that branding conveys, number of authors have criticized the manner in which nonprofit organizations have embraced commercial branding ideas and approaches. The first and most pervasive criticism is typically raised by members of the press, who feel that charities, in particular, can spend excessive sums building their organization's brand to the detriment of service provision. After all, they argue, the advertising budget could easily be spent on service provision. While this argument is a little facile, it is certainly an issue that charities need to be sensitive to and be prepared to counter, should the need arise.

More significantly, Spruill (2001) argues that branding can create barriers that prevent nonprofits from creating collaborative partnerships with each other for either service delivery or fundraising. Managers are understandably reticent about diluting their brand and are thus unwilling to develop partnerships as a consequence. Spruill also argues that branding can develop a spirit of 'unhealthy competition' for visibility, prompting others to undertake similar expenditure, none of which will directly help beneficiaries. There can also be a sense that the voice of smaller causes is buried under the noise created by high-profile 'names'. Meyers (1985) notes that such concerns prompted Planned Parenthood to drop the idea of licensing condoms, which could have earned about $300 000 a year in royalties.

Brand Strategy

Having discussed the concept of branding and how it can be of relevance to nonprofits, we will now move on to consider how a brand strategy is developed.

Brand Relationships

Thus far in the text we have implicitly assumed that it is only the nonprofit as a whole that will be branded. This need not be the case. While the nonprofit's name may constitute one level of branding, it is quite possible that distinct fundraising products could be branded, or even discrete components of the service the organization provides to beneficiaries. A number of approaches are thus possible.

- *Corporate umbrella brand.* Here the organization itself is branded. There are numerous examples of this, as it is by far the most common nonprofit practice. The United Way, Red Cross, UNICEF, and the World Wildlife Fund (WWF) all have strong and in some cases international corporate brands.

- *Family brand.* Nonprofits may elect to have separate brands for their fundraising and service provision products. Schemes such as Adopt A Dog or Sponsor a Granny have been branded by their respective nonprofits as distinctive fundraising vehicles. These may well be sub-divided to send a different message to distinct donor segments. Similarly, there may be branded components of service provision such as Talking Books or Lifeline, which could in turn have sub-brands for specific categories of service user.

- *Individual branding.* Finally, an organization can simply elect to brand aspects of its service provision or fundraising with separate and entirely unrelated brands. Such a strategy may be appropriate where the donor or service user population is diverse and/or where service provision is complex, with many different components. In such circumstances it is unlikely that a family or umbrella brand could be coherently developed and thus it would be more practical to simply brand each product.

In taking such decisions, it is important to bear in mind that there can be risks in relying too heavily on one brand. While we have noted that a strong brand can help mitigate the risk of unfavourable publicity should something go wrong, weaker brands may not weather the storm and any ill-performance or dissatisfaction can directly reflect on the organization. When an organization develops multiple brands this risk is mitigated since if public trust in one is damaged there are one or more opportunities to regain this through the work of the other brands in the portfolio. By developing multiple brands and a leadership in multiple target markets, the organization increases its chances of survival (Kotler and Andreason 1987).

Multiple brands must be managed in exactly the same way as multiple products. Gallagher and Weinberg (1991), for example, suggest employing the matrix depicted in Figure 6.5. Here each brand is evaluated for its contribution to the mission and to the economic viability of the organization. As with other models of portfolio, those brands falling in the lower right-hand corner of the matrix would be clear candidates for divestment, while those in the top left-hand corner would be clear candidates for investment. Those in the diagonal would require further evaluation to determine an appropriate strategy to adopt.

Differentiation

Whatever approach is ultimately adopted, each brand must be carefully differentiated from those of the competition. To achieve this, an organization must undertake a detailed analysis of the other provision in the market and identify in particular those organizations with similar names, brands, values, activities, and stakeholder groups. For each brand, the organization should look at how it compares with the nature of other provision and what, if anything, is distinctive about it.

In seeking to achieve this, organizations frequently employ a model such as that depicted in Figure 6.6. There are notable similarities between this and Aaker's six categories of meaning discussed earlier. It is simply a further way of conceptualizing a brand and thus seeking to identify components that either are, or could be, genuinely distinctive. It also draws a helpful distinction between the rational components of a brand, where perhaps

WHO CARES IF THEY CUT DOWN A FEW TREES?

Four of five children with leukaemia are saved by the rosy parlwinkle from the Madagascan rainforest. In fact plants create a quarter of all prescribed medicines.Yet more and more life-saving plants are becoming extinct as we destroy the rain forest. Who knows what potential cures for cancer, AIDS or heart disease are being lost forever? To find out what you can do to help WWF protect our forests, wild life and children call 01483-426333 or visit www.wwf.org.uk/whocares

TAKING ACTION FOR A LIVING PLANET

WWF

Barnado's

Barry Stark
Died: Age 2 years

When Barry was repeatedly beaten from the age of two, a large part of him died. His hope and ability to love died. His future died. 38 years later, he put a shotgun in his mouth and died for real. What a waste.

At Barnardo's we want to save children like Barry from a living death. We combat the effects of domestic violence on children through counselling and help give them back their future and life. This takes time. That's why Barnardo's works over the long term, helping over 50 000 children a year with nowhere else to turn.

Soon, you'll read a story, in this paper, about someone just like Barry. 'How sad', you'll say. There are thousands of future Barry sand they don't want your sympathy, they need your help.

NSPCC

Figure 6.5 Examples of brand building advertisements

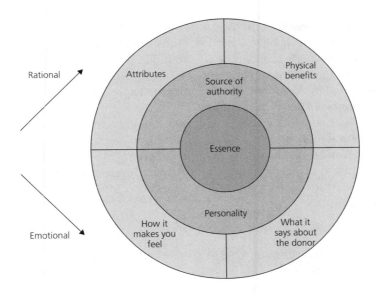

Figure 6.6 A model of brand

the donor is consciously aware of the rationale for their support, and the emotional aspects of a brand, which may impact at a more subconscious level. It comprises:

- *Brand essence.* This is the core of what the brand will stand for.
- *Source of authority and support.* The brand may be differentiated on the basis of the quality of the organization's authority (i.e. those whose views are expressed). A number of the large cancer research charities, for example, can draw on the authority of the medical staff and researchers they represent.
- *Attributes.*
- *Physical benefits.* These are the benefits to the donor or service user.
- *Personality.* These are the human attributes of the brand.
- *How it makes the individual feel.* Does the brand offer any emotional benefits to the donor or service user as a reward for their support?
- *What it says about the individual.* Does the brand convey an identity to the donor or service user by virtue of their support?

Brands may be differentiated by one or more of these components. The strongest brands tend to be those that can offer a strong sense of differentiation on all seven components, but on a practical level this is often very difficult to achieve.

Brand Partnerships

The majority of the largest nonprofit organizations in both the USA and UK have developed strong brands, either by a conscious evolution of strategy, or by default where, whether the organization likes it or not, a brand has evolved by virtue of the organization's presence in a given market. Other brands have been built through collaboration with for-profit commercial organizations. There are numerous examples of small nonprofits that have been helped to become household names by virtue of their association with a large corporate partner. American Express, in particular, has been very helpful to a number of fledgling nonprofits.

Equally, many nonprofits will elect to develop brand partnerships with corporates in return for a fee or some form of cause-related marketing agreement. In such circumstances the nonprofit brand is very much a partner in the agreement and may have more to offer the corporate by way of meaning and values than could ever be offered in return. Whether an agreement is worth entering into will be a function of the following advantages and disadvantages.

Advantages

- The relationship can generate considerable income for little financial or human cost on the part of the nonprofit.
- The positive brand images of the for-profit can be transferred, at least in part, to the nonprofit.

Disadvantages

- A nonprofit organization will probably have little say in how the branding process will evolve, since the branding strategies will typically be developed by the commercial partner to ensure that their specific objectives are met.
- There are very real risks that the image of the nonprofit could be damaged if the commercial partner is later found to be behaving inappropriately in some aspect of its operations. This can be particularly damaging where these activities are at odds with the mission of the nonprofit.

Voluntary Sector Brand Values

Before leaving the topic of brand management it is worth focusing for a moment on the voluntary sector context and discussing how the management of charity brands, in particular, might differ from the management of brands in other contexts. Recent research (Sargeant and Hudson 2003) has suggested that the management of brand values might be more complex.

Authors such as de Chernatony (1999) have argued that organizations should aim for clarity in presenting their values and how these might be distinctive from other players in a particular market. In the voluntary sector context, this process is complicated by the fact that being value[s]-based is one of the features that distinguishes charitable organizations from those in the public or private sectors (Aiken 2001). Indeed, there are felt to be key voluntary sector values that drive the distinctive way in which such organizations manage and organize themselves (Batsleer et al. 1991).

There may thus be organizational brand values that accrue by virtue of an organization's voluntary or charitable status. The very fact that organizations have elected to take this form imbues them, from the public's perspective, with a discrete set of values that are a function of their charity nature. Malloy and Agarwal (2001) argue that the dominant climate in the voluntary sector is based on a caring or feminine model, but there may well be other values common to all, such as trustworthiness or voluntarism.

Values can also be a function of the sub-sector in which the organization is operating, with the hospice movement, for example, espousing a very distinctive set of values around both the respect for and the enjoyment of what remains of life, for people with terminal illnesses. Similarly those nonprofits dealing with the needs of ethnic minorities frequently espouse the values of equality, opportunity, inclusiveness, and participation.

Finally, the organizational values literature suggests that each individual voluntary organization will have its own unique set of institutional values that accrue by virtue of variables such as its history, management style, and overall approach (Dose 1997; Saviour and Scott 1997).

It may therefore be appropriate to view the origins of voluntary sector values as those depicted in Figure 6.7, with a number being common to all voluntary organizations, some being derived from the nature of the cause, and some accruing by virtue of how the organization approaches its mission.

This structure is of more than passing interest since if certain values accrue to an organization's brand by virtue of that organization being a voluntary organization or charity, the need to focus on that value in individual marketing practice is greatly reduced. Equally, if some values apply at the level of certain categories of cause (e.g. animal welfare) the need to promote or manage that value becomes one for the sub-sector as a whole to address, rather than a single organization.

Clearly from a particular organization's perspective scarce marketing resources should be devoted to those values that are genuinely distinctive and differentiate the organization's brand from those of key competitors. Where values are shared with competitors

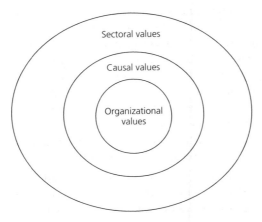

Figure 6.7 Structure of charity brand values

working with the same category of cause, there may be scope to develop collaborative marketing activity that reinforces (or manages) public perceptions of the work they undertake and the manner thereof. This may, for example, take the form of a coordinated approach to public relations activities and lobbying where genuine benefits would result for all parties. Finally, since some values undoubtedly accrue by virtue of an organization being voluntary or achieving charitable status, influencing such values would require a collective effort on the part of the sector and/or umbrella bodies. It is highly unlikely that one organization would, in isolation, be able to influence the nature and acceptance of this category of value.

Integrated Communications

While we have stressed on numerous occasions throughout this chapter the need for all communications to reflect the nature of the brand, we have not yet focused on the increasingly important topic of integrated communications; in other words, ensuring that all the communications an organization generates represent a coherent whole. This is particularly important where a nonprofit has elected to brand the organization. In such cases all the forms of communication the nonprofit generates should reflect the organization's overall brand. Too many nonprofits assume that they are dealing with discrete groups of stakeholders who will not have access to other communications that the organization might generate for other stakeholder groups, thus they do not see the need to be consistent from one form of communication to another. To be successful, however, the whole organization has to 'live the brand' and to reflect its various dimensions in every form of communication that leaves the organization.

Achieving consistency in approach is not easy, but there are a variety of steps that a nonprofit might take to ensure effective integration. These include:

- *Stakeholder consultation and buy-in*. In seeking to generate an organizational brand it is important that all the major stakeholder groups are consulted in respect of the form that this might take, the messages it would seek to communicate, and the values it would seek to espouse. Failure to consult widely and integrate stakeholder input will typically result in an inability on the part of the organization to secure the buy-in of all those who have a stake in the organization. This matters since, once created, it will be the individuals in these groups who will ultimately shape how the brand is perceived through their communications and dealings with others. Unless they actively support the initiative it is likely either to fail or be distorted to reflect the miscellany of different values and messages that disparate groups feel are most appropriate.

- *The generation of a brand book*. This document provides all the detail of what the brand is, what it stands for, and how it will be communicated; in effect all of the components we discussed earlier (see Figure 6.2). Brand books provide detail in respect of the design of the logo and where, when, and how it must be used. It also outlines in detail how the organization should convey its core values and how an appropriate style of communication may be fostered. It also provides information on where individual members of staff can turn to for advice if they are unsure how to implement any aspect of the guidelines.

- *Training for contact staff or volunteers.* As has been noted on many occasions throughout this chapter, all forms of communication can influence how the brand will be perceived. It is therefore essential that an organization develops and implements an appropriate programme of training for all those who will have contact with external stakeholder groups such as donors, volunteers, service users, the news media, etc. All such staff should ensure that they know how to operationalize the guidelines contained in the brand book in the context of their own role. This may require training in the style to be adopted in formal communications, or training in answering the phone, writing letters, press releases, etc.

- *Cross-functional briefings and meetings.* In many nonprofits, responsibility for external communications is split between the fundraising, campaigning, service provision, and corporate communications (e.g. branding) departments. Frequently each may have developed its own micro-marketing function, with considerable expertise having been amassed in relation to the task in question. The key barrier to ensuring effective integration is thus the extent to which each of these respective functions communicates (or not) with the others. There is therefore a need to establish regular contact between these groups of individuals to ensure that the approach adopted in one aspect of the organization's communications is consistent with that adopted in another. Regular team meetings and briefings are essential to achieve this.

- *Map a year in the life of . . .* The final lesson from professional practice is that it can be advantageous to nominate one individual who will 'pose' as a member of each key stakeholder group, signing on to the relevant stream of communications such individuals receive. This is undertaken anonymously so that no-one else within the organization is aware that this is happening. These individuals then keep a record of all the communications they receive from the organization. The reason for this is straightforward. Many brands are designed to build and develop relationships with stakeholders by adding to the emotional and functional value we discussed earlier. One department may feel it has created communications that do a pretty good job of this, carefully building up the recipient's knowledge and level of engagement over time. In most modern organizations, however, 'house lists' of particular stakeholder groups are often accessed by other parts of the organization. Members of the public, for example, who have agreed to participate in e-mail campaigns to lobby for social change, may also be approached for donations. They may also receive a copy of the trading catalogue and be invited to buy nonprofit merchandise. In some circumstances they could also be approached to become service users or volunteers to aid the cause. In short, many different departments will have access to individuals who originally joined the organization to campaign. Thus, while the campaign department may have a perfectly cogent strategy for relationship development, this can quickly lapse into the absurd when different and perhaps conflicting communications are received from other parts of the organization. While to a certain extent the team briefings referred to above may minimize the potential for conflict, it can be a very useful exercise to have an individual track what is actually received and for the team to reflect thereafter on whether a year in the life of a particular stakeholder is as the organization would wish it to be. If not, changes can be made.

■ SUMMARY

In this chapter, we have focused exclusively on the subject of branding. As we have seen, the process of branding a nonprofit organization bears many similarities to the process of developing an umbrella brand in the corporate sector. Many of the issues involved and indeed many of the models of brand developed in that context are of equal relevance to nonprofits.

However, it also seems clear that the branding of nonprofits may be inherently more complex. The need to reflect the needs and aspirations of a variety of stakeholder groups means that organizations, unlike their commercial counterparts, cannot simply take decisions that are optimal for a particular objective (e.g. increased market share or sales). Nonprofit brands communicate something of the values of different stakeholder groups and in the case of charities may even be shaped by the values of the sector as a whole, or of particular categories of cause.

To assist in managing a brand I have introduced a number of frameworks that can be used to plan both the content of a brand and also its embodiment in every contact that an organization has with external stakeholder groups. As we have seen, this includes a consideration of both verbal and nonverbal forms of communication and employing each to express one or more values associated with the brand. Managing these issues properly is important, since successful branding can lead to enhanced income generation and enhanced performance in the delivery of the mission. In short, branding can enhance many aspects of nonprofit performance while at the same time adding value for a multitude of different stakeholder groups: a genuine win-win situation for all.

■ DISCUSSION QUESTIONS

1. In your role as the communications director of a large environmental protection charity, you have been asked by your board of trustees to explain why it is necessary for the organization to allocate funds to brand-building communications. Prepare a brief presentation to the board outlining the benefits to the organization of continuing to develop its brand.

2. What are brand values? Why might projecting the right values be of particular concern to a nonprofit organization, and what additional complexities might exist in managing brand values in this context?

3. Is the development of an organizational brand always appropriate? Are there any circumstances under which it might not be appropriate to develop such a brand?

4. As the director of communications of a children's charity you have been approached by a large multinational organization which has indicated that it would be interested in partnering with your brand in return for a substantial initial donation and a small donation from each subsequent sale of jointly branded merchandise. What might be the advantages and disadvantages of entering into such a relationship? What questions would you ask of the potential corporate partner before proceeding with this deal?

5. What is meant by the term 'integrated communication'? Why is this an important issue, and how can a nonprofit organization ensure that its communications are effectively integrated?

■ REFERENCES

Aaker, J.L. (1997) 'Dimensions of Brand Personality', *Journal of Marketing Research*, August, 347–56.

Aiken, M. (2001) *Keeping Close to Your Values: Lessons from a Study Examining how Voluntary and Co-operative Organisations Reproduce their Organisational Values*, Milton Keynes, Open University.

Batsleer, J., Cornforth, C. and Paton R. (1991) *Issues in Voluntary and Non-profit Management*, Wokingham, Addison Wesley.

de Chernatony, L. (1999) 'Brand Management through Narrowing the Gap between Brand Identity and Brand Reputation', *Journal of Marketing Management*, Vol. 15, 157–79.

Dose, J.J. (1997) 'Work Values: An Integrative Framework and Illustrative Application to Organizational Socialisation', *Journal of Occupational and Organizational Psychology*, Vol. 70, No. 3, 219–40.

Frumkin, P. and Kim, M.T. (2001) 'Strategic Positioning and the Financing of Nonprofit Organizations: Is Efficiency Rewarded in the Contributions Marketplace?', *Public Administration Review*, Vol. 61 (May/June), 266–75.

Gallagher, K. and Weinberg C.B. (1991) 'Coping with Success: New Challenges for Nonprofit Marketing', *Sloan Management Review*, Vol. 33 (Fall), 27–42.

Hankinson, P. (2000) 'Brand Orientation in Charity Organizations: Qualitative Research into Key Charity Sectors', *International Journal of Nonprofit and Voluntary Sector Marketing*, Vol. 5, 207–19.

Hankinson, P. (2001) 'Brand Orientation in the Charity Sector: A Framework for Discussion and Research', *International Journal of Nonprofit and Voluntary Sector Marketing*, Vol. 6, No. 3, 231–42.

Kotler, P. and Andreasen, A. (1987) *Strategic Marketing For Nonprofit Organisations*, 3rd edn, Englewood Cliffs, NJ, Prentice Hall.

Malloy, D. C. and Agarwal, J. (2001) 'Ethical Climate in Nonprofit Organizations: Propositions and Implications', *Nonprofit Management and Leadership*, Vol. 12, No. 1, 39–54.

Meyers, W. (1985) 'The Nonprofits Drop The "Non"', *The New York Times*, 24 November, 14.

Polonsky, M.J. and Macdonald, E.K. (2000) 'Exploring the Link Between cause-related Marketing and Brand Building', *International Journal of Nonprofit and Voluntary Sector Marketing*, Vol. 5, No. 1, 46–57.

Ritchie, R.J.B. and Swami, S. (1998) 'A Brand New World', *International Journal of Nonprofit and Voluntary Sector Marketing*, Vol. 4, 26–42.

Sargeant, A. and Hudson, J. (2003) 'Exploring Brand Values in the Charity Sector: Just What is the Span of Control?' *ARNOVA Annual Conference*, Denver, CO, November.

Sargeant, A, and Jay, E. (2003) *An Empirical Investigation of Attrition Amongst Face-To-Face Recruits*, Cullompton, Sargeant Associates Ltd.

Saviour, L.N. and Scott, J.V.J. (1997) 'The Influence of Corporate Culture on Managerial Ethical Judgments', *Journal of Business Ethics*, Vol. 16, No. 8, 757–76.

Saxton, J. (1995) 'A Strong Charity Brand comes from Strong Beliefs and Values', *Journal of Brand Management*, Vol. 2, No. 4, 211–20.

Spruill, V. (2001) 'Build Brand Identity for Causes, not Groups', *Chronicle of Philanthropy*, Vol. 13 (June), 45.

7 Marketing Programmes and Services: The Operational Mix

OBJECTIVES

By the end of this chapter you should be able to:

(1) develop a marketing mix for a nonprofit product or service;

(2) discuss other approaches to grouping tactical marketing activities;

(3) write a marketing plan for a nonprofit product or service;

(4) suggest how the quality of a nonprofit service might be measured and evaluated;

(5) explain how a consideration of ethics might impact on nonprofit plans and activities.

Introduction

This is the final chapter of the text that will deal with marketing planning issues. In previous chapters we examined the first two stages of a marketing plan (i.e. 'Where are we now?' and 'Where do we want to be?'). We also addressed the strategic aspects of 'How will we get there?', focusing on overall direction, segmentation, positioning, competitive/collaborative strategy, and branding. In this chapter, we will examine the tactical marketing mix and a range of issues that nonprofits typically have to address in specifying exactly how their objectives will be achieved.

To structure the discussion, the chapter has been divided using the headings of a typical marketing mix. Since most nonprofits produce services rather than products, a service marketing perspective has been adopted. It is important to recognize, however, that many of the ideas expressed have equal relevance to both product and service contexts. It is also important to recognize that while a 'mix' can be a good way to group ideas, it is far from being a new idea. The notion of a marketing mix has been around for almost 50 years and has been criticized by many authors as too constricting or formulaic. The key to writing a successful marketing plan undoubtedly lies in applying a little common sense and grouping tactical plans in a way that makes sense for the organization in question. This frequently reflects the structure of the marketing department itself so that it is relatively easy to delineate individual responsibilities for implementation.

What follows is thus a standard structure that will work in most cases, albeit with some modification. The two key instances where it will probably not be appropriate are in Internet marketing (particularly where this is the primary route to market) and where the organization serves only a small number of high-value clients where it should instead look to manage specific aspects of its relationships with each client (see, for example, Payne et al. 1999). An appropriate e-marketing mix will be outlined later in this chapter.

Products/Services

The Components of Products and Services

The starting point for examining this component of the marketing mix lies in determining the requirements of the target market. What needs do the target segments have and how can they best be satisfied? Armed with this knowledge, marketers can then ensure that the products and services their organization provides are appropriately tailored to the needs of each of their customer or stakeholder groups.

The marketing literature presents a variety of frameworks for the analysis of the components of a product/service and these provide a useful guide for examining and defining the market entity that the organization is looking to provide. Kotler, for example, distinguishes between the core, tangible, and augmented aspects of a service while Levitt focuses on a service's generic, expected, and augmented components. In each case, the analysis is based on the idea that any service can be seen as offering a basic set of features from the point of view of the consumer. Beyond this, services are augmented by a variety of additional features that associate it with a particular supplier, differentiate it from competing services, and make it in some way distinctive.

Kotler's perspective is presented in Figure 7.1. Adopting this model in the nonprofit sector aids the marketer in clarifying the components of the service that they are offering to both recipients of goods and services and also to those that elect to fund such activities. The 'core' service from the perspective of the donor, for example, is arguably the knowledge that one has contributed to a worthwhile cause. In the case of healthcare, the core product is the diagnosis and programme of treatment prescribed.

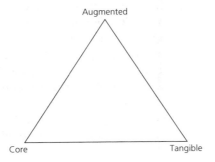

Figure 7.1 Components of a product

At this point, however, the service is only being defined in terms of the generic available in the market. One would hope for example that two or more competent physicians would reach the same conclusion in respect of a patient's ailment. Similarly most charities are capable of providing a 'feelgood' factor to one degree or another. In short, it is unlikely that the core service will vary much from one organization to another. It may be thought of as being simply the minimum necessary to satisfy the needs of the customer.

The tangible component of the service is of particular importance since recent research indicates that consumers are more likely to purchase and re-purchase a service if they can take away something tangible from the experience. Enhancing the tangible nature of the service can also serve to reduce risk from the perspective of the purchaser (see for example George and Berry (1981) and Palmer (1994)) and act as a useful reminder of their experience that can assist in word-of-mouth advertising among friends and colleagues. In the fundraising context the tangible part of the service would therefore include the 'thank you' tokens that are typically received for making a donation in the street. While rewarding a donor for his generosity, such tokens also serve the ancillary purpose of providing protection against further requests for donations.

In the healthcare context the concept of tangibility would more usefully relate to the quality of the environment provided for patients. Many hospitals and private clinics now give considerable thought to the physical design and layout of those areas where patients and their loved ones are likely to spend time. As obvious as this may sound, there is now a considerable body of research to suggest that in the absence of other evaluative criteria, patients will tend to rely on these tangible cues to judge the quality of the service they receive.

The reader will therefore appreciate that giving consideration to the tangible components of their service may be one way in which a nonprofit could look to differentiate its service from that supplied by potential competitors. Given that the core service is widely available, however, it is unlikely that simply adjusting the tangible components will in itself be enough to create and sustain an advantage over the competition. The augmented part of the service is the real key to this issue. While the consumer is paying for a certain core experience and will doubtless be happy if she receives it, the augmented component goes beyond what the consumer was expecting. It may be thought of as value added which can be used to draw a distinction in the minds of consumers between the service provided by one organization and that provided by another. Returning to our earlier examples for a moment, there may be many ways in which both organizations could augment their service. Donors could receive personalized mailings, individual attention from staff, invitations to visit a particular project to see how their money has been used, a commemorative plaque, etc. In the healthcare context the service could be augmented by the quality of information provided to relatives, allowing greater time for a patient–physician dialogue, access to support groups, personal follow-ups by hospital staff when the patient has returned home, etc. Augmenting the service in any of the ways described would be costly, but the rewards in terms of enhanced customer satisfaction and hence loyalty to the organization could well be worth the initial investment.

Together these three components form the basis of the market offering. Each component should be considered in isolation and as a part of the complete service offering.

This latter point is of particular significance since all three aspects of the service have the capability to communicate a message to target customer groups.

Service Quality

Of course the components of a service will not be the only issue a nonprofit will have to address. Marketers in this context will also want to ensure that an appropriate level of quality is maintained for the service, across all the stakeholder groups that will have contact with it. There are a number of reasons why this is an important consideration. First, nonprofit marketers will want to ensure that the quality of service reflects the values and mission of the organization (which often regard the satisfaction of stakeholder needs as being paramount). They will also be aware of the dramatic impact that the quality of the service can have on their ability to attract new service users and to retain them. This latter point is an issue we shall return to later in this chapter.

In its simplest form, service quality is a product of the effort that every member of the organization invests in satisfying customers. More specifically, service quality has been defined as 'the delivery of excellent or superior service relative to customer expectations' (Zeithaml and Bitner 1996) and 'Quality . . . is behaviour—an attitude—that says you . . . will never settle for anything less than the best in service for your stakeholders, whether they are customers, the community, your stockholders or the colleagues with whom you work every day' (Harvey 1995).

At the heart of these and other definitions of quality lies the suggestion that perceived quality is what the consumer sees and is the result of a comparison between expectations of service quality and the actual service received. To illustrate this, suppose that potential applicants to a particular university are promised in the prospectus the latest laboratory facilities, excellent tuition, access to a wide range of sports, and catering covering a broad spectrum of different traditions and tastes. When the students actually arrive on campus they discover that the catering is somewhat limited and mediocre, only outdoor sports are offered, and both the teaching and laboratory facilities are a little old-fashioned. The inevitable result is a great deal of student dissatisfaction. If, on the other hand, the university had painted a more modest picture of what would be provided, those students who did elect to study there would find their expectations met (or exceeded) and would undoubtedly be satisfied with their experience. This is an example of what Churchill and Suprenant (1982) regard as the 'disconfirmation paradigm' in action. While this is a concept that has recently received criticism in the literature, largely because there is no real evidence that the comparative process actually takes place, it does represent a useful starting point in our analysis.

Accepting for a moment that the disconfirmation paradigm is an appropriate way to model customer perceptions of delivered service quality, a number of interesting implications begin to emerge. Peters (1987) argues that on this basis, organizations should look to 'under-promise' and 'over-deliver'. In this way customer expectations will be low, their perceptions of delivered service quality high, and as a consequence their satisfaction will also be high. The problem with this argument is that expectations are learnt from experience, so this process will only work once. As soon as consumers perceive a high standard of service, they will come to expect it on subsequent occasions and could potentially be dissatisfied if their expectations are not fulfilled. As a result, this author contends that by far the safest way of ensuring customer satisfaction is simply to deliver consistently one's service promises. The second interesting consequence of the disconfirmation paradigm is that it leaves organizations looking to identify the criteria against which consumers build expectations. As Levitt (1981: 100) explains, this is not easy: 'The most important thing to know about intangible products is that the customers usually don't know what they're getting until they don't get it. Only then do they become aware of what they bargained for; only on dissatisfaction do they dwell . . .'.

Even where those factors important to overall satisfaction can be adequately identified, organizations still have the task of setting objective measures of quality and ensuring that they deliver against the targets that they set. Indeed, this is not an easy task, since while the quality of physical goods can be measured satisfactorily by monitoring variables such as durability or the number of physical defects (Crosby 1979), in the case of services there is an almost total absence of objective methods of assessment.

Some consolation can be drawn, however, since it is not only the service providers who have difficulty in assessing the quality of their services. Consumers can have equal difficulties in formulating their own individual assessments. While the disconfirmation model looks quite neat in theory, in practice consumers can make quality assessments on the most superficial of cues. To explain why this might be, it is worth looking at the work of Nelson (1974) who drew a useful distinction between two categories of consumer goods, namely:

- *those high in search qualities*—which consumers *can* evaluate prior to making a purchase (e.g. size, colour, feel, smell);
- *those high in experience qualities*—where the attributes can be discerned only during use, and hence (in most cases) only after purchase (e.g. taste, wearability, etc.).

For our purposes, however, Darby and Karni (1973) helpfully add a third category:

- *Credence qualities.* These are characteristics which are difficult to evaluate, even after consumption. Many nonprofits offer services which are high on credence qualities, e.g. a heart operation or a charity donation.

The existence of these three qualities can best be conceptualized on a continuum. As can be seen from Figure 7.2, different products/services have varying degrees of credence qualities. It will be inherently more difficult to assess the quality of a service that contains a high degree of credence qualities. Consumers may find it all but impossible to evaluate their experience. Nevertheless, marketers should not lose heart, since evidence suggests that in such cases consumers use a variety of surrogate variables to evaluate such services. In the case, for example, of a bypass operation consumers are unlikely to have the technical knowledge to appraise the skills of the surgeon—they might hence appraise service quality on the basis of the perceived professionalism of staff, the level of technology employed, the decor of their ward/building, etc. This is a simple but important concept to grasp as these criteria could quite easily be radically different from those that the hospital itself might use to evaluate the quality of the same operation (e.g. survival rates, number

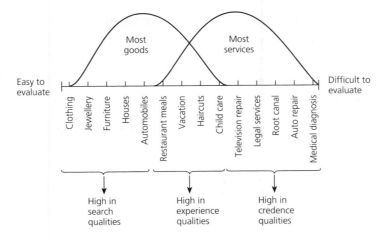

Figure 7.2 Continuum of evaluation for different types of products

Source: Zeithamil et al., *Services Marketing*, McGraw Hill, New York. Reproduced with the kind permission of McGraw Hill.

of medical complications, technical proficiency, use of resources, etc.). Nonprofits must monitor service quality not only against their own internal criteria but also in terms of those that are likely to be used by their customers. In the case of services that are high on credence qualities, these dimensions can usually only be identified through research.

The Measurement of Service Quality

Given the difficulties alluded to above, the reader could be forgiven for believing that the measurement of service quality is an almost impossible task. A variety of methods of measurement have been advocated, but there is still considerable disagreement in the literature in respect of the best method to use.

Ovretveit (1992: 23) argues in favour of a market-focused approach. As he puts it: 'The question is not the general "What do customers think about our service?" but the more specific "Which features of our service are the most important to potential, current, and past customers in relation to the actions which the service wishes to influence, and how does the service compare to the alternatives on these features?"'

It is therefore too simplistic merely to ask customers what they think about each dimension of the service. Each group of customers will have its own priorities in terms of those elements of the service that it perceives to be most important. Measuring every service component may therefore not be necessary and, where deficiencies are encountered, additional resources may be required only in those areas which will have the greatest impact on customer satisfaction.

It therefore seems clear that an organization looking to monitor service quality should

- identify its key customer groups or segments;
- identify the key components of the service;

- assess the relative importance of each component for each customer segment;
- set performance targets for each key component;
- measure actual service performance against each target;
- prioritize necessary improvements;
- allocate investment accordingly.

Following such a procedure should ensure that where deviations are detected against the desired targets, scarce resources can be targeted at only those aspects of the service that are perceived as of greatest importance. Of course, these factors will not be static over time and the process described above should be iterative.

While many of the steps appear quite straightforward, step (5) is somewhat problematic as in practice it is not an easy task to measure service quality. Three broad approaches are possible.

Counting Complaints

The simplest approach is to count the number of complaints that relate to each service provided, or each specific component thereof. This is clearly an unsatisfactory method of monitoring service quality as a relatively low proportion of customers will actually take the trouble to complain. Most will simply rate the service as poor and look for alternative suppliers.

Rating Service Attributes

A rather more sophisticated method of measuring service quality consists of deriving a list of service attributes and asking customers to rate their perceptions of each attribute, typically on a five- or seven-point scale.

In a study of student satisfaction with higher education institutions, Stewart (1991) utilized a series of attitudinal statements with a Likert scale for responses ranging from 'strongly agree' to 'strongly disagree'. The statements selected probed customer perceptions of each element of the traditional marketing mix, including:

- *product*—the variety of curriculum, course scheduling, student evaluations of faculty, opportunities for personal growth via professional and leadership activities, academic advising, student interaction with faculty and administrators, library holdings, and cultural, athletic, and social opportunities;
- *price*—tuition expenses—finance packages available;
- *place*—environmental issues—campus attractiveness and safety, availability of lounge facilities, study areas, and parking spaces; health and library service offerings; procedures for selecting dormitory and room-mate assignments; adequacy of meals/other catering;
- *promotion*—accuracy of promotional material—prospectus, departmental literature. Do students know where to go for advice, are they informed of extra-curricular activities on campus? Availability of information in respect of changes in curriculum procedures and requirements.

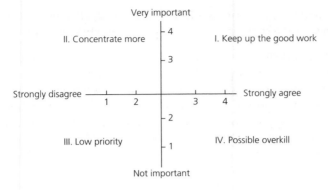

Figure 7.3 Importance/perception quadrants

Importantly, the author also advocated the gathering of data relating to the perceived importance of each element. For each of the components of the HE service, it is hence possible to plot the position of a given university's performance on a graph such as that in Figure 7.3.

Service components falling within the top right-hand segment are those that are both very important to customers and those areas where the university performs well. The level of service should clearly be maintained in these areas. Service components falling within the bottom right-hand quadrant are those where the university performs well, but are considered to be areas of little importance by customers. Institutions should hence give consideration to whether resources directed to these areas could be better employed elsewhere.

In the case of service components falling within the top left-hand quadrant, the advice would clearly be to concentrate any additional resources in these areas. They are perceived to be of considerable importance by customers, but the actual performance falls well short of that desired. Service components falling within the bottom left-hand area can be seen to be underperforming, but such underperformance may not be of particular significance, since these dimensions are also perceived to be of little importance by those surveyed.

The SERVQUAL Method

Perhaps the most famous of the techniques of service quality measurement is that proposed by Parasuraman et al. (1988). The authors posited the existence of four key service gaps (five if the aggregate gap is included). These gaps are together responsible for the difference between expected and perceived service quality.

- *Gap 1.* Not knowing what customers expect—the difference between consumer needs and management's perceptions of those needs.

- *Gap 2.* Not selecting the right service design—the difference between management perceptions of customer needs and the service standards set.

- *Gap 3.* Not delivering to service standards—the difference between service specifications and actual service delivery.

- *Gap 4.* Not matching performance to promises—the difference between the service promises made in external communications and the actual service delivered.

Parasuraman et al. (1988) evolved this concept of 'gaps' into a quantitative technique for measuring service quality known as SERVQUAL. This is based upon a generic 22-item questionnaire designed to cover the broad dimensions of service quality. The model has received widespread support in the literature, although it has been refined and adapted to make it suitable for application in a number of different sectors (see Babakus and Boller 1992). The SERVQUAL instrument is illustrated in Figure 7.4.

The idea behind the questionnaire is that

$$Q = P - E$$

where

Q = the perceived quality of each item

P = the performance achieved in each item

E = the customer's expectations of performance in each item.

To measure the quality of each service dimension one therefore subtracts the expectations score from the performance score for each item. A high positive result would hence indicate a high perceived standard of service, while a high negative score would indicate a low perceived standard of service. In testing the responses received to this instrument, the authors determined that service quality can best be viewed as having five underlying dimensions, namely:

- *tangibles*—physical facilities, equipment, and appearance of personnel;
- *reliability*—ability to perform the promised service dependably and accurately;
- *responsiveness*—willingness to help customers and provide prompt service;
- *assurance*—knowledge and courtesy of employees and their ability to inspire trust and confidence;
- *empathy*—caring, individualized attention the firm provides its customers.

Hence a number of the statements in the questionnaire can be viewed as addressing the issue of reliability, while others together address the issues of responsiveness, etc. As a result, the scale has a number of applications within a service environment. These include:

- *Tracking service trends.* SERVQUAL can be used over time to plot changes in customers' perceptions of key service components (i.e. responses to individual questions).
- *Analysing each service dimension.* Average 'difference' scores can be calculated for each of the five dimensions referred to above. The possibility also exists to average each of these to arrive at an overall measure of service quality which could then be tracked over time.
- *Identifying the relative importance of each service dimension.* A statistical technique known as regression can be used to isolate which of the five dimensions are felt by

Directions: This survey deals with your opinions of—services. Please show the extent to which you think firms offering—services should possess the features described by each statement. Do this by picking one of the seven numbers next to each statement. If you strongly agree that these firms should possess a feature, circle the number 7. If you strongly disagree that these firms should possess a feature, circle 1. If your feelings are not strong, circle one of the numbers in the middle. There are no right or wrong answers—all we are interested in is a number that best shows your expectations about firms offering—services.

		Strongly disagree				Strongly agree		
E1	They should have up-to-date equipment	1	2	3	4	5	6	7
E2	Their physical facilities should be visually appealing	1	2	3	4	5	6	7
E3	Their employees should be well dressed and appear neat	1	2	3	4	5	6	7
E4	The appearance of the physical facilities of these firms should be in keeping with the type of services provided	1	2	3	4	5	6	7
E5	When these firms promise to do somthing by a certain time, they should do so	1	2	3	4	5	6	7
E6	When customers have problems, these firms should be sympathetic and reassuring	1	2	3	4	5	6	7
E7	These firms should be dependable	1	2	3	4	5	6	7
E8	They should provide their services at the time they promise to do so	1	2	3	4	5	6	7
E9	They should keep their records accurately	1	2	3	4	5	6	7
E10	They shouldn't be expected to tell customers exactly when services will be performed (-)	1	2	3	4	5	6	7
E11	It is not realistic for customers to expect prompt service from employees of these firms (-)	1	2	3	4	5	6	7
E12	Their employees don't always have to be willing to help customers (-)	1	2	3	4	5	6	7
E13	It is okay if they are too busy to respond to customer requests promptly (-)	1	2	3	4	5	6	7
E14	Customers should be able to trust employees of these firms	1	2	3	4	5	6	7
E15	Customers should be able to feel safe in their transactions with these firm's employees	1	2	3	4	5	6	7
E16	Their employees should be polite	1	2	3	4	5	6	7
E17	Their employees should get adequate support from these firms to do their jobs well	1	2	3	4	5	6	7
E18	These firms should not be expected to give customers personal attention (-)	1	2	3	4	5	6	7
E19	Employees of these firms cannot be expected to give customers personal attention (-)	1	2	3	4	5	6	7
E20	It is unrealistic to expect employees to know what the needs of their customers are (-)	1	2	3	4	5	6	7
E21	It is unrealistic to expect these firms to have their customers' best interests at heart (-)	1	2	3	4	5	6	7
E22	They shouldn't be expected to have operating hours convenient to all their customers (-)	1	2	3	4	5	6	7

Figure 7.4 SERVQUAL

Source: © 2004 New York University. Reproduced with kind permission.

Directions: The following set of statements relate to your feelings about XYZ. For each statement please show the extent to which you believe XYZ has the feature described by the statement. Once again, circling a 7 means that you strongly agree that XYZ has that feature, and circling a 1 means that you strongly disagree. You may circle any of the numbers in the middle that show how strong your feelings are. There are no right or wrong answers—all we are interested in is a number that best shows your perceptions about XYZ.

P1	XYZ has up-to-date equipment	1	2	3	4	5	6	7
P2	XYZ's physical facilities are visually appealing	1	2	3	4	5	6	7
P3	XYZ's employees are well dressed and appear neat	1	2	3	4	5	6	7
P4	The appearance of the physical facilities of XYZ is in keeping with the type of services provided	1	2	3	4	5	6	7
P5	When XYZ promises to do something by a certain time, it does so	1	2	3	4	5	6	7
P6	When you have problems, XYZ is sympathetic and reassuring	1	2	3	4	5	6	7
P7	XYZ is dependable	1	2	3	4	5	6	7
P8	XYZ provides its services at the time it promises to do so	1	2	3	4	5	6	7
P9	XYZ keeps its records accurately	1	2	3	4	5	6	7
P10	XYZ does not tell customers exactly when services will be performed (-)	1	2	3	4	5	6	7
P11	You do not receive prompt service from XYZ's employees (-)	1	2	3	4	5	6	7
P12	Employees of XYZ are not always willing to help customers (-)	1	2	3	4	5	6	7
P13	Employees of XYZ are too busy to respond to customer requests promptly (-)	1	2	3	4	5	6	7
P14	You can trust employees of XYZ	1	2	3	4	5	6	7
P15	You feel safe in your transactions with XYZ's employees	1	2	3	4	5	6	7
P16	Employees of XYZ are polite	1	2	3	4	5	6	7
P17	Employees get adequate support from XYZ to do their jobs well	1	2	3	4	5	6	7
P18	XYZ does not give you individual attention (-)	1	2	3	4	5	6	7
P19	Employees of XYZ do not give you personal attention (-)	1	2	3	4	5	6	7
P20	Employees of XYZ do not know what your needs are (-)	1	2	3	4	5	6	7
P21	XYZ does not have your best interests at heart (-)	1	2	3	4	5	6	7
P22	XYZ does not have operating hours convenient to all their customers (-)	1	2	3	4	5	6	7

NB. The statements should appear in a random order in a questionnaire and those phrased in the negative (-) should be reverse-scored prior to date analysis.

Figure 7.4 (*Continued*)

customers to be of the greatest importance. Resource allocation can then be planned accordingly.

- *Determining whether specific groups of customers exist that prioritize differently the dimensions of service quality*. If this is the case, each group can be profiled to determine its demographic and/or lifestyle characteristics.

- *Tracking and comparing the service provided across different outlets and/or channels of distribution.*
- *Benchmarking against competitors.* A separate series of 'perceptions' questions could be included in the instrument for each key competitor and the resultant information used for benchmarking purposes.

SERVQUAL has been found to be very effective in a variety of different contexts including healthcare, charity service provision, and even in evaluating the service provided by the arts. It could therefore be used to good effect by nonprofits in a variety of the ways alluded to above.

Customer Value

We have so far in this chapter talked about customer perceptions of service quality and identified three ways in which this might be measured. The reader will recall that the latter two methods allow the researcher to identify those attributes of the service from which the customer derives the most value and it is this latter concept that we will focus on here.

Service organizations, whether they are profit-making or not, are unlikely to provide a service which has only one ingredient. When an arts customer buys a ticket for a museum, for example, the opportunity to view the exhibits is not the only component of the service purchased. Factors such as the ability to be able to interact with the displays, to understand something of the history of the items, and to be able to have an occasional dialogue with staff might also be significant components of the experience. Identifying which of the dimensions are of most importance is crucial, since it allows management to invest in those areas where customers derive the most value from their visit and cut costs in those areas which are not perceived to be of particular importance. This very simple idea has recently taken on a whole new significance because of the work of Jones and Sasser (1995). Consider the graph in Figure 7.5.

The figure illustrates the satisfaction ratings recently obtained from a survey of customers to a one-off exhibition at an art gallery. Now ask yourself the following questions.

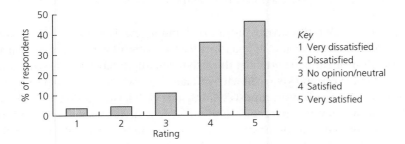

Figure 7.5 Customer satisfaction with an art gallery exhibition

Putting yourself in the position of the manager of that gallery for a moment, would you be happy with these figures?

The conventional wisdom has always been that you should be. After all, some 82 per cent of your customers are either satisfied or very satisfied. Consider an additional question.

Which category of customers should we be most concerned with?

Again the conventional wisdom has always been that we should work to improve the ratings that we are currently receiving from customers rating their satisfaction with the service as a one, two, or three. Clearly they are not satisfied with the service and we need to improve what we offer these groups of customers.

If you were then told that the customers who rate their satisfaction as a 5 are six times more likely to purchase from you again than the customers who rate their satisfaction only as a 4, would your opinion change?

In a study which embraced a variety of different sectors, Jones and Sasser concluded that this was a pattern of loyalty common to all the sectors studied. In the example quoted, even if *all* the customers who rated their satisfaction as a 5 repurchase, only 17 per cent of those who rated it as a 4 will do so. This revelation helps to focus the mind on the group of customers who should clearly be regarded as most important. If an organization can improve on the percentage of customers who rate their satisfaction as a 5, it can substantially improve on the levels of loyalty that will be exhibited as a result.

Before moving on, it is worth noting that the factor of six quoted above is not static across all industries and sectors; it will clearly depend on the availability of substitute services and the nature of the competition. For many nonprofit organizations, which provide unique services, the factor is likely to be considerably lower, but even if it should prove to be as low as two or three, a significant difference will still exist between the loyalty patterns exhibited by the customers who consider themselves satisfied and those who consider themselves very satisfied. It is interesting to note that recent research has explored this issue in the context of fundraising and concluded that donors who perceive themselves as very satisfied with the quality of service provided by the fundraising department are significantly more likely to remain loyal than those that perceive themselves as merely satisfied. The multiple isn't as high as the factor of six referred to above, but very satisfied donors are twice as likely to remain loyal as donors who are simply satisfied (Sargeant 2001).

The reason for elaborating on this research is a simple one. The key to moving customers from a 4 to a 5 is customer value. If you think back to some of your own experiences with service organizations and in particular those that you might have been asked to evaluate, you can probably very quickly recall why you failed to award a 5 yourself to a particular organization. The organization almost certainly met your basic requirements, but did not excel in one area that was of particular importance to you. As a result, organizations need to be particularly alert to those aspects of their service offering that customers perceive to be most important and ensure that they 'engineer in' value in these key areas. If loyalty is to be preserved and/or enhanced, customers must be made to feel that they have received an exceptional service.

Price

The second of the ingredients of the marketing mix concerns issues connected with price. In a not-for-profit context, price can take on many guises and could take the form of entrance fees, tuition fees, service charges, donations, contributions, etc. In many organizations, particularly those with a good or service to sell, the pricing decisions may be almost identical to those taken in the for-profit sector. For other organizations, however, the 'price' charged to the beneficiaries may well be kept to an absolute minimum and indeed may even be set at zero. Such practices definitely do not have parallels in the for-profit sector, unless they are an integral part of a coordinated attempt to gain market share at any cost—witness for example the newspaper price wars that took place in the UK in the mid-1990s.

Price versus Cost

To begin a discussion of price in the nonprofit context it is useful to start with an understanding of costs. All transactions with an organization, be it in relation to the sale of physical goods, or the handing over of a £20 donation, all have costs associated with them. These costs essentially break down into one of three distinct types (Rados 1981). In other words:

Total costs = OOP costs + opportunity costs + AO costs

where

OOP costs + out of pocket costs

and

AO = all other costs

To aid us in a discussion of these three different types of cost, we will consider the example of a charity donor who intends to attend a gala event in support of her local hospice. She understands that at the end of this event she will be asked to give around £50 to support the cause and this is what most organizations would consider to be the cost to her of her continuing support. They would be wrong! To get to the gala, our donor would incur some form of travelling expense, either on public transport or in her own car. She may also have to pay a babysitter and use the telephone to put off any other appointments which she might have had planned. All these may be viewed as OOP expenses.

Our donor will also incur opportunity costs by attending the gala. Put simply, opportunity costs are the value of an opportunity passed up or foregone. She may have had the opportunity of attending the theatre, going to a friend's birthday party, enjoying a candlelit dinner for two, or earning an extra few hours overtime at the office. While in only the latter example is she actually out of pocket, a value could equally well be placed on the enjoyment she would gain from any of the other three alternatives. Since she has decided to forgo these in favour of attending the charity gala, the value of the next most attractive alternative can be viewed as the opportunity cost of attending.

Of course, there may be other costs associated with the evening. She may arrive a little late to find that no car parking places remain and she may have to spend time walking from one nearby. If it is a wet evening, this may be more than just a slight inconvenience. When she actually gets to the gala, the seating may be uncomfortable, she may find the staff unwelcoming, and the best of the food could already have been eaten. What a night! This final category of costs we call AO costs and, when added to the opportunity costs and out-of-pocket costs, we can derive the total cost of the evening to our valiant donor.

It is important to recognize that total costs can often amount to significantly more than the actual price paid, because it is the perception of total price that is the important factor. While easily able to afford the £50 donation, the donor in this instance may well fail to attend similar events in the future as the sum of all the other costs could have persuaded her that the evening was too expensive. Charities, and indeed all nonprofits, need to be sensitive to these issues. There would be little point for example, in setting the price for theatre tickets, without considering variables such as the attractiveness of the performance (affecting the value of the opportunity cost), or the costs to the audience of physically getting to the venue. In the case of the latter, if there are theatres more conveniently located, audiences will not have to incur the same level of transportation cost and may take this into consideration when they decide which of their local theatres to attend. This is an important concept to grasp, since in manipulating price a nonprofit can often be more creative than merely tinkering with whatever charge it happens to make for the goods and services it provides. Staying with our theatre example, negotiation with third parties might result in free car parking, special late night transport (to get people home after the performance), or a discount at a local restaurant to enable the theatre to market the evening as a package and thereby impact on opportunity costs.

Setting the Price

There are a variety of ways in which an organization can go about setting price, namely:

- *cost plus*—identifying what it costs to provide the service and adding on a profit margin if appropriate;
- *what they can afford*—setting the price to match the organization's expectations of what the recipient group can afford to pay;
- *competitor matching*—identifying what competitors are demanding for their products/services and setting your own price accordingly;
- *pricing to achieve organizational objectives*—using price as a tool to affect the overall levels of demand for the service in the market. The higher the total cost (see above) to the market, the less demand for the service there is likely to be. Nonprofits can therefore use price to achieve their objectives in terms of the penetration a given service provision will have.

Price Discrimination

The methods of price setting outlined above all make the assumption that all the organization's customers will pay a set price. This is not necessarily the case. Often non-profits will have quite different categories of customers with widely ranging abilities to pay. Arts organizations, for example, will undoubtedly want to cultivate their student audience as they will ultimately form 'the audience of tomorrow' but they recognize, too, that this segment of the market is more susceptible to price, than say a professional couple in their fifties. The answer is to price discriminate between these two segments and to charge a different price to each segment of the market. Price discrimination is a widespread practice among nonprofits and there are a variety of bases on which such discrimination can be based:

- *By market segment.* As in the example above, the organization charges different segments of customers different prices for the service provided. Hence museums might offer discount packages to students, OAPs, family groups, schools, etc.
- *By place.* Theatre tickets are usually sold according to the desirability of their location. Customers will therefore pay very different prices for the same performance depending on where they elect to sit—the stalls, the dress circle, or up in the gods.
- *By time.* Discrimination by time could take may forms. Performance prices could vary at different times of the day; entrance fees could vary by season to encourage off-peak demand; last-minute discounts could be offered on unsold theatre tickets to fill the auditorium, etc.
- *By service category.* Often an organization will elect to offer several grades of service, many of which could be perceived as exclusive—the first night of a show for example, or a celebrity opening. Although the additional costs associated with the creation of such an exclusive event will clearly need to be taken into consideration when pricing, organizations often charge well in excess of what it actually costs them to provide these 'add-ons'. Certain categories of customers are often prepared to pay for the prestige of being able to take advantage of this exclusivity.

Place

The 'place' element of the marketing mix is concerned with issues such as the degree of accessibility required to a service, how the service will be distributed to clients, the level of control required over any intermediaries that might be used, and the geographical coverage for the service that is desired. While the place element of the marketing mix has a clear relevance for organizations of all kinds, whether profit-making or not, there are additional complexities to be encountered in the nonprofit sector. Each of these will now be considered.

Service Accessibility

Service accessibility refers to the degree to which the customers of a particular organization should have easy access to the service being provided. Because of the inseparable nature of services, there are often few choices for nonprofit organizations but to site themselves as close as possible to the target market. The difficulty for some nonprofits, however, is that they have two (or more) such targets. They must site themselves appropriately for both resource providers and resource consumers and often have to make trade-offs between the two.

In the case of resource providers, location is important for the following reasons:

- Many nonprofits rely on the services of volunteers and must clearly have regard for where such individuals might typically live. It is much easier to attract volunteers if they do not have far to travel from their home.

- Location can greatly facilitate fundraising. If a charity can be seen to have a local presence, it will be easier to raise funds from both individual and corporate donors (see Sargeant and Stephenson (1997)).

- Location also needs to be considered in respect of the accessibility that will be offered to donors to make a donation. Many charities thus adopt a fairly intensive pattern of distribution, attempting to make their collection boxes available in as many different locations as possible.

In terms of resource consumers, location is important for the following reasons:

- Nonprofits need to consider how accessible their services will be to members of their target market. Where the service is aimed at persons with some form of disability any service will clearly need to be provided as close to their home as possible. For many visually impaired persons, for example, the requirement to use public transport to access a day centre provision would deter many from attending.

- There is an intrinsic link between the physical locations selected and the coverage that might be gained of the target market. Organizations must thus consider the geographical spread of their recipient base and select those areas with the highest concentrations of need.

Channel/Route to Market

For many nonprofit organizations, obtaining an appropriate route to market can be problematic. For-profit organizations have the 'luxury' of a plethora of channels of distribution that could be appropriate. These might include wholesalers, retailers, agents, distributors, franchises, etc. A typical manufacturer will have to determine which particular channels are likely to suit its needs best and then seek to develop relationships with these to encourage intermediaries to stock and perhaps promote its product(s). The key difference in the for-profit sector is that manufacturers generally have a series of 'carrots' which they can use to motivate intermediaries to stock, such as variable commission rates, bulk discounts, merchandising assistance, dealer competitions, and so on. For most nonprofit organizations, these options do not exist. Many services for the elderly, for example, are distributed primarily through the auspices of social service or housing departments. Social workers receive no commission for passing on contacts to nonprofit organizations and do so simply because of the regard they have for their clients.

The additional complexity of managing nonprofit channels of distribution is well illustrated by the following case study.

CASE STUDY 7.1 NON-MAINTAINED SPECIAL SCHOOLS

Within the current legislative framework there are a number of schools within England and Wales which provide a specialist education for children with a variety of disabilities. Local education authorities (LEAs) currently have a duty to provide the best possible education for children, irrespective of their level of disability. This encourages local authorities to create provision within their area for children with common disabilities, such as learning disabilities. In the case of children with a less common disability it is possible that an LEA will be unable to find appropriate provision within one of its own schools. Under such circumstances the LEA may decide to send a child to a non-maintained special school, perhaps located outside their area. These organizations are charitable in status and rely for their funding on the fees paid by LEAs.

Under the terms of the 1981 Education Act, LEAs are under an obligation to integrate as many children as possible into mainstream schools, a move which, while it would clearly be in most children's interest, is certainly one which saves the LEA the expense of financing a number of special education places. Moreover, under the Act LEAs have a duty to take into account the wishes of parents in respect of a child's education. Thus if a decision in respect of a particular child is borderline, the wishes of the parent should influence the LEA to make the choice that the parents desire. In cases where the LEA and parents fail to reach agreement an appeals procedure may be instigated.

These extremely complex arrangements leave many non-maintained special schools with something of a marketing dilemma. Such organizations often have no alternative but to rely on the goodwill of intermediaries to pass on details of the services that they can provide. Advisory teachers employed by LEAs are the key source of information for parents, as are social workers and medical specialists, none of whom receive any remuneration from the non-maintained sector. Indeed one could argue that the one key intermediary, the LEA, has a vested interest in persuading parents to send children to a mainstream school as it could then avoid the substantially higher fees payable to the specialist sector. While there is no evidence that this actually occurs in practice, the potential for a conflict of interest is clear. Figure 7.6 illustrates the percentage of the school population that has been receiving a special education, year on year since 1979.

To compound this dramatic drop in numbers it is almost impossible for special schools to gain direct access to parents of potential students. Mailing lists of individuals with a particular disability simply do not exist and neither would it be desirable to create them. This makes it difficult for such organizations to communicate to parents the very real benefits that their schools can sometimes offer over a mainstream education.

continues

CASE STUDY 7.1 continued

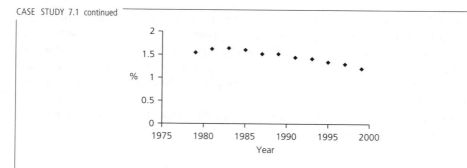

Figure 7.6 Percentage of pupil population placed in special schools

Faced with these difficulties, non-maintained special schools must therefore learn to deal with an extremely complex pattern of distribution, the majority of which they can exert no control over.

Customer Perceptions of the Channel

In its simplest form this might involve decisions about the decor of the premises (relatively simple surroundings may suggest to potential donors that donations are not being wasted on spurious decorations). More usually it may involve a consideration of the image that the channel might hold in the minds of potential customers. A decision may be taken, for example, not to use the technique of outbound telemarketing in a fundraising mix, since in the minds of many people it is still associated with the 'hard sell' techniques of the mid-1980s and therefore as an unacceptable intrusion.

Those nonprofits that are involved in fundraising activities may instead make use of a range of distribution channels, including direct marketing, agents, volunteers and (if collecting boxes are utilized) possibly a range of different retail outlets. Interestingly, Horne and Moss (1995) determined that collection box yields vary significantly between different categories of retail outlets and they should hence be selected with care. The retail types associated with the highest yields are (in descending order) take-aways, cafes, bars, newsagents, supermarkets, and ironmongers. Soft furnishing, sports and clothes shops were found to be the outlets with the smallest yields.

The Emergence of Electronic Channels

The comparatively recent emergence of a range of new technologies has opened up a whole new range of opportunities for nonprofits not only to communicate with their market, but also to deliver their services to their clients. Many nonprofits now boast websites where enquirers can download information about the organization, its services, staff, facilities, etc. While the majority of these electronic sources are as yet reactive, in the sense that they deal positively with enquiries, the opportunity exists in the future for nonprofits to take a more proactive stance and to actively market themselves through the

Internet. Indeed, a number of organizations are already making a very creative use of the medium. Cancer Research UK, for example, has recently created an *In Memoriam* feature on its website which allows individuals who have lost a loved one to cancer to create a virtual memorial and to collect donations in memory of that person to support Cancer Research's work.

A number of universities in the USA are now embracing the Internet as a means of delivering their programmes. Live conferences with staff and indeed whole educational programmes can now be delivered online. Such developments not only increase the number of fee-paying students that might be attracted to an institution, but because of the inherently convenient mode of delivery, many mature learners who would not have the time to return to a traditional classroom environment are being encouraged to return to their studies.

The WWF has also been benefiting from the creative use of new technology by the commercial organization 'e-cards'. The organization's website offers Internet surfers the opportunity to send an e-card to their friends and loved ones. An e-card is essentially an electronic postcard, and users can select the photograph that they would like to appear on their recipient's screen. An example is given in Figure 7.7. It costs the user nothing to send the card, but by participating in the scheme they earn a donation for the WWF by being exposed to advertising on the e-card order page. The service provides an excellent example of the considerable benefits that can accrue from partnerships between commercial and nonprofit organizations.

Figure 7.7 WWF e-card

Promotion

The promotional element of the mix is responsible for the communication of the marketing offer to the target group. Promotion is 'the process of presenting an integrated set of stimuli to a market with the intent of evoking a set of responses within that market set ... and ... setting up channels to receive, interpret and act upon messages from the market for the purposes of modifying present company messages and identifying new communication opportunities' (Delozier 1976).

It can be used for a variety of purposes within the marketing mix, typically:

- to inform potential customers of the existence and benefits of the service;
- to persuade potential customers that the benefits offered are genuine and will adequately meet their requirements;
- to remind members of the target group that the service exists and of the key benefits that it can offer;
- to differentiate the service in the minds of potential customers from the others currently on the market, i.e. to define clearly the positioning of the service.

Before moving on to examine the elements of the communication mix and how they can be utilized to achieve the purposes outlined above, it will be instructive to begin by a short analysis of the communication process. Figure 7.8 illustrates a simple model of communication.

The source of the communication message is simply the organization that intends to communicate with its market. To enable it to do so, it must decide on the message that it wishes to convey, i.e what does it want to convey about itself, and what action (if any) would it like members of the target group to take on receipt of the message. In a social marketing content, this might involve the organization in trying to get across the danger of unprotected sex exposing people to the risk of AIDS. The message might be a simple one—'unprotected sex puts you at risk of AIDS'. However, the reader will appreciate that simply transmitting this message to the target market is unlikely to be successful. To begin with, people react in different ways to fear appeals such as this and many might screen out the message as a result. Others might not perceive the message as being relevant to them because they do not perceive their lifestyle as putting them at risk. It is normal therefore for communications messages to be encoded.

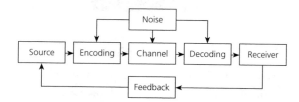

Figure 7.8 A simple model of communication

Encoding involves the source in deciding what the communications will actually contain to get across their message to consumers. In essence this is the creative treatment applied to the message to ensure that when it arrives at the receiver he decodes it as being of relevance to him and acts on it. This may be done by using ordinary-looking people in the advertising, conveying the selfishness of putting those you love at risk, explaining that AIDS can affect all sections of society, etc. Of course, there is no guarantee that when the message is received it will be decoded in the manner in which the source had originally intended. There are a variety of factors which can interfere with a communications message, and these are typically referred to as *noise*.

Noise acts to distort the message or to prevent its reception by the receiver. It can thus take many forms including:

- a lack of attention on the part of the receiver;
- heavy promotional spending by other competing organizations;
- selection of inappropriate media;
- poor creative treatment, resulting in ambiguous messages;
- poor perception of source—if it is not regarded as credible the message may be ignored;
- environmental distractions—the message may be received under conditions that make it impossible for the recipient to concentrate.

It is thus important for an organization to try to minimize the effects of noise by selecting the most appropriate communication channels available to reach its target market. It can also help reduce noise by giving adequate thought to the encoding process and making sure that the promotional budget allows it to gain an appropriate 'share of the voice'. Clearly this is not an easy process to manage and it is essential to ensure that there are mechanisms in place to gather adequate feedback from the target market. If messages are either not being received or are being decoded and wrongly interpreted, it will be essential for the source organization to take immediate corrective action. Indeed, it would be usual to test all forms of marketing communications prior to exposing them to the market, although even this is no guarantee of success. There is hence a need for ongoing monitoring of marketing communications.

It is clear from the model in Figure 7.8 that the promotional element of the marketing mix involves the establishment of a dialogue with customers, the quality of which can vary considerably depending on the nature of the communication channel selected and the degree to which noise has the capacity to interfere with message reception. Of course, this model is very general and does not address issues which relate to the use of specific promotional tools. These are essentially advertising, sales promotion, public relations, and direct marketing, collectively referred to as the communications mix. We will now give a brief consideration to each of these elements in turn.

Advertising

Kotler (1994: 627) defines advertising as 'any paid form of non-personal presentation and promotion of ideas, goods or services by an identified sponsor'. Advertising can be placed in a variety of media, including websites, television, radio, cinema, newspapers, magazines/trade press, and outdoor (poster and transport advertising). With an ever increasing number of promotional media becoming available, it is becoming more difficult to identify those which offer the most appropriate use of promotional resources. Essentially one is looking to find the medium which can reach the largest number of members of the target market at the lowest price. Thus the measure of 'CPT' (Cost Per Thousand) is used by many organizations to compare the use of various media. CPT is calculated as you would expect. If a full-page advertisement in a national newspaper circulated to three million readers is £9000, the cost per thousand is £3. This figure can then be used to compare the various media options available. It is a very simple measure and it is necessary to be very clear about the profile of the media audience. If the profile does not exactly match your requirements (and it rarely does), you may be underestimating the CPT figure since you could be communicating with a large number of people who are not in your target market.

Media can also be selected on the basis of how many competitors use the medium, since if a large number of competitors are present the returns accruing to each advertiser are likely to be less than they would be in a publication where it is possible to enjoy a wider 'share of the voice'. It may also be important for many nonprofits to consider the environment of the medium. Does the medium offer an environment that is appropriate for the message being conveyed? There would be little point, for example, in placing an advert for a modern art exhibition in a publication whose editorial was generally critical of such art forms. Similarly, the term 'environment' can be applied to the environment in which the message is received. Some media demand a lot of concentration of readers, such as specialist trade journals, making it possible to provide much more detailed information about the product/service in advertisements. Television advertising, on the other hand, offers little opportunity in this regard since it commands little attention. Indeed many people leave the room, perhaps to make a coffee, when commercial breaks begin.

Sales Promotion

The term 'sales promotion' in the nonprofit sector refers to any immediate stimulation to buy (or to give a donation) that might be provided at or near the point of sale.

The purpose of sales promotion is to prompt the customer to engage in a transaction with the nonprofit. It is thus more immediate in its effects and hence favoured in times of budgetary constraint since an immediate return on the investment can be demonstrated. The same, regrettably, cannot be said of advertising, whose effects are considerably less tangible and certainly longer-term. Sales promotion activity includes the provision of free gifts, discounts, premiums, leaflets, contests, display material, or demonstrations. The key to the selection of successful sales promotion activities lies in selecting something which reflects the needs and wants of the customer group and offers them something which they will find to be of value. This may be as simple as an introductory discount on a service to tempt customers into sampling, or it may be something more elaborate. In the fundraising context for example, the simple poppy which indicates a donation to the British Legion has a very powerful and emotive appeal. It offers a potential donor the opportunity to associate with a nation's grief and thanksgiving, and this promotion is so powerful most people in the public eye ensure that they wear their poppies for at least a week before Remembrance Sunday. The donor in this case is receiving a very real, if intangible, benefit. Other organizations allow donors to 'sample' their product and as a result guide dogs and even air ambulances can each have their part to play in a promotion. (The Cornish Air Ambulance Service recently charged donors for an opportunity to look inside the ambulance.) If the donor is able to share in a unique experience and is made to feel involved in the charity, fundraising will be greatly enhanced. It should also be noted that sales promotions can have a more mundane role to fulfil in that they allow volunteers to have something to sell and ensure (in the case of flags, pins, and stickers), that the donor is protected from further requests to give.

Public Relations

Public relations is often confused with publicity, crisis management, lobbying, etc. In fact, PR can embrace all these elements, but it should also be regarded as a somewhat wider function within an organization. One of the most frequently used definitions of PR is as follows: 'Public relations is the management function that evaluates the attitudes of important publics, identifies the policies and procedures of an individual or an organization with the public interest, and executes a programme of action to earn understanding and acceptance by these publics' (Public Relations News, 27 October 1947).

It is hence concerned with the development of each of the organization's publics and might typically involve an organization in proceeding through the stages outlined in Figure 7.9.

The process begins with an analysis of the current perceptions of each of an organization's publics. Those perceptions are then assessed to see how desirable they might be from the organization's perspective and, where weaknesses/ambiguities are identified, a programme of PR can be developed to address them. The process Kotler and Fox (1985) advocate also makes it clear that it is important for an organization to plan for potential crises, however unlikely these may be. If an organization has plans to deal with all potential contingencies, should the unthinkable happen it will be well placed to implement a cogent response.

A variety of PR tools may be utilized to develop the desired perceptions among its target publics. These include:

- *Production of written material.* This might include leaflets, flyers, magazines, annual reports, and volunteer newsletters.
- *Organizational identity media.* Most nonprofits today have some form of corporate identity which features prominently in the organization's stationery, brochures, signs, and business cards. These are what might be referred to as organizational identity media and it is essential that through the careful use of design, logos, etc., that all these media conform to a standard format and convey a consistent message to the publics targeted.

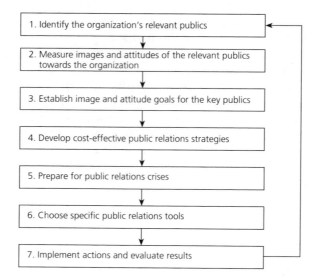

Figure 7.9 The public relations strategic planning process

Source: Kotler and Fox, *Strategic Marketing for Educational Institutions* © 1985. Adapted by permission of Prentice Hall, Inc, Upper Saddle River, NJ.

- *Publicity*. The PR department can often identify newsworthy activities within the organization and seek to promote these in the media. The problem with such 'free advertising' is that there is no guarantee the media will elect to cover it. Unlike advertising which must be sent to the media and paid for, publicity must be sent to the media and prayed for!

- *Provision of expert speakers*. Many nonprofits have unique expertise or act as the mouthpiece for a particular section of society. In such circumstances it is important that all the key media understand that this expertise exists, so that should an occasion arise where an expert comment is called for, they know exactly who to approach. For this reason, many universities now produce a publication called 'Who can Speak on What', or something similar, which can be distributed to regional and national media, in the hope they will use it to source subject specialists for expert comment.

- *Telephone helplines*. Many nonprofits who provide a service to members of the public are already providing very successful telephone helplines which provide help and guidance to those in need. Many of the medical charities, for example, provide a 24-hour helpline which sufferers and/or their relatives can ring for reassurance and guidance. Given that it now costs very little to provide a toll-free or freephone number many nonprofits are now prepared to cover the costs of this activity themselves as part of a coordinated PR strategy.

Nonprofits generally have very complex audiences to whom they must communicate their message. This audience may be made up of current and potential sponsors, the media, the business and local community, their own volunteers, and the recipients on whose behalf they are working. Given this complexity it is not surprising that PR takes such a prominent place in the marketing mixes of many nonprofit organizations. Unfortunately, PR has a much less obvious price tag than media advertising and its results are perhaps even more difficult to assess. It remains an important tool for many organizations however, primarily because of the impact it can have on the market. Messages carried through third parties are perceived by the public as having greater credibility than messages conveyed in advertising where the organization may have a tendency to portray itself in an overly positive light.

Direct Marketing

Currently a major growth area in marketing, direct marketing is increasing in importance for a great many organizations. Traditionally charities have been perceived as being particularly strong in this field, with their creative use of the marketing database putting them very much at the forefront of developments. Direct marketing can take many forms, the most common of which are briefly described below:

- *Direct mail.* With the increasing sophistication of database technology it is now possible to refine the contact strategies that nonprofits have with a wide range of customers. A theatre, for example, can look back over the purchase histories of its clients and write to those who it knows from past experience will be interested in certain categories of performance. Similarly, charities can use their knowledge of the database to treat high-value donors differently from low-value donors and target direct mailshots at the time of year that specific segments of donors find most acceptable. Indeed, nonprofits that make wise use of their database are moving away from a broadbrush approach to market segmentation and are beginning to develop almost one-to-one dialogues with their customers.

Most modern databases also allow a nonprofit to profile its customer base. While the data so gained can be used to help develop existing customers, it can also be used to good effect to target other potential customers in society who match the profile of existing customers. With a proliferation of consumer and industrial lists now available, nonprofits can target prospective customers in a way that could only be dreamed of a mere twenty years ago. This is a subject that will be returned to in more depth in Chapter 9.

- *Telemarketing.* While it is still comparatively rare for a nonprofit to attempt telemarketing activity in-house, unless it was on a very small scale, there are now a number of specialist agencies who offer telemarketing expertise to the nonprofit sector. It can be used for either inbound or outbound activity. Inbound activity remains the most common, whereby a freephone or toll-free number is provided for clients and/or donors to contact the organization free of charge. The number is frequently quoted in all other forms of marketing communication and the telemarketing service provided free of charge to make the exchange process more accessible to clients. Outbound telemarketing is still rather less common, although growing in popularity. At a recent general election, for example, the Conservative party made every effort to contact all the voters of a marginal seat in Cornwall by telephone to ensure that they were able to get their message across to potential waiverers.

It is interesting to note that at the time of writing, the Federal Trade Commission in the USA has just established a national 'Do Not Call' register of individuals who do not wish to be subjected to outbound telemarketing activity. It will thereafter be an offence for telemarketers to call this group of individuals. The take-up rate to subscribe to this service has been phenomenal, with millions of Americans signing up the service in its first 48 hours of operation. The UK has long had an equivalent service and individuals not wishing to receive telemarketing calls in this country can subscribe to the TPS (Telephone Preference Service) preventing subsequent access to their number. Organizations violating an individual's wish not to be disturbed in this way now commit a criminal offence.

- *E-Marketing.* We have already mentioned the increasing use of the Internet in our discussion of 'place'. While it can be an effective vehicle for service delivery it can also be a very effective communications medium. For this reason some organizations will place their consideration of e-marketing in the 'place' element of the mix, while others will consider the relevant issues under 'promotion'. As with so many of the frameworks we use in marketing it really doesn't matter where this material is presented as long as it is presented in a cogent and easy to operationalize fashion.

Where organizations are involved with marketing predominantly in an Internet environment it may be worth developing a separate e-marketing mix. One possible suggestion for the form this might take is presented in Figure 7.10. A plan may be developed for each distinctive facet of the mix to ensure that a high-impact experience is created for visitors to a given site.

Entertainment—the way in which the site is designed to be imaginative, fun and/or entertaining to use.

Informativeness—the extent to which the site informs and/or provides a helpful resource for those interested in a particular issue.

Organization—the extent to which the site is easy to use and convenient to search for information, services, etc.

Aesthetic design—the extent to which the use of colour, graphics, and creative design is appropriate on the site

Processing speed—the extent to which it is easy and quick to download pertinent materials and/or functionality. The number of steps it takes to make a purchase, order a service, or take action on a particular issue.

Security—the extent to which the site is secure and embues users with confidence in respect of how their personal data will be used.

Fulfilment—the detail of how actions taken online will be operationalized thereafter. For example, the accurate processing of the payment, despatch of an order, and communication thereafter. To achieve this satisfactorily, there needs to be an appropriate degree of linkage between the website and other IT systems that will be responsible for delivering the promises made by the site.

Figure 7.10 E-marketing mix

Of course, e-marketing is not restricted to the use of the Internet alone. Many organizations now make use of SMS or MMS (Short Message Service and Multimedia Message Service) messaging to communicate with either service users, members, campaigners, or donors. Individuals can receive text messages which alert them to the need to take action, or bring them up to date with the activities of the nonprofit. From a fundraising perspective, some nonprofits have set up arrangements with mobile operators where texting a certain number in reply to a message will result in a donation to their organization. Such techniques can be particularly effective at engaging with younger audiences who tend to be more comfortable with the latest technology.

We have also seen in recent years the testing of Web TV. While many countries, the UK included, now have a form of interactive television where viewers can make purchases or order services using their TV remotes, this is only the beginning of the revolution in traditional broadcasting. A number of US cities have piloted Web TV which moves beyond the fairly simplistic operation of interactive television to offer a genuine merger between web-based technology and traditional broadcasting. Users of Web TV are able to view television channels in the usual way, but may also switch from a TV programme to its associated website, engage in chat, make a purchase, and surf to related sites or sources of information before returning to the broadcast in question. From a nonprofit's perspective, such developments offer significant opportunities to interact with a variety of stakeholder groups. Their website, for example, might be featured on a television programme dealing with issues related to the cause or mission. Viewers can then leave the programme to visit the website, download information, make contact with service provision, sign up to a campaign, or even offer a donation.

- *Door-to-door.* Door-to-door canvassing and/or selling remains a popular way of fundraising for many, particularly 'local' charities. It can also be a very effective means of raising awareness of the activities of an organization, or canvassing to reach prospective volunteers.

- *Personal selling.* While this is perhaps less common in the nonprofit sector, there may be a number of organizations who find it desirable to maintain a direct salesforce which can negotiate on a one-to-one basis with prospective clients and/or funders. This is likely to be more appropriate where an organization has a small number of high-value clients or where the clients are narrowly concentrated in a small geographical area. In such circumstances the increased overhead of employing a salesteam may be justified in terms of the quality of the contact/service that will be provided.

People

To an organization providing a service to clients, the people element of the marketing mix is arguably the most important. After all, it may reasonably be argued that the people ARE the organization, whether they are paid employees or unpaid volunteers. Interestingly the latter category of staff are more prevalent than many people believe. Lynn and Davis-Smith (1992), for example, found that almost half of the adults in the UK will engage in some form of voluntary activity over the course of a typical year. Indeed Bruce and Raymer

(1992) found that, on average, for every paid employee retained, the larger charities utilize the services of 8.5 volunteers.

Ensuring that all staff, whatever their status, deliver a service of the highest quality is a key issue for all nonprofits. The inseperability of services makes it impossible to distinguish between service production and service delivery and it is the people of the organization who are therefore responsible for both. In this section of the marketing plan, the nonprofit must therefore give consideration to the people skills that it will need to provide its service and, indeed, to deliver every component of the marketing plan. This can then be matched against the profile of the existing human resource and appropriate gaps identified. The organization can then ensure that those 'gaps' are represented in the recruitment programme and that the appropriate person specifications are in place. On some occasions it may be possible to plug these gaps by the recruitment of full-time or part-time staff. On others it may be more appropriate to look to the recruitment of suitably qualified volunteers. Hind (1995) suggests that before recruiting paid staff, a process which results in a considerable drain on organizational resource, the organization should ensure that their recruitment is absolutely necessary. To determine this, he suggests that paid staff are necessary only under the following circumstances:

- when specialist expertise is required on an ongoing basis;
- when continuous attention is needed to tasks which must be performed in accordance with the organization's timetable and in compliance with its formal procedures and standards;
- when roles exist requiring the management of other staff or large groups of volunteers.

Of course, if the attraction of volunteers is the preferred option it is useful to understand something of an individual's typical motivations for volunteering. If the tasks for which volunteers are sought cannot be fulfilled by volunteers, an organization may be left with little choice but to pay for staff. Fenton et al. (1993) found that the following three categories of volunteer motivation are most common.

- *Demonstrative motivations.* Individuals who volunteer for this reason are essentially seeking some form of ego reward. They donate their time because they believe that some form of social recognition will follow.
- *Social motivations.* Researchers found that this was the most common form of motivation and involves individuals volunteering because they see it as an active form of giving to support charity. It is seen as an opportunity to socialize with other volunteers and to feel collectively that they are doing good.
- *Instrumental motivation.* Less commonly expressed than the other two, individuals who volunteer for this reason are doing so simply because they feel the need to help others. They feel they have a duty to help others less fortunate than themselves.

It is, of course, usually much easier to develop and retain existing staff/volunteers than it is to attain new ones. The second focus of this section of the plan is hence to identify the steps that need to be taken to retain existing personnel. By far the easiest way of achieving this is to survey those who decide to leave and, having discovered the reasons for dissatisfaction, implement any changes that may be necessary to ensure that problems are corrected. One can also ensure that an ongoing dialogue is maintained with existing staff so that they do not feel compelled to leave in the first place! In the case of volunteers, it would also be advisable to ensure that the organization responds to the various categories of motivation identified above and understands what the volunteers actually want to get out of their relationship with the organization. Retention strategies can then be developed, taking account of these needs.

Process

When marketers talk of process, they are talking about the process that a particular client group must go through to purchase and enjoy the service being provided. Clearly, for a service organization, every aspect of the encounter that a customer has with staff will be important. Each stage of the service will be evaluated by customers and many will have a substantial impact on the overall level of satisfaction experienced. The question is, however, which elements of the process are deemed by the customer to be most important? To answer this, it is often useful to draw a flow chart of the various components of the service that the customer experiences. An example is shown in Figure 7.11.

Although this is a gross simplification of the process that one might go through in purchasing and enjoying an evening at the theatre, it does at least serve to illustrate that the process consists of a number of specific encounters with the organization. Each of these may of course be broken down into a number of sub-encounters. Take, for example, the telephone reservation process; there are a number of components to this including the length of time you wait to have your call answered, the efficiency and friendliness of the operator, and the accuracy with which he performs his role. For the moment, however, we will stick with the general process depicted in Figure 7.11. The reader will appreciate that not every aspect of the service will be equally important. The provision of a cloakroom, clean toilets, and the existence of a bar may be relatively unimportant for the segment of customers addressed. If research is conducted which identifies those aspects of the service that the customer places most importance on, the organization can invest in those areas, ensure that they are of the highest quality, and hence enhance overall

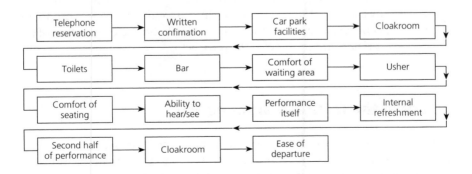

Figure 7.11 Flow chart of a visit to the theatre

customer satisfaction. Conversely, in those areas that are considered unimportant, the organization can look to minimize costs and perhaps even remove that aspect of the service altogether, utilizing the resource saved in other areas that are perceived as being important. The idea of engineering customer value in this way was first suggested by Porter (1985) who referred to the concept discussed above as the *value chain*. In his view it represents an essential tool for organizations to use in appraising their service process with a view to enhancing it.

Physical Evidence

The final ingredient of the service marketing mix is physical evidence. Since the service product is largely intangible, it is important for the organization to focus on those tangible cues that do exist and to ensure that they convey appropriate messages to the consumer about the quality of the service she is purchasing. As has already been identified above, in the absence of a physical product consumers will use tangible cues to make their judgements in respect of service quality. In a typical organization these cues may include the following.

- *Premises.* Thought will obviously be given in the healthcare context, for example, to the physical design of waiting areas. They should generally be clean, comfortable, and informative, in the sense that reading materials may be left for patients informing them of various aspects of the services that are available.
- *Facilities.* The appearance of the facilities on offer is also important. In selecting a school, for example, parents are unlikely to rely totally on the reputation that a school has in a given area. They are also likely to inspect the facilities it has to offer for themselves and may ask to see the sports/library and IT provisions.
- *Dress.* The presentation of the staff can help reinforce the corporate image that the organization is looking to project. Smart, attractively presented staff can infer quality, in the absence of other cues, and may reassure potential customers of the professionalism offered by a particular organization.
- *Reports.* The written communications of the organization may also be regarded as tangible cues. The annual report, the 'sales' brochure, will all be used to evaluate the service. In selecting a course of study at a university, for example, unless a visit to the site is planned, prospective students may have little more to build their perception of quality on than the presentation and contents of the prospectus.

Summary of the Tactical Marketing Mix

We have now examined each of the ingredients of a typical service marketing mix. In developing a marketing plan, an organization will need to give careful consideration to each of these seven elements, while at the same being careful not to fall into the trap of viewing each ingredient in isolation. The mix should be viewed as a collective whole and opportunities for synergy will only be exploited if it is regarded as such. Each ingredient of the mix should consistently reinforce the 'message' being conveyed by the others. To ensure that the plan represents a coherent whole, the author should ensure that the organization's approach to each of the seven Ps is presented in the plan in a clear and easy-to-read format. It should then become obvious whether flaws or ambiguities are present, and corrective action can be taken.

Ethics—An Additional Element of the Mix?

Before moving away from the concept of the mix to examine the remaining elements of a typical marketing plan, it is worth noting that a number of authors have suggested that an explicit consideration of ethics is warranted as a dimension of the marketing mix. The rationale here is that one of the distinguishing characteristics for many nonprofit organizations is the ethical nature of their operations. Since they do not have to seek to maximize profit they can (and perhaps should) take decisions that seek to maximize the benefit that accrues to society as a whole. In other words they are freed up to 'do the right thing' or take 'the right decision'. Of course it is then necessary to decide what exactly the 'right' decision might be.

The study of ethics involves determining right from wrong. Such decisions will be driven by an individual's own beliefs and values, those of the organization, and those of the wider society in which they live. In Judeo-Christian society, for example, these values may be derived from respect and compassion for the individual and a wider concern for the impact of one's actions on others. Ethics operate at a different level from the laws of a particular society since laws frequently provide for minimum standards of behaviour. They deal with the worst excesses of a society and with aspects of that society that are of wider interest and concern. They also reflect the prevailing view of the government, which one hopes in a democracy would in turn reflect the views of the majority of the members of that society.

Ethics by contrast operate at a 'higher' level. While a particular action may not be illegal, it may nevertheless be regarded by a given individual as wrong because it indirectly harms others, or is not in the best interests of the organization that employs them. It is this grey area beyond the realms of the law that is the domain of ethical judgements and where the fundraising profession has invested considerable time and effort to determine what does and does not, constitute appropriate behaviour.

My own perspective on the role of ethics in nonprofit marketing is that it should not be considered as a distinct element of the marketing mix. Rather, it should be regarded as something that pervades the mix as a whole (i.e. each of the elements described above). Organizations need to decide what constitutes appropriate behaviour and delineate what they are and are not prepared to do. Many nonprofits now enshrine this in an ethical policy which explicitly deals with the ethical issues likely to be encountered by staff. The document specifies both the general principles that will be applied and how staff should deal with specific examples. Many nonprofits also encourage their staff to join the relevant professional association and to adopt the code of ethics that their particular profession feels is appropriate. The ethical code developed by the Association of Fundraising Professionals is reproduced below.

AFP members aspire to:

- Practise their profession with integrity, honesty, truthfulness, and adherence to the absolute obligation to safeguard the public trust.
- Act according to the highest standards and visions of their organization, profession, and conscience.
- Put philanthropic mission above personal gain.
- Inspire others through their own sense of dedication and high purpose.
- Improve their professional knowledge and skills, so that their performance will better serve others.
- Demonstrate concern for the interests and well-being of individuals affected by their actions.
- Value the privacy, freedom of choice, and interests of all those affected by their actions.
- Foster cultural diversity and pluralistic values, and treat all people with dignity and respect.
- Affirm, through personal giving, a commitment to philanthropy and its role in society.
- Adhere to the spirit as well as the letter of all applicable laws and regulations.
- Advocate, within their own organizations, adherence to all applicable laws and regulations.
- Avoid even the appearance of any criminal offence or professional misconduct.
- Bring credit to the fundraising profession by their public demeanour.
- Encourage colleagues to embrace and practise these ethical principles and standards of professional practice.
- Be aware of the codes of ethics promulgated by other professional organizations that serve philanthropy.

Source: Association of Fundraising Professionals.

Any readers interested in a further exploration of the topic are advised to consult Anderson (1996) for a consideration of ethics in fundraising, Malaro (1994) for ethics in arts management and the Humanitarian Studies Unit (2001) for ethics in aid and development. The ethical literature in relation to healthcare and education is perhaps the best developed (see, for example, Weber (2001) and Nash (2002)).

Budget

Having detailed the steps that are necessary to achieve the marketing objectives, the writer of the plan should then be in a position to cost the various proposals and to derive an overall marketing budget for the planning period. Of course, in reality, life is just not that neat. Cost will undoubtedly have been in the minds of marketing planners even before they commenced the marketing audit. At the very least the development of a suitable budget is likely to have been an iterative process, with proposals being re-evaluated in the light of budgetary constraint.

There are a variety of ways of determining the marketing budget. The ideal would clearly be to specify the strategy and tactics that are felt necessary to achieve the marketing objectives, and then to cost these to arrive at an overall budget. This is usually referred to as the 'task method' of setting a marketing budget. In reality, this method is seldom employed since financial pressures from senior management, the budgeting/accounting practices of the organization, and uncertainty about resource attraction all hamper the derivation of an appropriate budget. In practice, therefore, budgets tend to be set by the following methods:

- *Percentage of last year's sales/donations.* There is a danger with this method that if the organization has been suffering from a poor performance of late, reducing the marketing budget in line with sales/donations could actually serve to worsen the situation. Clearly, when sales or donations fall there is a strong case for enhancing, not reducing, the marketing budget.
- *Percentage of budgeted year's sales/donations.*
- *Competitor matching.* The amounts spent on marketing by the competition are estimated, and the resource allocation is matched.
- *What can be afforded.* Perhaps the least rational of all the methods of budget calculation, this method involves the senior management of the organization deciding what they believe they can afford to allocate to the marketing function in a particular year. Little or no reference is made to the marketing objectives, nor to the activities of competitors.

Irrespective of the method used, it is usual to specify how the eventual budget has been allocated and to include such a specification in the marketing plan itself. It would also be normal for an allowance to be made for contingencies in the event that monitoring by the organization suggests that the objectives will not be met. Sufficient resources should then exist for some form of corrective action to be taken.

Scheduling

The reader will appreciate that a large number of tactics will have been specified in the main body of the plan. To ensure that these tactics are executed in a coordinated fashion over the duration of the plan, it is usual to present a schedule which clearly specifies when each activity will take place. This often takes the form of a Gantt chart (an example for a fundraising campaign is given in Figure 7.12). If the responsibilities for various marketing activities are split between different departments/sections of the organization, the schedule will act as an important coordination mechanism. Indeed, if responsibilities are split in this way it is usual to add an addition to the plan specifying the individual postholder who will have responsibility for the implementation of each component of the plan.

Activity	Jan.	Feb.	Mar.	Apr.	May	June	July	Aug.	Sept.	Oct.	Nov.	Dec.
Direct Mail		x	x							x	x	
Press advertising	x			x			x			x		x
Display advertising (Posters)											x	x
Telemarketing		x			x			x			x	x

Figure 7.12 Schedule of a fundraising campaign

Monitoring and Control

As soon as the plan has been implemented, marketing management will then take responsibility for monitoring the progress of the organization towards the goal specified. Managers will also need to concern themselves with the costs that have been incurred at each stage of implementation and monitor these against the budget. Thus control mechanisms need to be put into place to monitor (a) the actual sales/donations achieved, against the budget; (b) the actual costs incurred against those budgeted; (c) the performance of individual services against budget; and (d) the overall strategic direction that the organization is taking—i.e. will the overall corporate objectives be achieved in a manner commensurate with the organization's mission?

If variances are detected in any of these areas, corrective action can then be initiated, if necessary by utilizing the resource allocated for contingency.

■ DISCUSSION QUESTIONS

1. Distinguish, with examples, between marketing strategies and tactics.

2. What would you describe as the key components of the fundraising product?

3. With reference to your own organization (or one with which you are familiar) identify the key costs that will be experienced by both your donors and the recipients of your goods or services. What are the implications of these costs for your pricing decisions?

4. What channels of distribution might typically be used by:
   - A modern art museum?
   - A Third World charity looking to solicit funds?
   - A library service for elderly persons with a visual impairment?

5. In what ways might the communications mix utilized by a university development office (i.e the fundraising office within the university) differ from that adopted by a charity concerned with raising funds for cancer research?

6. 'Promotion is not the only element of the marketing mix that can communicate with customers. All seven elements of the service mix have the capacity to communicate with the customer'. Discuss.

7. What role should ethics play in the development of a nonprofit marketing mix? Why are ethics considered particularly important in the context of nonprofit management?

■ REFERENCES

Anderson, A. (1996) *Ethics for Fundraisers*, Indianapolis, IN, Indiana University Press.

Babakus, E. and Boller, G.W. (1992) 'An Empirical Assessment of the SERVQUAL Scale', *Journal of Business Research*, Vol. 24, 253–68.

Bruce, I. and Raymer, A. (1992) *Managing and Staffing Britain's Largest Charities*, VOLPROF, Centre for Voluntary Sector and Not-For-Profit Management, City University Business School, London.

Churchill, G.A. and Suprenant, C. (1982) 'An Investigation into the Determinants of Customer Satisfaction', *Journal of Marketing Research*, Vol. 19, 491–504.

Crosby, J. (1979) *Quality is Free*, New York, McGraw-Hill.

Darby, M.R. and Karni, E. (1973) 'Free Competition and the Optimal Amount of Fraud', *Journal of Law and Economics*, Vol. 16 (April), 67–86.

Delozier, M. (1976) *The Marketing Communication Process*, Maidenhead, McGraw-Hill.

Fenton, N., Golding, P. and Radley, A. (1993) 'Thinking about Charity: Report of a Pilot Study into Public Attitudes to Charities and Volunteering', in *Researching the Voluntary Sector*, West Malling, Charities Aid Foundation.

George, W.R. and Berry, L.L. (1981) 'Guidelines for the Advertising of Services', *Business Horizons*, Vol. 24, July/August, 52–6.

Harvey, T. (1995) 'Service Quality: The Culprit and the Cure', *Bank Marketing*, June, 24–8.

Hind, A. (1995) *The Governance and Management of Charities*, Barnet, Voluntary Sector Press.

Horne, S. and Moss, M. (1995) 'The Management of Collecting Boxes: Analysis of Performance and Site Location', *Journal of Nonprofit and Public Sector Marketing*, Vol. 3, No. 2, 47–62.

Humanitarian Studies Unit (2001) *Reflections on Humanitarian Action: Principles, Ethics and Contradictions*, Pluto Press.

Jones, T.O. and Sasser, W.E. (1995) 'Why Satisfied Customers Defect', *Harvard Business Review*, Nov/Dec, 88–99.

Kotler, P. (1994) *Marketing Management: Analysis, Planning, Implementation and Control*, Englewood Cliffs, NJ, Prentice Hall.

Kotler, P. and Fox, K. (1985) *Strategic Marketing for Educational Institutions*, Englewood Cliffs, NJ, Prentice Hall.

Lynn, P. and Davis-Smith J. (1992) *The 1991 National Survey of Voluntary Activity in the UK*, Berkhamstead, Volunteer Centre UK.

Malaro, M.C. (1994) *Museum Governance: Mission, Ethics, Policy*, Englewood Cliffs, NJ, Prentice Hall.

Nash, R.J. (2002) *Real World Ethics: Frameworks for Educators and Human Service Professionals*, Boston, MA, Teachers College Press.

Nelson, P. (1974) 'Advertising as Information', *Journal of Political Economy*, Vol. 81 (July/Aug), 729–54.

Palmer, A. (1994) *Principles of Service Marketing*, Maidenhead, McGraw-Hill.

Parasuraman, A., Zeithaml, V.A. and Berry, L.L. (1988) 'SERVQUAL: A Multiple Item Scale for Measuring Consumer Perceptions of Service Quality', *Journal of Retailing*, Vol. 64, No. 1, 12–40.

Payne, A., Christopher, M., Clark, M. and Peck, H. (1999) *Relationship Marketing For Competitive Advantage*, Oxford, Butterworth Heinemann.

Peters, T.J. (1987) *Thriving On Chaos: Handbook for a Management Revolution*, New York, Harper Collins.

Porter, M.E. (1985) *Competitive Advantage: Creating and Sustaining Superior Performance*, New York, Free Press.

Rados, D.L. (1981) *Marketing For Non-Profit Organizations*, Dover, MA, Auburn House.

Sargeant, A. (2001) 'Relationship Fundraising: How to Keep Donors Loyal', *Nonprofit Management and Leadership*, Vol. 12, No. 2, 177–92.

Sargeant, A. and Stephenson, H. (1997) 'Corporate Giving—Targeting the Likely Donor', *Journal of Nonprofit and Voluntary Sector Marketing*, Vol. 2, No. 1, 64–79.

Stewart, K.L. (1992) 'Applying a Marketing Orientation to a Higher Education Setting', *Journal of Professional Services Marketing*, Vol. 7, No. 2, 117–24.

Weber, L. (2001) *Business Ethics in Healthcare: Beyond Compliance*, Indianapolis, IN, Indiana University Press.

Zeithaml, V.A. and Bitner, M.J. (1996) *Services Marketing*, New York, McGraw-Hill.

Social Marketing: The Marketing of Ideas

OBJECTIVES

By the end of this chapter you should be able to:

(1) define social marketing;

(2) distinguish between social marketing and social communication;

(3) understand the contribution of market research techniques to the field of social behaviour;

(4) design a social marketing communications campaign.

Introduction

In Chapter 8 we concluded our work on the development of a marketing plan for products and services. We developed a generic framework and explored how a wide variety of non-profits might use this to market to an equally wide variety of different stakeholder groups. In this chapter, the last on marketing planning, we move away from a consideration of products and services and consider instead the marketing of ideas. We will explore the history of what has come to be known as 'social marketing', the social marketing mix, and some of the key findings from research studies conducted in this domain. We will focus particularly on the role of communications in this chapter, since the more traditional elements of the marketing mix have less relevance to the context of ideas.

What is Social Marketing?

Social marketing first emerged as a distinct concept in the early 1970s when Kotler and Zaltman (1971: 5) recognized that marketing tools and techniques typically applied to products and services could be applied equally well to the marketing of ideas. The authors define social marketing as 'the design, implementation, and control of programmes calculated to influence the acceptability of social ideas and involving considerations of product planning, pricing, communication, distribution, and marketing research.'

The wording of this definition is quite precise. The authors have deliberately avoided any reference to education or the facilitation of a change of attitudes or values. This is because social marketing is concerned with neither of these processes. The ultimate goal of any form of marketing is to influence behaviour. This may be to influence a particular individual to purchase an organization's product/service, or it may be to influence an individual to start recycling a proportion of his household waste. In either case, a concrete change in behaviour has resulted. Marketing and the variant social marketing are therefore conceptually different from the process of education, where the ultimate goal is knowledge, not necessarily a change in behaviour. Similarly, marketing should be viewed as distinct from a process designed merely to elicit a change of attitudes or values. Individuals or organizations concerned with this process may essentially be regarded as lobbyists, since once again behavioural changes are not involved.

To understand the key difference between marketing as we have discussed it thus far and social marketing, it is necessary to examine the question of objectives. In the generic marketing discussed thus far, some form of benefit has usually accrued to the marketing organization as the result of its marketing activity, e.g increased patronage, enhanced levels of voluntary donation, etc. Thus, even if the objective of the organization is not to make a profit and the work of the organization is philanthropic, some form of 'benefit' will nevertheless accrue to the marketing organization. In social marketing this is not the case. The marketing activity is aimed at society, with the aim of inducing a change in the behaviour in that society for the good of all.

Of course the word 'good' in the last paragraph is a relative term and it does rather depend on your viewpoint just how 'good' you would perceive the effects of social marketing to be. Indeed, a number of researchers have recently questioned the ethics and desirability of social marketing (see for example Laczniak et al. (1979). The reader will doubtless be relieved to learn that it is not my intention here to 'muddy the water' by entering into a complex philosophical debate. Rather it is important merely to realize that there is a distinction between the objectives of generic marketing and the objectives of social marketing. It is this distinction which makes the latter concept unique.

Fox and Kotler (1980) draw a further distinction between what they term 'social communication' and 'social marketing'. They view the former as a paradigm of thought which majors on the use of mass media advertising, public relations, and personal selling. The aim of social communication is simply to take advantage of all possible opportunities to communicate a message to a target group. The social marketing paradigm, however, adds at least four more dimensions which are typically missing from a purely social communication approach. These are as follows.

Marketing Research

The social marketer only begins work on a campaign after the target market has been thoroughly researched. The size of the overall market, its needs/wants, attitudes, behavioural patterns, and the likely costs and benefits of addressing individual market segments will be carefully evaluated. Appropriate campaigns can thereafter be designed for those segments it is felt most appropriate to address.

The power of effective marketing research cannot be understated. It can greatly improve the relevance and ultimate impact on behaviour of a social marketing campaign. It was recently identified, for example, that prostitutes in Tijuana, Mexico, had little fear that they might die of AIDS. Traditional social communications messages extolling the virtues of safe sex were therefore largely ineffectual with the members of this important target group. Research, however, identified that the prostitutes were very much afraid of leaving their children without mothers. The emphasis of the resulting social marketing campaign was hence switched from, 'I want to live' to 'I want to protect my child'.

Product Development

Assume, for example, that the purpose of a campaign is to influence consumers to adopt a recycling behaviour. The social communicator will tend to see the problem as a need to exhort people to change their behaviour. The social marketer, on the other hand, will also seek to promote the necessary means to more easily facilitate this change. The campaign would highlight the technology that is available to assist in recycling and offer practical opportunities for the behavioural change to be adopted at minimal cost. In short, the 'product' being promoted is not just a need to change behaviour, but also the means by which it is possible to do so.

Two decades ago, international health experts recognized that simply telling people about birth control was unlikely to have any significant impact on behaviour. Their early attempts were hindered by misconceptions about contraceptives, such as they would make women ill or children sick, the expense, or unfavourable religious beliefs. A social marketing approach was then adopted by many organizations which took account of these difficulties and segmented the market according to the sets of perceptions that were held. The emphasis was changed from mere mass communication to the creation of support frameworks which were tailored to the needs of each market segment.

A further example from social marketing folklore is the story of a project developed at Johns Hopkins University in partnership with USAID and a number of Mexican agencies. The aim was to encourage Latin teenagers to become more sexually responsible, something which had hitherto proved difficult to achieve by mere mass communication alone. The team therefore sought a route which might appeal to the teenagers, that would not be perceived as a 'lecture' on the subject. Moreover, the team wished to ensure that as high a percentage as possible of teenagers had access to appropriate advice. The solution was to create two pop songs, 'Stop' and 'When We Are Together', performed by Tatianna and Johnny, which contained lyrics that made it clear that sex does not have to be part of a loving relationship. The two songs were a great success and when teenagers purchased the record, the sleeve opened out into a poster which contained information about where to obtain birth control information.

The Use of Incentives

Social marketing can involve the use of incentives to encourage the desired behaviour change. Thus some campaigns in South America or the Third World have offered small gifts to those who agree to use a particular service. Similarly, price incentives have been offered to encourage take-up rates among the poorest groups in a given society. The use of such 'sales promotion' activities can pay rich dividends in a good social marketing campaign (see Sihombing 1994 or Schellstede 1986).

EXAMPLE

Health agencies in Tanzania have employed a voucher system to encourage poorer segments of society to protect themselves against malaria. During the past decade, insecticide-treated nets have become a key strategy for controlling the disease. Health agencies have attempted to subsidize the prices of nets through a voucher system that makes the nets affordable and helps establish a commercial market in their provision. The vouchers were targeted particularly at families with young children and/or pregnant women. When the scheme was initially introduced the voucher redemption rate was very high (97 per cent) but within two years this fell away considerably. The team responsible for the campaign concluded that vouchers were a feasible system for targeted subsidies, although considerable effort was required to achieve high levels of awareness and uptake. They also concluded that within a poor society vouchers may not necessarily ensure health equity unless they cover a high proportion of the total cost, since some cash is needed when using a voucher as part-payment. Poorer women among the target group are, as a consequence, less likely to take up the offer.

Facilitation

The social marketer is concerned not only with the communication of a message; she must also attempt to make the adoption of a behavioural change relatively easy to achieve. Thus community recycling initiatives which galvanize the whole community into action (and where individuals can draw support from each other) may be more effective than a simple advertising campaign alone. Similarly, if individuals are to be encouraged to adopt safer sexual practices, access to appropriate advice and contraception must be convenient and freely available. In Uganda, contraceptives were almost impossible to sell in conventional retail stores. Social marketers therefore created booths in traditional markets and sold contraceptives at prices acceptable to the target market.

Social Marketing Domains

Social marketing has been used to good effect to tackle many social issues worldwide. Perhaps the greatest success has been achieved with family planning campaigns to control the size of the population in a variety of countries. In Sri Lanka, for example, where market research indicated that although there was widespread support for birth control there was little knowledge of the techniques available, the government introduced a brand of condom called 'Preeth' (meaning happiness) and sold it to consumers at extremely low prices. The product was supported by promotions in local films, on radio, and in print, and the overall campaign proved to be very successful in lowering the birth rate in that country. The domain of social marketing is, however, not related merely to birth control issues. Social marketing campaigns have also tackled issues such as:

- HIV infection and sexual responsibility (e.g. Black 1979; Luthra 1991; Ramah and Cassidy 1992);

- the dangers of smoking (e.g. Elder 1994);
- drink driving (e.g. Braus 1995);
- pollution/business ethics (e.g. Abratt and Sacks 1988);
- recycling/energy conservation (McKenzie-Mohr 1994);
- drug/alcohol abuse (e.g. Smith 1992).

The reader will appreciate that many of these are difficult issues and the behaviours concerned may be firmly entrenched. Marketing may therefore offer no magic solution. Even with the most finely tuned social marketing campaign, the targeted behaviours may prove difficult, if not impossible, to change. According to Kotler and Andreasen (1991) there are three major dimensions which determine just how difficult it may be to achieve such a change:

- whether the behaviour is high or low involvement;
- whether the behaviour is a one-off (or one-time) or continuing;
- whether the behaviour is exhibited by individuals or groups.

Examples of each of the eight categories of social marketing produced by these dimensions are given in Table 8.1.

High Involvement versus low Involvement

The more 'involved' with a purchase decision a consumer is, the more thought they are likely to give to alternative solutions and the costs and benefits associated with each. It is thus important for marketers to recognize whether a decision is high or low involvement as this will impact on the amount of factual information provided. There is, however, regrettably no consensus on what constitutes 'involvement'. See, for example, Kapferer and Laurent (1985) or Ratchford (1987). Most researchers would agree though that consumers will be more 'involved' in a situation if they perceive it as having immediate

Table 8.1 A categorization of social behaviours

Behaviour	Low involvement	High involvement
One-time behaviour		
Individual	Donating money to a charity	Donating blood
Group	Election of a local council	Creation of a Neighbourhood Watch scheme
Continuing behaviour		
Individual	Not smoking in elevators	Stopping smoking or drug intake
	Recycling newspapers	Recycling all household waste
Group	Driving within the speed limit	Supporting a woman's right to abortion

Source: Kotler/Andreasen, *Strategic Marketing For Nonprofit Organisations*, 5th edn, © 1996. Adapted by permission of Prentice-Hall, Inc., Upper Saddle River, NJ.

and personal relevance to themselves. Moreover, if the situation is perceived as having a high degree of risk associated with it, the level of involvement will also be enhanced. The choice of a method of birth control, for example, would for most constitute a high involvement decision since it is of immediate personal relevance and the social and financial risks of an unwanted pregnancy are very real.

Low involvement decisions on the other hand are typically of little importance to the consumer as the outcome of the decision will not have a major impact on their lifestyle. Such decisions involve little thought, do not involve a detailed search for information in respect of the alternatives, and carry few penalties if the wrong decision is taken. Thus, in the social context, low involvement behaviours may be easier to change than those requiring high involvement. If a particular behaviour pattern is not deemed significant and changing it would expose the individual to little social risk, it will be easier for the marketer to encourage a change to take place. Persuading car drivers to switch to non-alcoholic lager might thus be somewhat easier than persuading them to switch to soft drinks, since they can still be seen to enjoy a pint with their friends at a party. They can hence offset any social pressure that they might feel to join in and have a drink.

Interestingly, there are a variety of products and services which are capable of evoking high levels of involvement purely on the basis of the emotional appeals that are associated with them. Tobacco is one such product, and understanding the reasons why this is so might significantly aid social marketers in a bid to reduce deaths from heart disease and lung cancer. Hirschman and Holbrook (1982) found, for example, that many smokers imagined themselves as 'Marlboro Men' and felt that their habit (and brand) was a statement of both their masculinity and their desire to imagine themselves as idealized cowboys. The weakening of this association might thus be one issue for social marketers to address.

One-time versus Continuing Behaviour

One-time behaviour changes are usually easier to instigate than longer term adjustments. They require the target merely to understand the communication message and to take action on the basis thereof. Of course, the easier it can be for the target audience to take the desired action, the more likely it is that they will actually take it. Communicating the benefits of a change in behaviour is therefore not enough in itself; thought must also be given to how easy an individual will find it to act on the information presented. Thus immunization programmes in the Third World will visit individual rural communities, rather than expecting people to travel to major towns and cities for treatment. In this way, as large a percentage of the population as possible can be affected. Similarly political parties of all persuasions will usually offer free rides to the polling station for the elderly or infirm to ensure that they turn out to vote—it is hoped, in the manner desired!

Persuading individuals to change their behaviour patterns permanently is a little more problematic. Over time, behaviour can become habitualized, in the sense that it happens without any thought on the part of the individual. Moreover, justification for the behaviour can become firmly entrenched in an individual's value systems. People have to be convinced of the need for them to change and the benefits that might accrue as a result. They also have to be convinced that these benefits will be substantive enough to warrant the effort necessary to instigate the change in behaviour. In the case of low involvement decisions, this may only involve an occasional reminder of the need to behave in a particular way. High involvement, continuing behaviours are the most difficult to change. In many cases these may prove impossible to alter without resorting to legislative change to provide a final backdrop of enforcement.

Individual versus Group

Group behaviour is inherently more difficult to change than the behaviour of particular individuals. The complex dynamic of relationships that exist within a societal group act to reinforce and legitimize the attitudes and values of the members of that group. Acceptance of any form of change can be interpreted as disloyalty to the collective identity of the group and individuals brave enough to deviate from the norm may have a number of social penalties imposed on them as a result.

To address changes in group behaviours, it is important to recognize the distinction between opinion leaders, opinion formers, and opinion followers. Communication strategies that acknowledge the significance of the opinion leaders and formers are far more likely to effect the desired change in behaviour.

Opinion Leaders

Opinion leaders are those individuals that have the ability to influence behaviour because of their perceived status within their social group. Reynolds and Darden (1971) identified that these individuals tend to be more gregarious and self-confident than non-leaders and, importantly from a marketing perspective, also tend to have a greater exposure to the mass media. Clearly if group behaviours are to be modified, it is the opinion leaders within those groups who must be targeted in particular with the communications message. Given that they tend to read more publications than others in society, are among the first to return promotional coupons, and have a propensity to take and enjoy risks, they are not impossible to identify.

Opinion Formers

Unlike opinion leaders, opinion formers exert influence over group behaviour because of their actual authority, education, or status. In essence, opinion formers may be looked to for advice because of the *formal* expertise that they have in a particular area. Thus government ministers, community group leaders, newspaper editors, etc. can all be viewed as opinion formers. Once again, since this group has a great capacity to be able to influence others, it will form an important target group in any social marketing campaign. Fortunately opinion formers are easier to identify than opinion leaders since, by virtue of their position, they normally seek to be seen as having an important impact on the attitudes and behaviours of others. Targeting them is therefore not problematic.

Opinion Followers

The majority of members of society can be categorized as opinion followers. They are unlikely to set a new trend in behaviour themselves unless such a behaviour change has previously been legitimized and endorsed by their societal group. They look for advice in respect of appropriate behaviours, both from opinion formers and opinion leaders.

Researching Social Behaviours

The research of social issues is undoubtedly one of the most difficult facets of marketing that nonprofit practitioners have to deal with. Many traditional primary research techniques are difficult, or even downright inappropriate, to apply in this field. People are understandably reluctant to talk about sensitive personal matters and when one considers that a high proportion of postal questionnaires asking respondents about the relatively innocuous topic of personal income will often be returned with the relevant section incomplete, something of the difficulty researchers face in this sensitive area becomes readily apparent. Various forms of questionnaire, including telephone/postal, will be particularly difficult to apply in this context, making the collection of quantitative data problematic.

For this reason, much social research is qualitative in nature and as a consequence conducted with smaller numbers of subjects, although often in considerably more depth. Of the techniques that are most helpful in accumulating this category of data, personal interviews and focus groups are probably the most commonly utilized (Weinreich 1999).

Interviews

Personal interviews with subjects from a particular societal group can play a pivotal role in a social marketing research project. Although they are relatively costly to administer, the researcher is able to take her time with the research and to establish a rapport with each subject before more intimate and personal details are probed later in their discussion. The researcher can also benefit from being able to observe the body language of the subject and hence be sensitive to those aspects which he finds it particularly difficult to talk about.

As we said in Chapter 3, interviews can be either fully structured, semi-structured, or conducted in a free format closely resembling an everyday conversation. In the first, the researcher has a prescriptive list of the questions that will be posed and has decided in advance the order in which they will be delivered. The interviewer has little or no authority to adjust the wording of the questions in each case, making it easier to compare the findings of the interviews undertaken, but potentially stifling a debate of any interesting issues that might emerge. For this reason, a semi-structured approach is more common since although the researcher must follow a prescribed pattern for the interview, there is more scope for her to tailor the conversation to follow up on matters of particular interest.

At the other end of the scale, a free format interview is one in which the researcher has only an idea of the subjects that will be covered, and the interview is conducted as far as possible as a natural conversation. These naturalistic 'conversations' are normally tape-recorded so that the researcher is free to concentrate on the development of the interaction between him and the subject. This technique is commonly used in social marketing research since the subject can more easily be put at their ease and approached with questions that reflect the natural order of the conversation taking place.

Focus Groups

Focus groups, by contrast, involve the researcher assembling a 'panel' of between six and eight members of the subject group. A trained facilitator then explores with this group the issues under research. The discussion is usually unstructured, in the sense that the researcher has a clear idea of the ground that must be covered, but is happy for the group to emphasize those aspects of the discussion that they find particularly exciting or of relevance to them. Once again it would be normal practice to either audio- or videotape the proceedings so that the facilitator is free to concentrate on the development of the discussion and ensure that each individual has the opportunity to contribute.

As with personal interviews, focus groups can be used to investigate difficult social issues and the key findings can be developed from a careful analysis of the tape of the discussion after it has taken place. Focus groups often yield valuable insight into the underlying motivations for particular categories of behaviour, and as participants begin to recognize that they are not alone in holding a particular view, open and honest discussions often emerge.

A good recent example of the use of focus groups to inform social marketing practice is reported in the case study below. In this case, the agency employed to design a campaign aimed at encouraging younger females to adopt safer sexual practices decided to use focus groups as the vehicle for discovering why it was that many such individuals were still failing to take adequate birth control precautions. Many of the focus group participants indicated that they would sometimes take a gamble by not using birth control and, especially when younger, did not use any form of contraception at all. The following statements represent a selection of direct quotes from focus group participants, giving some clue as to why this might be the case.

Luckily, I haven't gotten pregnant, but yeah, it's certainly been a gamble, you know, and if I'm in a situation where nothing's available, you know, just those situations you can get into . . . I know it's stupid but, you know, at the time that's not as real as the moment is.

I was so immature that it was like almost a game to me, to say, 'Oh, no, it won't matter this time,' you know. Or 'Don't worry about it' or 'I can't get pregnant.' I know so many girls that say, 'Oh, I can't get pregnant. I think I must be one of those women that can never get pregnant.' I thought that until I got pregnant.

When I first started having sex and stuff, I honestly believed that I could not get pregnant.

The quotes given above were used by the creative agency to directly inform the development of the poster in Figure 8.1. As the reader will appreciate, it was designed specifically to get across the vital statistic that 80 per cent of young women who do not use birth control become pregnant within a year. In short, it was designed to counter the thought that 'it can't happen to me'. The preliminary artwork for the poster was itself subsequently the subject of a focus group discussion to ensure that it was likely to be successful in imparting

Figure 8.1 Specimen poster from the 'Don't Kid Yourself' campaign

the required message to the target group. In this latter case, members of the group were asked to interpret the message contained in the poster.

Their responses were:

Your odds of getting pregnant are pretty good.
Start using birth control. You're not always lucky.
This one's really easy to understand. It's concrete and believable.
It's eye-catching. If I saw this somewhere I'd stop and look at it.

The full details of the campaign and its development are given in the case study below.

CASE STUDY 8.1

The 'Don't Kid Yourself' Campaign

The 'Don't Kid Yourself' campaign is the result of a collaboration among the Title X Family Planning grantees in Public Health Service Region VIII—Colorado, Montana, North Dakota, South Dakota, Utah, and Wyoming. The grantees pooled their funds in order to create a social marketing campaign to reduce unintended pregnancies in the region. They selected Weinreich Communications, a social marketing firm in Washington, DC, to plan, develop, and implement the programme. Every element of the 'Don't Kid Yourself' campaign was developed based upon social marketing research conducted by Weinreich Communications. An initial set of five focus groups were conducted in Butte and Salt Lake City with members of the target audience—low-income women aged 18 to 24. These focus groups provided insight into how they thought about birth control and pregnancy, as well as how best to reach them with campaign messages. Based on the results of the initial research, draft materials and campaign ideas were developed and tested in six additional focus groups before being finalized. In addition, eight individual interviews were conducted with target audience members to be used as a source of soundbites for the radio spots. The campaign was then pilot-tested in Butte and Salt Lake City.

In Salt Lake City, the number of phone calls to Planned Parenthood's clinics increased by 72 per cent during the two months the pilot campaign was implemented. In Butte, the number of people listing the Butte Family Planning clinic as a place they would go for answers about sexual health or birth control issues nearly doubled after the campaign.

The campaign included the following elements.

Radio Advertisements (10 30-second Spots)

Most of the radio ads used actual voices of members of the target audience to model attitudes, change misconceptions, and spark thoughts and conversations about the topic. Radio was selected as a key element of the campaign for several reasons. First, in the focus groups, nearly all participants said that they listened to the radio regularly. Second, radio allows the campaign to reach a very specific audience; it is possible to target precisely women aged 18 to 24 and reach a large percentage of that population. Third, because radio is ever-present in many people's lives, the target audience may hear messages when they are in a situation in which they should use birth control—the radio spot may thus serve as a reminder and make it more likely that they use it. Fourth, the spots may play when friends or partners are together and promote conversations about birth control issues. Finally, the older people

continues

CASE STUDY 8.1 continued

who are more likely to be offended by the ads are less likely to be listening to the same stations as the 18- to 24-year-olds.

Posters (4 Designs)

A set of four posters was developed to get the campaign message out through community organizations, including clinics, schools, businesses, government agencies, recreational facilities, and local 'hangouts'. The tagline on all the posters and visual materials, 'Don't Kid Yourself,' came from a focus group participant who was summing up the point of the poster visuals. Although she didn't realize it at the time, these words provide a clever *double entendre* for this campaign. This idea of 'kidding oneself' came up often in the focus groups, with many young women saying that they often had unprotected intercourse because they thought that pregnancy couldn't happen to them or that they would be safe 'just this once'. The bright neon colours, rough drawings, and text typeface of the posters were designed to draw attention from the 18- to 24-year-old age group and younger.

Newspaper Ads (4 Designs)

Four newspaper ads were designed in several different sizes. The focus group research showed that many of the women read particular types of newspapers or sections of the paper. Newspaper ads were felt to be helpful in reaching those who respond better to visual information, or who do not hear the radio ads. They also provided the phone number and campaign messages in a form that could be cut out and kept until someone is ready to call.

Drink Coasters

Bright pink drink coasters with campaign messages were designed for distribution to bars and clubs. The focus group participants said that bars, clubs, and coffeehouses were good places to reach women aged 18 to 24. These venues were particularly appropriate, since potential sexual partners or groups of friends might be drinking together and could use the coaster as a method of initiating conversations about birth control.

Brochures (2 Topics)

Two three-colour brochures were developed, based on the needs identified by focus group participants. One brochure presented birth control options, while the other assisted in talking to a sexual partner about birth control. They provided in-depth information and skills-building content at an appropriate reading level, using the target audience's language. The brochures also served as a proxy for those who would not come into the clinic to speak with a counsellor. They were placed in locations frequented by the target audience, including schools, grocery stores, bars and clubs, public libraries, and doctors' offices.

The Social Marketing Mix

The reader will appreciate that since in a social marketing context we are no longer concerned with physical products or even services, the traditional marketing mix introduced in Chapter 7 is more difficult to apply. While this is so, it is possible to extend and adapt the marketing mix to generate a greater relevance to the marketing of ideas

(Kotler and Roberto 2001). Since marketers seem to prefer to talk about 'P's, a six-P framework for use by those working in the social arena is proposed below.

Product

The product in this context is the idea that the marketer wishes to get across to stimulate a change in behaviour. Unlike traditional marketing, which advocates the development of the product carefully designed to mirror customer preferences, the social marketer strives to engineer a change that (in their opinion) would be good for society as a whole. The element of persuasion is therefore important since the behaviour change must be marketed on the basis of the benefits that could accrue either directly or indirectly as a result. The product might hence be a change in sexual behaviour, a change in recycling behaviour, or the stimulation of demand for health programmes to counter social problems such as drug or solvent abuse.

Price

The price may be regarded as the monetary costs associated with adopting a change in behaviour. Attendance on a health programme may require the individual to fund some of the treatments that might be suggested. More usually, however, the important costs of a change in behaviour will be social. Individuals may suffer embarrassment or even ridicule within their social group for responding to a social marketing campaign. One can even place a cost on the fear that individuals might have of attending a health programme such as an annual mammogram. Some women may simply feel that they could not deal with the stress of having a lump discovered and may take the conscious decision that it is better not to know.

Cost is also an issue in the realm of recycling; Shrum et al. (1994) conclude, after a review of the literature, that cost viewed in terms of inconvenience acts as a very powerful motivator to avoid recycling. Identifying all the potential costs is therefore important, as the social marketing campaign can take account of these and make every attempt to minimize them as far as possible.

A final point on price that experience has taught social marketers is that it is often better to make some form of charge for any products that they might be involved in distributing (Kotler et al. 2002). Simply giving away items runs the risk that little value will be placed on them. It is often better to sell items cheaply to encourage a perception of value among members of the target segment. Indeed, doing so may also help engage the support of the local infrastructure, which will be necessary if the programme is to have any form of long-term impact. It is therefore not unusual, for example, for a small charge to be made for contraception, even in some of the world's poorest societies.

Place

'Place' refers to the location at which any service component of the social marketing campaign will be delivered. In the case of many birth-control programmes, for example, access to the programme must be straightforward and provided at a location geographically close to the target market. Place can also refer to the channels of information that are used to reach the target market. Information on the dangers of HIV, for example, might be conveyed to the target market by distributing leaflets via schools, colleges, universities, general practitioners, family planning clinics, etc.

Promotion

Social marketers will make use of most of the promotional tools described in Chapter 4. Many campaigns utilize advertising, public relations, sales promotion, and direct marketing to communicate with their target audience. The mechanics of exactly how this might be achieved and the stages involved in developing a typical communications plan are outlined later in this chapter.

Partnerships

It has already been suggested that certain categories of behaviour are not easy to influence. Many nonprofits may simply be too small to make much of an impact on their own. They may lack the necessary resources in terms of both staff time and monetary backing. As a consequence, many nonprofits involved in social marketing look for potential partnerships with other organizations with similar goals. This may involve working closely with a wide variety of different organizations in both the private and public sectors. Clearly social marketers will need to identify and liaise with potential allies for a particular campaign to ensure that the overall approach to society is as coordinated as possible.

Policy

The difficulties of influencing continuing behaviours have already been alluded to above. In many cases the only method of achieving the desired outcome may be to compel individuals/groups to institute the change in behaviour required. Ultimately, it may become necessary for governments to ban all forms of tobacco advertising to reduce sales. Simply trying to persuade individuals to give up smoking of their own volition may work up to a point, but there will always be a few 'die-hard' smokers who simply will never have either the necessary will-power or desire to give up their habit. For these reasons, marketers also have to be aware of the social policies that influence behaviour and attempt to influence those who have the power to instigate legislative change.

Thus, it is possible to utilize an adapted marketing mix in a social marketing context. The familiar concepts of product, price, place, and promotion all have a role to play in the creation of an effective social marketing campaign, even where the provision of no physical products or services is involved.

Since previous chapters of this text have already examined the use of the marketing mix in different nonprofit contexts, the remainder of this chapter will focus on the development of a social marketing communications campaign and examine in detail the stages involved in its creation.

Designing a Communications Campaign

Seven steps are normally followed in designing a communications campaign. These are listed below:

1. specification of the target audience
2. communications objectives
3. specification of promotional message
4. media selection
5. schedule
6. budget
7. monitoring/control.

Each of these will now be examined in turn.

Specification of the Target Audience

Chapter 3 highlighted a variety of criteria that could be used to define the target audience. They may be specified in terms of their geographic, demographic, geo-demographic, behavioural, or lifestyle characteristics. However, in a social marketing context it would be also usual to specify in detail the behaviours within each segment and the current pattern thereof. With only finite resources available, social marketers will usually have to select only those segments that they perceive as being of particular importance. Bennett (1996), in a survey of twenty health education officers, identified that homosexual men were almost unanimously perceived as being the most important target for AIDS awareness campaigns and that resources were being allocated accordingly.

If a variety of segments are to be addressed, the behaviours of each should be identified so that planners can be clear about the point from which the behaviour change will be started. Such a specification will aid in setting campaign objectives and will be essential if the overall effectiveness of the campaign is to be assessed.

Communications Objectives

Communications objectives, like any other form of objective, should be specific, measurable, achievable, relevant, and timescaled. They are written to address various aspects of the campaign, so that the resulting communications strategy is focused on achieving the goals of the initiating organization. Colley (1961) developed a model for setting communications objectives entitled DAGMAR (Defining Advertising Goals for Measured

Advertising Results). Although Colley's ideas were originally developed to assist in the assessment of advertising effectiveness, the model he developed can be applied to all forms of social marketing promotion. Colley believed that the process of communications was essentially hierarchical in nature and hence, for our purposes, if an idea is to be effectively communicated consumers should be moved through the following five stages:

Unawareness—Awareness—Comprehension—Conviction—Action

Before a social idea can gain acceptance, the target audience must be appraised of the concept and made to realize that alternative behaviours exist. Third World communities thus need to be made aware that birth control methods exist and that pregnancy can be avoided. Similarly in the marketing of oral rehydration therapy, mothers in parts of Asia need to be made aware that diarrhoeal disease need not necessarily be fatal, given the proper (and rudimentary) treatment.

Simply making an audience aware of alternative behaviours is unlikely to be enough in itself to encourage a change, however. The social marketer must strive to ensure that the target audience actually understands the benefits that a change in behaviour could bring. Taboos or fallacies about the use of birth control methods must hence be overcome. Similarly, information about the success and simplicity of oral rehydration tablets in treating diarrhoeal disease must also be conveyed.

Having achieved a certain level of understanding in the target market, it is then necessary to generate a sense of conviction. Smokers, for example, may be aware of the dangers of their habit and understand the relationship between it and fatal diseases such as heart disease and cancer, but they may lack the necessary conviction to quit. Establishing conviction in such a high involvement decision is not an easy task, though, and a variety of carefully targeted messages may be necessary to secure it.

The final stage of Colley's model can be viewed as the ultimate goal: securing a change in behaviour. Communications messages could be used to guide their recipients through the steps necessary to effect a change in behaviour. A freephone number could be provided to give individually tailored advice to callers about health or welfare issues, for example.

Colley held the view that communications objectives could be written to reflect any of the five important stages of the model. One could hence write objectives in terms of the number of people who are aware that alternative behaviours are available/acceptable (awareness), the number of people who understand why a behavioural change might be necessary (comprehension), the number of people who express an intention to change in the future (conviction), and finally the number of people who actually implement a change in their behaviour (action). Social communication objectives typically address all four of these areas.

Specifying the Promotional Message

There are a number of considerations which must be addressed in the design of appropriate promotional messages. These include the level of involvement a particular behaviour invokes, the content of the message, and the manner in which it will be conveyed. Each of these issues will now be explored in turn.

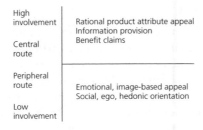

Figure 8.2 High-involvement versus low-involvement decisions

Source: Fill, C. (1995) *Marketing Communications*. Reproduced with the kind permission of Prentice Hall.

Level of Involvement

Fill (1995) argues that the effectiveness of a message from a receiver's perspective depends on two factors. The first is the amount and quality of information communicated, while the second is the overall judgement made about the manner in which it is presented. There is therefore a need to strike a balance between an individual's need for information and his need to enjoy the consumption thereof. However, different styles of message may be appropriate depending on the nature of the behaviour that it is intended to influence. As Figure 8.2 makes clear, decisions that are high-involvement in nature require that the individual is presented with detailed information about the options available and the benefits thereof. This is because such decisions will require the individual to use his cognitive functions and the decision-making processes are hence relatively (although not exclusively) rational in nature. What is termed a central route to persuasion is adopted, consisting of strong, well-documented, and supported arguments in favour of the idea being raised. After the recent BSE crisis in the UK, for example, numerous agencies were involved in a large social marketing campaign to convince the public that British beef was safe. Given that the question of which meat to eat had become a high-involvement decision for most UK households, it was decided to convey a series of very rational reasons why British beef was safe to eat, and considerable background detail was communicated to the public in an attempt to allay any fears.

Low-involvement decisions, on the other hand, require less thought from the individual and messages will hence be more effective if they concentrate on imagery. The aim here is to engender an emotional response which reflects an individual's ego or self-image, and marketers follow the peripheral route to persuasion through an emphasis on non-content message ingredients such as music, lighting, scenery, or the use of celebrity endorsements. The advertising that preceded the compulsory use of seatbelts in the UK focused on the use of powerful imagery which illustrated the pain and suffering that could be caused to family members by a failure to comply with the new regulations. Celebrity endorsement was also offered by Jimmy Saville who coined the catchy advertising strapline, 'Clunk click every trip'.

Content of the Message

There are a number of issues relating to message content that social marketers must consider, including the following.

One- and Two-sided Messages

Some promotional messages contain only one side of the argument. They convey only the positive impacts of the change in behaviour required, while ignoring any drawbacks completely. Other messages may be termed two-sided in that they present a more balanced view to the audience, showing both the advantages and disadvantages of a given behaviour change. In general, research would seem to indicate that one-sided messages are more effective where the recipient group already has a favourable view of the behaviour change, or where their level of education is low. Conversely the use of two-sided messages is preferred where the recipients are either highly educated or hold a very negative view of the behaviour change presented.

Drawing Conclusions

Marketers must also decide whether the message they intend to convey will draw a firm conclusion about the need for a change in behaviour, or whether the message will be left open and the individual encouraged to draw her own conclusions. There is no easy way in which to choose between these two options but a variety of factors have been found to impact on the most appropriate form of message to use (Hovland and Mandell 1952). Specifically, the desirability of drawing a conclusion for the audience has been found to depend on the following factors:

(1) *The level of education of the message recipients.* The higher the level of education possessed by the audience, the more likely it is that they will prefer to draw their own conclusions. There is a danger that members of a highly educated group will feel patronized by an approach which claims to know what is right for them. Those with lower levels of education, however, may be incapable of drawing the correct conclusion from the data presented for themselves and may require it to be drawn for them.

(2) *Level of complexity.* If the idea being marketed is technically complex or multifaceted, it may be less easy for the recipient to see the end to which they are being led. Guidance may hence have to be more specific where complexity is encountered. Similarly, completely new ideas may need a greater degree of explanation and conclusion-drawing than those that have been around for some time.

(3) *When action is required.* In the case of marketing the oral rehydration tablets mentioned earlier, the action required of the recipient is often immediate. Any delay in decision-making may substantially reduce the chances of saving a child's life. Promotional messages in such circumstances must therefore be forceful and the results of inaction spelt out very clearly. If, on the other hand, the timescale for action is somewhat longer, the necessity for immediate action is diminished and the need for firm conclusion-drawing is less pronounced.

(4) *Level of involvement.* As one would expect, high-involvement decisions are best approached by giving individuals the appropriate facts to make their decision alone. Any attempt to 'force' a change in behaviour on individuals in these circumstances is likely to be counter-productive. Indeed, recipients may actively resent such messages (see Sawyer and Howard 1991).

Framing the Presentation

In presenting any new social ideas to a potential audience, there will always be a variety of arguments that could be used to attempt to persuade. Of course, not all of these messages will have an equal impact on the target group; some will be seen as weak arguments, while others will not be as easy to counter. The issue for marketers then becomes the order in which these messages should be presented. Should a promotional message begin with the stronger points or the weaker ones?

Once again we must return to the question of the level of involvement that the audience has with the idea. If the audience has a low level of involvement it may be necessary to begin with a strong message to generate attention. It is also true that if the audience holds a strongly opposing view, a weak argument at the beginning of the message will only serve to raise counter-arguments in the minds of recipients, and the remainder of the message may be filtered out as a result. Of course, the converse of these points is also true. Messages which begin with weaker points and build up to the strongest arguments at the end tend to be more appropriate where the position adopted is not controversial, or where the issue evokes a strong but positive sense of involvement.

Social marketers must also decide whether to use positively framed messages (i.e. messages which refer primarily to the benefits of the desired change in behaviour) or negatively framed messages (which draw attention to the drawbacks of *not* implementing the change in behaviour). So, for example, a campaign directed at persuading people to stop smoking will need to decide whether the campaign will be positively framed and feature the details of how much better they will feel if they stop, or whether it should focus on the health implications of not giving up (negatively framed messages). Maheswaran and Meyers-Levy (1990) conclude that positively framed messages are more appropriate in situations where the individual does not have to process information (low involvement) and negatively framed messages more appropriate where a detailed level of information processing is required (high-involvement decisions).

The Nature of the Appeal

There are a variety of ways in which a social idea can be communicated in a promotional message. If individuals are highly educated, or where the decision is a high-involvement decision, we have already seen that a factual appeal may be the most appropriate to use. However, where the target audience is less well educated, or where the appeal is addressing low-involvement behaviours, the social marketer may find that an emotional appeal is more effective. Indeed, even where an appeal is largely factual there may still be scope for the social marketer to design campaigns which make an indirect use of fear, humour, or sexual imagery. The advantages and disadvantages of each of these approaches will now be considered in turn.

(1) *Fear appeals.* Fear is an emotion often evoked to good effect by social marketers. This may be an immediate fear, such as the fear of contracting a particular disease, or it may be more longer-term in nature and reflect a concern for issues that will have a greater impact on future generations (e.g. some recycling behaviours). Fear may also be categorized according to whether it is a health-related fear or a fear of social disapproval,

resulting from taking (or not taking) a particular form of action. Social marketers may utilize a variety of messages from each category.

Many researchers working in the field of fear in advertising have found that there is a negative relationship between the strength of a fear appeal and its ability to persuade a target market. In other words, appeals that evoke a strong sense of fear will be likely to be less effective than those which utilize fear only to a very mild extent. Schiffman and Kanuk (1994) explain this phenomenon as a reaction to what is termed *cognitive dissonance* in the minds of recipients. In the case of a strong fear appeal used to target cigarette smokers, the recipients cannot reconcile their need to continue using the product with the strong sense of fear the advertising has generated. In psychological terms they experience dissonance. The only way they can reconcile this dissonance is either by giving up the habit or rejecting the content of the fear message. As Schiffman and Kanuk (1994: 308) put it: 'Since giving up a comfortable habit is difficult, consumers more readily reject the threat. This they do by a variety of techniques including denial of its validity ("There still is no real proof that smoking causes cancer"), the belief that they are immune to personal disaster ("It can't happen to me") and a diffusing process that robs the claim of its true significance ("I play it safe by only using filter cigarettes").'

It is therefore important to test any campaign relying on a fear appeal to ensure that an appropriate level of fear is induced. Used properly, it can be an important weapon in a social marketer's armoury, since Sternthal and Craig (1982) conclude that fear appeals are a particularly powerful way of persuading audiences to change their attitudes. Regrettably, the relationship between the use of fear appeals and actual behaviour change is rather less clear-cut. For those who are interested, Janis (1967) provides a concise review of the literature in this area.

(2) *Appeals based on humour.* Numerous studies over the years have addressed whether humour can enhance the effectiveness of a promotional campaign. Helpfully, Weinberger and Gulas (1992) present a review of the relevant literature which concludes that:

- humour attracts attention;
- humour does not harm comprehension (indeed, in some cases it can aid it);
- humour is no more effective at increasing persuasion than other promotional messages;
- humour enhances 'liking'; individuals are more likely to develop a favourable impression of advertising that utilizes humour;
- humour that is relevant to the product is superior to humour unrelated to the product;
- audience characteristics (gender, ethnicity, age) affect the response to humorous appeals;
- the nature of the product affects the appropriateness of a humorous treatment;
- humour is more effective with existing products than with new products;
- humour is more effective with low-involvement decisions than those with a high involvement.

Figure 8.3 Health education council advertising
Source: Health Education Council.

EXAMPLE

In 2004 the UK's National Blood Service commissioned a national campaign to encourage young people to give blood. It explained the urgent and ongoing need for 2.5 million donations a year to meet hospital demand in England and Wales. The campaign was ongoing throughout the year and aimed to encourage 200 000 youngsters who had just reached their seventeenth birthdays to get into the habit of donating. Direct mail was the chosen medium, and the creative tapped into the desire of young adults to be treated as 'grown ups', using a powerful ransom-style note. An offbeat envelope proclaimed, 'We Want Your Blood'.

---

(3) *Sexual appeals*. The very nature of many social marketing campaigns ensures that a percentage of marketers working in this area have will have to address the level of sexual messages/imagery that will be contained in the messages they have to convey. The use of sex in advertising can take many forms, such as nudity, *double entendre*, or perhaps more subtle devices such as that depicted in Figure 8.3. The extent to which blatantly sexual imagery will be appropriate will vary from society to society and from year to year. In the mid-1980s, for example, visual sexual imagery was commonplace in many forms of advertising. By the end of the decade, advertisers had reverted to the use of more romantic imagery in response to an increased awareness of the threat of AIDS.

The key advantage of an appeal based on sex is simply that it is unrivalled in terms of its power to attract attention. Studies have shown that advertising with a sexual appeal is capable of arousing the immediate attention of both men and women. Regrettably, however, attention does not necessarily equate with interest in the product or idea being marketed. Social marketers may therefore find that they attract immediate interest among the target group, but ultimately they fail to learn anything about the ideas the marketer is attempting to communicate. Nudity in particular has been found to impact negatively on the ability to communicate a message.

If used, sexual imagery must therefore be used with care. Research suggests that the key seems to lie in:

- using the sexual content largely as a device to attract attention;
- using the sexual component only where it is necessary to display a product function—or the expression of an idea;
- using sex symbolically rather than overtly—sexual imagery tends to be more effective than overt portrayals of sex. Nudity is also less effective in advertising than the use of sexual symbolism.

(4) *Cartoons/animation.* Animation techniques have begun to rise in popularity in recent years. Although campaigns featuring animated characters have tended to address a younger audience, several big names have recently used animated campaigns aimed at adults to good effect in the for-profit sector. Tetley Tea, Direct Line (an insurance company) and National Savings are three campaigns for potentially very dull products that have been greatly enlivened by the use of creative animation. Thus, when considering the marketing of some social ideas, a greater degree of attention may be attracted if animated characters are utilized to convey the idea. Houston and Markland (1976), for example quote the example of Marcus Rabbit MD being used to convey immunization messages to parents of small children in Missouri, USA.

Media Selection

There are a variety of different media which can be utilized in a social marketing campaign, each with their own advantages and disadvantages. These include the following.

Television

If the campaign is to be directed at broad target groups within society, the cost of reaching each individual within that market will be comparatively low if television is selected as an appropriate medium. Television also lends a certain status to a campaign, in that organizations which advertise on television are generally perceived as being more reliable and trustworthy than those that don't. Thus the credibility of a social idea may be greatly enhanced by even an occasional airing on television. Of course, given that a typical television commercial is only a few seconds long, it may be necessary to repeat the message on several occasions to ensure that the idea has been effectively communicated. This in turn increases the absolute level of cost associated with the campaign and when one adds in the costs of producing the commercial in the first place, the overall cost can often be prohibitive.

In 2003 Elections Ontario ran a campaign with the ultimate goal of encouraging voter turnout at the forthcoming elections. The campaign centred around a series of TV commercials. In 'Restaurant' a twenty-something couple inquiring tentatively about the menu are interrupted by a brazen young man at a neighbouring table. 'A cheeseburger for this young lady', he instructs the server. 'On a Pita. And he'll have ... nothing.' 'Great, thank you,' murmurs the server, who bustles off as the couple exchange sheepish glances. In 'Hair Salon' a woman's meek request for a trim is overruled by a smirking boor in the waiting area who orders the stylist to go 'short, short and spiked, with some tiger-striped highlights'. Each spot is tagged coyly, 'When you don't vote, you let others speak for you'. The ads generated 250 000 calls to the organization's call centre and their website generated 47 million hits, representing 650 000 unique visitors. The campaign succeeded in adding about 600 000 names to the voters' register.

Print

Print media represent a very flexible communication opportunity for the marketer. Advertisements of all shapes and sizes can be presented utilizing a wide range of colours and effects. Adverts can be targeted specifically at those newspapers or magazines known to have a high readership among the target audience and, because of the enhanced segmentation this provides, messages can be tailored to suit the environment of the publication in which they are housed. Print also offers opportunities for inserts (which are incidentally six times more likely to be read than advertising carried on the pages of a magazine) and cut-out coupons, which can be completed to obtain further information, etc.

The weaknesses of press advertising relate to the fact that increases in circulations have tended to lag somewhat behind increases in advertising rates, gradually making print financially a less attractive option. The other major difficulty with press advertising is that readers of the publication will not necessarily read ads. Readers can, and do, select those advertisements which they feel they want to read. Magazines have the further weakness that it is often necessary to book space months in advance of the intended publication date. Given that at this stage the details of the promotional campaign are unlikely to have been finalized, this can create significant problems.

Radio

Expenditure on radio advertising has been cyclical over the past 15 years. It recovered from a dip in the mid-1980s to level off at approximately £160 million per annum in the UK in 1990. More recently the sector has experienced another rise in its fortunes and expenditures are currently closer to £200 million. Radio advertising is thus clearly becoming an increasingly attractive option for many organizations. Largely this is because it is possible to identify specific audiences tuning in to various stations at various times of the day. Radio campaigns are relatively cheap to produce and comparatively easy to modify, should this become necessary. Radio also has the advantage that it can often fire the imagination of the recipient, and effects can be achieved which would be unthinkable on television.

On the downside, radio advertising obviously lacks any form of visual stimulus which can be helpful in gaining attention. The other difficulty is that listening can often be a background activity and the level of attention advertising receives can, as a consequence, be low. Radio is a useful medium, however, for reinforcing other forms of promotional activity, because sound triggers can be used to aid recall of, for example, a television commercial.

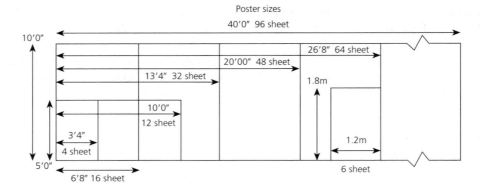

Figure 8.4 Poster advertising sheet specification

Source: © 2004 The Media Pocket Book, World Advertising Research Center, **www.warc.com.**

Outdoor

All forms of posters and signs are usually referred to as outdoor media. Outdoor media traditionally receive less attention than other types of media, and overall expenditure is a very small percentage of promotional spend in general. The amount of information that can be conveyed on a poster is relatively limited, and for this reason many poster campaigns elect to focus on the creative use of imagery. As with radio, poster campaigns can be very effective at reinforcing messages conveyed by other media and very large numbers of people have the opportunity to see (OTS) promotional messages conveyed in this way. Poster sites are sold on the basis of the number of 'sheets' that make up the display panel and these vary in size from 1 to 86 sheets (see Figure 8.4). Similarly a purchase is typically made of a package of sites, rather than a series of one-offs.

Posters can be much more effectively targeted than many people believe. The introduction of the OSCAR (Outdoor Site Classification and Audience Research) system in the UK enables advertisers to select those sites likely to be most effective at reaching their target audience. Locations can be selected on the basis of key demographic variables and targeting greatly enhanced as a result.

The key disadvantages of outdoor advertising are the long lead times. Many sites are booked up months or even years in advance, particularly if the site is one of the increasing number of three-dimensional displays, which tend to command a greater degree of attention. There are, of course, many other, often very creative, forms of outdoor advertising. One can book advertising space on the sides of most forms of transport, hire balloons, airships or even, as the Devon Wildlife Trust did recently, create a six-foot replica of a dodo and 'release' it into the wild!

Electronic

There has been a proliferation in the availability of other electronic media over the past twenty years. Aside from the fragmentation of the television industry and the growth in Web TV, advertising space can also now be bought on Internet sites and text messages sent to a variety of different users in a range of specific locations or contexts.

EXAMPLE

The UK's National Health Service (NHS) recently sought commercial sponsorship for a text message reminder service. The initiative was designed to save the NHS over £400 million through missed appointments with doctors and specialists each year. The NHS initially worked in partnership with milk drink brand Yakult and five other commercial organizations. The NHS Trusts who piloted the scheme encouraged out-patients to register their mobile phone numbers to take part in the service. Thirty NHS Trusts, representing 20 per cent of the NHS, adopted the service in its first year.

Schedule

To ensure that all the communications activities undertaken are fully integrated, it would be usual to specify the exact timings of each on a Gantt chart (see Chapter 7) which can then be utilized by those responsible for the campaign to ensure that not only does each activity commence on the prescribed date, but that opportunities for synergy are fully exploited. Thus, for example, if it is intended to run a brief television campaign, outdoor and radio advertising can be implemented as a follow-up in subsequent months to ensure that enhanced levels of awareness of the social idea are maintained cost-effectively for as long as possible in the minds of the target market.

It is also important to note that the original objectives for the campaign can impact on the schedule that it is intended to follow. Campaigns which are ground-breaking and designed to raise awareness of a totally new concept may thus require promotional effort to be concentrated in a major initial burst, to expose as many members of the target audience to the social ideas as early as possible. This can then be supported with periodic reminders at various points throughout the year. If, on the other hand, the campaign is designed merely to extend and develop an idea already established in the minds of the targets, the need for an expensive initial burst is likely to be greatly reduced. In such circumstances it is rather more likely that the promotional budget will be evenly allocated across the whole duration of the campaign, allowing a gradual infusion of learning to take place.

EXAMPLE

The Like Minds campaign in New Zealand was designed to improve the public's understanding and acceptance of mental illness and to counter negative stereotypes of people suffering with such a condition. Initial research identified that European, Maori, and Pacific Island views on mental health differed. A segmented approach to the campaign was therefore deemed necessary to reflect the attitudes of each key audience. The campaign was run in the native language of each community and featured personalities well known to each audience. The communications did however contain a common strapline, namely, 'One in five New Zealanders will be affected by mental illness. How much they suffer depends on you'. The campaign was timed to coincide with the launch of *A Beautiful Mind*—a film portraying Professor John Nash's struggle with schizophrenia. Post-campaign research showed a significant increase in agreement that 'People who've had a mental illness can still lead a normal life' (increased 7 per cent to 87 per cent); and 'I am feeling more accepting of people with mental illness' (up 5 per cent to 80 per cent).

Budget

As in the case of the marketing plan referred to in Chapter 7, it would be usual in a communications plan to specify the overall budget and the manner in which it will be allocated across the various activities to be undertaken. Variances between proposed and actual expenditure can then be easily monitored and, where necessary, corrective action initiated.

Evaluation and Control

There are four types of evaluation which would typically be undertaken in a social marketing context. These are:

1. *Formative evaluation.* This form of evaluation is undertaken to pre-test the materials that will be used during the campaign. This would typically include the copy, design and layout of any advertising, together with an assessment of the effectiveness of any sales promotion techniques that it is intended to use.

2. *Process evaluation.* The process of implementation will also be subject to review. Each stage of the communication plan will be evaluated to ensure that the campaign objectives will be achieved and that appropriate messages have been received and understood by members of the target market.

3. *Outcome evaluation.* This typically consists of a detailed analysis of whether or not the desired change in behaviour has been facilitated. Of course, there are many variables that could be examined for the purpose of outcome evaluation. These include:

   - the number and form of requests for information;
   - the source of requests for information—the profile of respondents;
   - the awareness, recall, and acceptance of the campaign messages; changes in attitude may also be measured;
   - the extent to which the target market has been exposed to the message—the coverage achieved by the campaign;
   - the nature and extent of behavioural change achieved within the target segment.

4. *Impact evaluation.* It may be impossible to measure the impact of a social marketing campaign in the short term. The campaign could be concerned with changing societal behaviours, which would only impact on society in the longer term. Thus, while one would obviously be concerned with the immediate impact on behaviour achieved by a campaign, it may also be necessary to track those behaviours over time to ensure that they are sustained. Some social marketers may even attempt to evaluate the benefits that have accrued to society as a result of the behavioural changes achieved. It is worth noting that such forms of evaluation are seldom used for communication programmes alone because the costs of conducting this form of research are formidable.

Control procedures are usually set up to monitor each stage of the campaign. The overall objectives would usually be broken down to derive a set of targets for each month (or aspect) of the campaign to achieve. Any deviance from these interim targets would be recorded and, if significant variations have occurred, corrective action may be implemented to ensure that the campaign objectives are met in full. Typically around five to ten per cent of the communications budget would be set aside to allow for such contingencies.

■ SUMMARY

In this chapter we have defined social marketing as the marketing of ideas with the specific intent of influencing social behaviours. It is this latter dimension which distinguishes the concept from mere education or lobbying activities. The relevance of social marketing to various social domains was established, including efforts to alter forms of sexual, smoking, drug/alcohol abuse, pollution, and recycling behaviours. In each case social marketers have no concrete product or service which they can 'sell' to a target market—they have only an idea which, if accepted by the selected segments, could impact favourably on the whole of society. Of course, one's perception of what would be a favourable outcome will differ from individual to individual and there are thus strong ethical dimensions to any social marketing campaign.

A number of factors were introduced that have been found to affect the extent to which it is possible to influence behaviour, namely whether the behaviour is high or low involvement, whether the behaviour is one-off or continuing, and whether the behaviour is exhibited by groups or individuals. Continuing behaviours exhibited by groups were introduced as being the most difficult to alter, largely because group dynamics serve to legitimize and support antisocial behaviours which may otherwise be discarded.

This chapter introduced the concept of a social marketing mix which could assist in changing these behaviours, adding two additional 'Ps' to the traditional 'four-P' mix, namely partnerships and policy. These additional elements together allow the social marketer to recognize the desirability for many organizations of forging links with others in order to exert greater influence over their target market. They also acknowledge what is often a final necessity—convincing governments to instigate legislative change, when less forceful attempts at persuasion have failed.

The chapter concluded with a review of the contents of a typical communications plan and the key considerations which must be borne in mind by a social marketer as each stage is developed. A surprising amount of research has been conducted into issues such as the suitability of various forms of emotional appeals, message order effects, and the manner in which information is presented. Only by taking account of such research can social marketers ensure that they benefit from knowledge gained through past failures and ensure that their particular campaign is as effective and efficient as possible.

■ DISCUSSION QUESTIONS

1. To what extent does the element of persuasion inherent in a social marketing campaign conflict with the marketing philosophy of satisfying customer requirements?

2. Distinguish social marketing from the processes of social communication, education, and lobbying.

3. What primary data would you advise a social marketing organization to gather in an attempt to inform the design of a campaign designed to reduce levels of teenage smoking? How might this data be gathered?

4. You are a consultant employed by the communications manager of Waste Concern, an organization whose primary aim is to encourage households to recycle as much of their domestic waste as possible. How could this organization proceed to segment the 'market' for its communications? For each segment you identify, design appropriate communications messages and specify the media that you would recommend the organization to utilize to deliver them.

5. Design a marketing communications plan for your own social marketing organization, or one with which you are familiar.

■ REFERENCES

Abratt, R. and Sacks, D. (1988) 'The Marketing Challenge: Towards being Profitable and Socially Responsible', *Journal of Business Ethics*, Vol. 7, 494–507.

Bennett, R. (1996) 'Implementation of HIV/AIDS Awareness and Prevention Campaigns: The Case of the London Boroughs', *Proceedings MEG Conference*, University of Strathclyde.

Black, T.R.L. (1979) 'The Application of Market Research in Contraceptive Social Marketing in a Rural Area of Kenya', *Journal of the Market Research Society*, Jan, 30–43.

Braus, P. (1995) 'Selling Good Behavior', *American Demographics*, Nov, 60–4.

Colley, R. (1961) *Defining Advertising Goals for Measured Advertising Results*, New York, Association of National Advertisers.

Elder, J.P. (1994) *Motivating Health Behavior*, Albany, NY, Delmar Publishers.

Fill, C. (1995) *Marketing Communications*, Hemel Hempstead, Prentice Hall.

Fox, K.A. and Kotler, P. (1980) 'The Marketing of Social Causes: The First 10 Years', *Journal of Marketing*, Vol. 44, No. 3, 24–33.

Hirschman, E.C. and Holbrook, M.B. (1982) 'Hedonic Consumption: Emerging Concepts, Methods and Propositions', *Journal of Marketing*, Vol. 46, 92–101.

Houston, F.S. and Markland, R. (1976) 'Public Agency Marketing—Improving The Adequacy of Infant Immunization', In Proceedings: *American Institute for Decision Sciences*, 461–63.

Hovland, C.I. and Mandell, W. (1952) 'An Empirical Comparison of Conclusion Drawing by the Communicator and the Audience', *Journal of Abnormal and Social Psychology*, Vol. 47 (July), 581–8.

Janis, I.L. (1967) 'Effects of Fear Arousal on Attitude Change: Recent Developments in Theory and Experimental Research', in Berkowitz, L. (ed.) *Advances in Experimental Social Psychology*, New York, Academic Press.

Kapferer, J.N. and Laurent, G. (1985) 'Consumer Involvement Profiles: A New Practical Approach To Consumer Involvement', *Journal of Advertising Research*, Vol. 25, No. 6, 48–56.

Kotler, P. and Andreasen, A. (1991) *Strategic Marketing Management For Nonprofit Organizations*, Englewood Cliffs, NJ, Prentice Hall.

Kotler, P. and Roberto, E.L. (2001) *Social Marketing: How To Create, Win and Dominate Markets*, New York, Free Press.

Kotler, P. and Zaltman, G. (1971) 'Social Marketing: An Approach to Planned Social Change', *Journal of Marketing*, Vol. 35, No. 2, 3–12.

Kotler, P., Roberto, E.L. and Lee, N. (2002) *Social Marketing: Improving The Quality of Life*, Sage Publications.

Laczniak, G.R., Lusch, R.F. and Murphy, P.E. (1979) 'Social Marketing: Its Ethical Dimensions', *Journal of Marketing*, Vol. 43, No. 1, 29–36.

Luthra, R. (1991) 'Contraceptive Social Marketing in the Third World: A Case of Multiple Transfer', *Gazette*, Vol. 3, 159–76.

Maheswaran, D. and Meyers-Levy, J. (1990) 'The Influences of Message Framing and Issue Involvement', *Journal of Marketing Research*, Vol. 27 (Aug), 361–7.

McKenzie-Mohr, D. (1994) 'Social Marketing for Sustainability: The Case for Residential Energy Conservation', *Futures*, March, 224–33.

Ramah, M. and Cassidy, C. (1992) 'Social Marketing and Prevention of AIDS', in *AIDS Prevention Through Education*, New York, Oxford University Press.

Ratchford, B. (1987) 'New Insights about the FCB Grid', *Journal of Advertising Research*, Aug/Sept, 24–38.

Reynolds, F.D. and Darden W.R. (1971) 'Mutually Adaptable Effects of Interpersonal Communication', *Journal of Marketing Research*, Vol. 8 (Nov), 449–54.

Sawyer, A.G. and Howard D.J. (1991) 'Effects of Omitting Conclusions in Advertisements to Involved and Uninvolved Audiences', *Journal of Marketing Research*, Vol. 28 (Nov), 464–74.

Schellstede, W. (1986) 'Social Marketing of Contraceptives', *Draper Fund Report*, December, 21–6.

Schiffman, L.G. and Kanut, L.L. (1994) *Consumer Behaviour*, 5th edn, Prentice Hall International Editions.

Shrum, L.J., Lowrey, T.M. and McCarty, J.A. (1994) 'Recycling as a Marketing Problem: A Framework for Strategy Development', *Psychology and Marketing*, Vol. 11, No. 4, 393–416.

Sihombing, B. (1994) *Overview of the Indonesian Family Planning Movement: The Blue Circle and Gold Circle Social Marketing Policies*, Jakarta, National Family Planning Coordinating Board.

Smith, M.A. (1992) *Reducing Alcohol Consumption Among University Students: Recruitment and Programme Design Strategies Based on Social Marketing Theory*, unpublished dissertation, University of Oregon.

Sternthal, B. and Craig, C.S. (1982) *Consumer Behavior: An Information Processing Perspective*, Englewood Cliffs, NJ, Prentice Hall.

Weinberger, M.G. and Gulas, C.S. (1992) 'The Impact of Humor in Advertising', *Journal of Advertising*, Vol. 21, No. 4, 35–59.

Weinreich, N.K. (1999) *Hands on Social Marketing: A Step by Step Guide*, Thousand Oaks, CA, Sage.

9 | Fundraising

OBJECTIVES

By the end of this chapter you should be able to:

(1) describe the changes currently taking place in the fundraising environment and appreciate the implications for fundraising strategy;

(2) distinguish between donor development and donor recruitment and plan fundraising activity for both;

(3) develop, plan, and implement corporate fundraising activity;

(4) develop, plan, and implement trust fundraising activity.

Introduction

Charities and their associated fundraising activity have a long history in the UK. Their origins can be traced to the seventeenth century and to the Charitable Uses Act of 1601, which introduced the term 'charity' into the legal and fiscal framework of the UK for the first time. Of course, over the years the law has been amended and clarified, but the preamble to the Act is still influential in determining whether causes can be considered charitable or not.

If the definition of 'charity' has remained relatively static over the past 400 years, the fundraising environment definitely has not! Early fundraising activity was largely limited to working with individuals and hence characterized by the building of networks of contacts and the cultivation of specific and carefully guarded relationships. Of course, much major gift fundraising is still conducted in this way, but even in this sphere the pattern of giving has become much more complex. To begin with, even a century ago the number of individuals who would have been worth cultivating in this way would have been relatively small. Wealth was historically concentrated in the hands of a few wealthy industrialists or landowners. Indeed, much early charitable activity was undertaken at the whims of such individuals who were free to indulge their own favourite causes as time and money permitted.

In the modern era, many new sources of charitable income have emerged. These are listed in Figure 9.1.

Of course not all of these sources of income come within the scope of a typical fundraiser's remit. The majority of fundraising departments have three or four key target

> - Individual donations
> - Legacies
> - Sale of goods and services
> - Rent/investment income
> - Tax benefits
> - Grants from:
>   - ☐ Central government
>   - ☐ Local government
>   - ☐ Europe
>   - ☐ Trusts/foundations
>   - ☐ National lottery

Figure 9.1 Sources of sector income

Source: Pharoah (1997). Reproduced by kind permission of The Charities Aid Foundation.

groups only and, in the case of larger charities, may be structured to reflect the needs of each. For this reason it is intended that this chapter will examine fundraising techniques that may be used with individual donors, corporate donors, and trusts/foundations. By way of an introduction, however, it would be useful to begin by examining the changing fundraising environment. As we saw earlier, a thorough understanding of the 'trading' environment is an essential prerequisite to the development of any form of marketing strategy.

The Fundraising Environment

Despite the range of funding sources outlined above, some charities face a genuine struggle for survival and many more are facing a situation where they are having to make cutbacks both in the variety and quality of the care that they provide. Why should this be so? There are a number of relevant factors which should be considered; primarily the

- slow growth in voluntary income attracting to the sector
- recent growth in the number of registered charities
- nature of the new causes entering the sector
- performance of the major players.

In respect of the first point, there appears to have been a slow but steady increase in the amount of voluntary income attracting to the charity sector. The difficulty fundraisers have lies in determining the exact extent of this increase. Definitional problems and the fact that various 'tracking' studies all employ different methodologies makes the identification of reliable data on this issue problematic. One of the more indicative studies (because of its sole focus on fundraising charities) produced by the Charities Aid Foundation indicates that the growth experienced by the top 500 charities was only 2.2 per cent in real terms from 2001–2.

Compounding the problem of the low growth in sector income has been the emergence in the late 1990s of ever-greater numbers of registered charities, many of which are looking to raise funds. At the time of writing, there are over 200 000 registered charities in the UK and although the number seems now to have peaked, fundraisers still face a very competitive environment.

In itself this would be less of a problem if the nature of these new causes reflected the profile of the causes already in existence. Sadly, this is not the case. Many of the new charities that have recently registered have causes that are altogether more appealing to the philanthropic public. Many schools, arts institutions, and hospitals are now actively seeking funds from individual and corporate donors, where they might have relied completely on the state no more than ten years ago. It is a sad fact that it is easier to raise funds to educate a child than to house the homeless or feed a starving farmer in the Third World, yet who is to say which cause is actually more worthwhile? Indeed the overall pattern of giving in the UK is somewhat distorted, at least from the perspective of some foreign eyes. The Donkey Sanctuary, for example, is able to attract higher levels of voluntary income than the mental health charity MENCAP, while the Battersea Dogs Home is able to attract significantly more support per annum than the Terrence Higgins Trust. It seems clear, therefore, that the nature of the cause can have a dramatic effect on the fundraising capacity of an individual charity. Given the emotive appeals and the prominence of many of the new organizations entering the sector, existing charities with less 'sexy' appeals will be worst hit by the changes.

A further factor that has contributed to the enhanced competitiveness of the sector is the performance of the major players. The sector's income is concentrated in large organizations, with almost 90 per cent of income generated by just 1 per cent of charities (Jas et al. 2002). The biggest charities consistently outperform the rest of the sector in terms of annual income growth rates, and such enhanced performance is a source of major concern to smaller charities. This unequal income distribution is illustrated in Figure 9.2.

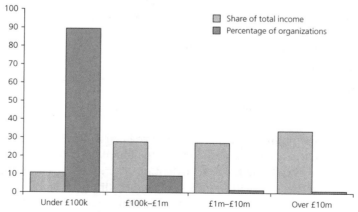

Figure 9.2 Percentage of organizations and share of total income by income band (%)

Source: © 2004 NCVO. Reproduced with kind permission.

There are of course many other factors which have recently impacted on fundraising activity, including the introduction of new database and communication technologies, new legislative frameworks, changes in tax law, and increasing levels of management sophistication. Considered together, these factors have all contributed to the creation of a very dynamic fundraising environment and one that fundraisers fail to take account of at their peril. It is for this reason that a detailed marketing audit (see Chapter 3) is as necessary a prerequisite to a fundraising plan as it is to the overall marketing plan of a nonprofit organization. The derivation of realistic (and appropriate) fundraising objectives and strategies will only be possible when an organization understands how the forces acting in the environment will impact on the actions that it decides to take. Fundraisers, in common with other marketers, cannot afford to operate in a vacuum.

The Fundraising Plan

The fundamental components of the marketing plan introduced in Chapter 3, namely the marketing audit, marketing objectives, strategies, and tactics, are all of equal relevance to the task of planning the activities that will be undertaken to raise funds for a particular organization. There is still a need for a comprehensive audit and the thoughtful derivation of fundraising objectives in the light of the information obtained.

Fundraisers will also wish to consider the overall strategies they wish to pursue to raise the level of funds indicated in the objectives. This will undoubtedly involve apportioning effort between the various potential types of funder and within these groups, the specific segments that will be addressed. The positioning of the organization within each segment will also warrant consideration at the strategic stage of the plan since it will be important to define clearly the values and imagery that the organization wishes to portray. It should also be made clear how these might differ from those of potential competitors for funds. At a tactical level, the fine detail of exactly how the objectives will be achieved is provided. In some organizations the tactical section of the plan is organized using the four- or seven-P framework proposed earlier, while more usually for a fundraising plan, it will be structured using headings that reflect each key fundraising target audience. A separate tactical marketing mix will then be delineated for each of these targets. To complicate matters a little further, however, it is also normal for a charity to draw a distinction under the heading of individual donors, between donor recruitment and donor development activity. In the case of the former, the aim of the marketing is to attract new donors into the organization for the first time, while in the case of the latter the aim is to retain and develop these donors over an extended period of time. The structure therefore proposed for a fundraising plan is summarized in Figure 9.3.

Since many of these issues have already been explored in preceding chapters, it is intended here to concentrate solely on the tactical aspects of fundraising, looking in particular at three target audiences; individuals, corporate organizations, and trusts/foundations.

```
Marketing audit
SWOT analysis
Fundraising objectives
Fundraising strategies
Fundraising tactics
(a)  Individual giving
        (i) Donor recruitment activity
            Tactical marketing mix
        (ii) Donor development activity
            Tactical marketing mix
(b)  Corporate giving
        Tactical marketing mix
(c)  Trust/foundation giving
        Tactical marketing mix
Budget
Schedule
Monitoring and control
```

Figure 9.3 Structure of a fundraising plan

Fundraising from Individual Donors

Donor Recruitment versus Donor Development

Recruiting donors into an organization for the first time is probably the most difficult task that fundraisers ever have to accomplish. Most donor recruitment activity is perceived as a business of some risk, since it is unlikely that the resources expended on it will be immediately recouped. Expenditure on donor recruitment activity should thus be viewed as a long-term investment. Charities rarely break even in conducting recruitment activity, but once 'warm' donors have been brought into the organization, the charity can begin to draw considerable benefit from the relationship it has with these individuals as this develops over time.

Not all 'warm' donors will be treated alike, however. A minority of those recruited will be worth substantially more to the organization than their peers, and where it has been identified that an individual might be prepared and able to commit large sums of money, it is likely that she will be isolated from the general donor base and 'developed' by specialist major-gift fundraisers. Even in the case of smaller charities which may not have this degree of specialization in their fundraising departments, it is still almost certain that such individuals will receive a highly personal service from the most senior members of fundraising staff.

The majority of newly recruited donors are likely only to have given quite small sums of money. Despite this, such individuals are clearly enthusiastic about the nature of the cause and therefore likely to respond again if asked to give in the future. Such individuals can therefore be targeted at intervals with requests to give further sums. Indeed, as time passes, they may also be targeted with requests to give on a regular basis through automatic bank payments, requests to encourage other supporters to join, or perhaps even a request to consider leaving the charity a legacy in their will. It is at this development stage that the relationship with these donors becomes truly profitable and begins to justify the initial investment.

Of course, given that donor development activity is inherently more profitable than donor recruitment, there is a danger that charities may not balance their efforts and investment levels correctly between the retention and development of their existing donors and the generation of a sufficient supply of new donors to refresh the database and provide revenue in times to come. While there are no clear rules about what proportion of fundraising expenditure should be allocated to each form of activity, it is likely that in an established charity the ratio will be 80:20 in favour of development. Both forms of fundraising are discussed below.

Donor Recruitment Activity

There are really two approaches to the targeting of donor recruitment activity, the choice of which will depend on both the length of time the charity has been established and the degree of sophistication achieved in terms of record keeping. The two possible approaches are either:

(1) *a priori*—where the organization decides in advance of fundraising activity those categories of individual who are likely to be worth targeting. This 'gut feel' approach may be the only one possible if the charity is new and has no record of dealing with donors, or where record-keeping has in the past been poor and where, hence, very little is known about existing donors to the organization;

(2) *post hoc*—where the organization analyses the profile of its existing donors and uses this information to help it select future prospects. This latter approach clearly requires the organization to have either kept accurate and detailed records in respect of its donors, or to be willing to conduct additional market research to capture such information.

The A Priori Approach

Considering first the *a priori* approach, the key question that fundraisers must ask is: 'What type of person will be likely to give to my cause?' The reader will appreciate from Chapter 5 that there are a variety of demographic, lifestyle, and behavioural variables that could be used to select potential donors, but of all these criteria, which are likely to be the most successful?

At the first level of refinement, fundraisers will be likely to want to isolate charity donors (and preferably high-value donors) from non-donors. They will then (of course) wish to isolate those that are likely to want to support their category of cause from the general mass of charity supporters. Fortunately a number of studies have been conducted that might guide them in the attainment of this goal.

A variety of demographic variables have been shown to impact on giving (Milliman and Turley 1993). The age of an individual appears to be directly related to his propensity both to engage in charity giving and the level at which such behaviour will take place (i.e. the sums donated) (Nichols 1992; Midlarsky and Hannah 1989). According to

Royer (1989) 60 per cent of charitable gifts in the USA come from people aged 60–76. A similarly skewed profile of charitable support has been reported in the UK.

Some writers account for the skewed age distribution of givers by explaining that older people experience less social interaction than their younger counterparts. This results from a physiological decline (impacting on mobility), age-related losses (including retirement and the death of a spouse; Atchlet 1987; Lemon et al. 1972), and a less positive self-image due to a reduced lack of control and self-determination (Ward 1977). Elderly members of society may thus be able to experience pseudo-social interaction through the relationships they build up with charities and in essence exchange one form of social interaction with another (Graney and Graney 1974; Caplow 1984). Given that the elderly of today are much more likely to be wealthy than their predecessors, this represents a considerable future opportunity for charities to address, and not necessarily a threat (Moschis 1992).

The variable 'gender' is also of relevance. Marx (2000) found that women are more likely to support human services organizations and to have a commitment to the organization. In the USA the Council of Economic Advisors determined that women tended to give more frequently than men, although they donate very similar amounts in aggregate. What this means in practice is that individual nonprofits looking at the behaviour of their database will notice that while they have more women on their database they appear to be less generous than men. This is simply because they are spreading their giving across a wider range of organizations. It is interesting to note that this pattern is mirrored in most other Western countries.

There are further attitudinal and behavioural differences. Braus (1994), for example, found that women tend to want more information about how the money is actually going to be used, prefer one-off donations as opposed to regular (or committed) giving, and to give more 'from the heart than the head' (48).

Not surprisingly, the variable social class/income is also an important determinant of charitable behaviour. While economic downturns constrain both the desire to give and the ability to do so (Galaradi 1989) this effect would appear to constrain the lower income earners rather than those towards the top of the social scale. Writers such as Mears (1992) and Jones and Posnett (1991) see giving as income elastic, although it is important to note that not only the amounts given will vary as one moves up the social strata, but also the rationale for support. Radley and Kennedy (1995) identified that the lower socio-economic groups tend to see the needy as a group to be pitied because of their treatment at the hand of fate. Promotional messages stressing the ability of even a small gift to alleviate pain and suffering are therefore likely to be most effective. The higher socio-economic groups, by contrast, particularly those from the professions, give not only for the amelioration of suffering but also for the longer-term change in their situation. Support is thus prompted by a need to make a change in a social structure, and promotional messages could perhaps reflect this motivation. Reed (1998) identified that in the UK higher income earners were most likely to give to Third World and environmental causes and least likely to support homelessness and children's charities. Authors such as Amato (1985) add that professional people tend to become more involved in their charitable giving.

This theme of involvement would also seem to be of importance to particularly high net worth individuals. Boris (1987: 239), in a study involving interviews with 100 wealthy philanthropists, identified that 'virtually every major philosophical current is reflected in the motives of donors', including feelings of civic responsibility, egoism, progressivism, and scientific problem-solving. In a similar study, Schervish and Herman (1988), in 140 interviews with individuals whose net worth was in excess of $1 million, identified nine 'logics' of philanthropy each implying a high degree of involvement with the causes selected for support.

Interestingly, in the USA the poor and extremely wealthy give a much higher proportion of their income than the middle class (Silver 1980) and those living in small town/rural settings are more willing to exhibit helping behaviours than city dwellers (Latane and Nida 1981).

The personality of a given individual does not in general appear to be a good indicator of charity support (Penrod 1983). A number of studies have, however, highlighted that the self-confident are more likely to help than other categories of individual (Berkowitz 1972). There is also evidence that intrinsically motivated people do more for charity than self-centred, external reward seekers (Reykowski 1982).

A number of studies have moved beyond this early approach and have utilized lifestyle and/or geo-demographic data to predict participation in giving. Schlegelmilch (1988) showed that attitudinal and lifestyle variables improve the prediction of whether an individual will give versus chance by 32 per cent and Yankelovich (1985) reported that the most important characteristics of the generous giver are all related to the donor's perceptions and values. Perceptions of financial security, discretionary funds, attendance at religious services, and whether an individual volunteers time for charity were all shown to be good indicators of a propensity to give. Hansler and Riggin (1989) also report success using the geo-demographic system VISION to segment potential support for the Arthritis Foundation.

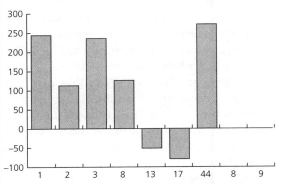

Segments above the line 0 (like No. 44—Prairie People) volunteer more often than 17 (Carports and Kids) and 13 (Little League and Barbecues)

Figure 9.4 VISION profile bar chart

Source: Hansler and Riggin (1989). Reprinted with permission from *Fund Raising Management Magazine*, 224 Seventh St, Garden City, New York, 11530, USA (516/746-6700).

A selection of VISION segments and their propensity to volunteer time to charity is shown in Figure 9.4.

The graph warrants a little explanation. The vertical axis has been arranged as an index, with the point (0) representing the average propensity to volunteer across the whole American population. Thus segments such as No. 44, which the suppliers of this system call 'Prairie People', are considerably more likely to volunteer time to charity than members of segment 17 ('Carports and Kids') or segment 13 ('Little League and Barbeques').

There are thus a variety of different variables that can be used to select segments of individuals who would be statistically more likely to give time or money to charity than others. All these variables could potentially be used to define a set of parameters that could be used to purchase a commercially available list of individuals. The charity could then target these individuals with a direct mailshot or advertising campaign, secure in the knowledge that they are statistically more likely to respond.

In all these studies, however, the only distinction that has been drawn is one between donors and non-donors. No attempt has been made to differentiate between those who might choose to support one category of cause and those who might choose to support another. There is a good reason for this! There is a very healthy debate at the present time surrounding this issue. Writers such as Schlegelmilch and Tynan (1989*a*, *b*) who carried out a survey of 800 Scottish households containing known donors, demonstrated that 'specific types of charities are not associated with specific segments'. They therefore concluded that charities were providing a commodity product since donors' needs appeared to be largely similar. It should be noted, however, that the authors tested only a limited number of psychographic variables and that these were not closely related to the charitable product. This latter point may explain why the academic research is so sharply at odds with the reported experience of practitioners within the sector. Pagan (1994), reports that the RNID (Royal National Institute for the Deaf) increased the response from its direct mail campaigns significantly by recognizing that their donors tend to have a religious interest and enjoy both gardening and reading the *Daily Telegraph*. Building these lifestyle variables into the criteria for donor selection from lists increased the response rate to 'cold' direct mail from 0.6 per cent to 3.3 per cent. In a further example, the Terrence Higgins Trust's donors appear to be predominantly young to middle-aged, male, with a high disposable income and a propensity to enjoy gourmet food. This is hardly a profile that would match that of many charitable organizations!

More recent work by Sargeant and Bater (1997) and Bennett (2003) found that lifestyle and values could indeed offer significant utility in distinguishing donors from one category of cause to another. These studies demonstrated empirically that charities may indeed segment the market very successfully on the basis of lifestyle variables. The authors also argue that in reality the scope for demographic segmentation of the charity market will depend on the nature of the cause.

Charities which exist to serve the needs of a very narrow set of recipients are likely to find it easier to segment the market on demographic grounds. The Police Dependants Trust, for example, has a very narrow recipient base and to suggest that potential donors could not be selected using the demographic variable 'occupation' would be intellectually puerile. Serving and ex-police officers would clearly be a key target market for this highly specialist organization. If, however, the charity appeals to a wider recipient group as, for example, does the Save The Children Fund or Barnardo's; demographic segmentation of potential donors becomes more problematic. In the latter case, one would appear to be competing for funds from a demographically homogeneous body of donors.

Any readers interested in reading a comprehensive review of the giving behaviour literature are advised to consult Sargeant and Wymer (2004) or Bendapudi and Singh (1996).

The Post Hoc Approach

The post hoc approach to targeting potential new donors involves the organization in conducting a detailed analysis of its own database/records, or in conducting some primary research. Here the aim is to profile those individuals who currently give to the charity and target others in society who exhibit broadly similar characteristics. Thus if the existing database is comprised primarily of married A/B women, other individuals who match that profile can be targeted by using those criteria to select appropriate media for marketing communications. In the case of direct marketing activity this may involve building these variables into the criteria for list selection, while for more general advertising activity, magazines, TV channels, and even poster sites can now be selected to offer greater penetration among the specific target groups.

Larger organizations may, however, be in a position to take this analysis one stage further. Consider Figure 9.5.

EXAMPLE

Compassion In World Farming (CIWF) was created in the 1960s to protest against the ill-treatment of farm animals resulting from intensive farming. In November 2003 the organization began a short telemarketing campaign to recruit new donors and increase its income. Telemarketing is rarely employed for donor recruitment and the approach was therefore highly unusual. The organization analysed its database and used the information it gleaned to select individuals from cold lists who had a similar profile to CIWF's core supporter base. A call guide was then developed by the telemarketing agency in collaboration with CIWF. The call guide focused on British live sheep exports, providing a series of facts on the cruel and illegal conditions in which they are transported and slaughtered. During the conversation, individuals were asked to make a £12 monthly donation. If they turned this down they were asked to make a lower donation. In total, 310 donors were recruited to an average annual donation of £67.54. Most of the donors were female, although donations made by men were 9 per cent higher than those made by their female counterparts.

Charities with larger databases will undoubtedly find that patterns of giving are not uniform. Individuals give wildly differing amounts to the causes that they elect to support, depending on their levels of disposable income and the enthusiasm with which they view their participation. A useful form of analysis might hence be to categorize donors according to the sums of money that they typically donate per annum. Thus a great number of donors may elect to give no more than £10 per annum. Substantially fewer will elect to give between £11 and £50 per annum and, at the top of the pyramid, only a very small percentage of donors will be found to be giving over £100 each per year. These categories are of course purely arbitrary and any charity conducting this analysis

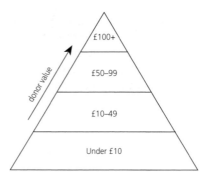

Figure 9.5 The donor pyramid

will need to set appropriate 'cut-off' points of its own. Wherever the lines are drawn, however, it is important to realize that it is the profile of the people at the top end of the pyramid that fundraisers should be most interested in. These are after all, the individuals who are giving the most to the charitable organization. If they have unique demographic, lifestyle, or behavioural characteristics it is important to use these as the criteria for list selection and not the criteria that define the profile of the database as a whole. By so doing the organization has a much better chance, not only of recruiting new donors, but also of recruiting those who have a greater propensity to give larger sums.

Experienced fundraisers will appreciate that even this is a very simplistic form of analysis, but it does form a useful starting point. In charities where data have been studiously gathered for a number of years, it may be possible to take this analysis one step further and instead of using the value of the 'average' annual gift to map out the pyramid given in Figure 9.5, it may be possible to use the variable 'lifetime value'. The simple variable 'average annual gift' is flawed since it neglects to take into consideration the longevity of the charity/donor relationship and the cash value of a donor's overall pattern of giving. The concept of lifetime value overcomes these shortcomings by deriving a monetary value for how much an individual donor will be worth to an organization over the duration of their relationship with it. As previously, the profile of those with a high lifetime value will be of inherently more interest to a charity than the profile of those with a low lifetime value.

The Opportunity

There are a variety of criteria that can be used to target potential new donors to an organization and the good news is that in practice comparatively few charities are yet making use of them. Data collected by Sargeant (1999) indicates that the variables currently utilized by the UK's top 500 fundraising charities are as illustrated in Table 9.1.

The comparatively low percentages of charities that reported using each method of identifying individual donors suggests that the targeting of new donors is still haphazard in many organizations. This view is supported by the fact that only 21 per cent of fundraisers were involved in profiling their database to assist them in the

Table 9.1 Criteria by which potential new donors are selected for contact

Criteria	% of respondents
Donor in some way connected to the cause	52.3
Known donor to other organizations	44.3
Geographic location	38.6
Income	30.4
Lifestyle	29.6
Age	28.2
Magazine readership	24.5
Gender	22.3
Match to database profile	21.2
Geo-demographic variable	18.4

Source: Sargeant (1999). Reproduced with kind permission.

pinpointing of other potential donors in the market. Given that almost 70 per cent of fundraising charities are currently engaged in the use of cold direct mail and a further 10 per cent in outbound telemarketing, there would appear to be a substantial opportunity for many organizations to hone the precision of their direct fundraising activities.

A particularly interesting aspect of these data is the relatively small but significant use of geo-demographic and lifestyle variables. These figures almost certainly reflect the increasing sector-wide usage of commercially available targeting systems, and bears testimony to the increasing sophistication of charity fundraising. This figure will doubtless increase over the next five to ten years.

EXAMPLE

The British Red Cross provides first aid and welfare services in the event of major emergencies in the UK. Overseas it assists with the aftermath of natural and man-made disasters such as earthquakes, famine, and war. The organization is part of the International Red Cross and Red Crescent Movement, the world's largest independent humanitarian organization. In June 2003 the British Red Cross launched the 'Tutti Fratelli' direct mail campaign to increase donations from current supporters. It drew on the origins of the Red Cross in nineteenth-century Europe and aimed to give supporters a stronger, more emotional bond to the organization's humanitarian principles. The mail pack included a letter, a contribution form, and two colour pictures. One of them was a print of Jean Henry Dunant tending the wounded on both the French and Austrian sides during the Battle of Solferino in 1859. Dunant, a Swiss businessman, insisted on treating casualties from both armies, prompting the Italian women working with him to declare 'Tutti Fratelli' ('we are all brothers'). This humanitarian act inspired the founding of the Red Cross Movement in 1863. Donors received a pack with an enclosed letter that began with a bold statement 'Tutti Fratelli—This is what you said when you first made a donation to our work'. The aim was to reinforce the principle that the Red Cross should help anyone in need, regardless of their background. The Red Cross achieved a return on its investment of 3:1.

Fundraising from Existing Donors

Donor recruitment is but one aspect of charity fundraising. Once donors have been recruited, the charity must then manage its relationship with those donors over time. The key to this management process is market segmentation (see May 1988).

Most charities now have a database (at least in the broadest sense of the word) but surprisingly few organizations appear to be using it to its full potential (Sargeant 1995). By segmenting the database and putting the data to work a charity can substantially increase its revenues. At the heart of segmentation in this context is what May (1988: 68) calls 'the ability to ask different donor groups for different amounts of money at different times'. This section will examine in some detail the mechanics of how this can be achieved.

Assuming that a given charity has compiled a database, a number of criteria could be applied to that database to select donors for targeting with a particular campaign. Many of the variables we have already encountered such as age, gender, income, geographic location, geo-demographic coding, occupation, lifestyle, etc. could be used for this purpose. Mailings with specific themes could be sent to target groups which experience suggests would be most receptive. In the context of database segmentation there are, however, a number of other variables that should be utilized, namely:

- original source of gift
- amount of highest/most recent donation
- date of most recent gift
- frequency of donation
- preferred timing of donation
- nature of the relationship required.

Considering each of these points in turn, data in respect of the original source of gift is useful since all individuals who give are unlikely to behave in a similar way. Direct mail donors, special event attendees, enquirers, sufferers, etc. will react differently to certain types of contact. If, for example, a donor has a history of attending fundraising events, but will not participate in other forms of fundraising activity, this fact needs to be recognized and taken account of in any future contact strategy.

Similarly, the amount of the highest gift can enable a charity to develop a donor from a low value category (say £5 per annum or £2 per month) to a higher value category (say £20 per annum or £10 per month). It is now common practice for charities to ask for specific amounts when they write to donors. Often there are three or four levels of giving included in a mailing and the donor is asked to tick a box to indicate the amount enclosed. Each level of giving is usually accompanied by a 'shopping list' explanation of the impact that it will have on the recipient base. Most charities also ensure that a final tick box allows the donor to choose to give any other amount they deemed appropriate. Asking for a specific sum has however been found to enhance the overall level of giving as donors are 'guided' to appropriate levels of support (Nichols 1995). This is one of the reasons why so many television campaigns carry details on the screen of what a £5 donation, £10 donation, or £2 per month donation will accomplish. Of course when donors have been recruited to the organization, the level of donation suggested through tick boxes can be slowly increased over time. This may in turn require that several different variants of a mailing are produced in order that each value category of donor can be persuaded to give at a level at which they will find appropriate. This level should vary upwards with the passage of time. As a general rule, it is normal for a donor to be encouraged to give two or three times at the same level before any attempt is made to develop them in this way.

The date of the most recent gift is also an important database variable since to a certain extent it will control the date of the next contact that a charity will have with a particular donor. At the most simplistic level, this will help ensure that a donor who wrote a cheque for £100 yesterday is not burdened with another request for cash help tomorrow. Donors expect that the charities they support will maintain a dialogue with them and data needs to be managed intelligently to ensure that this is indeed the case.

Allied to this latter variable is the frequency at which particular individuals give donations. Often this may be once, twice, or three times a year and the patterns preferred by donors need to be respected. If one individual has a consistent record of giving twice a year it would seem a little foolish to write to them three or four times a year. Donors should be approached at a frequency that they find most comfortable to support. This makes the donor feel better about their relationship with the charity and avoids wasting valuable fundraising resource. A further point worthy of note in this section is the timing of individual donations. Many charitable donations are made in recognition of an anniversary or a special event such as Christmas. Once again, if a pattern begins to emerge, it would be sensible to respect the donor's wishes only to give at a set time of the year and thus to approach them only at those times. It is worth noting, however, that there are exceptions to this rule. Some charities do consciously make an effort to increase the frequency of donation as a further means of donor development, and this can often be more effective than asking directly for higher gift amounts. It is also very common now for charities to seek to 'upgrade' donors to a regular gift commitment arranged through an automated bank payment. Regular (usually monthly) gifts like this are convenient for the donor as they require little administration, and advantageous for the charity as they mean that the donor does not have to be approached with a new request for funds each time. Monthly givers tend to have a high lifetime value as the monthly gift is likely to continue for a lengthy period. This form of giving appeals particularly to younger segments of the population as they are comfortable with automated banking routines and appreciate the speed and convenience of this sort of arrangement.

It can be advantageous to combine a number of the preceding variables. If, for example, a charity focuses only on the amount of the last donation it might treat someone who gave £50 in January as a £10 donor if they happen to have given £10 in March. In fundraising terms this represents a big mistake since different categories of donors should receive different forms of communication, the 'value' of which reflects the level of support offered. Thus individuals who give more than £50 per year may receive different forms of communication than those who only give £10 a year.

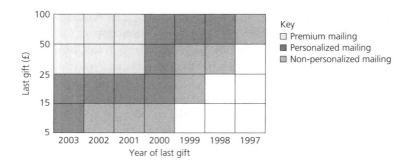

Figure 9.6 Simple two variable segmentation system

There are a number of ways in which variables can be combined to ensure that the problem highlighted above is overcome. The easiest way of achieving this, with most databases, is simply to combine two variables and develop a coding system that defines each resulting segment of donors (see May 1988). Such methods of segmentation are widely used (Sargeant 1995) but, as will be explained, they are fundamentally flawed. Supposing for a moment that a charity has employed such a simple system of segmentation, they would be in a position to produce a graph such as the one reproduced in Figure 9.6.

In this example the charity has determined that low-value donors will receive a simple non-personalized mailing, higher-value donors a personalized mailing with an extra item, and the highest value donors will receive a highly personalized mailing including a small premium gift. Each shaded box thus represents a particular segment. In this example, any individual who has given more than £25 within the last three years would receive a premium gift from the charity. Donors who gave a smaller sum, or who gave over £25 over three years ago, would simply receive a personalized mailing. Low-value donors, or those who have given a considerable time ago, will receive a non-personalized simple mailing. Finally, donors who had not given for a considerable time would be dropped from the database altogether. As Rivlin (1990) points out, such a system has the merit of being very simple to manage and the two most important factors in fundraising are taken account of.

Before highlighting the difficulties associated with this form of approach, however, it is worth elaborating a little on the last point. Many charities are very adept at managing the data on their database and are loath to part company with donors who either give at consistently low levels, or who last gave some considerable time ago. These donors are probably costing the organization more to support than they have ever contributed in return, though in the case of regular but low-level givers there is a chance that they might ultimately leave a legacy gift to the charity in their will and thereby 'repay' the investment the charity has made! Such unprofitable individuals should be identified and efforts made to ensure that they are at least not proving a cost to the charity, by decreasing the frequency and quality of the communications they receive.

Individuals who have not given for some time can also be used in reciprocal mailings. A great many charities will hence swop details of donors who have exhibited a disappointing level of commitment. Reciprocals have historically been justified by the need to offer donors more 'appropriate' choices to stimulate their giving. If this sounds unlikely, it must be remembered that if a donor appears on a charity's database as a low-value giver, they will be a low-value giver for one of two reasons. They either have no money, in which case no amount of reciprocation will stimulate them further, or the organization they are presently giving to doesn't really 'push the right buttons' for them. The argument goes that if they are swapped with other charities, eventually they will be solicited by an organization that they will really feel passionate about and that the value of their giving will go up as a consequence.

However, there are concrete economic reasons to stay away from reciprocal mailings. It is apparent from research into donor lifetime values (Sargeant and MacKenzie 1998) that on average donors entered into a reciprocal programme will lose between 10–20 per cent of their lifetime value thereafter. This is simply because a donor's charitable pot becomes divided over a wider number of charities and ultimately the focal organization will be squeezed out completely as other opportunities and priorities present themselves. Calculating the accumulated loss of value and factoring this into the decision of whether or not to undertake reciprocal mailings as against genuinely cold acquisition may lead to a change in strategy. The loss of potential income from existing supporters must be carefully weighed against the income generated from soliciting others. Sadly, few organizations take this long-term view and most continue to rely on short-term metrics such as immediate return on investment (ROI) response rates, and cost per donor acquired. Such figures can greatly distort the true picture and yield a sub-optimal fundraising strategy as a consequence.

To return to the problems associated with the approach taken in Figure 9.6, consider for a moment the case of the two donors in Table 9.2.

Using the classification system postulated above, both these donors would be classified in the same segment since the value of their last donation was between £15 and £25 and it was made in both cases during 1999. Using this simple form of segmentation, they would therefore be treated alike by the charity concerned. The profiles of these donors are hardly alike, however, and Donor A is of considerably more value to the organization than donor B. Although building in the additional variable of 'frequency of donation' would solve this problem, it would be administratively burdensome for a charity since it would lead to a doubling of the number of segments that must be tracked. Rivlin

Table 9.2 A history of two individual donors

Donor A		Donor B	
Date	Amount	Date	Amount
Jan. 1997	£20	Feb. 1999	£20
May. 1997	£24		
Nov. 1997	£20		
Feb. 1999	£18		
May. 1999	£22		

(1990) therefore proposes that charities should undertake a regression analysis that could incorporate as many variables as were felt to be relevant. The aim in this respect is to build up a picture of the net worth of each donor and hence to estimate how much that person will give both over the next twelve months and even (if records permit), how much they might be expected to give over the lifetime of their association with the charity. Typically a charity may develop five such value segments and have a separate strategy for approaching each. Clearly the two donors in the example would then be classified into different segments, each of which could be addressed with an appropriate contact strategy. Fortunately many software tools will perform this form of analysis, eliminating the need for fundraisers to have a detailed understanding of the statistics involved to use them effectively.

The final variable that can be used to assist in donor development is the catch-all 'nature of the relationship that is required'. The very highest-value donors may be looking for personal forms of contact with the charity, while others will be content to receive regular newsletters, telephone calls, or mailshots. Some will want to be active in campaigning and lobbying, and some might want to volunteer. Surprisingly few organizations, however, actually ask donors what form they would like their relationship with the charity to take. Would donors prefer to be contacted at set times of the year? Do they prefer to be prompted to give by regular requests for donations? Are they interested in visiting the charity? Would they like to receive newsletters/updates? Are they concerned always to receive an acknowledgement of their gift? Would they like to transfer to monthly giving? Figure 9.7 contains a copy of a mailing distributed to donors to the charity Botton Village soon after they have made a donation for the first time. It shows clearly how donors can be offered quite differentiated forms of contact strategy, which not only enthuses the donor about the service he has received, but also conserves valuable fundraising resource, as materials will not be despatched to donors who have no interest in receiving them. The information Botton Village gathers can then be combined with data pertaining to the value of each individual donor and he can then be allocated to one of a variety of different segments, each of which will be developed with an appropriate contact strategy in the months that follow.

Work by Sargeant (1999) suggests that as with donor recruitment activity, comparatively few fundraising charities are taking full advantage of the opportunities to segment their database and to develop appropriate standards of care for differing categories of donors. Table 9.3 indicates the variables that charities typically hold on their databases, together with those that are utilized to aid in the selection of donors to receive a particular campaign.

As one would expect, charities collect a variety of data in respect of the amounts that individuals have given to their organization. Variables such as the amount and frequency of donation, together with a detailed giving history, clearly predominate. What is surprising, however, is the extent to which this information is underutilized in the development of fundraising appeals when there is considerable evidence in the literature that effective fundraising appeals are based on a sound contact strategy which can be tailored to the needs of individual groups (or segments) of donors (see Nichols 1991). Indeed, perhaps the most disappointing aspect of Table 9.3 is the fact that while almost all charities record the amount of the most recent donation, only half

Let Botton help you

Your support means a great deal to us and we want to help you in return. Please decide exactly how you want us to stay in touch by ticking the relevant boxes below.

Choose when you want to hear from us

1. **At the moment we send you four issues of** *Botton Village Life* **a year:**
   - ☐ *I would prefer to hear from you just once a year, at Christmas.*
   - ☐ *I would like you to keep me up to date with Botton's news through Botton Village Life, but I do not wish to receive appeals.*

2. **If you only receive a newsletter once a year, you may like us to contact you more often:**
   - ☐ *I would like to receive Botton Village Life four times a year.*

3. **If you would rather NOT receive information:**
   - ☐ *I would prefer you not to write to me again.*

4. **Choose whether you'll help us find new friends:**
   From time to time we agree with other carefully selected charities to write to some of each other's supporters. This can be a very valuable way to find new friends.
   - ☐ *I would prefer not to hear from any other organisations.*

Choose what you'd like to receive

5. **Our video of life in Botton**
   Our latest video, *Botton Village: This Is Our Home* – set against the changing seasons in the rural beauty of Danby Dale – will help you to get to know us better. It tells the story of our community through the lives of our villagers and is a charming portrait of special people and the challenges they meet in sharing life together.
   - ☐ *Please send me your video on a month's free loan.*
   - ☐ *Please send me my own copy. I enclose a cheque for £7.50.*

6. **Our** *Sounds of Botton* **audio tape**
   Our tape follows villager Jane Hill as she tours the village and meets her friends. It will give you a unique insight into life at Botton.
   - ☐ *Please send me a free copy of the Sounds of Botton tape.*

7. **Our information for visitors**
   Visitors are always welcome at Botton. If you can, please give us a ring in advance on (01287) 660871. We can supply details of the opening times of our workshops and a map of how to get to Botton.
   - ☐ *Please send me your information for visitors.*

How else can we help?

8. **Explaining the methods of giving you can use**
   Please send me:
   - ☐ A Gift Aid form for gifts of £250 upwards.
   Please note our charity is not eligible for Gift Aid 2000.

9. **Providing a helpful guide to making a Will**
   We produce *The Simple Guide to Making a Will* which is full of useful, impartial information. Of course, if you do decide to remember Botton in your Will, we would be very grateful.
   - ☐ *Please send me my free copy of The Simple Guide to Making a Will, currently applicable only in England and Wales.*
   I would like the ☐ standard print ☐ large-print version.

10. **Sending you past issues of our newsletter**
    Interesting stories from the village's history feature in past issues of our newsletter, *Botton Village Life*. You may ask for any of the past issues you would like, or another copy of ones you may have mislaid or passed on to a friend.
    - ☐ *Please send me a set of back issues (1-20).*
    - ☐ *Please send me issue no _____ (nos 21 upwards).*

11. **Giving you details about Camphill in the UK**
    Botton Village is just one of the many communities which are part of the Camphill movement. If you want to know about other Camphill centres, we will be happy to help.
    - ☐ *Please send me the booklet An Introduction to Camphill Communities and a list of centres.*

   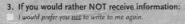

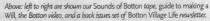

Above: left to right are shown our Sounds of Botton tape, guide to making a Will, the Botton video, and a back issues set of Botton Village Life newsletter.

Do you want a word with someone?

Our office team of Fran, Rebecca, Jackie, Kelly, Joanne and Sue is here to help you. Just ring our helpline (01287 661294) or our switchboard (01287 660871), 9am to 4pm weekdays, and one of us will be pleased to talk to you. Do let us know if you have moved to a new address, if we are sending you more than one copy of our newsletter by mistake, or if there is anything else you would like to tell us.

Botton Village is part of The Camphill Village Trust Limited, a non-profit-making company limited by guarantee 539694 in England and registered as a charity, number 232402.

Figure 9.7 Botton village donor response form

Source: Botton village donor communication. Reproduced with kind permission of the Camphill Village Trust.

Table 9.3 Charity use of database variables

Variable	% of respondents holding data on charity database	% of respondents utilizing data in the selection of donors to receive a particular campaign
Date of last donation	97	65
Amount of most recent donation	95	59
Frequency of donation	78	50
Gender	54	15
Nature of connection with the organization (if any)	52	35
Preferred mode of donation	44	14
Record of correspondence	36	14
Marital status	27	6
Age	27	16
Preferred date of donation	21	18
Income/profession	12	14
Hobbies/interests	10	8
Net worth of donor/lifetime value	10	7
Presence of children in the household	4	1
Attitudinal data	4	3
Religion	4	4
Media consumption	3	1
Membership of voluntary organizations	3	0
Level of education	1	1
Other	3	3

Source: Sargeant (1999). Reproduced with kind permission.

will actually use this information to guide their choice of future contact strategy. In fundraising as in the commercial world, some customers are worth far more to an organization than others. This should at the very least be reflected in the choice of the standard of care that high-value donors receive. The defection of a high-value donor to a competing organization will after all cost an organization far more (and in more than simply cash terms), than the defection of a low-value donor. Correspondingly, more effort should therefore be applied to the encouragement of loyalty among higher value donors.

Donor Recognition

With this latter point in mind it is worth briefly considering the question of how loyalty might be developed. At its most basic level, the key to loyalty lies in maintaining a meaningful dialogue with donors over time. Donors (particularly high-value donors) need to feel that they are appreciated and that their 'efforts' on the charity's behalf have actually made an impact. Moreover, they expect the charity to recall their past deeds and understand a little about them as individuals. Thus more successful fundraisers utilize every opportunity they can to develop and extend a dialogue with their donors. A colleague from a major wildlife charity ensures that he speaks personally to each of his major donors at least twice a year. In the early stages of his relationship with a high-value donor, he keeps a careful record of the donor's family circumstances (name of spouse, age of children, etc.) and any hobbies/interests that they might have. As any good salesperson will know, such intelligence is an invaluable tool as it allows the fundraiser to continue a conversation with a donor the next time they speak to them without the need to perform a devastating feat of memory. This particular colleague uses the information on hobbies and interests for a second purpose—if he comes across a newspaper or magazine article that he thinks would be of interest he will forward it to the donor concerned. A very low-cost mechanism for enhancing value!

There are a variety of other more formalized ways in which donors can be 'rewarded' either for their loyalty or for the amounts that they give. Some of the more common forms of what are termed 'donor recognition programmes' are listed below.

- *Newsletters.* Currently the most common form of 'reward', these serve to inform donors of the use to which their funds have been put and can act as a useful reminder of the donor's association with a charity, particularly if newsletters are sent at intervals complementary to other forms of contact.

- *Invitations to events.* Where charities have a site that donors may visit, donors may be extended an open invitation to visit, or alternatively open days can be held when donors can be specifically encouraged to visit. This category of reward may also take the form of invitations to special functions such as general meetings, dinners, galas, etc.

- *Citations in charity literature.* Often the annual reports of charities will feature the names of the highest value donors. Donors can also be thanked through acknowledgements in charity magazines or other promotional material.

- *Personalized communications.* As indicated above, higher value donors may receive uniquely personalized communications and may only be contacted by the most senior fundraising staff within the charity.

- *Premium materials/gifts, etc.* These are most effective where the premium directly relates to the nature of the cause and, while they should always be used with caution, are capable of adding considerable value to the charity/donor relationship.

- *Plaques/certificates of acknowledgement.* This is still a practice in its infancy in the UK, but is relatively commonplace in the USA. High-value donors will be sent either a bronze, silver, or gold plaque to acknowledge their donation, depending on the overall value thereof.

Despite the opportunities, donor recognition is still a practice which is under-developed in the UK. While a few large charities have become very adept at building long-term relationships, particularly with high-value donors, many still perceive that all their donors should be treated the same irrespective of their overall value to the organization.

CASE STUDY 9.1 CELEBRATING THE MILLION—A CASE STUDY OF THE RSPB

Background

The RSPB celebrated the recruitment of its millionth member in 1997. Given that in 1988 the organization had a mere 500 000 individuals on its database, something of a sea-change must have taken place in the manner in which the organization promoted itself to its target markets.

Central to the RSPB strategy was the development of a formal five-year plan. The organization began in 1992 by undertaking a comprehensive review of its operations and carefully defining all the key conservation issues that it was necessary to address during the next five-year period. From this, it was then able to calculate the income stream that would be required, and planners quickly realized that for all the objectives to be met they would have to double their net income by the year 2000.

Historically over 90 per cent of the RSPB's income had been derived directly from individuals in the form of membership subscriptions, donations, and legacies. Faced with what seemed like the impossibility of achieving a quantum leap in the levels of income attracted from these sources, the RSPB decided to undertake a complete review of *all* its fundraising activity. The audit identified three key areas in which improvements could be made:

1. *Face-to-face fundraising*. With visitors to RSPB reserves, local groups and high-value donors.

2. *Corporate fundraising*. Where a potential existed to develop ongoing relationships with companies rather than one off sponsorship.

3. *Database marketing*. Fundraisers were very much aware of the powerful correlation between the number of members in the organization and the net income attracted. While membership subscriptions were in themselves an important source of revenue, committed members were often also willing to give additional sums to support various appeals that the organization might run.

Aggressive targets were set for each of these three areas, and the decision was taken to attempt to double the number of members to over one million during the next five-year period. Improvements were also to be made to the Return On Investment (ROI) that would be achieved in the medium- to long-term. The key to achieving these goals can best be considered separately as recruitment and development activity.

Database Strategy—Recruitment

The RSPB, in common with most charities, takes full advantage of every opportunity to encourage new members to join and uses a variety of promotional techniques to assist it in this goal, including face-to-face recruitment at reserves and press, radio, and television advertising. By far the majority of new members, however, are recruited through direct mail activity.

To help it target this latter activity, the charity makes prolific use of marketing research data. For the RSPB the starting point is clearly the data already held on its database such as gender, age, and geographical location. In itself, however, this information is still very general in nature and insufficient to effectively target direct mail activity. Additional research is hence periodically undertaken with representative samples of members/donors to establish both their lifestyle and attitudinal profiles. The former is useful since it can greatly help in developing list selection criteria, and the latter because the data may be input to a variety of multivariate statistical techniques including cluster analysis. Using this technique, the RSPB was able to determine that it is serving four distinct attitudinal

continues

segments of donors:

1. *Enthusiasts.* Individuals who are committed RSPB members and make every effort to attend the programme of events that the organization arranges. For this group the social interaction with other members is perhaps almost as important as a passionate interest in the conservation of wild birds.

2. *Birdwatchers.* These individuals support the RSPB because they are active birdwatchers and see membership as a natural complement to their hobby. They tend not to attend meetings or events, but are no less active conservationists.

3. *Garden bird enthusiasts (A).* Individuals, probably in their 50s or 60s, who enjoy nature and who join the RSPB to support its conservation work. They are enthusiasts as opposed to experts on wild birds, but this in no sense detracts from their enjoyment of their hobby.

4. *Garden bird enthusiasts (B).* This group is very similar to the above, but it differs in two important respects. Members are generally younger than members of segment (A) and support the RSPB for its work in protecting the environment rather than preserving bird life.

Importantly, it proved possible to utilize this information to tailor the promotional messages used to contact specific target audiences. However, even when the RSPB had decided on the content of an individual mailing for each segment, considerable effort had to be expended to ensure that it had the desired effect. Focus group discussions were therefore utilized to ensure appropriate promotional themes and two or more versions of a mailing would be tested with a representative sample of the chosen segment of members. Figure 9.8 illustrates three envelope designs that were piloted for a membership recruitment campaign. In this case it was only the envelope design that varied although the RSPB also tested the effectiveness of any promotional incentives it might include, such as a pen, sticker, video offer, etc. to ensure that any additional expenditure would be justified by the higher response rate it generated. Through research the RSPB has thus been able to greatly refine the precision of its recruitment activity.

Database Strategy—Membership/Donor Development

The first year of a new membership is critical. When members are recruited, the primary objective in their first year is to get them to renew. Since over 80 per cent of members now join by direct debit, this task is much easier than it would have been, even a few years ago—natural attrition has now been all but eliminated. During this critical period, efforts are made to welcome members into the organization and get them used to the level of involvement that they will have in the years that follow. Later in the first year of membership, members may also be approached with a view to soliciting an additional donation from them for the first time. The timing of this 'ask' has been found to be critical.

A piece of marketing research demonstrated that new members are significantly more likely to donate when they feel that the RSPB has fulfilled its part of the membership 'bargain' first. People who receive their first appeal mailing before the receipt of their first quarterly magazine were found to be 50 per cent less likely to respond. RSPB marketers therefore ensured that all new members receive at least one quarterly magazine before soliciting any form of additional donation.

The organization also strives to recognize that the four attitudinal segments identified earlier will each have different levels of knowledge about birds and wildlife habitats. Sending an early campaign letter to members of the garden bird enthusiast segment asking them to support the corncrake is unlikely to generate a good response because it is a bird they are likely never to have heard of. A more general 'soft' appeal is therefore deemed more appropriate for this particular segment. As levels of

continues

CASE STUDY 9.1 continued

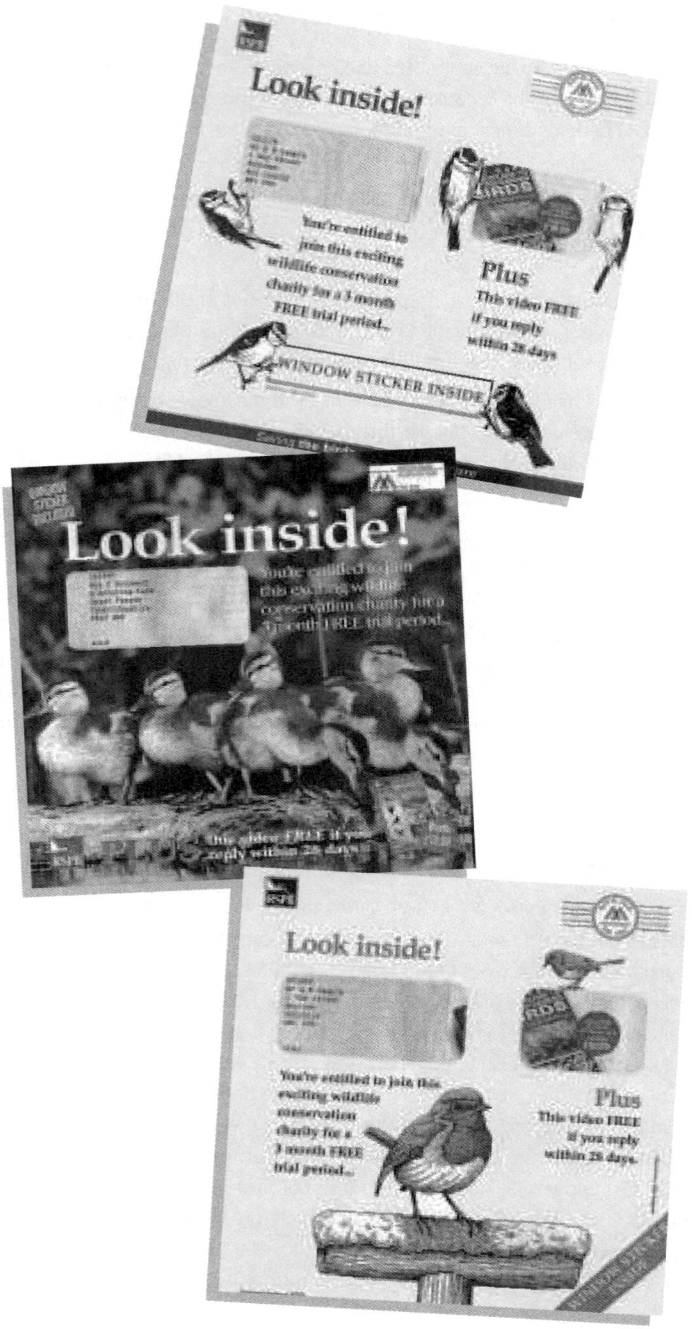

Figure 9.8 Pre-tested RSPB envelopes

continues

knowledge and awareness are cultivated over time, the nature of the appeal mailing is adjusted accordingly.

Using the techniques of CHAID and cluster analysis the RSPB can also identify the distinguishing characteristics of donors/members and use this knowledge to understand how best to present their services to them. In particular, behavioural, attitudinal, and demographic variables have all been found to offer utility in distinguishing between legacy donors, high-value givers, members who will take out an affinity credit card, etc. In effect, the charity can hence look at the profile of a particular new member and know (with a fair degree of certainty) how that individual is likely to behave over time. RSPB fundraisers can thus determine whether a new member is a good legacy prospect, affinity card prospect, etc., and tailor the communications strategy to bring them to this point.

Donor recognition is also a significant issue for RSPB fundraisers. Donors are individually thanked for each donation and feedback is regularly provided, either on an individual basis or through the *Birds* magazine, to keep donors informed as to the progress of a particular project and how their funds have been used.

All these key strategies allow the RSPB to maintain a highly individual dialogue with particular segments of members/donors and, perhaps more importantly, to build a closer relationship with each. Indeed, these relationships can be enhanced in a variety of other ways. Fundraising mailings can be structured to prompt gifts at specific levels. Such prompts are usually at odd number levels (e.g. £18.33) designed to reflect very specific and tangible benefits to bird populations. Although the RSPB team has found it difficult to develop donors past their own comfort level of giving, they have found it possible to increase the prompt levels *slowly* upwards and to increase the number of times people give. It is also possible to segment the database and to draw a distinction between different value levels of giving. Higher-value donors will thus receive a different version of an appeal mailing featuring higher-level prompts.

High-value donors are often targeted with a uniquely individualized mailing. While the nature of the appeal will be identical, the RSPB feels that by recognizing the importance of this category of donor and making them feel special, it can greatly enhance its relationship with this group over time. As an example, the RSPB launched a land purchase appeal, which was targeted at a significant proportion of the database. Lower value donors received a standard mailing pack, while donors who had given over £1000 during the previous year were sent a pack of correspondence relating to the land purchase, including the relevant council papers. Research had shown that donors in this category were more responsive to reasoned/rational argument and the mailing was hence designed specifically to appeal to them. It also served to indicate to this segment that the RSPB valued their commitment to the point at which it was willing to treat them a little differently from the other more general categories of supporter.

Nor is it just the high-value donors to whom the charity is now devoting attention. The RSPB had long recognized that it had a core of members who were either unable or unwilling to become donors. In many cases, it was felt that this might reflect the financial circumstances of the individual rather than any less commitment to the cause. In recognition of this, the RSPB now promotes ways in which individuals can help without spending money, e.g. tax-efficient giving, selling raffle tickets, or taking out an RSPB Visa card. Many individuals who could not afford to give additional sums have been found to be more than happy to donate the time it takes to sell a pack of raffle tickets on the charity's behalf. Indeed, while the funds that this activity raises are worthwhile in themselves, this activity serves a greater purpose in that it brings a further segment of members into a much closer relationship with their charity. By so doing, there is a very real possibility that other forms of giving, such as legacies, may increase over the long term.

continues

CASE STUDY 9.1 continued

At the core of all this activity is the RSPB's desire to make the most of its relationships with its supporters—and this is very much regarded as a two-way process. Aside from refining the precision of its direct marketing activity, the charity has also continually invested in the development of its customer care. Ongoing research with members/donors ensures that the service provided by the organization closely matches that demanded by its customers. Only by ensuring that the relationship becomes mutually beneficial can fundraisers be sure that newly recruited donors will ultimately renew their membership and recommend the organization to others. A 'sales' oriented approach based on exploitation would clearly be in no-one's interest and would ultimately be self-defeating.

Individual Fundraising Approaches

So far in this chapter we have talked about how to target individual donors predominantly with some form of direct marketing activity. Before concluding this section therefore it is worth noting that a plethora of other fundraising techniques exist, many of which do not require anything like the degree of fundraising sophistication alluded to above. It is worth noting that despite widespread participation in many of the forms of giving listed in Table 9.4, the revenues and costs generated by each activity will vary considerably from charity to charity. The CAF data is however a useful starting point for fundraisers in determining which techniques might be worth investigation and further development.

Two points are particularly worth noting from this table. First, while the various forms of charity collection remain important modes of giving, the revenues generated by such activities are considerably lower than many people believe. While the costs of street collections are usually minimal since they are undertaken by unpaid volunteers, they are perhaps a more useful device for raising a general awareness of the charity than for raising much needed funds. Second, the importance of trading income is often underplayed. A significant percentage of overall charity income is generated by this means and although trading operations often differ widely in terms of profitability from one charity to another, it is clear that they can prove a very lucrative source of funds.

Fundraising from Corporate Donors

Patterns of Corporate Support

Recent survey work conducted by the Directory of Social Change (2002) suggested that the overall level of corporate support for the voluntary sector has remained relatively stable in the last ten years, even if it continues to total less than 0.25 per cent of a typical company's pre-tax profit. Approximately £300 million is given in cash and non-cash assistance to the sector each year, although there is considerable debate surrounding the dispersion of these funds throughout the sector. The great diversity of forms that corporate support can take proves difficult to quantify and differing research methodologies therefore tend

Table 9.4 Modes of individual giving

Method of giving	% of all respondents giving by the method	% of total donations
Door-to-door collections	37	6
Street collections	32	4
Buying raffle tickets	31	7
Sponsoring someone in an event	23	6
Church collection	14	8
Buy in charity shop	14	11
Pub collection	11	2
Shop counter collection	11	1
Attend charity event	11	5
Buy in jumble sale	7	5
Subscription/membership fees	6	6
Buy through catalogue	5	10
Collection at work	5	2
Television appeal	4	3
Buy goods for charitable organizations	3	4
Appeal letters	2	2
Appeal advertising	1	4
Affinity card	1	0.5
Telephone appeal	0.5	0.5

Source: Walker and Pharoah (2002).

to generate quite different results. The most common forms that corporate support can take are listed below.

- *Cash support.*
- *Sponsorship.* This form of giving enables a charity function or event to take place that might not otherwise happen. Usually arrangements are made that will benefit both parties, perhaps through the provision of an adequate level of publicity and accompanying acknowledgements for the sponsor.
- *Secondment.* Staff may be seconded to work with voluntary organizations.
- *Training.* This category includes payments for start-up costs and training of charity personnel.
- *Administrative support.* Corporate staff may be involved in administering support programmes.
- *In-kind assistance.* Companies may elect to donate stocks and/or equipment for use in the pursuit of charitable causes.

Table 9.5 Breakdown of company donations by recipient group

Category of voluntary activity	% share of total support
Culture and recreation	11.7
Education and research	31.2
Health	26.8
Social services	12.9
Environment	4.9
Development and housing	4.4
Law, advocacy, and politics	1.1
Philanthropic intermediaries	1.1
International	4.9
Religion	0.2

Source: Passey (1995). Reproduced with the kind permission of the Charities Aid Foundation.

- *Joint promotions*. These include forms of joint sales promotions and the development of affinity card links.

After quantifying the value of donations by all the means listed above, Passey (1995) determined that total corporate support was allocated in the proportions illustrated in Table 9.5. The data show quite clearly that certain categories of cause will find it far easier to raise funds from corporate donors than others. To examine why this might be so, it is useful to look at the underlying reasons why corporate donors elect to give to charity and how these patterns of thought have changed over the years.

The literature suggests that there may be two distinct motivations for corporate giving. Ostergard (1994) reports that two paradigms of thought exist, as follows.

The Responsibility-oriented Paradigm

Historically this paradigm has predominated (Stroup and Neubert 1987). Under this paradigm, corporate giving is viewed as a genuinely philanthropic activity where the primary objective is for the business to give something back to its community. Donations are made only because a particular cause is felt to be worthwhile and not because any form of gain will accrue to the donor. Indeed the causes supported may often bear no relationship to the business interests of the giver. The Exxon Education Foundation, for example, was widely admired until the late 1980s, for being far removed from the world of big business. The programmes supported by the foundation bore absolutely no relation to the nature of Exxon's business interests. After the 1989 Exxon Valdez oil spill it became painfully clear, however, to Exxon executives just how short-sighted this view had been. The company had missed an opportunity to forge links with charities that might conceivably have offered it a number of future benefits. With no long-term relationships having been established, for example with environmental groups, Exxon had nowhere to turn for advice and soon became the brunt of a torrent of criticism. By contrast Arco (a key competitor to Exxon) had been developing strategic links with environmental groups for a number of years and as a result has established a 'hotline' for advice should the unthinkable happen. They were also able to adapt their operational strategy to incorporate the advice offered by the environmentalists and hence minimize the future risk to their corporate identity. Arco had recognized the 'need' for a shift towards an opportunity-based paradigm (Sterne 1994).

The Opportunity-based Paradigm

The opportunity-based paradigm first began to emerge in the late 1960s and early 1970s, with a number of organizations beginning to look for benefits of one form or another to accrue from their charitable giving. More recently, authors such as Jones (1996) have noted what they call the emergence of 'strategic giving' that reflects what they perceive as a move towards fiscal efficiency and measurable effectiveness in charitable giving. Other writers, such as Pifer (1987), Mescon and Tilson (1987), and Wokutch and Spencer (1987) identified a general shift towards what has become known as 'dual agenda' giving, whereby organizations will be predisposed to give to charities that have a good fit with their own strategic objectives. As an example, Hunt (1986) points out that Hallmark chooses to support fine arts and design programmes in the hope that a supply of both employees and customers will be generated as a result.

It was in 1981, however, when in an attempt to raise funds for the restoration of the Statue of Liberty that a new dimension of corporate philanthropy really began to emerge. American Express referred to their programme of support as cause-related marketing (CRM), a phrase that switched the emphasis from purely what the business could do for the charity to an equal focus on what the charity could do for the business. In defining cause-related marketing in an address to his fellow business leaders, the senior vice-president of American Express warned that 'if your primary goal is to make money for a worthy cause, stay away from it. It's not meant to be philanthropy. Its objective is to make money for your business' (Kelley 1991). Varadarajan and Menon (1988: 60) define cause-related marketing as a 'process of formulating and implementing marketing activities that are characterized by an offer from the firm to contribute a specified amount to a designated cause when customers engage in revenue providing exchanges that satisfy organizational and individual objectives.'

CRM is thus concerned with the development of a win-win partnership where both parties derive broadly equal benefit. Those organizations that subscribe to the opportunity-based paradigm will therefore be entering their relationship with a charity with a very clear idea of the set of benefits that they would expect to see accrue as a result. In general, there are four key categories of benefit that can accrue for a business as a result of its association with a charity.

(1) *Long-term strategic benefits*. Giving to some research charities may, for example, facilitate the development of a new technology that may be used by the donor organization in future. There may also be occasions when the recruitment of particular individuals is facilitated since an organization has been shown to 'care', or where highly skilled and qualified members of staff may be retained in the organization by virtue of a substantial

investment in the socio/cultural infrastructure within the local community. Sterne (1994) reported that in the case of the Synoptics Corporation in the USA a rapid expansion programme made the recruitment of senior executives problematic. Potential applicants came not only with job expectations, but also other expectations of the company. The expectations of such employees therefore became a key driving force behind the creation of a community relations strategy which encompassed corporate giving, volunteering, matching gifts, and employee recognition programmes.

(2) *Community expectations.* There have been a number of well publicized examples where community expectations have led to a corporate donation either because the company has felt obligated to give, or more commonly, where it was felt that to give would enhance community relations to the point where the company could increasingly become a master of its own destiny. Richards (1995) cites the example of Proctor and Gamble. With the advent of a new social responsibility programme, headlines such as 'P&G know-how in fight against crime' and 'Procter to spend £15 000 on drugs booklet' have been commonplace in the press. This has had the fortunate effect that P&G now finds it easier to have a say in the future of Newcastle, where the firm is based.

(3) *Employee responsibility.* In many cases the organization may be motivated to give by the desires/concerns of its own employees. In this sense, corporate giving can be seen to 'articulate' the social responsibilities of employees. An often-cited example of this phenomenon is the Reebok Human Rights Now Tour with Sting and Bruce Springsteen in the late 1980s. The tour probably didn't sell many shoes, but it gave the organization's young stakeholders a reason to be proud of their work. In a further example, Hallmark cards developed a long-term relationship with The Children's Society. The charity are regular participants in the organization's sales conferences, which the company feels act as an excellent motivator for its sales force since, the more they sell, the more the good cause benefits. The British Red Cross has even put in appearances at the AGM of city solicitors Freshmans. The aim here is for the company to provide a feel-good factor for delegates at the same time as explaining the benefits to shareholders of their continuing support.

(4) *Enhancing the bottom line.* If the company can be seen to 'care' by its key customer groups, there is a general expectation that sales may be enhanced as a result. Fendley and Hewitt (1994) cite the example of the NSPCC who assisted the Yorkshire Building Society to introduce a new savings product for young savers. By using the NSPCC's Happy Kids brand, which already extends to a range of children's clothing and greeting cards, the savings product gained something of an advantage in an already crowded market. In this case the NSPCC received £1 for each account that was opened and 10 per cent of the gross interest paid twice a year. This one deal alone was estimated to have been worth at least £80 000 in its first year. Other successful examples in the UK of such practices include deals between the children's charity NCH and corporate sponsors Bisto and Securicor, estimated to be worth £125 000 and £110 000 respectively and a deal between White Horse and the RSPCA, worth in excess of £50 000.

There are a variety of reasons why businesses might elect to support charity, but it would be a mistake to believe, certainly in the UK, that the opportunity-based paradigm is as widespread as the popular press might have one believe. In fact, the majority of corporate giving in the UK is still undertaken for purely philanthropic reasons. The key motivation for many corporate supporters is therefore no more hard-headed or objective than would be the case in most individual giving decisions (see Sargeant 1997). What is interesting, however, is that while it is the responsibility-based paradigm which remains the most dominant, organizations that give for this reason tend to give far smaller amounts on average than those that subscribe to the opportunity-based paradigm. Charities therefore need to give adequate consideration to which category of corporate donor they are likely to want to attract and tailor their approach accordingly. In the case of the former, literature which plays on many of the emotional appeals utilized with individual donors might be the most appropriate, while with the latter a more rational approach highlighting the benefits that can be offered in terms of press coverage, exposure in charity publications, networking with influential figures, etc. would clearly be preferable.

The key problem is deciding which would be the best approach to use. The rationale for giving does not appear to be related to the size of the organization or the category of industry in which particular firms are operating. The only answer at present would appear to be a painstaking research process that carefully categorizes prospects according to their likely interests.

Targeting Corporate Donors

Stage 1

As the reader will by now appreciate, there are a number of stages involved in soliciting corporate support. The first stage involves the charity in defining what it is looking to gain from potential corporate supporters. While this may only be a target for cash donations, as was noted earlier corporate giving can take a number of different forms and it is hence important to be clear about exactly what the charity is hoping to get out of relationships from the outset.

The corollary of this is a consideration of exactly what the charity has to offer potential supporters—or, at least, what it is prepared to offer. Some charities may wish to maintain a degree of distance between it and its corporate supporters to avoid the risk of being put in a compromising situation in the future. Environmental charities in particular need to be very careful of those corporate organizations they initiate links with, and the degree of 'cosiness' that can be seen to develop between them. Then, should the need arise, they can still campaign for a change in industrial policies and even be overtly critical of the donor.

Stage 2

The second stage is perhaps the most difficult, for it is at this point that the charity needs to begin generating a list of potential contacts from whom it could look to solicit donations. Tables 9.6 and 9.7 contain a useful starting point in this analysis. Table 9.6 indicates those categories of business organization that typically offer the most support to charities, while Table 9.7 indicates those criteria that are normally used by such organizations to screen appeals that are targeted in their direction.

Many corporate organizations will only give to causes that they perceive as local, perhaps because the charity is based in the locality of one of their manufacturing plants.

Table 9.6 Corporate support by industrial category (SIC)

Industrial category	Number of companies responding	Total corporate support (£000)	% of total support	Median corporate support (£000)
Manufacturing	56	49,013.0	32.9	213.5
Finance, insurance, and real estate	40	46,344.8	31.1	295.0
Mining	11	18,534.0	12.4	331.0
Retail trade	14	18,431.0	12.4	421.0
Business services	11	7,931.7	5.3	75.0
Transport and communication	18	7,283.0	4.9	183.5
Construction	5	1,375.9	0.9	39.0
Wholesale trade	8	922.9	0.5	118.3
Agriculture	0	0	0	n/a
Public administration	0	0	0	n/a

Source: Passey (1995). Reproduced with the kind permission of the Charities Aid Foundation.

Table 9.7 Criteria used to select charities for support

Criteria	% of cases
Local cause	62.5
Relevant to business	43.8
Relevant to staff	31.3
Size of organization	18.8

Source: Sargeant and Stephenson (1997) 'Corporate Giving—Targeting the Likely Donor', *Journal of Nonprofit and Voluntary Sector Marketing*, Vol. 2, No. 1, 64–79. Reproduced with the kind permission of Henry Stewart Publications, London.

Similarly, the cause must usually be perceived as being of relevance to the business and/or one that attract the interests of staff. A significant number of corporate donors will also assess the relative size of the charity partner, essentially for one of two reasons. Smaller firms will want to feel that their donation will have an impact and consequently they may elect only to support charities that are relatively small in size, compared with their own annual turnovers. Larger organizations, on the other hand, may be looking for charity partners that can enhance their overall profile and they will hence be favourably disposed to approaches from the largest players in each charity 'market'.

At this stage of the process, the aim is for the charity to compile a list of loosely qualified 'suspects' who might be disposed to giving. This list will later be subjected to a higher degree of scrutiny (see below).

Stage 3

The third stage of the corporate fundraising process involves the charity in refining its list of contacts. Kotler and Andreasen (1991) propose a matrix that can assist fundraisers in this process (see Figure 9.9).

Clearly not every corporate organization identified in the initial search stage will be equally likely to offer potential support. Neither will all organizations have an equal capacity for giving. Some organizations will quite rightly be regarded as hotter prospects than others and will therefore need to be isolated to receive perhaps a more personalized form of contact strategy. Plotting the position of each prospect in Figure 9.9 can therefore assist a charity in prioritizing its prospects.

The matrix is constructed in a very similar way to the portfolio matrix introduced earlier. The charity must first identify those factors that will comprise each of the axes and then derive a score for each prospect, which can then be used to plot their overall position in the matrix. In the case of the 'Giving Potential' axis, there are a variety of factors which will impact on a firm's ability to give, including financial performance, attitude of directors, giving policy, past record of giving, etc. Each of these factors can then be weighted for importance and each firm awarded a score in terms of how well they meet each criteria. An aggregate score for the horizontal axis can then be derived. Similarly there will be a variety of factors that will impact on the interest that the donor is likely to have in a particular charity. These might include similarity of mission, similarity of target audiences, the need for favourable publicity, etc. Again a score can be derived for each factor and an overall score for the axis determined. At this point the prospect's position in the matrix can be plotted.

Organizations falling in the top left-hand corner of the matrix are obviously candidates for personal attention from a charity's most senior fundraisers, and a close and long-term relationship should be developed with these companies. Companies falling within the

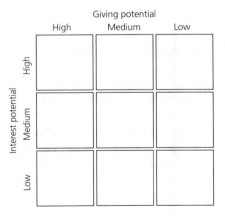

Figure 9.9 Classifying corporate donors by level of interest and giving potential

Source: Kotler/Andreasen, *Strategic Marketing for Nonprofit Organisations*, 5th edn © 1996. Adapted by permission of Prentice Hall, Inc, Upper Saddle River, NJ.

central diagonal are clearly worth contacting but may merit less attention in terms of a fundraiser's time. Indeed, many of these organizations may be communicated with through the medium of direct mail, with subsequent personal follow-up if the response warrants it. Companies falling within the lower right-hand corner of the matrix may either be contacted purely by direct mail (as this is comparatively inexpensive) or they may be dropped altogether from the charity's list of prospects.

Stage 4

As indicated above, the fourth stage of the process involves the design and implementation of appropriate contact strategies for each category of prospects. This may involve the use of a variety of media including personal sales visits, direct mail, and telemarketing. It will also involve a careful tailoring of the 'offer' to ensure that only those aspects that will have the most relevance for the potential prospect are emphasized.

Stage 5

Stage 5 involves a careful monitoring of the overall process. This should be ongoing, so that if the desired response/success rates are not being achieved, questions can be asked and appropriate corrective action taken. The organization will also find it instructive to monitor the profile of those respondents who respond both favourably and unfavourably. This data will be invaluable in helping the charity to refine its selection of suitable corporate prospects in the future.

The recruitment of new corporate donors represents the beginning of a series of relationships, and charities must also give consideration to how these relationships will be developed over time. In particular, the following questions are worth asking from the outset. Will particular members of staff be given responsibility for managing the relationships with specific corporate clients? Are appropriate mechanisms in place for providing the desired feedback to donors? What control procedures will be necessary to monitor the success of the relationship?

Fundraising from Trusts/Foundations

Charitable trusts and foundations are organizations that exist to manage funds donated by an organization or individual (the donor or settlor), for the benefit of some beneficiary group. The beneficiaries are usually specified by the donor and it is the responsibility of the management of the trust (the trustees) to ensure that its funds are indeed used for this purpose. A great many trusts in the UK exist not to service directly the needs of the beneficiary group themselves, but rather to give grants to individuals or other charities in the furtherance of their objectives.

There are about 10 000 charitable trusts and foundations in the UK and they give in the region of £2 billion in grants each year, which makes them as important an income source as local authorities or central government departments. Data suggest that grant-making trusts are responsible for supplying roughly 13 per cent of an 'average' UK charity's income. They represent, however, a very diverse population and while a few organizations give in excess of £10 million per annum, the majority of trusts are quite small in size and highly specialized in terms of the categories of cause that they will support.

In approaching trusts, a seven-stage process is recommended.

Audit of Potential Projects

The first stage in trust fundraising will involve a careful analysis of all the activities that the organization is planning to carry out with beneficiary groups over the short- to medium term (most trusts will not support projects which are likely to extend beyond a three-year period). Those activities that can clearly be identified as specific projects should be isolated and evaluated for how attractive they are likely to be to an external funder. It is worth noting that many trusts will prefer not to fund projects which in their opinion are high-profile enough to warrant the attraction of commercial support, and many will also shy away from the support of projects consisting largely of overhead costs or those which they believe should be government-aided. Trusts are, however, interested in projects that are likely to have a high impact with the beneficiary group, are particularly innovative, and which can demonstrate an impact in a relatively short period of time.

Where potentially suitable projects have been identified fundraisers will need to work closely with other charity staff to justify the need for each project and to derive a series of strong arguments in respect of why each is worthy of support.

Initial Trust Search

Having identified potentially suitable projects, the next stage is to compile a shortlist of trusts that are, on the face of it, worthy of an initial approach. There are a variety of sources of information on trusts which can be used for this purpose and these tend to vary substantially in quality from country to country. In the UK the most commonly used source of trust information is the *Directory of Grant Making Trusts* (now available online or as a CD-Rom in addition to the traditional book version), which provides the contact details for key trusts, information in respect of their giving behaviour, appropriate dates for application and, importantly, the categories of cause supported. Other UK sources of information about trusts include the Charity Commission, local authorities, and the Directory Of Trustees. Most other industrialized countries also have publications that can be scanned to locate trusts (e.g. the Foundation Directory in the USA) and there is now even an International Foundation Directory in existence, for the benefit of those seeking to launch a more global appeal!

Network Search

The third stage in the process involves a charity in searching for any formal or informal links it might have with the trusts identified in Stage 2. This is particularly important as the use of informal contacts can often have a very positive impact on the outcome of a grant decision.

In his review of the status of trustees in the whole charity sector, Vincent (1988) was critical of the decisions made by trustees of grant making trusts: 'Is this (the decision) a matter of the personal whims of the trustee, or is there some objectivity in their decision-making? At the present time it is very much a question of who you know.'

While few would doubt that all trusts would give serious consideration to a well crafted proposal which was clearly covered by the objects of their organization, it is certainly the case that the exploitation of any personal contacts that might exist would certainly help to oil the wheels of decision-making. It must be remembered that charitable trusts receive many thousands of requests for support each year, and wherever possible it is important to stand out a little from this crowd. Many medium-sized or large trusts have comparatively large numbers of trustees and paid administrative staff to help share the burden. The greater the number of trustees, the greater the likelihood that one or more of them might be known to someone associated with your own charity. It is therefore worthwhile circulating the details of the larger trusts to whom an application will be made to all key personnel, volunteers, or trustees who might conceivably have a contact. This could then be utilized to ensure that the application is made to the trust at the highest possible level. Every avenue should be explored at this stage to exploit any such contacts.

Prioritization and Matching of Prospects

Experience suggests that many trusts will have certain cut-off dates by which an application must be made. Others will be prepared to offer only small amounts of funding. Still others may offer funding for only a limited period of time. This variation will require fundraisers to prioritize those trusts to whom contact should be made, so that the best possible use can be made of fundraising resources. Trusts should also be matched against those projects (identified in Stage 1) that they are most likely to want to support.

Selection of Contact Strategy

The importance of networking has already been highlighted. It is clear that wherever possible the approach to a grant-making trust should be a personal one and ideally one that exploits an existing personal relationship between a trustee and someone associated with the applicant charity. Approaches where a personal contact is involved are clearly those that warrant the greatest effort, since they are also likely to be the approaches that generate the most positive responses.

Where more personal forms of contact are not possible, it may still be possible to engage the trust administrator in a dialogue before the application is made. Often this can generate valuable information as the administrator will undoubtedly know the categories of project that are most likely to appeal to his trustees. In their role as gatekeeper they will also have a good understanding of what the trustees consider to be the key components of a successful application. This is all valuable intelligence, which can help in Stage 6—the application.

The Application

The written application should be carefully formulated and take account of any intelligence about the trust gathered at all of the preceding stages of the process. Applications to the larger trusts should always be made first since it is always more difficult to acquire early funding and a few large donations to a project in the early stages can have the fortunate effect of encouraging other, smaller trusts to contribute as time goes on. Applications to smaller trusts, which will typically only be made by letter, are thus normally left until last.

Applying to these smaller organizations is a little more problematic, since fundraisers are unlikely to be familiar with the individual needs and preferences of this category of organization. There is a need therefore to ensure that these written applications are crafted with a particularly high standard of care. Research with the administrators of 350 grant-making trusts conducted by Sargeant and Bater (1997) provides a useful insight into some of the more common pitfalls to avoid.

- *Not reading the requirements*. The temptation to adopt a shotgun approach to trust fundraising should be avoided. The production of vague letters of application that are then distributed *en masse* are unlikely to bear fruit and will almost certainly antagonize trust administrators who receive numerous such letters each day. Letters should be carefully crafted, taking account of the individual interests of each trust. Indeed, only those trusts should be targeted for whom the project is appropriate.

- *Providing too much/too little information*. Good applications should be short, concise, and to the point. They should provide the trustees with all the information they require but avoid the temptation to oversell the project and bombard the trustees with needless amounts of background information. This will simply not be read and will only serve to detract from the overall quality of the application.

- *Poor presentation*. A significant number of trust administrators complain that they receive scruffy, handwritten applications that are difficult to decipher. Applications should be neat, well presented, and legible. They should not, however, be too 'plush' as this might create the impression that the applicant organization is awash with resources and does not require the funding anyway!

- *Not making the ask*! A surprising number of fundraisers avoid all the other pitfalls, but neglect anywhere in the application to state the total amount of funding that is requested. Many others fail to supply sufficient detail in respect of how the funds will be used. This is the one aspect of the application that is usually expected to be provided in some detail, as trustees need to evaluate each proposal they receive in terms of the impact it is likely to have with the beneficiary group. The 'ask' therefore needs to be clear and quantified.

Follow-up

The final stage of the process involves the charity in carefully recording details of both its successful and unsuccessful applications. Even data pertaining to the latter can be immensely valuable as it may prove possible to contact the trusts concerned again at some later date. The experience gained at this stage can hence help inform the approach that is used on subsequent occasions. It may even be possible to obtain feedback from trusts to ascertain why a particular project was rejected. Any such approach needs to be handled with care, though, as many trusts prefer not to divulge such information.

Perhaps more importantly, however, when a successful application for funding has been made, fundraisers will need to ensure that appropriate mechanisms for feedback are put in place so that the trust can be informed as to the progress of the project they are supporting. Only some 50 per cent of trusts will actually require such feedback as a condition of their support, but it is good practice to ensure that it is provided to all. Even if trustees are unable to accept invitations to visit a project, or to read in great detail the impact it has had, the fact that the charity has taken the trouble to maintain a dialogue will undoubtedly pay dividends when subsequent applications are submitted in the future.

■ SUMMARY

In this chapter we have examined three key areas of fundraising activity: fundraising from individuals, corporate organizations, and grant-making trusts/foundations. In the case of the former a distinction was drawn between donor recruitment and donor development activity. It has been argued that while it would be rare for donor recruitment campaigns to break even, a careful profiling of existing donors to an organization can greatly enhance the response rates likely to be obtained. Moreover, if charity records permit, even greater utility can be gained by profiling only those individuals with a propensity to donate higher sums, and using this as the template from which to design the donor recruitment activity.

In the case of donor development, it has been argued here that charities should differentiate the standard of care, and hence the approach that is used to develop donors based on the worth of each individual to the organization. In particular, fundraising strategy should recognize the importance of keeping high-value donors loyal to the organization and to achieve this the design of an appropriate donor recognition programme may be warranted.

A structure for planning the approach to corporate donors was also introduced, highlighting the importance of market segmentation as an aid to the targeting of organizations most likely to respond. Two key paradigms of corporate giving were described, with the responsibility-oriented paradigm being shown to predominate. It was noted however that organizations that give because they view their involvement with a charity as an 'opportunity' tend to give more on average than those with a more philanthropic perspective.

The chapter concluded with an analysis of trust fundraising. A structure for planning trust fundraising was introduced, and the practicalities of fundraising from this target group were discussed.

There are thus many different categories of donor that a charity can elect to target. The appropriate balance for fundraisers to achieve among these three groups will undoubtedly depend on the size of the charity and the nature of its cause. Some categories of cause are inherently more appealing to individual donors, while others have an appeal that is perhaps more suited to the cultivation of corporate donors or charitable trusts. Whatever the balance that is most appropriate in a particular instance, there can be no substitute for a formal planned approach to the fundraising activity to be conducted.

■ DISCUSSION QUESTIONS

1. With reference to an organization of your choice, identify the key environmental influences currently acting on the fundraising function.

2. Why is it important for fundraisers to segment the donor market? What criteria might be employed for this purpose?

3. What do you understand by the term 'donor recognition programme'? Develop and outline such a programme for an organization with which you are familiar.

4. Many charities are now treating 'major' donors rather differently from those who give only small amounts to their organization. Are there any circumstances under which such a strategy would not be appropriate?

5. In your role as the fundraising director of a major charity, what advice would you offer to a junior colleague who is about to commence fundraising from grant-making trusts for the first time?

■ REFERENCES

Amato, P.R. (1985) 'An Investigation of Planned Helping Behavior', *Journal of Research in Psychology*, Vol. 19, 232–52.

Atchlet, R.C. (1987) *Ageing: Continuity and Change*, Belmont, CA, Wadsworth Publishing Company.

Bendapudi, N. and Singh, S.N. (1996) 'Enhancing Helping Behavior: An Integrative Framework for Promotion Planning', *Journal of Marketing*, Vol. 60, No. 3, 33–54.

Bennett, R. (2003) 'Factors Underlying the Inclination to Donate to Particular Types of Charity', *International Journal of Nonprofit and Voluntary Sector Marketing*, Vol. 8, No. 1, 12–29.

Berkowitz, L. (1972) 'Social Norms, Feelings and Other Factors Affecting Helping and Altruism', in *Advances in Experimental Psychology*, Berkowitz, L. (ed.), New York, Academic Press.

Boris, E.T. (1987) 'The Values of the Wealthy: Philanthropic Attitudes as a Reflection of Political Philosophy in American Culture', in *The Constitution and The Independent Sector*, Washington, DC, Independent Sector, 237–47.

Braus, P. (1994) 'Will Boomers give Generously', *American Demographics*, Vol. 16, No. 7, 48–52, 57.

Caplow, T. (1984) 'Rule Enforcement without Visible Means: Christmas Gift Giving in Middletown', *American Journal of Sociology*, Vol. 80, No. 6, 1306–23.

Fendley, A. and Hewitt, M. (1994) 'When Charity Begins with a Pitch', *Marketing*, 23 June, 14–15.

Galaradi, T. (1989) 'What may lay Ahead for DM Fundraising?', *DM News*, Vol. 11, No. 1, 92, 100.

Graney, M.J. and Graney, E.E. (1974) 'Communications Activity Substitutions in Ageing', *Journal of Communications*, Vol. 24, 88–96.

Hansler, D.F. and Riggin, D.L. (1989) Geo-Demographics: Targeting the Market, *FundRaising Management*, Vol. 20, 35–40, 43.

Hunt, A. (1986) 'Strategic Philanthropy', *Across the Board*, July/Aug, Vol. 23, 23–30.

Jas, P., Wilding, K.,Wainwright, S., Passey, A. and Hems. L. (2002) *The UK Voluntary Sector Almanac*, London, NCVO Publications.

Jones, A. and Posnett, J. (1991) 'Charitable Giving by UK Households: Evidence from the Family Expenditure Survey', *Applied Economics*, Vol. 23, 343–51.

Kelley, B. (1991) 'Cause-Related Marketing', *Sales and Sales Management*, March, 60.

Kotler, P. and Andreasen, A. (1991) *Strategic Marketing for Non-Profit Organizations*, Englewood Cliffs, NJ, Prentice Hall.

Latane, B. and Nida, S. (1981) 'Ten Years of Research on Group Size and Helping', *Psychological Bulletin*, Vol. 89, No. 2, 308–24.

Lemon, B.W., Bengtson, V.L. and Peterson, J. (1972) 'An Exploration of the Activity Theory of Ageing: Activity Types and Life Satisfaction Among In-Movers to a Retirement Community', *Journal of Gerontology*, Vol. 27, No. 4, 511–23.

Marx J.D. (2000) 'Women and Human Services Giving', *Social Work*, January, Vol. 45, No. 1, 23–31.

May, L. (1988) 'How to Build a Simple Segmentation System', *Fundraising Management*, May, 67–71, 111.

Mears, P. (1992) 'Understanding Strong Donors', *Fund Raising Management*, April, 45–8.

Mescon, T.S. and Tilson, D.J. (1987) 'Corporate Philanthropy: A Strategic Approach to the Bottom Line', *California Management Review*, Vol. 29 (Winter), 49–61.

Midlarsky, E. and Hannah, M.E. (1989) 'The Generous Elderly: Naturalistic Studies of Donations across the Life Span', *Psychology and Ageing*, Vol. 4, No. 3, 346–51.

Milliman, R.E. and Turley, L.W. (1993) 'Using Demographic Segmentation Variables to Identify Financial Donors for Mental Health Services', *Public Mental Health Marketing*, Vol. 2, No. 3, 69–73.

Moschis, G.P. (1992) *Marketing to Older Consumers*, Westport, CT, Quorum Books.

Nichols, J.E. (1991) *Targeted Fundraising*, Illinois, Precept Press.

Nichols, J.E. (1992) 'Targeting Older America', *Fund Raising Management*, Vol. 23, No. 3, 38–41.

Nichols, J.E. (1995) 'Developing Relationships with Donors', *Fundraising Management*, Vol. 18 (August), 19, 47.

Ostergard, P.M. (1994) 'Fasten Your Seat Belts', *Fundraising Management*, March, 36–8.

Pagan, L. (1994) 'Testing Out Support', *Marketing*, 12 May, 43.

Passey, A. (1995) 'Corporate Support of the UK Voluntary Sector', in CAF (1995) *Dimensions of the Voluntary Sector*, West Malling, Charities Aid Foundation, 57–61.

Penrod, S. (1983) *Social Psychology*, Englewood Cliffs, NJ, Prentice Hall.

Pifer, A. (1987) 'Philanthropy, Voluntarism and Changing Times', *Journal of the American Academy of Arts and Sciences*, Winter, 119–31.

Radley, A. and Kennedy, M. (1995) 'Charitable Giving by Individuals: A Study of Attitudes and Practice', *Human Relations*, Vol. 48, No. 6, 685–709.

Reed, D. (1998) 'Giving is Receiving', *Precision Marketing*, 9 February, 17–18.

Reykowski, J. (1982) 'Development of Prosocial Motivation', in Eisenberg N. (ed.), *The Development of Prosocial Behaviour*, New York, Academic Press, 377–93.

Richards, A. (1995) 'Does Charity Pay?', *Marketing*, 21 Sept, 24–5.

Rivlin, A. (1990) 'New Ways to Manage a Database', *Fundraising Management*, July, 33–8.

Royer, M. (1989) 'Please Give Generously, Okay?', *NSFRE Journal*, Summer, 17–20.

Sargeant, A. (1995) 'Market Segmentation in the Charity Sector—An Examination of Common Practice', *Proceedings of the MEG Annual Conference*, Bradford, July, 693–702.

Sargeant, A. (1997) 'Banishing the Battleship Ladies! The Emergence of a New Paradigm of Corporate Giving', *Proceedings, Academy of Marketing Conference*, Manchester, July, 903–16.

Sargeant, A. and Bater, K. (1997) 'Trust Fundraising—Learning to Say Thank you', *Journal of Nonprofit and Voluntary Sector Marketing*, Vol. 3, No. 2, 122–35.

Sargeant, A. and McKenzie, J. (1998) 'A Lifetime of Giving: An Analysis of Donor lifetime Value', West Malling, Charities Aid Foundation.

Sargeant, A. (1999) 'Market Segmentation—Are UK Charities Making the Most of the Potential?', *Henley Working Paper*, 03/99.

Sargeant, A. and Wymer, W. (2004) 'Understanding Giving: A New Framework for Conceptualizing Donor Behaviour', Henley Working Paper, 02/04.

Schervish, P. G. and Herman, A. (1988) *Empowerment and Beneficence: Strategies of Living and Giving Among the Wealthy*, Final Report: The Study on Wealth and Philanthropy, Presentation of findings from the Study on Wealth and Philanthropy submitted to the T.B. Murphy Foundation Charitable Trust.

Schlegelmilch, B.B. (1988) 'Targeting of Fund-Raising Appeals—How To Identify Donors', *European Journal of Marketing*, Vol. 22, No. 1, 23–42.

Schlegelmilch, B. and Tynan, C. (1989*a*) 'Market Segment Oriented Fundraising Strategies: An Empirical Analysis', *Marketing Intelligence and Planning*, Vol. 7, No. 11, 16–24.

Schlegelmilch, B. and Tynan, C. (1989*b*) 'The Scope for Market Segmentation Within The Charity Market: An Empircal Analysis', *Managerial and Decision Economics*, Vol. 10, 127–34.

Silver, M. (1980) *Affluence, Altruism and Atrophy*, New York, New York University Press.

Sterne, L. (1994) 'Giving as they Grow', *Foundation News and Commentary*, Vol. 35, No. 5, 42–3.

Stroup, M.A. and Neubert, R.L. (1987) 'The Evolution of Social Responsibility', Business Horizons, Vol. 30 (March), 22–4.

Varadarajan, P.R. and Menon, A. (1988) 'Cause-Related Marketing: A Co-alignment of Marketing Strategy and Corporate Philanthropy', *Journal of Marketing*, Vol. 52, No. 3, 58–74.

Vincent, R. (1988) 'Charity Administration: Is it Time for an Institute of Charity Trustees?', *New Law Journal*, Vol. 29 (April), 2–4.

Ward, R.A. (1977) 'The Impact of Subjective Age and Stigma on Older Persons', *Journal of Gerontology*, Vol. 32, 227–32.

Wokutch, R.E. and Spencer, B.A. (1987) 'Corporate Saints and Sinners', *California Management Review*, Vol. 29 (Winter), 72.

Yankelovich, Skelly, and White Inc. (1985) 'The Charitable Behavior of Americans', Management Survey, Washington DC, Independent Sector.

10 Arts Marketing

OBJECTIVES

By the end of this chapter you should be able to:

(1) understand the contribution that marketing can make to the development of the arts;

(2) categorize and profile arts audiences for a variety of different events;

(3) understand how data mining techniques and customer relationship management (CRM) tools can be employed within a box office database to facilitate the achievement of arts marketing objectives;

(4) describe the arts funding framework and appreciate the role of marketing in securing funding from statutory and corporate sources.

Introduction

It is the purpose of this chapter to explore many of the key issues currently of relevance to marketing in the arts sector. To achieve this, the chapter is divided into two major components. In the first, the relevance of marketing will be explored to the issue of audience development. The text will examine the available audience research and use this as the basis for a discussion of the formulation of appropriate marketing strategy, before moving on to consider the utility that might be offered in the completion of this task by the box office database and the use of data mining and CRM tools. The second component of the chapter considers marketing's application to the attraction of funding. In particular its relevance to securing both statutory funding and corporate sponsorship will be examined. The chapter will begin by exploring the nature of arts marketing and how its application may differ from that observed in other parts of the nonprofit sector.

Defining the Arts

It is important to begin this section by defining what we understand by the term 'arts'. For the purposes of this text, the definition first provided by the 810th US

Congress (and later adopted by the Arts Council in the UK) will be employed, namely:

The term "the arts" includes, but is not limited to, music (instrumental and vocal), dance, drama, folk art, creative writing, architecture and allied fields, painting, sculpture, photography, graphic and craft arts, industrial design, costume and fashion design, motion pictures, television, radio, tape and sound recording, the arts related to the presentation, performance, execution and exhibition of such major art forms, and the study and application of the arts to the human environment. (ACGB 1993)

Thus the term 'arts marketing' can be considered as embracing a wide variety of human endeavours, many of which are nonprofit-making in nature. While the focus of this text is quite clearly nonprofit, many of the ideas that will be presented here will be equally applicable to all arts organizations, whether they are profit-making or not. Indeed, whatever the goals of a particular organization, managed wisely they are all capable of making a substantial contribution to the health of the society in which they operate. The arts form an integral part of the fabric of the world in which we live. They help define the origin of societies across the globe and they legitimize and give meaning to a whole range of intellectual and individual feelings and ideas. They therefore offer opportunities for expression and personal fulfilment in a way unrivalled by any other facet of society.

In looking to market the arts, one therefore has to be sensitive to the nature of the 'product' in a way that is unparalleled in the realm of most consumer goods and services. In no other context does one have to be so sensitive to the need to preserve the essence of what is being marketed, even if from a commercial standpoint the restrictions that this imposes may be a recipe for 'failure'. Many arts organizations continue to provide access to material that is likely to appeal to only a very small segment of society. Indeed, still others may support new and emerging art forms for which an audience has yet to develop. They undertake these endeavours because they strongly believe in the merit of what they are doing and the contribution it will make to society in the medium- to long term.

Despite a plethora of changes in funding frameworks and philosophical arguments about the legitimacy of many forms of art, the arts sectors in most Western societies continue to experience growth. In the USA, following the birth of the first official federal arts agency, the National Endowment for the Arts (NEA) in 1965, the number of arts organizations increased almost exponentially over just a few years. The number of symphony orchestras went from 110 to 230, nonprofit theatres from 56 to 420, dance companies from 37 to 450, and opera companies from 27 to 120 (Reiss 1994).

A similar pattern has emerged in the UK where there has also been a proliferation of arts organizations, the majority of which may be said to be nonprofit-making in nature. While this growth is undoubtedly to be commended, it is important to realize that government funding for the arts has in many countries (including the UK) declined in real terms. This has put pressure on fledgling arts organizations to become self-sufficient at an early stage through the attraction of ever larger audiences. Against this backdrop, the reader could be forgiven for imagining that historically the marketing concept has been warmly embraced by arts professionals. The reader would be mistaken!

Why the Reticence?

It is fair to say that arts organizations have lagged some way behind most other categories of nonprofit in recognizing the utility of the marketing concept. Even as recently as ten years ago, in some arts circles one would have been severely chastised for even daring to mention the word marketing. Why should this be so? Why should arts organizations have been so reticent in accepting the need to market their services and products?

To answer this question, it is necessary to return to a point made in the first chapter of this text. It should be remembered that many organizations in the not-for-profit sector continue to equate marketing with selling, and feel that such techniques cheapen the work that they are involved with. The same views have been held, perhaps even more acutely, by arts managers, who feel that their productions should somehow be above the need for any form of commercial approach. As Diggle (1984: 18) puts it, there was a 'religious school of thought that held art to be sacred, that audiences were made by God and any attempt to improve their sizes was profanity'.

What was particularly interesting about this school of thought was that it tended to originate from artists in search of a living, or artistic directors who never bothered to consider the nature of the potential audience until the opening night and who then wondered why their auditorium was half-empty! Of course it would be too simplistic to suggest that it is possible to apply blindly marketing tools and techniques to the arts product without any form of modification. In the arts sector there are a number of 'balances' that must be struck between the view of the arts that suggests that they have inherent worth and are worth preserving at all costs and the view that suggests that the arts, like any other form of human activity, should be forced to 'pay their own way' and that a consideration of likely audiences should therefore be paramount. This idea of balance needs to be examined in relation to performances, portrayal, and audience.

Balance in Performance

Examining first the question of the art forms or performances that should be made available to society, it seems clear that there is an inherent conflict here between the marketing concept on the one hand and the whole ethos of the arts on the other. Should arts organizations start with a thorough analysis of what their potential audiences are likely to want and then build into their programmes a mix of all the art forms desired, or should they steadfastly continue to produce art forms that they believe would be good for the society they serve, irrespective of the level of demand that will be forthcoming? Mokwa et al. (1980: 6) hold to the former view: 'Most might deny that the arts have lived too long in a world comprised of faith, hope, and charity—the quicksand of the arts. Faith—that the arts have values, Hope—that someone will recognize the values and come to view them, Charity—that someone will pay for them (and) absorb the deficits. The faith is valid and must be kept, but the hope is of a blind nature and the charity is not forthcoming as it is needed.'

Searles (1980: 610), however, supports the latter view: 'If the audience were to decide, our arts world would become narrower and narrower and increasingly sterile. All of us need to be pulled, pushed, or even thrown into new artistic experiences. This part of life—the content and makeup of the US arts world—is simply too important to be entrusted to the non-artist.'

Without the creative freedom to explore new art forms, creative teams will be incapable of enriching the society in which they work, yet without the income that the more popular art forms are capable of generating, individual arts organizations may simply fail to survive. There is clearly, therefore, a need to reconcile these two extremes of opinion and to strike some form of balance between the preferences of audiences on the one hand and the needs of those producing the arts on the other. To quote Diggle (1984: 23): 'The whole art of programming for an arts organization is based on a sensitive appreciation of who the market is, what it wants now *and what it may be persuaded to want in the future* and the relating of those perceptions to what the organization is capable of delivering.'

It would be foolish for any arts organization, no matter how pure its ideals; to completely neglect the current needs of potential audiences. Given the current funding constraints facing the sector, it is simply not realistic to design a comprehensive arts programme without recognizing the need to achieve a balance between those activities that are likely to generate a surplus and those that are likely to make a loss. Only by satisfying current audience desires can an arts organization achieve an adequate revenue stream to support the equally worthwhile fringe activities for which large audiences do simply not exist. Moreover, if audiences can be encouraged to attend a venue to view a more 'popular' art form, it may be possible to persuade a number of them to return to sample other, perhaps more obscure, forms of art. The adoption of such a strategy therefore guarantees that the organization will have sufficient revenue to support less popular art forms and that as wide an audience as possible can be encouraged to view them. The facilitation of this process is the real contribution that marketing can make to the sector.

Of course, marketing still has to fight for the right to make this contribution, and there are often healthy debates in many organizations between the artistic and marketing directors, each of whom approaches the design of the next portfolio from a radically different perspective. As Keith Cooper, the first director of public affairs and marketing at the Royal Opera House, put it: 'Art and commerce have not been happy bedfellows. If we were to be completely commercial I might have to say to the opera director: "We can only do the popular productions, we can't do the modern works because they don't sell so many seats". Of course I don't say that because it doesn't get me anywhere' (Ford 1993).

Despite the difficulties, there are many examples of organizations that have successfully achieved this balance in performance. The Kooemba Jdarra Theatre Company is one such organization, where marketing has successfully integrated the needs of customers with the needs of its contemporary performers.

CASE STUDY 10.1

Kooemba Jdarra Theatre Company

Based in Brisbane, Australia, Kooemba Jdarra Theatre Company is dedicated to developing and pro-ducing contemporary performances that present the stories of Aboriginal and Torres Strait Islander Queenslanders (Figure 10.1). Since its incorporation in 1993, the company has maintained a strong commitment to professionalism and excellence in the arts.

Figure 10.1 A Kooemba Jdarra Theatre Company production
Source: © Kooemba Jdarra Theatre Company 2004. Reproduced by kind permission.

Kooemba Jdarra is recognized by its peers as the major developer and producer of contemporary Indigenous Australian texts and has enjoyed many successes in the areas of: community workshops held throughout the state; community festivals and celebrations; the development and production of over 22 new Indigenous texts and inter, intra-state and international tours of its work.

Although enjoying a strong, consistent, artistic record, Kooemba Jdarra had reached a plateau in the development of new audiences for its product. In 2001 Kooemba's strategic planning incorporated a strong marketing focus in order to address this lack of growth. A permanent marketing position was created and an integrated marketing and communications approach was adopted for all of Kooemba's activities, including the development of new products.

Many arts organizations would avidly resist the concept of audience needs dictating the develop-ment of products. However, Kooemba, whose cultural roots are firmly embedded in more than 60 000 years of history, embraced the possibilities that a marketing approach could contribute to the cre-ativity, vibrancy, and maintenance of Indigenous Australian culture. At the same time the company

continues

remained committed to ensuring a strong focus on artistic and cultural integrity within this marketing approach.

Examples of recent productions developed for specific market segments include *Piccaninni Dreaming* and *Yarnin Up*. *Piccaninni Dreaming* was specifically developed to deliver a culturally appropriate performance for the primary school education market, while *Yarnin' Up* was developed as a product suitable for touring to regional and remote Indigenous communities throughout Western Australia, the Northern Territory, and Queensland.

To augment its marketing approach for the development of product, Kooemba Jdarra stringently undertook a variety of market research strategies to engage with audiences in order to assess the success of its productions. Focus groups, direct mail surveys, telephone surveys, and exit surveys have been employed to ascertain both the number of audience members engaged in viewing Kooemba's performances, and the level of success of that engagement. A useful by-product of this research has been the collection of valuable data on Kooemba, which supports the company's activities in the areas of lobbying and advocacy.

Kooemba's strong cultural responsibility for the incorporation of community participation and a history of valuing community opinion diverts the focus of the company from one of individual artistic vision to one of collective community vision. This collective vision, coupled with a culture unencumbered by embedded Western theatre protocols, provides freedom for Kooemba to develop a new form of creativity within its management. It is perhaps this freedom that allows marketing to be perceived as a valuable tool in the development of cultural product, rather than being perceived as a dangerous step into the world of commercialization. The irony is that one of the most contemporary Western business approaches is being embraced by, and successfully serving the needs of, one of the world's oldest cultures.

Case study authored by Vera Ding: Reproduced by kind permission of the author.

Balance in Portrayal

Aside from the need to achieve a balance in terms of the arts forms supported, there is often a need to decide on the extent to which an organization is prepared to 'exploit' art for commercial purposes. Just how far should our arts bodies go, for example, in popularizing artistic work to make it more accessible? Many museums, for example, have altered the way in which they present their exhibits in a bid to open up their artefacts to a wider audience. As a consequence, many larger museums now offer displays that have much in common with theme parks. There are interactive displays, videos, special effects, and a whole new range of promotional merchandise, including children's toys and cheap replicas of historic artefacts. While no-one can deny that this has had the desired effect in terms of encouraging larger numbers of the public to view, there are legitimate concerns that in presenting art in this way, one is actually degrading it. Consumers have simply been encouraged to collect momentary experiences without any real reflection, and to move hurriedly from one 'fix' of culture to another. As Strehler (1990: 211) comments: 'Reducing the presentation of an artistic work to instantaneous, consumable entertainment is consistent with the undeniable needs of the consumers, but misses the primary cultural purpose of revealing its deeper causes.'

In short, something of the original experience that the artist intended is lost in the drive to popularization. It is for individual arts organizations to decide how far they are willing to permit this to happen and to reach some form of balance.

Balance in Audience

The third 'balance' is arguably the most difficult to achieve. As will shortly be demonstrated, the mission of many arts organizations requires them to expand the potential audience for their offerings with almost missionary zeal. Indeed, many of the traditional sources of funding for arts activities require that a substantial amount of development work be undertaken to ensure that 'non-standard' audiences are encouraged to attend. Historically this has proven to be problematic, as certain groups within society appear to be openly hostile to much arts-related activity. In an attempt to change attitudes, organizations have had to commit valuable marketing resource to the cause and as a result have perhaps neglected their existing core audience. Mokwa et al. (1980: 10) phrases this more eloquently, narrating a story of a ship lost at sea for weeks:

... its crew dying of thirst because of no fresh water. Finally, sighting another vessel, the thirsty captain signalled: 'Water, water ... dying of thirst!' The other ship signalled back: 'Cast down your bucket where you are.' Thinking he was misunderstood, the first captain repeated: 'Water, water ... send us water!' 'Cast down your bucket where you are,' came the response again. The same messages were repeated again before the first captain thought to cast down his bucket. It came up full of fresh drinkable water. Although adrift on the ocean, the ship was in a sea of fresh water forming the nearly shoreless mouth of the Amazon River.

The moral of the tale, according to the authors, is that arts administrators tend to continue to look elsewhere for their help, rather than exploiting the potential close to home. Arts organizations need to strike a balance between prospecting for new audiences and looking after and cultivating their existing ones. If properly developed, this latter segment can generate much revenue that can in turn be redirected to the task of encouraging other, more reticent, segments of society to attend as well.

The Vicious Circle

The achievement of an appropriate balance in each of the areas alluded to above continues, however, to evade many organizations and has therefore contributed substantially to marketing's delay in gaining acceptance within the sector. Indeed, even where a role for marketing has been recognized, the level of resources organizations are prepared to commit to the task is often pathetically inadequate. This in turn leads to patterns of performance that fail to meet expectations and a general air of, 'Well, I told you marketing wouldn't work, didn't I!' As long ago as 1991, Marketing the Arts Nationally and Regionally (MANAR) recognized this problem, describing it as a 'vicious circle'. It is illustrated in Figure 10.2.

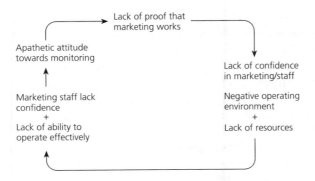

Figure 10.2 The vicious circle

Source: © MANAR 2004.

The circle can be viewed as beginning with a lack of resources being applied to the marketing task. This in turn leads to staff being unable to market the organization effectively, which in turn gives rise to a lack of confidence on the part of the relevant personnel. Since staff no longer feel they can make a difference to the enhancement of their organization, they are perhaps less than enthusiastic about monitoring their efforts. Without effective monitoring, there is no evidence to offer senior management that marketing activity is worthwhile and they become increasingly sceptical about both the abilities of their marketing staff to deliver and the desirability of investing valuable income in that area. As a consequence, inadequate resources continue to be made available and the whole process becomes self-perpetuating.

Of course, one could also become trapped in the circle by virtue of the cultural hostility that might exist towards the marketing function. Without the commitment of senior management to the marketing function, perhaps because of the misconceptions alluded to above, adequate resources will never be made available. This is to be regretted since the quality of marketing undertaken by an arts organization has recently taken on a new significance. As will be shown later, the criteria applied by the UK's major arts funding bodies require potential applicants to demonstrate their expertise in this area. Marketing can therefore no longer be avoided.

The Arts Audience

There has been relatively little academic research conducted to date on the analysis and segmentation of arts audiences. Much of the data that is available is unpublished, of dubious quality, or highly focused on a small group of broad demographic variables. This is to be regretted, since an understanding of the type of person who attends specific types of arts events, and their motivations for so doing, will allow an organization to develop a targeted marketing plan that will reach the prospective audience cost-effectively and with the message that they will find most persuasive (Reiss 1994). As the reader will appreciate from the previous chapter, arts organizations also need to be clear that it should be possible to segment both the market for non-attenders (who may require specific types of recruitment activity) and the market for existing attenders (who may require specific forms of development). In the case of the latter category Ashbrand (1993) reports that the McCarter Theater in Princeton, New Jersey, has been able both to increase its cash flow and achieve a 20 per cent rise in subscription sales by installing software that enables the theatre management to target shows at individuals they know have an interest in that particular art form. Communications can hence be specifically tailored to the needs of individual groups within the overall customer database. Moreover, relationships can be built and maintained with those individuals who are worth the most to the arts organization by virtue of their frequent attendance.

A review of the available research in respect of arts audiences will therefore be instructive and help suggest how an arts organization might attract and develop the potential audience for its own specific services. Moreover, the review should also highlight those audience characteristics that may be deemed to be most important and hence key to the design of an appropriate box-office database, a subject that will be developed more fully later.

Audience research may broadly be divided into the following three categories:

1. studies that delineate specific segments of arts attenders
2. studies that examine the motivation of arts attenders
3. studies that attempt to profile and categorize non-attenders.

Each of these key groups will now be examined in turn.

Segmenting Arts Attenders

Given the great diversity in art forms, there is a clear potential to segment the market for different categories thereof. Most 'high' art forms, for example, tend to appeal to individuals who have higher levels of education and income than the majority of the population (Useem and DiMaggio 1978). It is also the case that a significantly higher proportion of professional people attend art forms such as the theatre, concerts, or the opera. These findings have been demonstrated by a number of studies in the USA and in the UK and have also been verified by the BMRB (British Market Research Bureau). This latter source of information in respect of audience profiles can be a useful starting point for marketers looking to define a market for the first time. Other commercially available sources of information such as Mintel or Keynote can also prove useful in defining, at least in general terms, what a potential audience might look like.

Useful though this preliminary investigation of arts audiences might be, the reader will recall from the preceding chapter that within the broad spectrum of individuals who might be predisposed to attending a particular category of event, there might be further sub-segments, many of which may be worth exploiting with a separate marketing mix. As an example, Seminik and Young (1979) studied the potential to segment arts audiences utilizing data gathered from a survey of patrons of two large opera companies. The authors concluded that three distinct segments of attender existed:

(1) *Season ticket subscribers* (73.8 per cent of the sample). These individuals rely for their information about performances on direct mailings from the opera companies themselves. Members of this segment tend to be older, from higher socio-economic groups and have a higher degree of education than the other two segments. Season ticket subscribers attend the opera because they view themselves as fans.

(2) *Infrequent attenders* (11.6 per cent of the sample). These individuals rely for information about performances on word-of-mouth recommendation from friends and acquaintances. They do not regard themselves as 'fans' in the same way as season ticket subscribers, and will attend only if a big name star is performing.

(3) *Non-subscribing frequent attenders* (14.6 per cent of the sample). These individuals also rely on word-of-mouth recommendations for information. This group also regards itself as being a general fan of the opera, but is younger and less well educated than the season ticket subscriber segment.

These findings are important in so far as they suggest that an arts organization could draw a distinction between each category and apply a mix of attraction and retention activities to each. This idea is illustrated in Figure 10.3.

Subscribers are clearly committed to attendance at a particular venue. They are likely to have the most frequent pattern of attendance and be worth a significant sum of money to an arts organization over the duration of their relationship with it. The loss of even a small percentage of the members of this segment per annum will therefore result in a significant drop in revenue. It is therefore important that considerable effort is expended in keeping this segment loyal. As they are already enthusiastic about the arts 'product', they do not need to be 're-convinced' of its merits. Instead the focus with this group should be in establishing and building a meaningful relationship that builds loyalty and keeps retention rates high.

Non-subscribing frequent attenders are somewhat more problematic. Evidence suggests that this segment will attend a very wide variety of different categories of event

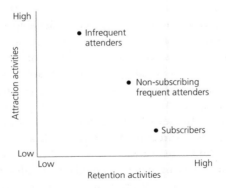

Figure 10.3 A classification of arts consumers

and it may be difficult to build loyalty in the face of competition from other venues perceived as of equal value. A mix of attraction and retention activities might hence be more appropriate.

Infrequent attenders are likely to have to be convinced of the 'need' to attend specific events and the focus with this category will hence lie in attraction. They will therefore need to be informed of the merits of a particular performance, why it represents a particular opportunity, and the status of the 'star' who is performing. Efforts to develop this group further are likely to be futile since they will tend only to attend performances that are perceived as in some way unique. It is interesting to note that many arts managers would disagree with this assessment, arguing that infrequent attenders could be developed over time and eventually become subscribers. There is no evidence, however, that this is the case. Ryans and Weinberg (1978) in a five-year study of theatre audiences, attempted to verify their hypothesis that an entry pattern to subscriptions existed. The researchers felt that subscribers would begin as single ticket buyers, progress to the purchase of several tickets in a season, and then ultimately become a season ticket holder. They found, quite surprisingly, that there was a high incidence of sudden subscribers (those who subscribed without attending previously) and were hence forced to conclude that their perception of an entry pattern to the arts was invalid.

Additional studies that have examined attendance patterns at other forms of arts events have derived similar findings to those given above. Importantly, Kaali-Nagy and Garrison (1972) were among the first to recognize that the Pareto principle can be applied equally well to arts audiences and, in their study of the Los Angeles Music Center, found that 10 per cent of patrons accounted for nearly 45 per cent of the attendance pattern of their sample. The authors thus concluded that a relatively small number of people constituted the core of the Center's audience. Importantly these findings have been replicated at other venues and indeed in other countries (see for example Sargeant 1997).

Businesses will be familiar with the Pareto rule and will ensure that they expend considerable effort on those customers who generate the majority of their income. The same does not yet seem to apply to arts organizations, though, especially theatres. If there are certain segments of society that may be deemed regular attenders of arts events, these segments should surely be the focus of considerable effort. Such segments are by their very nature the easiest to encourage to attend and may hence be readily developed over time. Indeed Dawson (1980: 7) identified what he saw as a paradox in arts management, namely that of 'the missionary effort (taking place) to develop arts audiences from those marginally interested and the near exclusion of effort to develop the fullest possible response from that segment of society most likely to support the arts.'

This latter point is worthy of some elaboration since many arts organizations continue to fail to recognize the need to focus on those customers who are potentially worth the most to their organization. After all, a customer who spends £500 a year with an organization is certainly worth more than a customer who spends only £5 over the same period. Many die-hard artistic directors may regard this as heresy, but they would be wrong to do so! It is important to realize that a careful cultivation of high-worth customers can yield valuable revenue that can then be applied meaningfully to the more missionary aspects of an organization's work. In short, marketing does not mean the abandonment of artistic values, but can actually enrich them.

Audience Motivation

The second important category of research into arts audiences concerns an examination of their motivations for attendance. An understanding of why people attend and what

---

Questionnaire

1. Are You
☐ Male   ☐ Female

2. Year of Birth _____

3. Are you presently
☐ In full-time employment
☐ In part-time employment
☐ Retired
☐ Housewife
☐ Other

4. Are you
☐ Single
☐ Married
☐ Other

5. How many people are there in your household? _____

6. Do you have children living with you at home?
☐ Yes   ☐ No

If yes, how many? _____

What are their ages? _____   _____   _____   _____   _____   _____

7. What are your hobbies and interests?
_____
_____
_____
_____

8. What is/was your main occupation? _____

9. At what age did you complete your full-time education?
☐ Aged 16 or younger
☐ Aged 17/18
☐ Aged 18/20
☐ Aged 21+

Figure 10.4 Theatre audience questionnaire

10. How likely are you to attend any of the following categories of performance at the XYZ theatre? Please indicate your level of interest using the following scale.

1 = Not at all likely
2 = Not very likely
3 = No opinion/neutral
4 = Somewhat likely
5 = Very likely

Category of Performance	Likelihood of Attendance				
	1	2	3	4	5
Classic Plays					
New Plays					
Comedies					
Musical Comedies					
Dance					
Ballet					
Other (Please Specify) _____					

11. When you attend the theatre, how important are each of the following factors in influencing your selection of which theatre to attend? Please use the following scale to select your response.

1 = Not at all important
2 = Not very important
3 = No opinion/neutral
4 = Important
5 = Very important

Factor	Importance				
	1	2	3	4	5
Category/Type of Performance					
Reputation of Performers					
Presence of a ÔBig NameÕ					
Cost of Tickets					
Ease of Booking					
Presence of a Bar					
Cleanliness of the Theatre					
Comfort of the Seating					

12. On how many occasions would you attend the theatre in a typical year? _____

13. For what reason do you normally attend the theatre? Please tick any boxes that apply.

☐ To Socialize with Friends and Relatives   ☐ To Enjoy a Night Out
☐ To Celebrate a Special Occasion   ☐ I Enjoy Attending Arts Events
☐ To Learn Something   ☐ Other (Please Specify) _____

Figure 10.4 (*Continued*)

14. To what extent would each of the following factors be likely to encourage you to attend the theatre more often?

Factor	Would Encourage More Regular Attendance	Would Not Encourage More Regular Attendance	No Opinion/ Unsure
Lower Prices			
Easier Booking Facilities			
Availability of a Season Ticket			
Early Booking Facility			
Availability of Discounts			
Better Range of Performances			
Other (Please Specify) _____			

15. How likely are you to attend any of the arts venues listed below during the next 12 months? Please use the following scale for your reply.

1 = Not at all likely
2 = Not very likely
3 = No opinion/neutral
4 = Somewhat likely
5 = Very likely

Venue	Likelihood of Attendance				
	1	2	3	4	5
Museums					
Concerts					
Art Gallery					
Cinema					
Arts Centre					

Figure 10.4 (*Continued*)

features they will be looking for in an arts event can greatly aid marketing planning, since the 'product' can be carefully adapted to the target market and promotional messages can reflect the themes that a particular audience is likely to find most appealing. Valuable though this data might be, however, comparatively few arts organizations are likely to have access to it, and there are only a few secondary studies available for consultation. If this form of data is required therefore there may be no alternative but to conduct primary research.

Usually such research will either take the form of focus groups or questionnaires (both these forms of research are discussed fully in Chapter 4). An excerpt from a postal questionnaire that was employed to profile theatre audiences in the South-West of England is given in Figure 10.4.

The use of even a simple questionnaire such as the one illustrated in Figure 10.4 can pay enormous dividends for an arts organization. Demographic data from Questions 1–6 can be cross-tabulated with the responses to Question 10 to yield a profile of those most likely to attend a particular category of event. Moreover, data from Question 12 can also be of value in allowing the researcher to profile more frequent attenders for the purposes described in the previous section.

For our purposes, however, we are now interested in ascertaining whether a particular series of motivations might exist for attending the theatre. At a simplistic level we could simply examine the pattern of responses to Question 13, but this would tell us little about how these motivations might vary between different categories of individual, and this latter information is essential for the derivation of a meaningful communications campaign. Fortunately, however, there are a variety of statistical techniques that can be used to help facilitate a more sophisticated level of analysis. One of the more useful, but often-neglected, forms of analysis is cluster analysis. An example of its application is given in the case study below.

CASE STUDY 10.2

In Search of the Socialite

This case reports the results of theatre audience research conducted in the South-West of England. A similar questionnaire to that illustrated in Figure 10.4 was administered to 500 known theatre-goers in an attempt to identify whether specific segments of theatre audience existed, each of which might have differing motivations for its pattern of attendance. The technique of cluster analysis was therefore selected, as this allows the market researcher to identify potential market segments among the total group of individuals who respond (in this case) to a questionnaire. The cluster analysis algorithm begins by searching the dataset for those two individuals who answered the questionnaire most alike, and pairs off these two individuals. It then looks for the next two most similar patterns of responses and pairs these two individuals off. As the programme works through the dataset, it continues to look for the next closest match in terms of the pattern of responses. This may involve paring off two more individuals, matching one individual to one of the newly created pairings, or even creating groups of 4, 8, 16, etc. as appropriate. This 'matching up' process continues until all the respondents are finally reunited in one large mass. Consider the example shown in Figure 10.5. In this case there are only eight respondents to a questionnaire that we wish to analyse.

The analysis proceeds as described above from Stage 1 where only individual responses exist to Stage 8 where they are all combined as one group. While in itself this might appear a fruitless task, the algorithm helpfully records the level of difference that is being combined at each stage. Between Stage 1 and Stage 2 it is comparatively easy to find respondents who have given almost identical responses to the questionnaire. Between Stages 5 and 6, it remains comparatively easy, but within each group of individuals there is almost certainly now an element of variation in the pattern of responses (a difference of opinion!). Between Stages 7 and 8 this variation will undoubtedly be more pronounced as individuals with increasingly divergent responses are combined into the same group.

The trick in using this technique is to examine the measures of difference at each stage in the process and when the amount of difference between the individuals within a group jumps sharply, to recognize that the pattern of responses within a new pairing is no longer coherent. In plain English, one has to recognize when oranges begin to be combined with bananas! If, for example, the amount of difference

_____ continues

CASE STUDY 10.2 continued

measured in the responses within each group is seen to jump sharply between Stages 6 and 7, the researcher would recognize that there would appear to be three distinct segments of respondents among the eight individuals analysed. Any attempt to further reduce the number of segments to two would be inappropriate since the software then begins to combine into one group: individuals who are not alike at all. Ideally the amount of difference in response within a segment should be as small as possible, and the amount of difference between the segments as large as possible. In our example a three-cluster solution is thus recommended—Segment 1 containing respondents 1, 2, 3, 4, and 5, Segment 2 containing only respondent 6, and Segment 3 containing respondents 7 and 8. In reality, the number of respondents would have to be much greater for the analysis to be meaningful, and a segment containing only a few respondents would normally be discounted, but the example serves to illustrate how the clustering algorithm works.

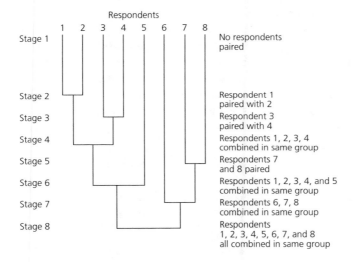

Figure 10.5 The process of cluster analysis

In an effort to make this clearer, examine for a moment Table 10.1. The table contains the results of the cluster analysis conducted on the theatre-goers in the South-West of England. Having performed the cluster analysis, it appeared that three distinct groups of customers existed. The table presents the typical answer of each segment to each of the questions contained in the original questionnaire.

continues

CASE STUDY 10.2 continued

Table 10.1 Cluster profile of theatre-goers in south-west England

Variable	Cluster 1	Cluster 2	Cluster 3
Demographics			
Education	16–18	16	21+
Age of children at home	Even distribution	Parents—younger children 11–20	Even distribution
Age	Predominantly younger (35 and under)	Predominantly middle aged (36–45)	Older (46+)
Marital status	Single	Married	Even distribution
Gender	Even distribution	Even distribution	Even distribution
Preferred performance type			
Dance	Very likely	Neutral	Somewhat likely
New play	Somewhat likely	Somewhat likely	Very likely
Drama	Somewhat likely	Neutral	Very likely
Ballet	Somewhat likely	Not at all likely	Not very likely
Classic plays	Somewhat likely	Neutral	Very likely
Musical comedy	Even distribution	Very likely	Not at all likely
Comedies	Neutral	Neutral	Neutral
Other arts venues attended			
Art gallery	Very likely	Not very likely	Likely
Cinema	Very likely	Unlikely	Neutral
Concerts	Somewhat likely	Neutral	Very likely
Museums	Neutral	Neutral	Neutral
Facilities Required			
Bar	Neutral	Neutral	Very important
Ease of booking	Neutral	Neutral	Important
Cleanliness of theatre	Important	Important	Neutral
Comfort of seating	Important	Important	Fairly important
Factors capable of encouraging attendance			
Lower price	No	Neutral	Yes
Ease of ordering	Yes	No	Yes
Purchase of a season ticket	Yes	No	No
Ticket availability guaranteed	Neutral	No	No
Early booking	Neutral	No	Neutral
Availability of discounts	Neutral	Neutral	Yes
Better range of performances	Neutral	Neutral	Neutral
Attendance pattern			
Frequency of attendance	Medium	Low	High
Segment size			
Percentage of total	27%	24%	49%

continues

CASE STUDY 10.2 continued

Table 10.2 Reasons for audience attendance at theatre events

Reason	Segment 1 (%)	Segment 2 (%)	Segment 3 (%)
To socialize with friends and relatives	28	63	56
To celebrate a special occasion	38	75	48
To learn something	45	27	43
A night out	43	50	26
Enjoy arts events	52	20	25

Note: Please note that the column totals do not add up to 100% since respondents were asked to tick any reasons that they felt applied.

Importantly, motivations for attending the theatre were also found to vary quite considerably between the segments identified. Table 10.2 contains the details.

Armed with this information, it is then possible to proceed to naming each segment. In this case, the categories of Nouveau Sophisticats, Blue Mooners, and Ageing Socialites suggested themselves. A brief profile of each segment is given below.

1. Nouveau Sophisticats (27 per cent of the total population)

The youngest of the three segments, it comprises young adults, many of whom may still be in full-time education. Of the three segments, this is the most likely to be single and committed to attendance at a wide range of different arts events. Members have an interest in most forms of art and would potentially consider viewing any type of performance at their local theatre.

They require few additional facilities from the theatre but expect the accommodation to be clean and comfortable. Given that people in this segment appear committed to the arts in general, they are less susceptible to price than other groups and are more likely to consider the purchase of a season ticket as a positive means of encouraging them to attend on a regular basis. It may also be the case that this segment are less susceptible to price than other segments because they already attract substantial discounts. Many theatres are, for example, willing to offer a discount on performances for those still in full-time education.

Implications for Marketing

This group is possibly the easiest to target since they are regular attenders at arts events, and leaflets distributed at other arts venues may well attract this audience. As members of this group are committed to the arts, promotional messages must surely concentrate on raising awareness of the scope and range of events available locally. Advertising themes such as product quality, variety, pleasant surroundings, aesthetics, and the theatre's facilities may be particularly appropriate.

2. Blue Mooners (24 per cent of the total population)

The least well-educated segment, blue mooners are so named because they are only infrequent attenders (i.e. they attend only 'once in a blue moon'.) They are likely to be married couples, possibly with teenage children, who view a trip to the theatre as a special occasion. They do not appear to be committed to a wide range of art forms and prefer to see only a limited number of types of performance at their local theatre. In particular, they are likely to attend musical comedies and modern

continues

plays. They share with Nouveau Sophisticats a need for few additional features in the theatre itself but do require clean and comfortable surroundings. This is to be expected, given the motivation of this segment for attendance at a theatrical performance. Blue Mooners are also less susceptible than other groups to any promotional method that might be aimed at encouraging them to attend on a more regular basis. Clearly there is little demand in this segment for the theatrical product except for a special occasion and this is reflected in the fact that this segment exhibits the lowest attendance rate (i.e. once a year or less).

Implications for Marketing

This is potentially the most difficult segment to motivate to attend on a more regular basis and indeed the research suggests that promotional methods aimed at persuading this group to attend more frequently will largely be ineffective. Clearly theatre management will want to make every effort to develop this segment into more frequent attenders by providing an experience of memorable quality that the individual will consider worthy of repeating. However, given that many individuals in this segment will make their purchase decision quite late and do not see early booking as an advantage, it seems probable that advertisements in local press and local radio may be most appropriate (research suggests that radio advertisements are particularly well suited to enhancing theatre audiences as the date of performance draws near).

3. Ageing Socialites (49 per cent of the population)

The oldest segment (predominantly aged over 45), Ageing Socialites have a particular interest in all types of play and would also consider viewing other related art forms such as concerts, ballet, and dance. They appear, however, not to be so interested in the various forms of comedy.

The primary motivation of this group is to share in a social occasion and hence the presence of a bar is particularly important so they can share a drink during the performance. Theatre attendance clearly forms an integral part of their social life and this is reflected in the fact that they exhibit a higher rate of attendance than members of the other two segments. The exact nature of the performance seems less important to this group, who instead cite price, discounts, and ease of ordering as being among the most important factors that might influence their decision to attend.

Implications for Marketing

Members of this group are clearly motivated by the social aspects of an evening's performance and successful promotional messages will reflect this. The theatre could also emphasize the facilities it has to offer and suggest how these can enhance the social value of the evening. Potential themes include service, comfort, ease, enjoyment, attention, entertainment, friendship, status, leisure, etc. In terms of marketing strategy, an evening at the theatre could be repositioned as a venue through which individuals could meet and socialize. Promotional brochures and leaflets could be changed to reflect the social exchange that many individuals seem to require, and illustrations of artwork related to each performance or photographs of the performers themselves might be supplemented (or replaced by), pictures of patrons relaxing in the bar and being seen to enjoy themselves. If it is the interaction that is important to the largest percentage of the audience, then such a theme should at the very least feature in a season's brochure.

It is worth emphasizing this latter point. If this segment is worth the most to an arts organization, it logically follows that the organization would wish to demonstrate periodically that it is capable of meeting their needs. An emphasis on the social aspects of an evening's entertainment could hence pay

continues

dividends in encouraging more frequent attendance. It is also worth noting that the senior socialite segment has a high propensity to attend a variety of events on an extremely frequent basis. This suggests that many arts organizations would gain considerable utility from cooperation in the form of list-sharing. It would appear that the highest-value customers will likely also be the highest-value customers of other related arts organizations.

The idea developed in the case that the social aspects of attendance at an arts event are important is not without support in the literature. In an interesting study of attendance at live musical events, Levy et al. (1980) conducted a series of in-depth interviews with middle-class music lovers. The authors found that audiences tended to prefer this type of event because of the perceived immediacy and involvement in the creative process. The social aspect of attendance was also found to be important, although in the case of what the authors call 'high culture' events (such as opera), this manifested itself quite formally, perhaps through the inclusion of a dinner, or a meeting with friends in the interval, in the plan for the evening as a whole. In the case of rock concerts, the social aspects were equally important but rather less formal—including travelling with friends to the event, and smoking, drinking, and eating together at the event.

Clearly the exact relevance of the social aspect of the entertainment will vary between one category of the arts and another. The key point for marketers to recognize is that this social component exists and can be extremely important to an audience. Thus, if carefully cultivated it can pay enormous dividends.

Non-attenders

Mention has already been made of the need for many arts organizations to broaden their appeal through societal groups that would not normally consider attending an arts event. Indeed the ability to be able to attract non-traditional audiences may be a requirement for the attraction of funding. Identifying and categorizing non-users can therefore be of equal utility to an arts organization, since different forms of non-user may prove susceptible to different forms of approach in an attempt to persuade them to sample the arts for the first time. Diggle (1984) makes a particularly strong argument for this approach in recognition of the fact that many arts organizations have a mission to develop audiences across as wide a spectrum of society as possible. He concludes that there are three segments of non-attenders:

1. *The intenders*. These individuals have a positive perception of the arts and plan to go to a venue or performance at some stage in the future, but for various reasons never quite seem to get around to it. Clearly, an organization wishing to develop this group may need to find some way to incentivize them, perhaps through the creative use of sales promotion-type techniques.

2. *The indifferent.* This group has no strong opinions about the arts and has no great motivation to set about attending. They are an interesting group, however, because they tend not to have negative perceptions of the arts and may be suitable candidates for development if positive attitudes can be encouraged.

3. *The hostile.* From an arts marketer's perspective this segment will hardly be worth pursuing at all. They have clear and firmly established negative attitudes towards the arts and will tend to dislike most art forms altogether. Clearly, if an arts organization is to make an effective use of its marketing resource there will be little point in focusing specifically on this segment.

Of course, there may be some merit in attempting to address all of the segments that Diggle identifies, but the approach will be radically different in each case. In the case of the intenders, the barrier to achieving attendance is relatively small. Members of this segment need either to be given some incentive to attend, or it needs to be made easier for them to do so. Interestingly, the Royal National Theatre identified a need some years ago to encourage a sub-group of intenders to attend its performances. In particular, they identified that students in the London area constituted an important audience for the theatre's work, not only because they represented the potential audience of tomorrow, but also because they could potentially become an important part of the audience today. To get them to attend, however, was no easy matter, as a number of barriers needed to be overcome. Price was clearly a key barrier, but the theatre also determined that inertia and the fact that this target group was unlikely to consider booking an evening's entertainment in advance were key problems that had to be overcome. The case study below describes the marketing approach that was adopted in an effort to circumvent these difficulties.

CASE STUDY 10.3

Royal National Theatre—Student Rep Scheme

The National Theatre has implemented a new strategy designed to develop fully the potential of its student audience. The theatre has set up a student representative scheme, the aim of which is to encourage a larger proportion of the capital's student population to attend its performances. The scheme was originally developed in partnership with *Time Out* as there was felt to be considerable synergy between what the two organizations could offer students in the London area.

The basic premise was that there should be as many representatives in London as possible in universities and colleges. Each representative would act on behalf of *Time Out* and the National to raise awareness among their peers about the services that both organizations could offer. At the most basic level of involvement, representatives would be expected to circulate publicity material and to ensure that posters were regularly displayed on their campus detailing forthcoming productions, events, etc.

continues

CASE STUDY 10.3 continued

To recruit its reps, the National produced a student leaflet, providing full details of all student services including the rep scheme. These leaflets were distributed at Freshers fairs each year, which members of National staff also attended to raise awareness of the theatre among as many students as possible. Potential reps were asked to send in details about themselves and why they wanted to join the scheme. Applicants were subsequently invited to attend for a brief informal interview. Successful students then joined the scheme and attended regular meetings held alternately at the National and *Time Out* to be appraised of the new productions, student events, and promotions. The National now has 50 reps and they meet once a month during term time.

Each rep is expected to promote the services that the National can offer to students, including its very popular Student Standby scheme. By utilizing this scheme, students can gain access to performances at substantially reduced rates. Although, with the exception of the first preview of all new productions, it is not possible to purchase these tickets in advance (they can only be bought on the day, 45 minutes before curtain up), students can access a performance that might typically cost £27 for only £7.50. It is also interesting to note that the scheme operates on the basis of the best available ticket, so students can often access some of the best seats in the house for the cost of their £7.50 admission fee.

The availability of student standby is promoted by the student reps through 'Standby' posters, which warn students in advance of what is likely to be available. These posters are updated each week and posted to reps for display. Availability is also flagged up in the student section of *Time Out*. Take-up of student standby has significantly improved as a result of the scheme and importantly for the theatre, take-up does not seem to be related to the general popularity of a particular production. This is important, since while students are afforded the opportunity to view a performance at a heavily subsidized rate, their presence may enhance the experience for all, as they increase the overall size of the audience thereby contributing to the quality of the ambience in the auditorium.

Aside from the dissemination of information, reps can often help in other ways, such as by organizing trips to National performances. One student rep recently organized a group of 67 students who might otherwise not have thought to come. It is very clear that reps can provide an additional impetus to encourage others to attend. At colleges where there are strong drama groups, however, it may not be necessary for reps to organize trips as their peers will attend anyway to complement their studies. At such institutions, the reps elect to promote awareness of other National services such as the Platform performances. These consist of 45-minute talks by writers or directors immediately in advance of a show, something that would clearly be of interest to a typical drama student.

To encourage rep loyalty, the National and *Time Out* provide a number of incentives. Student reps get access to the building, to marketing staff, and to special offers or deals that they would not normally have access to. They also qualify for a free ticket to a performance when they book a group of 12 people or more. There are therefore small 'perks' and rewards, but the scheme remains essentially voluntary.

Since its conception the scheme has continued to build each year and loyalty rates are high. If people join the scheme in the first year of their degree, they tend to continue in years 2 and 3. By doing so, they become increasingly valuable to the National as they begin to extend their contacts throughout the Student Union and the student publication office. This assists them to enhance the profile of the National, and a small number of reps even contribute reviews to student publications (see Figure 10.6). To assist the students who wish to do this, the National provides free press tickets to its preview performances.

continues

Modern times

Christina Patrick on sexliesandInternet

I'm no renowned theatre critic. Yet. But on average I see around three plays a week. That's a hell of a lot of plays per year. Some are great, some are mediocre and a few I walk out of.

Closer is without a doubt the best thing I've seen on stage this year. It's very rarely that something blows me away like this. If I made this many notes in lectures I might actually survive my degree, but somehow I need to condense ten pages of frantic scribblings on the brilliance in front of my eyes into a readable review. Tough one.

Closer is a brutally realistic and painfully clear presentation on human communication, interaction and relationships. It's incisively funny, packed with wry observational humour and unnerving insight into the human mind and its irrational workings.

There are four people: Dan and Larry and Anna and Alice, and for two hours we follow their interwoven lives through love, hate, abuse, loss, sex, revenge and a thousand emotions in between that for once aren't some epic tragedy but shown in their true habitat: real life. Communication is searingly direct and personal or detached and incomprehending.

Men want a girl who looks like a boy. She must come like a train, but with elegance... Liza Walker's tense combination of fragile child and toughened punk breathes complex life into Alice, the lost soul who meets obituarist Dan in a road accident and falls deeply, unaccountably and savagely in love with him. He uses her life story for a novel and they move up the ladder of partial success, meeting Anna (Sally Dexter), a photographer, who took Dan's dustcover picture, and Larry, a doctor at the hospital where Alice and Dan met, while their lives start to become increasingly entangled in a pleasingly balanced sort of way. Dan brings Anna and Larry together through a deliciously foul mouthed Internet sequence where Dan pretends to be a whore-ish Anna and we can see the whole "conversation" on a giant screen behind the men:

Mid 30s. Dark hair. Big mouth. Epic tits.
Perfectly timed pause.
Define epic.

It's fascinating to see the people behind the anonymous Internet connections, the harsh green words on the screen describing the most intimate acts... We are complicit in their mutual fantasies, caught in the humour of people exposing their most private thoughts, and then Marber hits you with Dan's instantly quotable sledgehammer sentences:

Life without risk is death. The best sex is anonymous. We live as we dream, alone.

Marber set out to write a Jonsonian city comedy of manners, and what he has produced is an acerbic and icily accurate reflection of modern life and thought. Phrases like "I fucking love you" for us have to be the currency of this strange thing called love, the old words are too tired, we can only inject new life into them with obscenities that are so widely used that perhaps they aren't even obscene anymore. Language is direct—more "fucks" per minute than the BBC would tolerate.

Private moments are shown to us in cringing detail: Larry's confession of sex with a New York prostitute is quickly followed by Anna's confession of her affair with Dan and the ensuing vicious interrogation: Was it good? Better than me? Where? When? The connections weave in and out of the play, covering modern sexual mores and the assumptions behind the roles men and women play and create for themselves.

The actors are all perfectly adequate, with superb comic timing, particularly Sally Dexter: "You're a man. You'd come if the tooth fairy winked at you." She has real stage presence and brings complex human depth the Anna, who would otherwise be in danger of becoming a creaky stereotype.

This play covers so many ideas—it manages to be intellectually incendiary yet still hold a taut and compelling narrative. It reminds us how "every human life has a million stories" and of the demands we make on ourselves and those we love or think we love: love, that crazy, warped, nebulous, mythical quality that still fuels our lives. It has been deconstructed and challenged by modern time, but somehow, despite all the evidence, we want to believe.

Figure 10.6 Student review of National Theatre performance

continues

CASE STUDY 10.3 continued

The student rep scheme has become an integral part of the theatre's overall marketing mix, and marketing staff regard it an important tool for ensuring that students are encouraged to attend the National as frequently as possible. Thereafter, by providing them with a memorable experience, the theatre hopes that their loyalty will be retained when they complete their degree and that they will continue to patronize the National for many years to come.

In the 'indifferent' category, the marketing task is clearly one of changing attitudes. An interesting piece of research by Cooper and Tower (1994: 306) suggested that many who are indifferent to the arts may not attend because:

- they lack confidence in their ability to enjoy the arts, possibly because of a lack of education or any form of background in the subject;
- of social pressure from peer groups acting to dissuade individuals from sampling the arts;
- there is a feeling that the arts are only for the upper classes;
- of the positive alternative of television, which has achieved the status of myth and 'meta medium' and which comprises many consumers' social and intellectual universe.

If a more positive attitude towards the arts could be cultivated, there is a high probability that in future the members of this group could be persuaded to attend. Members of this segment will, however, need considerable encouragement and the process of persuasion may require a substantial investment in both human and financial resources. There are a number of development strategies that could be adopted with this group.

(1) *Investment in education.* Links could be forged with schools and colleges to encourage young people to sample (and even participate in) the arts. School parties could be encouraged to visit arts organizations and interact with staff in workshops/seminars, etc. Staff could provide guest 'lectures' in schools which support the national curriculum and in the case of some larger organizations, educational material could even be produced to help young people to appreciate the art form in question. One art gallery in the USA produced a series of Impressionist kits consisting of slides of 12 paintings, biographies of the artists, texts on the movement, and suggested questions for discussion.

Exposure to the arts in this way can be non-threatening and may serve to demystify the arts for a new generation of young people. Indeed if an interest can be cultivated, a proportion of them may even persuade friends and relatives to sample an art form for the first time.

(2) *Facility enhancement.* A second option concerns altering the nature of the art facility itself. While this is not a move to be taken lightly, some arts organizations, particularly those with display material, can optimize the use thereof to attract new audiences. Ricklefs (1975: 169) cites the example of Washington's National Gallery, which started a separate exhibition department with a full-time architect with this very thought in mind. The aim was to enhance for the public the enjoyment of the artworks on display and by so doing to make them accessible to a wider proportion of society. As an example,

to provide the rustic background for a show of Alaskan native art, the gallery acquired weathered boards from a man who made his living tearing down old barns. Stone statues were placed on deer hides and the lights were arranged to simulate the Arctic sunlight. 'In the old days (they) just hung things on the wall, 'said one impressed viewer'.

Of course there is a need not to alienate traditional audiences by being seen to cheapen the arts through the use of gimmicks, but in the example quoted above, the reader will note that the gallery had gone to great lengths to ensure that the ambience supporting their works was as authentic as possible. In short the changes introduced served to enhance the experience for both new and existing customers.

(3) *Portfolio enhancement*. It may also be possible to encourage new audiences to attend a given venue by extending the range of art forms that are supported. Most categories of art contain forms that are perceived as more accessible by the general public. If these are from time to time included in the portfolio, new customers might be attracted who might otherwise not have attended. Moreover if they enjoy their experience they may be persuaded to sample other art forms that would hitherto have lacked an appeal. In the case of museums, travelling exhibitions could for example be booked. Often these are of great public interest and while they might represent something of a financial gamble, because of the expense of the hire, can yield great benefits in terms of both the revenue generated and the wider spectrum of the public attracted to view. Once again, if only a small percentage of these individuals are persuaded to return to sample another (perhaps local) exhibition in the future, the recruitment strategy will have been effective.

There are therefore a variety of strategies that could be adopted to attract the indifferents to attend the arts, although none of those suggested is without some form of financial risk. Individual organizations will therefore need to determine the extent to which they are prepared to focus on recruitment activity and decide on the allocation of budgets accordingly.

The remaining category of non-attender, the hostile, is almost certainly the only category that will not be worth some form of recruitment expenditure. This group has absolutely no interest in the arts and is openly hostile towards any attempts to encourage them to attend. Many in this category may view the arts as inappropriate for their social grouping, a waste of public funds, or worse! Targeting this segment is hence likely to be a waste of valuable marketing resource which, as has been shown above, could be gainfully employed elsewhere.

CASE STUDY 10.4

Broadening Audience Participation at the Horniman Museum

Victorian tea trader Frederick John Horniman began collecting specimens and artefacts from around the world in the 1860s. Horniman's mission was to bring the world to Forest Hill in South London, and he opened part of his family house to the public so they could view the riches he had collected. As the

continues

CASE STUDY 10.4 continued

collections increased they outgrew his home and in 1898 Horniman commissioned Charles Harrison Townsend to design a new museum (Figure 10.7).

Figure 10.7 View of the Horniman Museum

The museum opened in 1901 and was dedicated with the surrounding land as a free gift to the people of London by Frederick Horniman forever for their recreation, instruction, and enjoyment. The original collections comprised natural history specimens, cultural artifacts, and musical instruments. Over the last 100 years the museum has added significantly to the original bequest, with Horniman's original collections comprising only 10 per cent of current ethnography and musical instrument holdings. The museum now holds in total some 350 000 objects and related items. The collections have been recognized as being of national importance, with the anthropology and music collections having Designated status.

Further buildings were added to the original during the course of the last century, notably in 1911 when a new building was donated by Frederick's son Emslie. In 1999 the museum demolished some of the later additions and embarked on a Centenary Development to create a new extension and several

continues

associated spaces. This new development opened on 14 June 2002, doubling the public space of the museum.

The museum was constituted a charitable trust in 1989 and is run by a board of trustees. It has an annual turnover of around £4 million, and is largely funded by the government through the Department of Culture, Media, and Sport. As such, the museum's agenda is set by the government to a great extent both in terms of its educational objectives (where the museum caters for the requirements of the schools syllabus) and in terms of the visitors it sets out to attract.

The Department of Culture, Media, and Sport (DCMS) currently require the museums they fund to market themselves in such a way that they attract the widest audience—but especially to bring in people who don't tend normally to visit museums. In the case of long-established museums like the Horniman, over the years there has been something of a shift in audiences, away from the people whom museums were designed to serve—often the 'working classes' that museum founders wished to inspire and educate. Today the 'traditional' museum visitor tends to be predominantly white and 'ABC1'—i.e. from the better educated higher income social groups. The DCMS would like to see more museum visitors from 'C2DE' socio-economic groups and from minority ethnic groups. The current DCMS targets represent the most recent attempt to address this issue.

At first glance, this would seem to be a tough requirement for museum marketers generally, and perhaps especially for those at the Horniman—founded at the height of the British Empire, situated in what was in 1901 a wealthy London suburb of villas and gardens, and housing an idiosyncratic personal collection of exotic curiosities from 'strange' lands; very much an exploration of 'otherness' from the perspective of white Victorians.

However, Horniman staff have found that their museum is in fact in a unique position to fulfil the DCMS agenda. Forest Hill is now part of Lewisham, one of the most culturally mixed boroughs of London and one with a fairly high level of social deprivation. Much of the Horniman's collection is relevant to this multicultural local population; as Marcus Pugh, the Horniman's Head of Development and Marketing, says, 'We are blessed with a collection that actually reflects the communities we now serve.' The depth and variety of the Horniman's anthropology collection in particular enables the museum to fulfil a key role in promoting cultural understanding and integration.

A number of routes have been employed to ensure that diverse 'new' audiences are attracted to the museum and to encourage repeat visitors from within the local community. The museum is free to enter (this was one of Horniman's original requirements) and the recent extension of the museum was designed in part to increase the 'recreational' appeal of the site in addition to its 'educational' function. The museum site comprises the exhibition halls and extensive landscaped gardens. One feature of the new formation of the building is that the gardens have been directly linked to the museum. Previously the museum entrance was off the main road—to access the gardens required a walk to a separate entrance. The two facilities have even, at various times, been administered by different bodies! The new arrangement brings the visitor through to the museum entrance from the gardens and a cross-fertilization is already in evidence, with gardens visitors also visiting the museum, and museum visitors (who tend to have more of a learning agenda) discovering the gardens. Marketing staff are now developing this further by promoting the integration of the museum collection and the gardens, for instance linking the environment section of the museum to practical observations that can be made outside.

One of the main features of the new development was the building of a new space in which to house major temporary exhibitions. This was designed primarily to get more of the collection on view but also to bring large-scale touring exhibitions to the museum. In marketing terms, it allows

continues

staff more opportunities and facilitates the attraction of new audiences as it means the museum can offer a new angle on a regular basis and provide something original and different to see. These temporary exhibitions can be used to access new audiences and segments of the community that would not necessarily be attracted by the permanent Horniman 'product'. An exhibition on Caribbean and Amazonian culture is currently planned, and will include a celebration of Caribbean heritage through an active programme of community involvement.

The temporary exhibitions, which will play a high-profile part in the museum's offering in the years to come, should also encourage repeat visits. Local people often visit on a generational cycle, with individuals who were introduced to the Horniman through a school visit returning with their own children, and then again with their grandchildren. Such developments are likely to prompt these visitors back more regularly in future years.

The temporary exhibition hall (and the other facilities introduced as a result of the new development) will also allow Horniman staff to involve local companies with the museum for the first time. The new exhibition gallery has a real synergy with commercial sponsorship; it is flexible, exhibitions can be tailored to incorporate sponsors needs to an extent, and the exhibitions will be high profile. Museum staff now have a more complete package of products to offer corporate donors and can offer entertainment facilities and space for corporate events.

The Horniman attracts around 260 000 visitors each year. The museum undertakes an annual audience survey of approximately 400 individuals. This has revealed that the mix of visitors the museum attracts reflects closely the mix of the community the Horniman serves. Situated in the heart of one of the most diverse communities in London, this is not a statistic many other urban museums in the UK can boast. This, combined with dramatically increasing visitor numbers (an increase of 100 per cent since the Horniman's relaunch), it is hoped will encourage the DCMS, and other funders, that they are supporting a thriving museum which is continually evolving to serve its growing and changing audiences.

The Box Office Database

Getting Started

A marketing database is an organized collection of comprehensive data about individual customers, prospects, or suspects that is current, accessible, and actionable for such marketing purposes as lead generation, lead qualification, sale of a product or service, or maintenance of customer relationships.   (Kotler 1994)

Given Kotler's definition above, the creation of a digital database is the single most important investment that an arts organization can make. As we have seen in the previous chapter, the benefits offered in terms of a more detailed understanding of consumer behaviour can lead to an infinitely more effective use of marketing resources. In the context of the arts, however, the use of the database and the employment of customer relationship management (CRM) tools is somewhat different, as will be illustrated below.

Before taking the decision to invest in a database, it is important that an arts organization identifies clearly:

- what the primary purpose of the database will be
- what secondary functions the database will be expected to fulfil

- the other systems with which the database must interact—e.g. accounting
- the categories of data it is intended to store
- the volume of data it is intended to store
- the forms of analysis and/or segmentation the database will be expected to accomplish
- the forms of marketing it is intended to support
- the range of outputs that will be expected.

An understanding of these issues should enable an organization to select between the various options open to it in the acquisition of appropriate database software. For a typical arts organization, these are likely to include:

- *The purchase or lease of a commercially available software package.* There are a great many packages currently on the market and their number continues to grow. Packages will support many forms of direct marketing activity including direct mail and telemarketing. Other more sophisticated systems will aid in market research and even allow the development of geo-demographic profiles of the customers on the system.
- *The use of proprietary software.* This differs from packaged software in that it is usually developed by highly specialized third parties such as marketing computer bureaux. These organizations usually lease the software and work with the user to help them carry out their marketing activity and analysis.
- *Designing a custom database.* This is clearly the most expensive of the three options and therefore beyond the reach of most arts organizations. Moreover, one would need a very strong argument in favour of this alternative since the range of proprietary or packaged software is likely to meet all but the most specialized of needs perfectly adequately. Circumstances which are likely to warrant this considerable investment include the necessity to link with a wide range of other systems, the desire for a particularly specialized function, and/or the sheer size of the database to be created.

For the majority of arts organizations, however, the purchase of a commercially available package is likely to be the most appropriate option both because of the quality of the options currently available and the relatively low cost thereof.

What Information should be Stored?

Data in respect of customers is typically held in files which usually require the user to follow a set format. Each variable that is stored e.g. age, gender, etc. will have a specific field into which such information must be entered. More sophisticated packages also contain a number of user-definable fields so that the database can to a certain extent be customized to the needs of the individual organization. In the case of most box office systems, the data fields depicted in Figure 10.8 are likely to be of most relevance.

Name:

Title: Initials: First Name: Surname:
Qualiþcations (any suffix)

Addresses: Home, Business and Temporary Addresses
Number: Building Name: Street/Road: District: Post Town: County: Postcode.

Phone Numbers: STD Code and Number

Age/Year of Birth:

Social Grade: A, B, C1, C2, D, E

Profiling Classification: e.g. ACORN or Mosaic Code

Buyer Types:

the type of customer and their interests, including:
    the performances/events attended—what they booked, how they heard of it, etc.
    the relationship of the customer to the venue—i.e. subscriber, member, board member,
    respondent to particular campaign, etc.

the type of ticket bought:
child, student, pensioner, unemployed, any other concession

the number of tickets bought and price paid:
including the part of the auditorium normally occupied, prices paid, frequency of purchase

the payment method:

the time of booking:

Additional Records: for any other information, e.g. fundraising, sponsorship, and information
about contacts

Figure 10.8 Customer record

Source: The Market Research Society and Tomlinson (1994). Reproduced with kind permission.

It is interesting to note that the collection of customers' telephone numbers has recently taken on a new significance as many new telephone systems are equipped with a facility known as caller recognition. This allows the system to recognize the person calling by their telephone number and to display the relevant customer file in front of an operator so that he can welcome the caller by name. Not only is this a more personal service, since the operator has immediate access to the customer record, the time taken to process an enquiry is considerably shortened—something of benefit to both parties to the transaction.

Database Applications

Once installed and operational, a database can be used for a variety of purposes. These include building customer loyalty; cross-selling; up-selling; and effective targeting.

Building Customer Loyalty

Box office data can be used to add value to a client's experience with an arts organization. Frequent attenders can be rewarded for their loyalty by offering them concessions, invitations to special events, and even loyalty points which can be exchanged for either merchandise or seats at subsequent performances. It may come as a surprise to learn that even the Royal Opera House now operates such a scheme. Of course, the creation of consumer rewards must be handled with care—it would hardly be appropriate for example to offer a scheme entitled Aria Miles, or in the case of a ballet company, Pirouette Points. Loyal customers to these art forms are entitled to be rewarded for their loyalty, but in a manner that is wholly appropriate for the art form in question. Often the safest way of achieving this is through the provision of points which can be redeemed for additional tickets or free seat upgrades. Indeed given that few performances will completely sell out, a loyalty scheme can often operate at minimal cost.

Cross-selling

Cross-selling can take two different forms in arts marketing. The first might involve the marketer in encouraging customers for one category of event to attend and view another. Thus ballet customers could be informed of upcoming classical music concerts in an attempt to broaden their attendance pattern. More usually though, cross-selling may involve developing a link with a second organization and the sharing of names/addresses so that customers are informed of appropriate events taking place at other venues in the area. While this might on the face of it sound like commercial suicide, a review by DiMaggio et al. (1978) of 270 audience studies confirmed that high-value patrons of one art form are also likely to be high-value patrons of another. The sensitive sharing of names and addresses can therefore work to the benefit of both organizations.

Up-selling

Up-selling involves the marketer in trying to develop the arts customer to a higher level of value. In other words, an attempt could be made to persuade customers to take higher value seats, or to attend on a more frequent basis. Ashbrand (1993) cites the example of the McCarter Theater in Princetown, New Jersey, which installed a new client/server system that facilitated an increase in subscription sales by 20 per cent. As the curtain rises on each performance, the system allows sales and marketing staff to begin work generating a list of all ticket holders. Current subscription holders are separated from those who do not currently have a subscription and the latter category are targeted for a marketing campaign the following day. Clearly, if the audience have enjoyed the evening's performance, they will be more likely to accept a subscription package while the enjoyment is still fresh in their minds.

Effective Targeting

When an organization recognizes the buying behaviour of its clients, it can utilize this knowledge in targeting specific campaigns at those it knows will be most likely to respond. Offers and information pertinent to performances of ballet can therefore be targeted only at those customers who enjoy this art form. Similarly advanced information in respect of the annual pantomime can be targeted at those individuals known either to have small children, or to have attended such categories of performance in the past.

In addition, the comments made in respect of profiling in the previous chapter are equally pertinent here. Attenders at specific categories of events can be profiled and the data used to inform the purchase of lists of other individuals who might also be predisposed to attending such categories of event.

Data Mining

The establishment of a marketing database can open up remarkable insight for marketers into the nature of the customers they are interacting with and key facets of their behaviour. In other words, the database can be a key learning tool and organizations can 'mine' customer data for new and actionable information.

The term 'data mining' refers to 'the extraction of previously unknown yet comprehensible and actionable information from large repositories of data, used to make crucial (marketing) decisions and support their implementation, including formulating tactical and strategic marketing initiatives and measuring their success' (Edelstein 1999: 15).

As this definition makes clear, data mining techniques are usually applied in the context of a large amount of data, typically stored in what is known as a data warehouse. A data warehouse is simply a system kept separate from the operational systems of an organization, and is available solely for the task of being interrogated for information. Many commercial organizations now establish warehouses of data and then apply a range of statistical tools (such as the cluster analysis we described earlier) to try and find relationships between the variables stored on the database that would simply not be detectable by other means. Some organizations may also seek to supplement this data with other profiling information about customers and also input this into their analysis.

In the context of arts marketing, data mining could therefore answer questions such as

- What are the lifestyle interests of my customers?
- What is the profile of my high-value customers?
- Do certain types of people attend certain types of performance?
- Are there segments of people on the database who are responsive to certain forms of communication?
- What is the best way to develop customer value across the database?

To discern this information it is necessary to have a large database at your disposal and for a copy of this to be available offline so that the necessary manipulation of data can take place. Organizations employing data mining also need to have a fair amount of historic data about the behaviour of their customers and this data must be clean (i.e. contain few errors or omissions).

In the context of the arts and wider nonprofit sector, there are relatively few large databases that are big enough to support data mining in the commercial sense, but many organizations can, and do, mine their databases for the answers to particular questions to inform their marketing strategy.

Customer Relationship Management

Customer relationship management, or CRM as it is now widely known in marketing textbooks, is a collective term for methodologies, technologies, and e-commerce capabilities used to manage customer relationships (Foss and Stone 2001). In the context of arts marketing it is therefore about how one establishes and builds an appropriate relationship with all the customers who patronize the organization. CRM tools can help to identify customer relationships that will never be profitable, usually because over time it costs more to communicate with these individuals than they ever contribute in revenue. It can also help develop the value of all the customers who *will* be profitable to deal with.

The detail of CRM methodologies is beyond the scope of this text, but good CRM involves thinking through the marketing process as the customer experiences it and thus designing appropriate systems to deal with enquiries, to welcome new customers, to get to know those customers, to develop those customers, to manage any problems they might have and, if the relationship fails, to try to win back customers who have stopped purchasing from the organization.

CRM thus moves beyond the simple management of the customer database we alluded to above; it is more about thinking through the systems and processes that are in place to manage customer relationships. Organizations embracing CRM also need to consider the fit of the people they employ with customer needs and to reflect on the technology that will be necessary to support their decision making and any marketing plans they might develop. CRM effectively integrates all these ingredients.

Attracting Funding

The Arts Funding Framework

The funding framework for the arts in the UK is complex. Arts funders include central government, national assemblies, local authorities, the lottery, and private bursaries. Arts organizations will typically generate income through a number of streams: earned income, government subsidy, private donations, and business sponsorship.

In operating this 'mixed economy' in arts funding, the UK occupies the middle ground between heavy dependence on the State—as in European countries such as France and Germany—and almost entire reliance on private investment, as in the USA.

The Arts Councils

The Arts Councils of England, Scotland, Northern Ireland, and Wales are entrusted with the power to hand out money provided by government and the National Lottery to arts bodies and institutions. Since 1999 the assemblies in Wales and Northern Ireland and the parliament in Scotland have taken on the role of giving the arts councils each a block grant, which they can then distribute to the arts in respective countries as they see fit. Individual funding decisions are thus taken at 'arm's length' from the government, which in theory enables them to be free to operate without government interference. In a recent move, the Arts Council of England unveiled its plans to merge with the country's 10 regional arts boards with the aim of creating a 'streamlined' service and significant cost savings. Nine regional offices will continue, with a head office in London working exclusively on a national level.

The Arts Councils' objectives are

- to develop and improve the knowledge, understanding, and practice of the arts;
- to increase the accessibility of the arts to the public throughout Britain;
- to advise and cooperate with departments of government, local authorities, and other bodies.

The criteria for funding encourages applicants to give consideration to many of the 'balances' alluded to earlier. Arts organizations are expected to recognize the need to make a contribution to the cultural traditions of the region in which they operate. To do so will involve a careful identification of the nature of the existing local provision and an analysis of any gaps that would contribute to the range of experiences available. These gaps can then be compared with the resources available in-house to identify any opportunities that might exist for development.

Aside from the need to demonstrate a contribution to the cultural health of a region, potential applicants must also demonstrate the quality of their management and in particular the quality of their marketing management. They must be able to show that they have the capability to communicate effectively with target audiences and attract (and involve) reasonable numbers of customers given the nature of the performances/attractions provided. Marketing can therefore no longer be viewed as a peripheral activity. It must permeate the core of an organization's thinking and, moreover, be shown to have done so.

Local Authorities

Local authorities are the second largest supporter of the arts in the UK. They play a central role in supporting the arts regionally, not only through direct funding of arts organizations and events, but also through the provision and management of arts venues and the promotion of arts events. Local authority funding of the arts is discretionary; they are able to support the arts but it is not an official requirement. All local authorities operate differently, with their own structures, policies, grant criteria, and schemes.

Commercial Sponsorship

No chapter on arts marketing would be complete without a brief discussion of arts sponsorship, which remains for many organizations an important source of income. Sponsorship involves a company in exchanging (usually cash) support for a series of benefits which the arts organization, by virtue of the nature of its portfolio, or the profile of the audience it expects to attract, is able to provide.

From the corporate perspective, sponsorship can offer a number of benefits, many of which are so attractive in nature that a sizeable proportion of a marketing budget may be parted with to acquire them. The following benefits are the most common and form the basis of most solicitations initiated by arts organizations.

Sponsorship can be used very effectively

- to build up awareness of a corporate name or brand;
- to add value to that name or brand by demonstrating good citizenship;
- to generate favourable publicity for the sponsor;
- to romance important customers/distributors/staff through the provision of executive entertainment.

This latter point is worthy of elaboration, since some organizations look to their sponsorship as a means of being able to offer hospitality to important clients. As a condition of its support, the corporate sponsor insists on access to reserved seating, a special performance, or other such benefit. It can then offer free seats to selected individuals. Not only can this be an effective and non-threatening way of securing new business, it can also help reward staff, distributors, or intermediaries for their efforts over the preceding months. Corporate sponsorship was instrumental, for example, in allowing the management of an exhibition centre to meet the costs of hiring a touring exhibition of Chinese dinosaurs. The key condition of the support was that the sponsor would be able to host a dinner for its key personnel and clients in the building and that the evening would include an opportunity to view the dinosaur exhibition privately. Indeed the dinner was scheduled so that these individuals were actually the first to view what proved to be an enormously popular exhibition.

More commonly, however, the business places greater emphasis on the generation of favourable publicity, since if this is timed correctly, a direct impact on sales can often be measured.

Thorntons, an independent confectionery company with a national network of its own retail outlets, has its headquarters in Belper, near Derby. When the Derby playhouse approached it . . . for sponsorship of its Xmas show *Charlie and the Chocolate Factory*, a very successful deal was struck. For Thorntons, a highly appropriate connection at a time of year when sales are at their most intense. And for Derby Playhouse, not only a sizeable injection of funds, but some excellent photo-opportunities when the cast of 'Oompah-Loompahs' visited the factory and tried their hands at chocolate-making in the real world.   (Hill et al. 1995)

Any arts organization looking to secure sponsorship for the first time would therefore be well advised to seek organizations that have some synergy either with the nature of their productions or the target audience they are attempting to serve. This should not be the end of the search, however. In the author's experience it is also well worth consulting information sources such as market reports, trade and quality press, and the Internet, since useful intelligence can often result. Companies often support arts organizations that on the face of it, would seem difficult to justify. AT&T, for example, have a history of supporting arts organizations which seemingly would be able to offer little in return. The company supported the Almeida (a small 300-seat venue in North London) in staging an obscure Russian satire by Sergeyevich Griboyedov. When one understands, however, that AT&T take credit for producing the first transistor, the first laser, and the first commercial satellite, one begins to understand that the company is not afraid to take risks and this is reflected in the pattern of sponsorship it chooses to provide. The company likes to take risks with its sponsorship monies and to support performances that might otherwise not be seen. Nor is AT&T alone in its somewhat unorthodox pattern of sponsorship, making it essential for arts organizations serious about seeking sponsorship to look beyond the most 'obvious' lists of prospects to approach.

Before leaving the question of sponsorship, however, it is important to sound a word of caution. While arts organizations will doubtless be grateful for any offer of support they receive, there are wider considerations than the mere receipt of money. The culture and/or history of an organization may make it inappropriate for gifts to be accepted from certain categories of corporate organization. Those involved in dubious environmental practices, or organizations with less than reputable connections to the Third World, are particular candidates for avoidance, although altogether more subtle reasons will often be found to exist. As with other forms of corporate fundraising, there is therefore no substitute for the careful research into potential sponsors prior to the initial contact. This can conserve valuable marketing resources and avoid considerable embarrassment if the decision must be taken to withdraw at a later stage.

■ SUMMARY

In this chapter we have examined the relevance of marketing to the arts sector. It was argued that although many of the tools and techniques of marketing are of direct relevance, there is a need to adapt the fundamental marketing concept to accommodate the need for arts organizations to take a longer-term view of the needs of the society in which they are located. It was further suggested that this modification to the marketing concept could best be articulated as a need to achieve a series of balances: the balance of performances in a portfolio, the balance in portrayal of the arts, and the balance in terms of audiences attracted.

In respect of this latter point, the results of a number of audience studies were introduced and their implications for marketing strategy discussed. The reader was also introduced to the technique of cluster analysis as a tool to delineate sub-segments of behaviour and motivation within an overall arts audience.

The development and use of a box office database was also discussed and suggestions were offered in respect of both the most appropriate information to hold and how this might best be used for the purposes of building customer loyalty, cross-selling, up-selling, and the targeting of individuals who might be most likely to respond to particular campaigns.

The final part of the chapter examined marketing's application to the attraction of funding. The criteria for Arts Council funding were noted and the significance of marketing in allowing an organization to satisfy these was noted. The chapter concluded with a discussion of the role of corporate sponsorship and the benefits that could accrue to both the sponsor and the sponsored.

■ DISCUSSION QUESTIONS

1. Why has the arts sector been slow to recognize the significance of marketing, both as a guiding philosophy and as a functional area of management?

2. How might an understanding of the audience motivations for attending an arts event inform the development of an appropriate marketing mix? Illustrate your answer with examples.

3. You have been asked to give a talk to the Arts Marketing Association about the importance of segmenting a box-office database. What would be the key dimensions that such a talk would need to address?

4. What factors would normally be considered in the selection of appropriate database software?

5. With reference to your own arts organization, or one with which you are familiar, suggest appropriate fields of data that marketing management should look to create in the design of its customer records.

■ REFERENCES

Arts Council of Great Britain (1993) *A Creative Future: The Way Forward for the Arts: Crafts and Media in England*, London, HMSO.

Ashbrand, D. (1994) 'Client Server System Boosts Theatre Ticket Sales', *Infoworld*, Vol. 5, No. 52/1, 50, 55.

Cooper, G.A. and Tower, R. (1994) 'Inside the Consumer Mind: Consumer Attitudes to the Arts', *Journal of the Market Research Society*, Vol. 34, No. 4, 299–311.

Dawson, W.M. (1980) 'The Arts and Marketing' in Mokwa, M.P, Prieve, E.A. and Dawson, W.M. (1980) *Marketing the Arts*, New York, Praeger Press.

Diggle, K. (1984) *Arts Marketing*, London, Rhinegold Publishing.

DiMaggio, P., Useem, M. and Brown, P. (1978) *Audience Studies of the Performing Arts and Museums: A Critical Review*, Washington DC, National Endowment for the Arts.

Edelstein, H.A. (1999) *Introduction to Data Mining and Knowledge Discovery*, Chicago, Two Crows Corporation.

Ford, C. (1993) 'Tuning up for Promotion', *Incentive Today*, Sept., 14–16.

Foss, B. and Stone, M. (2001) *Successful Customer Relationship Marketing: New Thinking, New Strategies, New Tools For Getting Closer To Your Customers*, London, Kogan Page.

Hill, E., O'Sullivan, C. and O'Sullivan, T. (1995) *Creative Arts Marketing*, Oxford, Butterworth Heinemann.

Kaali-Nagy, C. and Garrison, L.C. (1972) 'Profiles of Users and Non-Users of the Los Angeles Music Center', *California Management Review*, Vol. 15, Winter, 133–43.

Kotler, P. (1994) *Marketing Management: Analysis, Planning, Implementation and Control*, 8th edn, Englewood Cliffs, NJ, Prentice Hall.

Levy, S.J., Czepiel, J.A. and Rook, D.W. (1980) 'Social Division and Aesthetic Specialisation: The Middle Class and Musical Events, *in Symbolic Consumer Behaviour, Proceedings of the Association for Consumer Research Conference on Consumer Aesthetics and Symbolic Consumption*, May, 103–7.

MANAR (1991) National Arts and Media Strategy: Discussion Document on Marketing the Arts, London, Arts Council.

Mokwa, M.P, Prieve, E.A. and Dawson, W.M. (1980) *Marketing the Arts*, New York, Praeger Press.

Reiss, A.H. (1994) 'The Arts Look Ahead', *Fundraising Management*, Vol. 25, No. 1, 27–31.

Ricklefs, R. (1975) 'Museums Merchandise more Shows and Wares to Broaden Patronage', *Wall Street Journal*, Vol. XCIII, No. 32, 14 Aug.

Ryans, A. and Weinberg, C. (1978) 'Consumer Dynamics in Nonprofit Organisations', *Journal of Consumer Research*, Vol. 5, 89–95.

Sargeant, A. (1997) 'Marketing the Arts—A Classification of UK Theatre Audiences', *Journal of Non Profit and Public Sector Marketing*, Vol. 5, No. 1, 45–62.

Searles, P.D. (1980) 'Marketing Principles in the Arts', in Mokwa, M.P, Prieve, E.A. and Dawson, W.M. (1980) *Marketing the Arts*, New York, Praeger Press.

Semenik, R.J. and Young, C.E. (1979) 'Market Segmentation in Arts Organisations', *Proceedings of the 1979 American Marketing Association Conference*, 474–8.

Strehler, G. (1990) 'The Marketing Oriented Diffusion of Art and Culture: Potential Risks and Benefits', *Marketing and Research Today*, Nov., 209–12.

Useem, M. and DiMaggio, P. (1978) 'A Critical Review of the Content Quality and Use of Audience Studies,' in *Research in the Arts, Proceedings of the Conference on Policy Related Studies of the National Endowment For The Arts*, Baltimore, Walters Arts Gallery, 30–2.

11 | Education

OBJECTIVES

By the end of this chapter you should be able to:

(1) describe the impact of key environmental changes on the marketing of education institutions;

(2) describe how an educational institution might proceed to attain a market orientation;

(3) define key educational publics and their impact on schools, colleges, and universities;

(4) understand the process by which parents/students decide on appropriate educational provision;

(5) design a marketing mix for use by a school, college or university;

(6) develop appropriate control procedures to ensure that the objectives of a marketing plan are met.

Introduction

It is proposed to begin this chapter by introducing some of the major changes that have taken place in British education over the past 30 years. While such an introduction could be criticized on the grounds of being geocentric, an understanding of the environment in which educational establishments now operate provides an essential background against which to assess the immediate benefits that might accrue from addressing issues such as the attainment of a marketing orientation and, particularly, a focus on students as customers. Indeed, while the specific nature of the pattern of education provision will vary considerably from country to country, many of the same forces for change are in evidence. It is thus hoped that the subsequent discussion in this chapter will be equally relevant for all educational institutions, irrespective of the country in which they are based. This chapter will therefore examine what might be viewed as the generic difficulties experienced by educational establishments in achieving a market orientation, and define the needs of the key publics on which a focus must be developed. The chapter will also examine the decision-making process as it applies to two key publics: prospective students and their parents. It will conclude with an overview of the unique nature of the educational product and discuss some of the difficulties that are likely to be encountered in the design of an appropriate educational marketing mix.

Recent Changes in the UK Education Framework

Primary/Secondary Education

In the UK, the Education Act of 1988 unleashed the power of market forces on the management of schools for the first time. Prior to the introduction of the Act the pattern of primary and secondary education could perhaps best be described as a series of small markets each dominated by a monopoly player. Since implementation however, this position has altered, in some regions, quite dramatically. In essence, the Act has shifted power away from the schools and the staff working in those schools towards pupils and parents. Parents now have the ability to select the school they feel is right for their child and, provided that the necessary place exists and that the child in question meets any entrance requirements, such as a particular religious affiliation, their wishes are usually respected.

Of course, in practice there are real constraints which reduce the level of parental choice. In many cases, the number of local schools might be very small, making it difficult to exercise genuine choice. Alternatively parents may not have the resources necessary to transport their child to a school more distant from their home. The Act has, however, had a dramatic effect in many parts of the country and school roles have genuinely begun to reflect the local pattern of parental choice, favouring 'good' schools over those which are felt to perform less well. Since the system of government funding is now based on a simple formula which reflects the numbers of children enrolled, a failure to recruit can starve a school of resources for IT, library, and sports facilities. Under these circumstances a greater percentage of the school's income will be absorbed by fixed costs, such as the maintenance of school buildings or staff salaries, which must be paid irrespective of the number of pupils enrolled. Competition is thus a real issue for many organizations and marketing has a crucial role to play in encouraging parents and pupils to view a particular school in a favourable light.

In an age where there is considerable public interest in levels of school discipline and when a school's reputation can often hang on this issue alone, effective communication with local communities also takes on a new significance. Relationships need to be built with all stakeholder groups in the locality to ensure that strong positive images of the role of a particular school and its pupils are developed over time. Moreover, a good public image, while it will doubtless aid in the attraction of students, will also help to attract and retain new staff. It is no secret that many UK schools now find it difficult to attract suitably qualified professionals because of their poor reputation. This may have been generated by the attainment of low academic standards, by a lack of resources, by poor management, or by a perceived threat of violence by pupils. In many cases the perception may be an accurate one and therefore difficult to counter, whereas in others the reputation might be entirely unjustified and marketing may thus have a role to play in correcting any erroneous elements.

In recent years the publication of league tables of school performance has had a key role to play in providing additional guidance to parents about which school(s) they might select for their child. Not only is data in respect of exam performance now available, but so is a range of other key indicators, including the 'improvements' that schools are able to prove in their pupils' educational attainment. This measure compares educational attainment at the point of recruitment with changes in subsequent years of the child's education. While at the time of writing, a number of private schools now top both league tables, a selection of inner-city comprehensives have been able to demonstrate a substantial improvement in educational standards. As parents begin to navigate their way around this data, it is likely that parental choice will continue to be exercised in areas of the country where, as was noted above, a genuine choice of school exists.

Further Education

The pattern of post-16 education has also experienced considerable change in recent years. In England, further education (FE) colleges have traditionally bridged the gap between school and university. While most have always offered a traditional route to higher education (HE), the strength of the FE colleges has always been their vocational provision. Students could study a range of courses that would give them a practical grounding in business, engineering, sports/leisure, nursing, beauty therapy, and a wide range of other disciplines. These vocational courses were practically based and while they led to valuable qualifications in their own right, were often used by young adults to gain a place at a university in competition with students who selected the more traditional A-level route. The FE college provided an entirely different learning environment, not unlike that which would ultimately be encountered at university, and which importantly could offer students a degree of flexibility not available in schools. Methods of assessment tended to be more varied and courses could usually be studied in full-, part-time or day release modes, making it possible to work towards a university place while at the same time experiencing employment for the first time.

FE colleges also played a vital role in their communities, providing a full range of academic and practical courses for adult learners who were interested in acquiring an additional qualification or developing new skills. Often this study may have been undertaken purely for the pleasure of learning something new, with no other goal in mind. In recent times, however, much of this provision has been adapted and extended and new routes towards part-time qualifications have been established. With many more adult learners wishing to gain a place in higher education, FE colleges responded by creating a range of Access courses, the successful completion of which helps to gain a place at university.

While much of the foregoing description of FE still holds, considerable change has recently impacted on the sector. The recent introduction by the government of the 'vocational A-level' has now blurred the academic/vocational divide and since these qualifications are designed to develop in students the skills demanded by the modern employer, many schools have taken the decision to add one or more of these to their sixth form portfolio. Schools that could once have been regarded as feeder institutions to FE have hence now to be regarded as competitors. Indeed given that many schools have a vested interested in promoting their own post-16 provision, FE colleges may find it increasingly difficult to gain access to potential students to communicate the benefits of what they have to offer.

At the other end of the scale, the division in portfolios between further and higher education institutions has also eroded. Government demands for a rapid expansion of access to higher education fuelled the development of partnerships between FE colleges and universities. It is now not uncommon to find the first year of a degree programme being delivered in an FE college and many postgraduate professional qualifications are now also franchised to FE providers. While the development of some FE/HE partnerships has clearly facilitated this blurring in distinction between the two portfolios, it has also led to the creation of considerable additional competition. FE colleges now compete directly with HE providers in their geographic regions for students.

These changes have led to a great deal of marketing complexity, reflected in the almost exponential increase over the past ten years in the number of institutions now making marketing appointments at a senior level. There are, after all, considerable dilemmas facing an institution that must now compete directly with both schools and universities. Marketing resources are now split between an ever-increasing number of target markets and even where sufficient resources are likely to be available it is often difficult to decide on a suitable strategy to adopt. The development of a coherent positioning strategy is particularly problematic.

There have also been changes to the way in which FE is funded, deliberately aimed at encouraging competition between colleges which have traditionally operated within their own geographical boundaries. Funding now depends not only on absolute measures of success, but also on patterns of relative success between competing institutions. Moreover, the funding mechanism itself has altered, placing a greater emphasis on student outcomes. No longer is funding awarded simply for the number of students on a course; the emphasis is now on the achievements of those students at the end of their studies. High drop-out or failure rates can now have a dramatic effect on the level of funding received. There has therefore never been a greater need to instil a market orientation among college administrators and staff. Simply recruiting greater numbers of students is no longer an appropriate goal.

Higher Education

Over the past thirty years, the pattern of higher education in the UK has changed almost beyond all recognition. A plethora of different providers now exist, catering for an equally diverse population of students. Higher education institutions (HEIs) have been forced by government policy to forge closer links with industry, research funders, and markets for education overseas. In an attempt to categorize this change, Bargh et al. (1996) draw a distinction between what they perceive as a trend towards massification and a trend towards marketization.

Massification

The growth of the HE student population has been spectacular. Total student numbers have risen from a mere 50 000 in 1939 (about 25 per cent of whom were studying medicine or dentistry) to 324 000 at the time of the Robbins report in 1963, to over 1.4 million today. The ability to experience higher education is no longer the privilege of a select few. What was, certainly until the early 1960s, very much an elite system has now been transformed into a mass system with levels of access that rival those attained in most European countries and North America.

Given the great rise in student numbers, change has been forced on the pattern of institutions providing the education. In the late 1950s there were no more than 24 universities providing a very narrow range of highly specialized courses. After the expansion of the system recommended by Robbins, the number increased to 45, and after the ending of the so-called binary divide between universities and polytechnics in 1992, 93 such institutions then existed. When one considers that there are also a further 60 HEIs not classified as universities and well over 400 further education colleges, as mentioned previously, which have a stake in higher education, the move to a mass system of provision is all but complete. Nor has change merely been confined to a growth in the number of providers. While the sector comprised only a handful of institutions, all governed by similar academic and professional values, there was little variation in the 'character' of each institution. The arrival of a situation where there are nearly a hundred different universities has encouraged a greater degree of heterogeneity. One university is no longer much like another, and considerable scope now exists for the development of a unique institutional 'personality'.

In 1963 the average British university had a mere 2750 students. Today the average university has well over 8000 full-time equivalents and approaching 20 000 students in total enrolled. The small and historically intimate nature of most institutions has therefore been lost and the expansion in student numbers has led to the creation of ever-larger sites and even split-site campuses. The task of managing this change has fallen to increasing numbers of professional administrators. New management frameworks have been implemented and this has in turn led to the erosion of what was once almost purely an academic culture, with its own unique set of attitudes, beliefs, and behaviours.

One of the key reasons for the growth in student numbers after Robbins was the creation of a mandatory award system that would subsidize the course fees of HE students and greatly assist students in meeting their costs of living over the duration of their studies. This had the impact not only of encouraging participation, but also of persuading students that distance was no longer a problem and that study could therefore be undertaken at whichever UK institution they desired. The home-based student therefore became the exception rather than the rule, and moving away from home began to be seen as part of the natural process of growing up and gaining one's independence.

The difficulty for HEIs and indeed successive governments after Robbins has been that a greater freedom of student choice, both to enter higher education *and* to study those subjects that were individually most attractive, has meant that demand for subjects deemed to be of crucial importance to the future health of the economy, such as the sciences or engineering, was often sadly lacking. Faced with additional spaces on these programmes, universities switched their attention in these areas to the attraction of overseas students for the first time. Since the fees were subsidized (at least until the Thatcher government took office), the attainment of a British education was a very attractive option. The experience gained by universities of recruiting overseas students at this time was later to pay dividends since the recruitment of overseas students has recently taken on a whole new significance. Not only are such individuals no longer subsidized by the UK government, the fees charged to overseas students are now set at rates that often greatly surpass those charged to UK or EC nationals. Moreover, at the undergraduate level, the government now controls the overall number of home students that a given university is expected to attract. Under- or over-recruitment is now penalized by the funding framework. Once the quota of home students has been recruited, the only way that the revenue stream from a particular course can then be increased is through the recruitment of overseas students who, since they are full-fee paying, are not included in the institutional quota. Such students therefore constitute an important and extremely profitable target market.

The nature of the academic product has also changed. More than a quarter of all students are now mature students and the number of part-time students has increased sharply, particularly on postgraduate programmes. The Internet has greatly enhanced distance-learning opportunities. The nature of provision has changed to reflect the needs of key new customer groups. There has also been a general blurring of the distinction between academic, vocational, and continuing education as HEIs have attempted to respond (in most cases) to the needs of their various constituencies.

Marketization

In recent years, successive government policy has encouraged the development of a market culture. Institutions are now in a position where they must compete for scarce resources and even consider alternative sources of funding, such as that provided by private enterprise. Moreover, the new market comprising of 93 competing institutions has afforded HE customers an unprecedented level of choice. This has already led to the creation of an unoffocial 'Ivy League' of institutions, a process recently encouraged by the decision of a number of foreign governments to limit the number of campuses to which they are prepared to send students (O'Leary 1996).

At the undergraduate level, the decision by the UK government to charge fees to all but the most underprivileged of students put great pressure on institutions to communicate to potential students the benefits of continuing their education and of studying at their particular campus. Indeed, at the time of writing, the UK government has just taken the decision to introduce variable fees, thereby allowing the 'better' institutions to charge more for their provision. Since students must now bear the cost of their studies, at least in the longer term, it is fair to assume that greater consideration will be given to *where* these studies will take place. There are also internal marketing implications for this policy change. As students must now pay varying amounts for their education, they are likely to have higher expectations of the quality of service they will receive. Institutional managers and teaching staff need to be especially sensitive to the needs of their fee-paying clients.

In addition, universities and other institutions that provide higher education are now subject to an unprecedented level of external scrutiny; the demands made of them have expanded and expectations have changed. League tables are now published in respect of the quality of both teaching and research and prospective students, or their sponsors, can use this information to allow them to make a more informed choice. The level of research funding provided to each university is now highly dependent on the research rating achieved, and this is set to become more so. There is a very real threat that the traditions of both teaching and research being conducted alongside one another at every UK institution will shortly come to an end, creating new categories of university, some of which will be perceived as being more desirable than others. Senior management will therefore have to ensure that appropriate strategies are put in place now to ensure that their desired positioning is maintained and developed over time. This will only be achievable if both the internal and external marketing activity is focused on this goal and coordinated to ensure that the *whole* institution moves forward in the direction required.

The remainder of this chapter will therefore examine how providers might respond to these challenges, commencing with what for most institutions will be the key marketing issue, namely how a market orientation might be achieved. As will shortly be demonstrated, introducing such a radical change of emphasis is perhaps more difficult in this sector than in any other, given both its history and the traditional freedoms afforded to its academic staff.

Higher Education in the USA

While the preceding discussion focused on the UK, the issues identified above are matters of great concern to most government education departments, irrespective of the country in which they are based. In the USA, for example, competition is a key issue, since while student demand for places at the top 50 US degree-awarding institutions still outstrips supply, the picture elsewhere in the sector is radically different. The vast majority of institutions continue to have to actively solicit student interest. There are currently over 3000 degree-awarding institutions in the USA, each contributing to the production of over 2.5 million new bachelor degrees every year. The sheer number of institutions and the wide range of courses on offer make it essential that HEIs communicate effectively with their target markets and carve out a clear positioning which serves to differentiate their provision from that offered by others, especially those within the same geographic region.

In addition to competition, the USA continues to experience a healthy growth in what has now become a large market for part-time and adult education. Moreover, fees are as much an issue in the USA as in the UK and, faced with strong domestic competition, many HEIs are now just as much concerned with the expansion of overseas recruitment as their UK counterparts.

We may thus conclude that the issues identified above will be of equal concern to educational management in many other countries. While the structure of the educational system will certainly differ, the forces shaping the development of change will be likely to exhibit strong degrees of similarity. Indeed, as we move increasingly towards a global market for education, this level of similarity can only grow in significance.

Changing Perspectives on Marketing in Higher Education

It is against this backdrop that the need for marketing can be assessed. Perhaps marketing's greatest contribution lies in its ability to facilitate the exchange process that takes place between the HEI and each of the customer groups it addresses. It can provide a detailed understanding of the needs of such customers and ensure that the institution addresses these needs in as efficient and comprehensive a manner as possible. In the competitive environment in which most HEIs now operate, enhanced customer satisfaction may be one of the few remaining ways in which institutions can create and sustain a credible source of competitive advantage. Marketing can help deliver this satisfaction, and much more besides. Indeed, in the education context, Kotler and Fox (1985) found that marketing can offer an HEI four major benefits, namely:

1. greater success in fulfilling the institution's mission
2. improved satisfaction of the institution's publics
3. improved attraction of marketing resources
4. improved efficiency in marketing activities.

Despite the benefits, however, the HE sector has been slow to embrace the concept and although many institutions have now appointed marketing officers, the actual influence that such professionals can have is often severely limited. In a major study of marketing in further and higher education, Heist (1995) traces the evolution of the marketing function over 40 years. The authors recognize that although certain behaviours are symptomatic of a particular historical phase, examples of each stage of development are still very much in evidence.

- *Beginnings*. The impact of the Robbins report, as highlighted above, was to completely change the pattern of educational provision. Universities were faced with a need for expansion and the need to explain this to the local communities in which they were based. It became necessary to negotiate with a variety of groups to plan the expansion, such as resident groups, traders, local authorities, etc. In response, many universities appointed administrators whose primary function was to manage the institution's relationship with these publics.

- *Placating the press*. This phase began in the late 1960s in response to developments such as the student revolt and subsequent critique by the press of university management, whom press reports accused of being too soft on the troublemakers who had instigated the problems. For the first time, media professionals were appointed, often ex-journalists themselves, to manage the difficult relationship that ensued with the press. Their primary role was to ensure that potentially damaging publicity was, as far as possible, deflected.

- *Winning hearts and minds*. By the mid-1970s, the press relations function had risen in importance. Senior management began to recognize the importance of a proactive rather than a purely reactive approach. In recognition of this, the press office function in many institutions was renamed 'external relations'. These new departments were empowered to generate favourable publicity for the institution and to coordinate any lobbying activity that might prove necessary. The public image of many universities had been badly damaged by the years of student revolt and a key external relations function was to rebuild the image of higher education. There was, however, also a need to communicate to government and other funders the desirability of maintaining the level of funding attracting to the sector. The mid-1970s were characterized by a period of serious public expenditure constraint.

- *Selling the system*. It was not until the early 1980s that institutions recognized that their relationships with the press and government funders were not the only relationships that should be fostered at a senior level within a university. Changes in government policy had raised the significance of overseas recruitment, soliciting donations from alumni and selling short courses and conferences, etc. At around this time, the first attempts were therefore witnessed to coordinate this diverse activity into a unified external relations function. Media or marketing professionals began to be recruited to manage all these important aspects of activity, and depending on the nature of the institution some commonality in reporting structures was achieved. This will be returned to below.

- *Marketing institutions*. By the late 1980s, a new trend in the marketing of education had begun to emerge. Universities started to integrate marketing, both as a philosophy and a management function, into the way in which their institution is managed. Formal planning and an adherence to an institutional mission became the norm across the sector and newly created marketing departments now help coordinate both departmental and institutional contact with key customer groups. Moreover, in more enlightened organizations, these marketing departments have established a two-way dialogue with academic departments, ensuring that genuine customer input is fed back to those who have the responsibility for the design and creation of new course programmes. Without over-riding academic freedom, these mechanisms serve to ensure that the programmes offered to the market reflect the needs of those who will ultimately consume them.

Achieving a Market Orientation in Higher Education

At the time of writing, comparatively few universities appear to have reached the final of these stages of development. There are usually a number of reasons as to why this might be so.

- *Academic values*. Marketing is still perceived by many as being incompatible with the educational mission and some academics continue to equate marketing with selling, and feel that their institution should be 'above' such practices. Others feel that marketing should not be necessary because they have a strong belief in the desirability of their subject and their right to deliver it as they see fit. Academics, by virtue of their professional status, tend to be more concerned with the future of their discipline and will often focus on the narrow interests thereof. As Jarratt (1985: 33) noted, in many universities there exist 'large and powerful academic departments together with individual academics who sometimes see their academic discipline as more important than the long-term well-being of the university which houses them' Boxall (1991: 12) concurs:

The activities and priorities of universities have traditionally been determined primarily by the preferences and aspirations of their academic staff, given voice through various faculties and internal committees. Indeed, the very essence of a university has been the self-determining community of academic professionals, whose rights to set their own agenda were enshrined in the unwritten charter of academic freedom.

- *Conflict between management and academic interests.* Difficulties are also encountered because of the split in responsibility for dealings with customers between departments and the institution's central administrative function. In most institutions, responsibility for marketing is split between these two areas, and this can give rise to a degree of tension. Many departments have the desire to be masters of their own destiny and hence want to take responsibility for all marketing activity, while others express reluctance and would be delighted if those working for the university's central administration could deal with the whole process. For their part, university marketers usually want to maintain some control over the activities of individual departments, but are reluctant to have too much 'local' involvement as their role within the university has usually to be more strategic in nature. There is therefore a need to achieve some form of balance in this relationship, although in practice this can be difficult given the antipathy that can exist between academic and administrative staff: 'In almost all HE institutions there is a "them and us" aspect to the manager–academic relationship, which will vary from nothing more sinister than staff club banter . . . to real conflict and tension especially at a time of cuts' (Palfreyman and Warner 1996: 12).

- *The lack of a strategic perspective.* Given the usually high number of subject specialisms that can be found in a particular university, it is often the case that it is only the senior administration of the institution who have the capacity to take a strategic perspective and are uniquely placed to do so (Lockwood and Davies 1985). The problem, however, lies in convincing academic staff of the need for this perspective and the need to implement any strategy that might be suggested as a result of it. Many academics fail to recognize that the desirability of offering new courses in their individual disciplines must be viewed against the capacity of other developments in other subject areas, to offer even greater utility for one or more of the institution's customer groups. Clearly only those developments which are optimal from the perspective of the whole institution should be supported. Very often, however, the power to make such decisions is vested in a university committee structure heavily dominated by academics, each fighting for the welfare of their own specific discipline. 'Universities are commonly not outwardly market oriented—courses are sometimes established and maintained for the status of a department or an institution, rather than where there is clear evidence of an economic level of long-term demand' (Moore 1989: 120).

- *The diversity of marketing activity.* The point has already been made above that responsibility for marketing activity can be shared between individual departments and marketers working for the central administration. Regrettably, however, marketing activity is also conducted by a variety of other players, making coordination difficult. In a typical university these might include:

- *The development office*. Staff in this department of a university will typically be involved in raising funds from both individual and corporate donors. They also have responsibility for the fostering of links with alumni.

- *The international office*. The responsibility for overseas recruitment is often devolved to an international officer, who will travel extensively, visiting institutions in other countries and attending educational fairs, etc.

- *Schools liaison office*. Liaison with feeder institutions remains an important activity in aiding student recruitment. Dedicated staff will tour local schools, giving presentations and offering advice in respect of university course options.

- *Admissions office*. Usually split between undergraduate and postgraduate admissions, the latter is of particular significance. Postgraduate admissions staff are often the first point of contact for students wishing to obtain information about the taught or research degrees currently being offered. The office will also deal with correspondence and applications from individual students. In this sense, it acts as a liaison between the academic department and the individual applicant and will probably also issue the final notice of acceptance or rejection.

- *Press office*. Most universities have dedicated staff whose sole function is to foster good relations with the press. Since their role is almost certainly now a proactive one, such individuals are constantly monitoring the work of academic departments to ascertain whether opportunities exist to promote the teaching, development, or research work being undertaken.

- *Business relations*. Many university missions now address the need for the institution to make a contribution to the economic health of the country and/or region in which the institution is based. This often involves working closely with commercial enterprise to conduct joint research, train staff, or sell the expertise of university academics who might undertake paid/unpaid consultancy. Since successive governments have been keen to provide increasing numbers of undergraduates with business experience, this function may also have the responsibility for arranging and supervising student projects and placements.

- *Research office*. Given the importance of research income (particularly for the established universities), it would now be highly unusual to find a university that did not have a fairly senior member of staff responsible for the administration of research grants and the coordination of bids to the respective funding agencies.

- *The conference office*. The potential to generate a very lucrative revenue stream from offering university facilities, both teaching and residential, to clients seeking a conference facility has long been recognized. The marketing of the site and its facilities will usually be the responsibility of a dedicated team.

While this list is not exhaustive, it does serve to illustrate the great diversity in marketing activity that would normally be undertaken in a typical university. Coordination can therefore be a very significant issue for senior management to address.

- *The influence of research*. The remuneration systems within the majority of universities, and indeed the academic system in general, continues to reward individuals for excellence in research to the near exclusion of all else. While many universities include in their reward structures the criteria of excellence in teaching and/or administration, in reality, the quality of an individual's research output is still of over-riding concern. Given this, the concept of rewarding an individual for the quality of any marketing activity they might have responsibility for, is almost laughable! As one colleague put it recently, 'you can't even gain promotion for being an excellent teacher—what chance marketing?'

The incentive for many academics to devote time to marketing is therefore sadly lacking and many staff prefer, understandably, to concentrate on those aspects of their role for which they will gain some reward. Active researchers therefore jealously guard their time and can be reluctant to engage in 'peripheral' activities such as visiting schools, attending education fairs, or interviewing business clients. It is ironic that since administrative workloads in HE often reflect the level of research an individual is able to generate, it is can often be the least able members of staff who find their time being allocated to marketing and administration activity.

CASE STUDY 11.1 STARTING THE PROCESS—ACHIEVING CHANGE IN AN 'ESTABLISHED' UNIVERSITY

There are several difficulties that will be encountered in achieving a marketing orientation in an HE setting. Whatever the route undertaken, it is likely to be fraught with difficulty and often subject to outright condemnation by senior members of academic staff. What follows is a description of the process that was initiated by a major, long-established UK university in its bid to become market-oriented. In essence, the senior management of the university recognized the need to focus on the needs of individual customer groups, so that the university could respond more personally to their needs. They also saw the need to design new programmes that would be attractive to the market and to be more aggressive in promoting certain aspects of the institutions work and provision. The following steps were therefore initiated.

(1) *Managing the Process*. A marketing committee was established to consider how the process of change might be initiated, involving senior academics and administrators and a marketing facilitator. It was felt important to demonstrate the importance with which this change was viewed and hence both the Vice-Chancellor and Registrar were in attendance.

(2) *Marketing Audit*. The marketing committee initiated a university-wide audit of marketing activity. This audit had both strategic and tactical perspectives and was designed to gather data in respect of the external changes that would impact on the university over the next five-to-ten-year period. Data was also gathered in respect of the competition, the needs of each key customer grouping, and the relative success/failure of past marketing activity. The methodology employed consisted of a series of personal interviews with staff, students, alumni, members of the local residential/business communities, and research funders. A questionnaire was also completed by each Head of Department (see Figure 11.1).

continues

CASE STUDY 11.1 continued

Departmental Guide to the Process of Auditing Marketing Activities

Introduction

The purpose of this document is to guide you through the process of carrying out a marketing audit for your department. It should be remembered that the central purpose of the audit is to assist you in determining 'where you are now' in marketing terms and what the opportunities may be for future development. Not every question asked will be of relevance for your department but you should distinguish between those that you perceive as having no relevance and those which you are unable to answer due to a lack of information.

The Macro Environment

1. The wider environment

Factor	Details
What political (government) decisions are likely to impact on your department within the next three years?	
What macro-economic factors might impact on your department within the next three years?	
Are there any technological developments, planned, or likely, which will occur over the next three years that could affect your department's activities?	

Customer Segments

2. Please indicate for each programme your department offers, both the total number of enquiries received and the number of students to finally enrol.

Course	1992/3		1993/4		1994/5		1995/6		1996/7	
	Enqs	Enrl	Enqs	Enrl	Enqs	Enrl	Enqs	Enrl	Enqs	Enrl

3. Examining the table above, do any trends emerge? If so, please give details.

Figure 11.1 Departmental marketing audit

continues

4. For each programme your department offers, please indicate the profile of the student body over the past five years.

Programme Title					
	1992/3	1993/4	1994/5	1995/6	1996/7
Number of Male Students					
Number of Female Students					
Number of Full-time Students					
Number of Part-time Students					
Number of Mature Students					
Number of Overseas Students					

5. Examining the table(s) above, are any trends in enrolment evident? Please give details.

6. In the case of each programme, please indicate where your current students Þrst heard of your provision.

Course	Primary Methods of Communication

7. From which regions of the country do you presently recruit for your undergraduate programmes? Do you tend to recruit from certain types of school?

8. For each programme please indicate where you are currently advertising/promoting the programme.

Course	Location of Advertising/Promotional Activity (if any)

9. Comparing your answers to questions 6 and 7, can you identify any promotional activity which would appear to be ineffective? Could this be improved?

10. Comparing your answers to questions 6 and 7, can you identify communication channels that could be enhanced with an additional spend? If so, please specify.

11. Can you identify any changes which might be likely to take place in the markets for your programmes over the next three years? How are these changes being monitored? What actions do you propose to take as a result?

12. For each programme, please indicate the two institutions which you would describe as your closest competitors.

Course	Competitors

13. Do you have copies of the most recent literature produced by these institutions?

☐ Yes   ☐ No

Figure 11.1 (*Continued*)

continues

14. Is this information circulated to course coordinators and admissions tutors?

☐ Yes ☐ No

15. What unique features can your department offer that the two competitors identified above cannot?

16. What unique features can competitor 1 offer that [your university] cannot? (If necessary please specify this by programme.)

17. What unique features can competitor 2 offer that [your university] cannot? (If necessary please specify this by programme.)

18. How has a knowledge of these features been integrated in the design of marketing communications?

19. If your department has an undergraduate programme (or programmes), how have the numbers of applications compared with those made to other institutions over the past five years?

Programme Title					
Institution	1992/3	1993/4	1994/5	1995/6	1996/7

20. What forms of promotion do each of your key competitors currently undertake?

Competitor 1 (Insert name)	Competitor 2 (Insert name)

Research

21. Over each of the past five years, what is the average amount of research funding that has been attracted per staff member? (i.e. the total research income generated, divided by the number of full-time staff or equivalents.)

	1992/3	1993/4	1994/5	1995/6	1996/7
Research Income per Staff Member					

22. How do the current year's þgures compare with the national average?

☐ Well Above
☐ Above
☐ Equivalent
☐ Below
☐ Well Below

Figure 11.1 (*Continued*)

continues

23. If the figures are below, or well below, the national average, what steps will be taken to increase the level of research funding being attracted?

24. Do mechanisms exist within your department to monitor the success of individual applications for funding and to learn from the design/content etc. of those that proved successful? If yes, please give details.

25. Have members of staff from funding bodies been invited to the department to meet members of staff and discuss application procedures over the past three years? If so, please give details.

26. Do opportunities exist to involve the business community in research? Are these opportunities currently being exploited?

Other Customer Groups

27. Are there any aspects of your department activities which you feel could be of value to the local/national business community? If so, please give details.

28. What mechanisms currently exist to promote these features/facilities to the business community?

29. Could the university offer additional assistance in this regard? If so, please give details.

30. Which professional bodies do your staff belong to? Do you know the CPD requirements set out by these professional bodies for their members? Are you an accredited provider for these institutions?

Own Marketing Activity

31. Has your department considered any of the following activities:

Activity	Yes (and currently use)	Yes (and rejected)	No
Attending Educational Fairs (UK)			
Attending Educational Fairs (Overseas)			
Providing Guest Lectures in Schools			
Providing Guest Lectures for Professional Bodies			
Providing Events for School/College Tutors			
Providing Events/Competitions for Schools (not open days)			
Advertising Undergraduate Courses			
Advertising Postgraduate Courses and/ or Research			
Releasing Occasional Press Releases through External Relations			
Links with Overseas Institutions			
Providing Speakers for High Profile Events— e.g. International Conferences			

32. If activities have been considered and rejected, please indicate why this decision was taken.

Figure 11.1 (*Continued*)

continues

33. On what basis are admissions tutors selected within your department? Are these qualities relevant to the target market?

34. What additional expertise would assist you in making your marketing more effective?

35. What market research would typically be undertaken by your department prior to the introduction of a proposed new programme?

36. What market research in respect of any key customer group would normally be undertaken by your department on an annual basis?

SWOT Analysis

This completes the marketing audit process. You should now have access to a variety of marketing intelligence data. This information should now be interpreted in terms of whether it represents a:

Strength
Weakness
Opportunity
Threat

Strengths and weaknesses are factors which relate to the internal aspects of your department's activities. The opportunities and threats relate to the information gathered about the environment external to the university (e.g. competitor activity).

Looking back over the data gathered, please interpret it in terms of whether you consider it to be a strength, weakness, opportunity, or threat. You should also list any other relevant factors which occur to you as you complete this section.

Strengths	Weaknesses
a)	a)
b)	b)
c)	c)
d)	d)
e)	e)

Opportunities	Threats
a)	a)
b)	b)
c)	c)
d)	d)
e)	e)

Figure 11.1 (*Continued*)

(3) *SWOT Analysis*. Once the data had been gathered, a comprehensive SWOT analysis was conducted, revealing three major weaknesses that urgently needed to be addressed:

(a) *The lack of a coordinated marketing intelligence system*. Most departments and administrative functions having contact with university clients maintained their own databases or records of such contact. There was no way in which the data could be shared between all those who might have an interest therein. Moreover, there existed no mechanism within the university to conduct any

continues

form of primary marketing research. As a result the institution had almost no understanding of the needs of any of its key customer groups.

(b) *Habitual under-recruitment in key subject areas.* Much of the university's provision was either unattractive to potential students or poorly marketed. The university was also found to be struggling to recruit overseas students in key subject areas and hence to maintain and build market share in many foreign markets.

(c) *The lack of a coherent identity.* The university lacked a corporate identity, and communications with customer groups were often visually poor and lacking in a common theme. A university logo was in existence, but its use was uncoordinated and not informed through research. Moreover, university managers (and academics) were all found to have their own views on how the university should position itself in the market and this diversity tended to be reflected in the communications they had with their market.

(4) *Agreement of an Action Plan.* In the light of the audit findings, an action plan was agreed to implement change. Specifically the following steps were taken.

(a) *Creation of a Marketing Forum.* Heads of Department, admissions tutors, and all those involved in some way with the marketing of the university were invited to attend an occasional meeting of a new marketing forum. The format of the forum was initially flexible, being agreed upon by the participants themselves. Its role developed into a facility for individuals to share their own experiences with marketing, discuss best practice, and analyse individual problems that had been encountered. Membership of the forum was open and meetings were held at lunchtimes to minimize the inconvenience to individual schedules.

(b) *Appointment of a University Marketing Officer.* It was intended that this person would form an integral part of the external relations team and have input into university marketing at both a strategic and a tactical level. Specifically, she was to be given responsibility for the coordination of the effort to achieve a market orientation and to help shape the future positioning strategy of the university. At a tactical level, she would also be available to advise departments which required individual guidance and assistance.

(c) *The Creation of a New Permanent External Affairs Committee.* It was decided to add an additional committee to the university's existing governance structure. The new committee would have ultimate responsibility for all university marketing activity (i.e. all those aspects listed above). As such, the new body was designed to provide a mechanism to ensure that all marketing activity was coordinated and appropriate, given the institution's long-term strategic plan. Reporting directly to Senate, with all senior staff in attendance, the committee was also to include representatives of the key customer groups. The president of the Students Union and representatives from local industry and commerce were thus invited to sit as members of the committee. It was further determined that given the diversity of marketing activity undertaken, it was unlikely that time would permit the committee to have anything other than a decision-making role. Three working groups, or sub-committees, were thus also established, the purpose of each was to address one of the three key weaknesses highlighted above, i.e. student recruitment, creation of a marketing intelligence system, and the development and coordination of a corporate image.

(d) *Provision of Marketing Training.* The university's staff development unit was instructed to provide an ongoing programme of marketing training throughout the academic year. Enrolment

continues

CASE STUDY 11.1 continued

was open to all academic and administrative staff and training was structured to allow individuals to study towards a recognized qualification, or merely to deepen their knowledge of a particular aspect of marketing, depending on their individual requirements.

(e) *Control Mechanisms Implemented*. The university recognized that many departments required marketing communications support, in respect of how to plan and implement the promotion of their individual courses. Since each department had traditionally planned in a vacuum, the university had on one occasion placed four different advertisements in one magazine, each of which painted a slightly different picture of life on its campus. It was thus decided that all promotional activity would have to be cleared centrally by the new marketing officer, who would also offer advice in respect of the appropriateness of the activities planned. She could also ensure that the university gained as much synergy as possible from all its activities and obtained the best possible financial deals from the media. The effectiveness of all the forms of promotion utilized was also to be monitored centrally, so that the advice given to departments could ultimately be informed by experience gained in the market.

The university also developed a set of guidelines designed to govern the use of the university logo and other materials that might be used in communications with customer groups. The aim was to standardize the production of literature so that it was immediately apparent that each brochure was part of a wider institutional 'family' of publications.

The reader will note that the changes implemented in the case represent a 'softly, softly' approach to achieving change and quite a different route to that which might typically be taken in industry. Senior management recognized the need not to overtly push academic staff towards the attainment of a market orientation. They felt that the provision of training, in-house marketing consultancy (by the new marketing officer), and marketing intelligence should demonstrate the practical benefits that marketing could provide. This in turn, it was felt, would help generate a much more positive perspective on what marketing could offer the institution, and thus gradually begin to alter its culture.

Key Educational Publics

Previously in this chapter the term 'customer' has been used to refer to those groups of individuals or organizations served by another organization. In the educational context, however, institutions often have contact with groups or individuals who, while they may not be involved in an exchange process with an educational institution (in a strict sense of the word), still have a vested interest in the work carried out by these bodies and its management. It may therefore be helpful, in attempting to achieve a market orientation, to develop a focus not only on customers, but also more generally on key educational publics. Kotler and Fox (1985: 24) define the term 'public' as 'a distinct group of people and/or organizations that has an actual or potential interest in and/or effect on an institution'.

Educational institutions probably have the most diverse range of publics of any category of nonprofit. When one considers that each of these will be likely to have a unique set of expectations of an institution, the complexity of educational marketing can begin to be appreciated.

School Publics

Looking first at school publics, Davies and Ellison (1991) suggest that the following target groups are worthy of particular consideration by marketers.

Internal Publics

- *Governors*. Governors have the capacity to shape the future direction of the school and as such have a need to be informed about ongoing developments. They also need to be informed about changes taking place in the external environment and from time to time lobbied about the desirability of a particular response. Governors may also need marketing support to communicate policy decisions and the underlying rationale for them to other school publics, such as pupils, staff, parents, and increasingly, the wider community.

- *Staff*. As the providers of the educational service, staff are arguably the most important of all the educational publics. It is staff who interact on a daily basis with the key customers of the school: parents and pupils. The attitudes and behaviour of staff can therefore have a profound impact on the performance of a school and its role in a community. Of late, the role of the staff has taken on a particular significance since school performance is now measured in league table terms. Since these league tables consist almost entirely of lists of quantitative criteria such as performance in exam results, there is a danger that schools could concentrate too heavily on these aspects of their role. Teaching staff have traditionally been able to take a more holistic view of the development of individual children and taken steps to ensure that social, artistic, physical, and academic concerns are all addressed. Since these aspects are all key components of the academic product, institutions need to ensure that staff are encouraged to continue to give consideration to these 'softer' aspects of their role.

- *Regular visitors and helpers*. School visitors and helpers play a vital role in shaping the image that the school has within a community. If these individuals leave the school with a favourable impression they are likely to impart it to others and hence enhance the overall image and reputation of the institution.

- *Current pupils*. It is current pupils, however, who have the greatest capacity to shape the nature of the relationship of a school with its community. Their attitude, appearance, and behaviour all communicate something of the quality of the educational experience the school is providing. Current pupils often need to be reminded of this fact and persuaded that it is ultimately in their best interests to ensure that the school is seen in as positive a light as possible.

- *Current parents*. Parents represent a key public for both primary and secondary schools. In both cases they now have the right to select the institution at which their child will be educated. Schools therefore need to reassure parents that the right decision has been taken and to enable them to do this an ongoing dialogue must be maintained. It has to be recognized that parental expectations of a school have now changed and they expect to have a greater influence over the child's education. Communications with the school must thus be both frequent and informative. The days of the preparation of report cards, which read simply 'could do better', have long since passed.

External Publics

- *Prospective parents*. The parents of prospective students are a key focus of external marketing activity. For a detailed discussion of the nature of the relationship that should be developed with this target public, see the section below on influencing student buying behaviour.

- *Prospective staff*. For many schools, the recruitment of appropriately qualified staff is a significant issue. In a competitive market the school will have to ensure that it effectively markets its location, the quality/behaviour of its pupils, and the management culture of the school, alongside the more traditional package of direct benefits that every employer now offers.

- *Other educational institutions*. Effective liaison with feeder institutions can play a major role in recruitment activity. Often, designated secondary school teachers will be given responsibility for developing relationships with key feeder schools in the immediate area. The cultivation of this relationship may involve regular visits to such institutions and meetings with staff, parents, and pupils, in a bid to make the transition from one school to another as seamless as possible.

- *The local community*. The local community is a public which is increasing in importance. While schools have always been concerned to be seen to be living in harmony with local residents, the role of community liaison has in the past has been reactive in nature. Since parents often build their perception of particular schools from listening to the local grapevine, influencing this grapevine proactively has now become a priority. The advent of community education has also compelled schools to specifically develop this target group. Many schools now market evening courses designed to meet the needs of local people and draw in valuable income.

- *Commerce and industry*. With educational funding becoming increasingly restricted, many schools have now registered as charities and are attempting to solicit support from corporate donors in the same way as other charitable organizations. The educational standards set and the overall reputation of a given school will doubtless exert considerable influence over a decision of whether or not support will be granted. Good links with industry and commerce are also important to find work placements for those students who require them. If a school has a bad reputation, employers are likely to be less willing to offer its pupils placements, particularly when the administration of the same can often be burdensome.

- *The local education authority*. While the role of the LEA has declined in significance in recent years, they remain key school publics by virtue of the access that they can provide to discretionary funding. They are also important targets since schools may have the desire to influence funding policies at a local level and will therefore want to develop close links that can be exploited for lobbying purposes, as and when the need arises.

University/College Publics

The list of important publics for those institutions involved in the delivery of FE or HE is even longer. To those identified above we may add research funders, alumni, accredited organizations, and local/national media, although not even this list should be regarded as exhaustive.

- *Research funders*. Research funders constitute an important public, particularly for universities to address. These fall generally into one of two categories. The first are quasi-governmental organizations that exist to act as a conduit to channel government support into those projects or departments deemed most worthy of support. The destination of this form of funding is now highly dependant on the performance of a department (or more accurately a unit of assessment), in the Research Assessment Exercise (RAE). Other government funding is available through the research councils and this may be bid for on an ad-hoc basis as projects present themselves. The second category of research funders is essentially grant-making trusts which exist to support particular forms of research. The process of applying for funds from such organizations is usually, although not always, competitive.

    While one would hope that decisions taken in respect of research funding would always be objective and based on the quality of past research and/or the application submitted, the impact of a favourable image and an institution's record of gaining publicity for its research should not be underestimated.

- *Alumni*.The careful cultivation of alumni can serve a number of purposes. Good alumni relations can greatly aid student recruitment, particularly in some overseas markets where personal recommendations are of great importance. Alumni can also be a valuable source of publicity for the university, as the achievements of past students are often newsworthy. Moreover, an alumni network can unlock doors that lead to research funding, consultancy, student placements, and even quite sizeable donations of cash support.

- *Accredited organizations*. With the expansion of higher education a great many institutions now accredit colleges to teach one or more aspects of their provision. Franchise or accreditation arrangements are now common. In the former a college delivers a course programme on a university's behalf, while under the latter arrangement, a university agrees to recognize a college course as meeting a particular standard, and awards an appropriate qualification to participants on completion. In recent years the development of such arrangements has been popular in the UK, but also with educational establishments abroad. Indeed, there has been a phenomenal growth in overseas links, primarily because they can prove extremely lucrative, not only in terms of the revenue generated, but also in terms of the number of future university applicants generated. As a consequence, responsibility for the development of such links tends now to be administered at a most senior level within the majority of HE institutions.

- *Local/national media*. Given the significance of the output of qualified individuals from colleges and universities to the national economy, it is no surprise that there is considerable media interest in the activities of universities. The activities and successes of individual students are often of great interest, as are the nature of the relationships that a university has with all its other publics. Carefully managed, the publicity this generates can have a very positive impact on the overall image of the institution.

In a short text such as this, it is impossible to examine in great detail the manner in which relationships with all the 'publics' identified above could be developed. The remainder of this chapter will therefore concentrate on the impact that marketing can have on arguably the most important of these—potential students.

Influencing Student Buying Behaviour

Chapman (1986) was among the first to apply the buying behaviour literature to the education sector. He suggested that in selecting a suitable institution at which to study, students (and/or their parents) pass through a number of uniquely definable stages.

- *Stage 1: Pre-search behaviour.* Students will give early consideration to their choice of the next educational establishment to attend although, at this stage, little or no effort is made to gather information about the various options available. Students will passively 'register' the existence of information to which they are exposed. This may be general institutional advertising, or it may be casual discussions with family or friends. It is at this stage, however, that attitudes towards different providers will begin to be formed. This is a crucial stage of the process, since these attitudes, be they positive or negative, will help the student in the future to develop her own shortlist of potential institutions at which to study.

The marketing task at this point is to ensure that the institution maintains a relatively high profile within its target markets. Favourable publicity about the activities of students and/or staff, links with feeder institutions, open days, special events, etc. can all help create and reinforce positive attitudes towards an organization. Similarly, the local grapevine can often be persuaded to act in an institution's favour through the careful cultivation of links with the broader community.

- *Stage 2: Search behaviour.* By the time students actively seek out course information, the evidence suggests that a shortlist of potential providers has already been formed. For the student it is then only a matter of comparing between this limited number of choices. They will utilize a variety of sources of information to help them in this task and look for data in respect of a wide range of decision criteria. Since these criteria will vary substantially between the various levels of education, this is a matter that will be returned to in some detail below.

EXAMPLE

De Montford University has attempted to attract more early applications from students and meet increasingly competitive performance targets with a new marketing strategy. The institution decided to enhance the coherence of its message by targeting potential students with a mixed strategy campaign. It abandoned traditional broad-based communications in favour of relevant press and radio activity using niche media. It decided to use niche youth-friendly publications and programmes to attract youngsters, including buying space on sixth-formers' homework diaries and placing postcards in colleges. The university also aimed to improve its overall branding stategy by ensuring its message remained consistent across all faculties.

- *Stage 3: Application decision.* Having researched the options available, the student will then utilize the decision-making criteria referred to above to identify a small number of institutions to which an application will be made. At this stage the selected institutions will respond by either rejecting the application or making an offer of a place. It is often the case that this offer will be dependent on a specified level of performance in forthcoming examinations.

The marketing task at this point is to ensure that applications are dealt with as promptly and 'personally' as possible. In higher education, while almost all undergraduate applications are dealt with by the Universities and College Admissions Service (UCAS), the time taken to respond by a particular institution can still make a substantial difference. This is particularly true of postgraduate education, where many students are keen to guarantee themselves a place as soon as the decision to study has been taken. In a market where a great similarity in portfolios now exists between institutions, those that are seen to provide a high standard of 'customer care' and that respond quickly to communications will undoubtedly gain an advantage.

- *Stage 4: Choice decision.* The next stage of the process involves the student in accepting one or more of the offers that has been made. In most cases, this acceptance does not form the basis of a binding contract with the education provider, and hence multiple acceptances are common.

It is absolutely essential that providers realize at this point that they will be competing with only a small number of other institutions. Since many still fail to maintain a dialogue with prospective students from the time at which an offer is issued, until the student arrives on campus, there remains a substantial marketing opportunity. Institutions that maintain a dialogue, perhaps by sending copies of information sheets, newsletters, course information and/or reading lists, have all recognized the importance of such communications in psychologically bonding a student to their institution. The reader will recall the issue of 'tangibility' in service marketing from Chapter 4. High-quality, informative communications that help prepare students for their forthcoming programmes of study can greatly raise the level of tangibility and serve to reduce the inevitable stress that will result from having to choose between the final few institutions.

EXAMPLE

In 2003, London Metropolitan University launched a direct marketing campaign to take on rival institutions in London and lure students during the clearing period. The initiative was the first conducted for the university since it was created by the merger of London Guildhall University and the University of North London in 2002. The campaign targeted 19–21-year-olds who had recently received their A-level results. A series of responsive ads featuring the strapline 'Find your place in London' were placed in the national and local press. The campaign was supported by extensive outdoor activity, ambient direct marketing, and London-wide cinema and radio push.

- *Stage 5: Matriculation decision.* At the final stage of the process, the student has to decide at which institution she will study and register as a student on the campus. At this stage the marketing task is to welcome new students and ensure that the transition to their new way of life is as smooth as possible. At an undergraduate level, universities have many years of experience of running informative and often highly entertaining 'Freshers Week' programmes to help ensure that students make new friends and settle in before the commencement of their studies.

The needs of mature, overseas, and post-graduate students are likely to be somewhat different. Many may need help to arrange accommodation (often for their whole family), medical care, English language support, religious services, and more specific help to identify all the key university services that they are likely to need during their stay. An increasing number of institutions have come to recognize the needs of these individuals and now operate separate induction programmes that ensure, as far as possible, that these are catered for.

While all the stages of the decision-making process are important and marketing has a clear role to play in each, the key communication issue for most institutions (and certainly the allocation of the largest proportion of the marketing budget) revolves around Stages 1 and 2. Institutions need to ensure that they communicate effectively with students early in their decision-making process. The difficulty for most providers, however, lies in deciding exactly what to say and to whom. The remainder of this section will attempt to shed some light on this issue, by analysing in some detail how decisions in respect of education provision are taken in the cases of primary, secondary, and higher education.

Primary Education

The key decision makers in respect of the appropriate provider of a primary education are now (by virtue of the Education Act), the parents of the individual child. Interestingly parents have been shown to give consideration to this issue at a very early stage in their child's development. Indeed, many will have decided on an appropriate primary school well before their child reaches the age of two years (Bussell 1994). Given this, one may legitimately ask what sources of information a parent might use in reaching their decision. After all, most appear to have been taken before any direct contact with a school has been initiated. Bussell found that the key source of information utilized by parents was the local grapevine, emphasizing once again the importance for schools of maintaining close relationships with their local community.

Petch (1996), in a series of 400 interviews with parents, determined that the following evaluative criteria were used by parents to compare between the various options available.

- *Happiness.* Parents' perceptions of the atmosphere in a particular school are important. Most parents will at some stage visit prospective providers, even if the visit serves only to confirm an earlier decision. Since most visits can be timed to allow classroom activity to be viewed, the happiness of the pupils can be, albeit subjectively, assessed.

- *Location*. Parents have been shown (for obvious reasons) to favour schools that are geographically closer to the family home.
- *Discipline*. The level of discipline imposed on students is a significant factor for parents. Most like to feel that good standards of discipline are rigorously enforced.
- *Facilities*. These can include computing, library, and recreational resources provided.
- *Friends*. The placement of children belonging to friends of the family can be relevant.
- *Siblings*. The school selected for an older brother/sister can influence a decision.
- *Teachers*. The perceived quality of the teaching staff is another criterion.
- *Reputation*. The overall reputation of the school is also considered.
- *Safety*. The perceived safety of the environment created by the school is another factor.

Secondary Education

By the stage at which decisions have to be taken in respect of secondary education, the child herself now has considerably more say. Studies by Thomas and Dennison (1991) and Alston (1985) both confirm the importance of the child in the decision-making process. Children appear to be influenced by visits from secondary school teachers and visits to their potential new schools. The most important factors in influencing a child's decision are, however, where friends will study, the facilities offered and, surprisingly, the existence of a uniform. Children appear not to want to attend a school where the pupils appear scruffy, or where they feel bullying might occur (West and Varlaam 1991).

The impact of written communications should also not be underestimated in communicating with potential pupils. West and Varlaam (1991) found that 70 per cent of children had read the school brochures of potential new schools. This fact has important implications for the style in which such publications are produced, since they should obviously be written in a manner easily accessible by 11/12-year-olds.

The decision in respect of which school to attend appears to be taken before the last year of primary education (Stillman and Maychell 1986), with a surprising amount of agreement between children and their parents over which school should be selected. Indeed, West et al. (1995) found that parents and children agree in 83 per cent of cases. Despite the increasing involvement of the child in the decision, however, the levels of parental input and concern remain high. Over 87 per cent will visit the school their child will ultimately attend and 94 per cent will take the time to read the school brochure. Of the factors that have the most influence on parental choice, discipline, exam results, and happiness are all primary considerations (see for example West et al. 1995; West and Varlaam 1991; or Hammond and Dennison 1995).

Higher Education

Undergraduate Students

Grabowski (1981), in a comprehensive review of the literature, found that the following factors all appeared to have an impact on student choice:

- athletic facilities
- academic reputation
- quality of college faculty
- economic status of family
- availability of financial aid
- conversations with former students
- geographic location
- opinions of high-school teachers and counsellors
- effectiveness of the institution in getting jobs for its graduates
- institution's competition
- interviews
- older brothers and sisters who attended the institution
- parents and family preferences
- physical plant and facilities
- activities of recruiters
- size of establishment
- social activities
- specific academic programmes
- visits to campus.

While the knowledge that all these factors have the capacity to influence a decision is helpful, it does not leave an HE marketer with a sense of how to prioritize their effort. The available research suggests that prospectuses are the most crucial form of marketing communication, but it is important to recognize that they often serve only to confirm decisions that have already been made (Chapman and Johnson 1979).

In respect of some of the other factors listed, Chapman and Franklin (1981) and Kealy and Rockel (1987) agree that parents, peers, high-school personnel, and campus visits are all of primary importance in influencing the decision-making process. Palihawadana and Westwell (1996) meanwhile conclude that perceived job prospects upon graduation are a powerful determinant of student choice.

Given the diverse nature of the conclusions drawn by these studies, it would seem sensible for institutions to conduct their own research. It may be that the criteria that have the capacity to exert the greatest influence on the decision-making process will vary depending on the subject matter being studied and the academic abilities and background of a particular individual. Quite clearly, once the factors that *are* of importance in a particular case are identified, the knowledge can be employed to good effect in designing promotional campaigns and deciding on an appropriate allocation of scare marketing resource. The case study of the Camborne School of Mines illustrates this point well.

CASE STUDY 11.2 DIGGING FOR GOLD—THE CAMBORNE SCHOOL OF MINES

Camborne School of Mines (CSM) has a long and proud tradition of educating young people for careers in various roles within the mining and geological sector. Long established as one of the finest providers of such education, the school enjoys a high profile throughout the world and all the major employers in the field seek its graduates. Indeed, in university circles it is now something of a rarity since employers actively compete to be the first to meet a particular student group on the annual 'milk round'. Indeed, competition for CSM graduates has been so keen that this process has to be carefully managed to avoid upsetting individual employers by being seen to give an advantage to one at the expense of another. Given this level of demand the reader will not be surprised to learn that historically CSM has had no difficulty in recruiting students to its world-renowned facility, and the attitude of staff during the early 1990s probably reflected this. Staff were comfortable with both the ability of the students they were able to attract and the overall numbers they attracted. In short, there was felt to be no real need for marketing as they understood it.

By the mid-1990s, however, CSM began to notice a dramatic decline in its student numbers. A variety of environmental factors and organizational complacency in respect of recruitment had led to a decrease in applications to all categories of course throughout the School. The details of this decline for the three major programmes offered by the School are given in Figures 11.2–11.4.

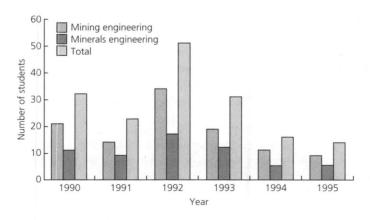

Figure 11.2 First year engineering degree enrolments

continues

CASE STUDY 11.2 continued

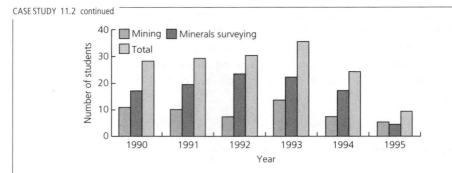

Figure 11.3 HND engineering enrolment

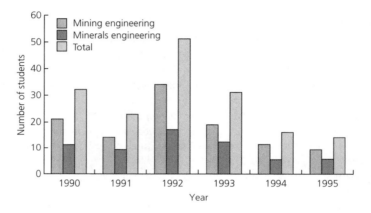

Figure 11.4 HND science enrolment

As can be seen from the figures, CSM offers a variety of engineering and science-based courses at both HND and degree level. By 1995 however, it can also be seen that the recruitment levels on these courses had fallen to an all-time low. At that time the management of the School were seriously doubting their ability to be able to maintain the range of courses available to students and there were even concerns that the total number of staff employed would in future be difficult to justify. Indeed, having extrapolated the trends suggested by the graphs, there were very real concerns that the School would not prove to be economically viable in 1996.

It was at this point that the management of the School began a thorough review of the changes in the market for their courses and the implications for their own marketing strategy. The key problem, they determined through research, was the image that both mining and the School itself projected. With respect to the latter, the School was felt to have a problem with its name. While there was no question of it being able to change this, because of high levels of awareness throughout the mining industry, the three ingredients of Camborne, School, and Mines, were all not likely to be particularly attractive to the average 18-year-old. Many would have difficulty in identifying where Camborne was, and even those who could would probably be put off by its distance from major centres of population.

continues

CASE STUDY 11.2 continued

The word 'school' also has associations with a lower level of education, and to make matters worse, mining as a career was also found to have a long series of negatives associated with it, as the early 1990s had seen the collapse of much of the remaining mining industry in the UK, leaving school-leavers with the impression that mining was a dead or dying industry.

Mining as a career was simply not highly regarded by school-leavers and tended to be regarded as 'dirty' or in some way inferior to other forms of engineering. Indeed, as a subject, mining engineering was found to be less popular than the study of Serbo Croat or Celtic Studies! CSM further determined that even where these negative perceptions were absent many students simply failed to understand what exactly was on offer in terms of course content. Potential students had no real idea of what studying minerals engineering and mining engineering was likely to entail. The School was therefore facing a serious communications problem. It was failing to attract students because of a whole series of negative images (which acted to persuade those who might otherwise have studied at Camborne to choose a different subject of study) and a complete lack of understanding of what was on offer.

It was therefore clear to CSM management that they had to take immediate action both to correct the erroneous views of the mining career and to ensure that potential students understood exactly what they could be studying at Camborne. However, this was felt to be insufficient to reverse the negative trend. CSM needed to understand more about *why* students elected to study with them and use this knowledge to their advantage. What were the positive aspects that the School could offer? To assist them in determining what these might be, the School conducted some marketing research among its existing students. This yielded valuable intelligence in respect of the factors that influenced the decision to study at Camborne, and the key results are illustrated in Figure 11.5.

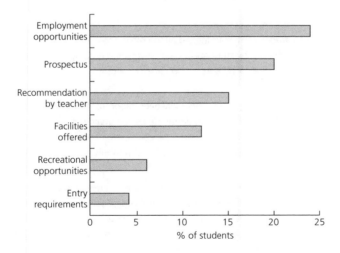

Figure 11.5 Reasons for applying to CSM

The results made it clear the key role that science teachers in schools have to play in informing students about the courses on offer and their relative merits. They are an important customer segment, as they have the power to appraise students of an option they might not have considered, or to help provide criteria against which to assess the various course options available. Similarly, the CSM and

continues

Exeter University (of which CSM is now part) prospectuses were found to be key forms of communication. Historically the CSM had always produced its own full-colour prospectus and the results of the survey indicated to management that this should be continued and that, moreover, any move to make cutbacks in either the quality of the prospectus or the quantity distributed should be strongly resisted.

Interestingly, however, almost a quarter of the students surveyed indicated that they studied at Camborne because of the job prospects that it could offer on completion of their degree/HND. Through talking to its students about these issues, CSM management further determined that many in their second or final years could command large sums of money for short periods of vacation employment. In one case, a student had been able to travel to Australia during his vacation and earned £600 per week during his stay. CSM further determined that the salaries their graduates could attract far exceeded the normal salary expectations of an average graduate, irrespective of the chosen subject of study. Salaries for graduate mining engineers were typically of the order of £30 000 and posts in a variety of different countries were available. Moreover, because of a worldwide skill shortage in this area, and the excellent reputation of the CSM with employers, almost all the students in a typical intake would be able to find employment within six months of completing their course.

The one key benefit that the School could offer its students was thus almost a guarantee of well-paid employment both during and after the completion of their studies. It was decided to take full advantage of this major benefit in a bid to enhance recruitment to the CSM's engineering courses at both HND and degree levels and it was this message that was to form the core of all the communications that the School had with its market during the 1995/6 academic year. In tactical terms, these communications included:

- *An aggressive PR campaign*. This addressed all the major local and national media. The initial PR focused on the success achieved by students in gaining vacation employment overseas and the sums of money involved. This proved to be a very popular story and it was covered by a wide variety of media.

- *Advertising*. While advertising had traditionally been taboo for universities, since it was felt that to be seen advertising might somehow degrade the perceived quality of the institution, CSM flouted 'the rules' and began advertising its undergraduate courses for the first time. Advertisements not only outlined the CSM courses available, but once again communicated the successes achieved by its students.

- *Personal selling*. Given the results of the student survey, it was felt appropriate to be more proactive in CSM's dealings with schools. Staff were encouraged to forge closer links with key feeder institutions and, where possible, to make regular visits and talk to prospective students. Packs of information were also produced which directly related to the content of GCSE and A-level syllabi and which were all designed to cultivate an interest in minerals and mining as a career.

The results of the push during 1995/6 were astounding. Figures 11.6 and 11.7 illustrate the impact that the new proactive marketing stance had on levels of student recruitment. A significant upturn was experienced on all engineering courses. CSM management are convinced that this upturn is directly attributable to the enhanced marketing activity undertaken, and not to random fluctuations in the market. Their proof for this assumption is the recruitment pattern experienced on the science courses, which did not form part of the 1995/6 marketing push. The recruitment trends for this set of courses are shown in Figure 11.8, with a clear and continuing decline indicated.

continues

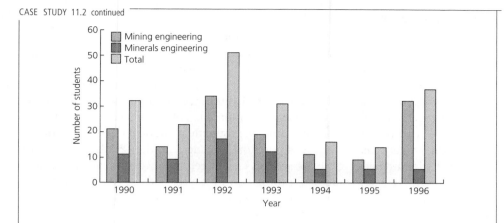

Figure 11.6 First year engineering degree enrolment

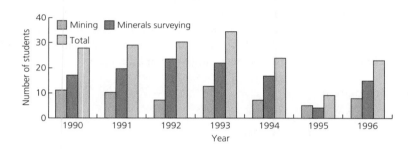

Figure 11.7 HND engineering enrolment

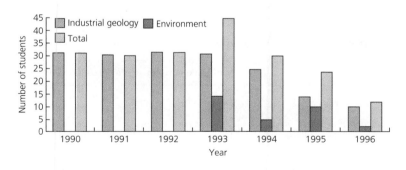

Figure 11.8 HND science enrolment

Postgraduate Students

Fortunately the criteria used by postgraduate students to select an institution appear a little more uniform. In the largest study of its kind, HEIST (1995) found that the factors cited in Table 11.1 were cited as having the most influence.

At a postgraduate level, the nature of the course content would seem to be altogether more important than at an undergraduate level. Intense promotional activity is therefore likely to be much less effective than an early consideration of customer needs/wants and a course design that reflects these. Interestingly, postgraduate students appear to seriously consider only a very small number of potential providers. In the USA Houston (1979) found that the number of graduate schools considered by a student averages around three, with only two key sources of information in respect of these being utilized. Key sources of information were found to include prospectuses and peer-related contacts, a finding replicated in the UK by Palihawadana (1992).

Overseas Students

The preceding discussion focused primarily on the recruitment of home students to university courses. Since most institutions now actively recruit overseas students it is worth examining for a moment what is known about the purchase behaviour of this specific group. HEIST (1995) reports that the following variables all have the capacity to influence a decision. They are listed below in descending order of importance.

- academic reputation
- content of the course
- international reputation of the institution
- guaranteed accommodation
- entry requirements
- cost of living
- level of fees.

Table 11.1 Factors influencing postgraduate student choice

Factor	% of students citing as primary consideration
Course content	32
Location	19
Availability of funding	12
Reputation of institution	10
Only institution offering course	7
Recommendation	4
Other	16

Source: O'Neill (1995). Reproduced with the kind permission of Heist, Leeds, UK.

There are a number of interesting points that emerge from this analysis. First, it would appear that the primary reason for studying overseas is to gain a qualification from a prestigious institution that will be recognized within the home country. This has implications for HE marketers in so far as most are geocentric in their approach. There is a clear need to do more than simply 'sell' in an overseas market. Institutions also need to build up a 'presence' within each market with a communications mix, the target of which is sufficiently broad to include students, parents, governments, sponsors, and employers. It is no accident that more enlightened universities now offer graduation ceremonies in other countries for overseas students and their families to attend. Such events can raise the profile of an institution and attract favourable publicity. Of course, one needs sufficient numbers of students to make this work, but since many foreign institutions now offer degrees awarded in partnership with UK universities, the opportunities to provide this kind of event are set to increase. It is no longer enough for providers to rely solely on their home reputation—a reputation in each target market must be built and maintained.

The second point worthy of note from the table is the importance of cost to the overseas student. Since most universities operate a very simple cost plus approach to their pricing, there may be in the future an opportunity to offer greater flexibility in respect of the pricing of each programme. How many institutions, for example, currently charge lower fees for those courses for which it is difficult to recruit? An end to rigid accounting practices and a more flexible market-based approach could well pay dividends in overseas markets.

It is also interesting to note a further point that emerged from the HEIST study. Around 25 per cent of international students currently studying in the UK have at some time previously studied in this country. Of these, some four-fifths were studying in the country at the time of their HE application. These facts have a major significance for HE providers in that they emphasize the importance of the schools' liaison function in developing close links with potential feeder institutions.

As one would expect, given the often great geographical distance between the country of origin and the institution at which students decide to study, the range of information sources that a student will utilize are diverse. The other contributory factor to the use of this range of information sources is undoubtedly the element of risk associated with study at an overseas institution. In most cases the student will never have visited the institution and hence cannot 'sample' the lifestyle that will be encountered, except through publications and websites. Moreover, living and working in a foreign culture can be a daunting prospect and students need much more reassurance that they are making the right decision. It is not surprising therefore that personal contacts are among the most significant influences on the decision-making process. Indeed, HEIST (1995) determined that personal sources were often the trigger to considering a particular institution in the first place. The results of the study are reported in Table 11.2.

The key recruitment tactic employed by educational institutions addressing overseas markets has long been attendance at overseas exhibitions. Academics and administrators travel to a selection of fairs and meet individual students. For a great many institutions this will be the only contact that they will have with their market in a given year. Only a minority will take the trouble to establish a regular programme of visits to feeder institutions, only a few will have regular contacts with British Council employees,

Table 11.2 First source of information about overseas institution

Source of information	% of students indicating
Friend	18.5
Education directories	13.8
Prospectus	8.0
Member of family	7.8
British council	7.4
Subject lecturer	5.7
Careers adviser	5.3
Exhibition in own country	5.3
University links with feeder institution	4.7
Through the media	4.7

Source: Allen and Higgins (1994). Reproduced with the kind permission of Heist, Leeds, UK.

careers advisers, and employers, and still less will actually make their presence known by advertising in the local press. What is perhaps most deplorable, however, is the fact that many universities continue not to exploit their local alumni. The achievements of many overseas students would be newsworthy in their home countries and most students return enthusing about their experiences. This enthusiasm could be employed to much greater effect in raising local awareness of the institution and making it a topic of conversation with many of those listed in Table 11.2. Universities must learn to adopt a broader focus within each of their target markets and to give adequate consideration to communicating with all those who can influence the decision-making process if they are to continue to meet their recruitment targets.

Education Marketing—Planning and Control

Marketing Strategy

It is apparent from the above that the task of marketing an educational institution is more complex than that for almost any other category of nonprofit. A diversity of publics with an equally diverse set of needs and wants make it almost impossible to derive one plan that will adequately serve the needs of the whole institution. It is therefore normal practice to address the marketing strategy that will be followed at an institutional level and to delegate authority for the production of individual tactical plans to specific departments or centres. Each of these can then develop a tactical mix that will be appropriate for the educational publics that they deal with on a daily basis.

Clearly, decisions must be taken at a strategic level in respect of the overall direction in which the institution will be taken, perhaps utilizing Ansoff as a framework (see Ansoff

1968). Market segmentation and positioning are also likely to be centrally decided as they are both likely to have profound implications for the development of subsequent tactical plans. In particular the positioning selected by an education institution will pervade every aspect of the work that it subsequently engages in. Unlike many consumer markets where individual offerings can be separately positioned, in education markets it is rare to be able to escape from the overall 'image' that a particular supplier has in the market. While most students recognize that departments in a university will vary in quality and will try to take a subject rather than an institutional perspective, it would be a brave marketer who would claim that the overall positioning of the university, in terms of perceived quality and status, does not have a considerable impact on student choice. There are a small number of institutions, for example, who tend to be selected as a fallback position by students if they fail to be accepted at one of the Oxbridge universities. Interestingly these institutions are continually selected as second choice, irrespective of the subject being studied. At a postgraduate level this phenomenon is perhaps less in evidence, since students are often motivated to apply by the research ranking achieved by an individual department. Even in these cases, however, students are doubtless mindful of how the institution will be perceived in the minds of potential employers on completion of their studies.

The positioning can also have a profound impact on the success or failure of fundraising initiatives and attempts to work closely with commerce/industry. Those institutions that are perceived as being either of high quality or as in some way unique are likely to have the greatest success in these areas.

The difficulty for senior managers, however, is that the positioning strategy selected needs to be consistent and hence capable of implementation in each of the very diverse markets that the institution serves. Accomplishing this is no easy matter, the temptation being to select a positioning strategy based on vague academic values such as excellence in teaching or research. There cannot be many institutions that do not perceive themselves as striving for excellence in both these key areas! A good positioning strategy should be unique and summarize neatly the key facets of the organization, thus allowing some scope for modification in response to the requirements of each individual market.

Marketing Tactics

The responsibility for the development of tactical plans will vary considerably from institution to institution. In schools, it is likely that one plan will be developed centrally with the help of senior teaching staff and administrators. In the case of an FE college a central institutional plan is also likely to exist, although responsibility for marketing individual courses is likely to be devolved to the members of academic staff who have the responsibility for coordinating each programme. In a university, the picture is likely to be more complex, with separate tactical plans being developed by a multitude of different administrative and academic departments. In this environment it is absolutely essential that some mechanism exists to coordinate the actions of each. Greater coordination can lead to a considerable number of benefits, including the placement of joint advertising (leading to overall cost reductions), greater buying power, a sharing of ideas and experience, and the careful planning of support activities. A department within one well-known institution recently advertised its presence in clearing for the first time and was swamped with high numbers of phone calls. No additional administrative staff had been devoted to the task of dealing with enquiries and none of the operators who took the calls were even aware that the advert had been placed. What could have been a very effective promotion was thus sabotaged by a failure to communicate with other key 'marketing' staff.

Control

The issue of control is of particular significance for educational institutions. Given the great diversity in marketing functions throughout the organization it is crucial that effective control mechanisms are put in place to ensure that the institution as a whole moves in the direction that has been envisaged. Where control is lacking, there can be a risk of strategic drift, where decisions are taken on an incremental basis by individual managers or academics with very different perspectives of the global situation. A lack of control can also result in an organization paying little attention to costs, the returns being generated by each marketing activity, and both the efficiency and effectiveness thereof.

Control activity can best be categorized as follows:

(1) *Strategic control*. At a strategic level, the emphasis is largely on ensuring that the organization 'gets to where it wants to be'. Senior management will have taken a range of decisions relating to the strategic direction of the institution, segmentation issues, and positioning. They will also have had considerable input to portfolio matters, pricing, and promotion. Strategic control therefore needs to ensure that the decisions taken were implemented in the manner envisaged and that the desired effect in terms of the strategic health of the organization has been realized (i.e. that the marketing activity has been effective). The key strategic control is thus the marketing audit referred to earlier, which should be undertaken on a regular basis.

(2) *Efficiency control*. Institutions will also want to ensure that they are making an efficient use of their resources. Marketing activity could well be effective in the sense that it is aiding the achievement of the institutional objectives, but it may be costing the organization more than is necessary. The efficiency of the marketing activity undertaken is thus an important issue on which to focus control. Typically this might be undertaken at a functional level, measuring, for example, the efficiency of various forms of promotional activity, e.g. attendance at overseas fairs, advertising, direct mailshots, etc. Desired levels of efficiency can be compared against actual and remedial action instigated where necessary.

(3) *Profitability control*. The profitability of each activity also needs to be controlled. Setting targets for each course, department, faculty, etc. may be one way of achieving this. Alternatively, an institution-wide perspective could be adopted and profitability measured by key customer segment.

(4) *Annual plan control*. A key focus of control activity is the annual institutional plan. Marketers need to measure:

- *Sales/market shares*. Actual figures should be compared with the budgeted figures.

- *Sales/expense analysis*. In many institutions this is referred to as the allowable cost per sale. Organizations need to decide in advance just how much they are prepared to spend to secure each sale, and monitor performance against this target.

- *Conversion rates*. Institutions will wish to ensure that a sufficient number of enquiries are actually converted into sales. If the conversion rate appears to be dropping in one department, this may indicate that its portfolio is becoming less attractive, or that its marketing is of poor quality.

- *Drop-out rates*. A key test of the quality of marketing activity in education is the extent to which it allows individuals to self-select the courses that are right for them. Monitoring drop-out rates can hence be a helpful control mechanism in ensuring that a high quality of contact is maintained with each target group. Individuals should have no difficulty in determining in advance which courses are right for them and taking action accordingly.

Despite the length of the above list, however, it is important that a balance be struck between ensuring that adequate control mechanisms exist and allowing individual marketing functions sufficient scope to develop their own creativity. Departments should be encouraged to explore the utility of new marketing techniques and not be afraid to experiment with new ideas, even if this means an occasional 'failure'. The control procedures employed within a particular organization should therefore allow sufficient scope for this to take place without compromising the integrity of the overall institutional position.

▓ SUMMARY

In this chapter we have examined a number of the key environmental influences for change on education at all levels within the UK. Issues of competition and enhanced student choice are now matters of concern to all education marketers irrespective of where they might happen to work within the sector. Importantly, these changes should not be viewed as taking place only in the UK—in many other countries the same environmental forces are shaping the manner in which educational frameworks are developed and maintained. Against this backdrop, it was argued here that the most important marketing issue for educational institutions to address is the early attainment of a genuine market orientation. This involves organizations in fostering greater degrees of collaboration between internal departments, monitoring the performance and activities of key competitors, and developing a focus on a wide range of institutional publics.

To date, research undertaken into the needs/wants of these publics has been comparatively sparse, although the findings of a number of the more important studies have been reported here. If institutions are to successfully develop course provisions that are attractive to the market they need to have a detailed understanding of the market needs. Indeed, an understanding of how and when decisions are taken in respect of educational provision is essential if providers are to effectively market their provision to the key organizational publics of potential students and their parents. Only when such knowledge has been gained can organizations hope to develop meaningful strategic and tactical plans that will capture the imagination of their market and ultimately lead to superior marketing performance.

■ DISCUSSION QUESTIONS

1. What are likely to be the key institutional barriers to the attainment of a marketing orientation in the education sector? How might these be overcome?

2. How might a competitive focus be accomplished? What categories of data should an educational institution try to capture in respect of its key competitors?

3. To what extent might marketing, at a philosophical level, be likely to conflict with the traditional concept of academic freedom? Are the two necessarily incompatible?

4. For your own institution, or one with which you are familiar, list its key publics. How might relationships with each of these key publics be developed and maintained over time?

5. Why is the concept of marketing 'control' of particular relevance to higher education institutions? What difficulties are likely to be encountered in attempting to control the marketing activities undertaken? How could these difficulties be overcome?

■ REFERENCES

Allen, A. and Higgins, T. (1994) Higher Education—The International Student Experience, HEIST, Leeds.

Alston, C. (1985) *The Views of Parents Before Transfer*, Secondary Transfer Project, Bulletin 3 (RS991/85), Inner London Education Authority.

Ansoff, I. (1968) *Corporate Strategy*, London, Penguin Books.

Bargh C., Scott P. and Smith, D. (1996) *Governing Universities, Changing the Culture?*, SRHE and Open University Press, Buckingham.

Boxall, M. (1991) 'Positioning the Institution in the Marketplace', in *Universities in the Marketplace*, CUA Corporate Planning Forum, Conference of University Administrators in Association with Touche Ross.

Bussell, H. (1994) 'Parents and Primary Schools: A Study of Customer Choice', *Proceedings of 1994 Marketing Education Group Conference*, Coleraine.

Chapman, R. (1986) 'Toward a Theory of College Selection: A Model of College Search and Choice Behaviour', in *Advances in Consumer Research*, Vol. 13, ed. R.J. Lutz, and Association for Consumer Research, Provo, UT.

Chapman, R.G. and Franklin, M.S. (1981) 'Measuring the Impact of High School Visits: A Preliminary Investigation', AMA Educators Conference Proceedings, Chicago.

Chapman, D.W. and Johnson, R.H. (1979) 'Influences on Students' College Choice: A Case Study', Ann Arbor, MI, Project CHOICE, School of Education, University of Michigan.

Davies, B. and Ellison, L. (1991) *Marketing the Secondary School*, Longman Industry and Public Services Management, Harlow.

Grabowski, S.M. (1981) *Marketing in Higher Education*, AAHE ERIC Higher Education Research Report, No. 5, Washington.

Hammond, T. and Dennison, W. (1995) 'School Choice in Less Populated Areas', *Educational Management and Administration*, Vol. 23, No. 2, 104–13.

Heist (1995) The Role of Marketing in the University and College Sector, Heist, Leeds.

Jarratt (1985) Report of the Steering Committee for Efficiency Studies in Universities, CVCP, London.

Kealy, M.J. and Rockel, M.L. (1987) 'Student Perceptions of College Quality: The Influence of College Recruitment Policies', *Journal of Higher Education*, Vol. 58, No. 6, 683–1103.

Kotler, P. and Fox, K. (1985) *Strategic Marketing for Educational Institutions*, Englewood Cliffs, NJ, Prentice Hall.

Lockwood, G. and Davies, J. (1985) *Universities, The Management Challenge*, NFER Nelson, Windsor.

O'Leary, J. (1996) 'The Future of Higher Education', *Higher Education Quarterly*, Vol. 43, No. 2, 108–24.

Palihawadana, D. (1992) 'Marketing Higher Education: A Case Study Relating to the Strathclyde Business School', unpublished PhD thesis, Dept of Marketing, University of Strathclyde, Glasgow.

Palihawadana, D. and Westwell, R. (1996) 'Information Search and Choice Behaviour in Higher Education', MEG Conference Proceedings, 1165–211.

Petch, A. (1986) 'Parental Choice at Entry to Primary School', Research Papers in Education, Vol. 1, No. 1, 26–41.

Stillman, A. and Maychell, K. (1986) *Choosing Schools: Parents, LEAs and the 1980 Education Act*, NFER Nelson.

Thomas, A. and Dennison, W. (1991) 'Parental or Pupil Choice—Who Really Decides in Urban Schools? *Education Management and Administration*, Vol. 19, No. 4, 243–51.

West, A., David, M., Hailes, J. and Ribbens, J. (1995) 'Parents and the Process of Choosing Secondary Schools: Implications for Schools', *Education Management and Administration*, Vol. 23, No. 1, 28–38.

West, A. and Varlaam, A. (1991) 'Choosing a Secondary School: Parents of Junior School Children', *Educational Research*, Vol. 33, No. 1, 22–30.

12 Healthcare Marketing

OBJECTIVES

By the end of this chapter you should be able to:

(1) understand and describe the healthcare environment;

(2) understand and describe the importance of service quality in obtaining a competitive advantage in healthcare;

(3) understand and describe the changing relationship between healthcare providers and their patients;

(4) design, develop, and implement a marketing plan for a primary healthcare organization;

(5) design, develop, and implement a marketing plan for a nonprofit hospital.

Introduction

The relevance of the marketing concept to the delivery of healthcare services has long been recognized, and it was as long ago as 1971 when the first journal article on the subject by Zaltman and Vertinsky appeared in the *Journal Of Marketing*. Since then, a variety of other writers have entered the fray and two key healthcare marketing textbooks by MacStravic (1975) and Kotler and Clarke (1987) have now been added to our bookshelves. These were followed by a deluge of new journal articles covering almost every conceivable aspect of the subject.

Despite the academic interest in the subject, however, marketing has still not been fully embraced by the healthcare community. Many of the common misconceptions of marketing alluded to in Chapter 1 are still widely held and much of the sector still suffers from an acutely malignant form of product orientation!

Many healthcare organizations still have no conception of the term 'customer', and remain steadfastly focused on management issues related to the product/service being provided. The reader will recall from Chapter 1 that the primary goal of any product-driven organization is to 'deliver goods that it thinks would be good for the market' (Kotler and Clarke 1987: 29). In the delivery of healthcare, this approach essentially regards the patient as being in passive receipt of his treatment and affords little scope for a genuine interaction to take place between the healthcare provider and its patients. There is, regrettably, a considerable amount of evidence to support the proposition that much of the UK's healthcare provision, in particular, is delivered in such a manner. Teasdale (1992: 62), for example, notes that: 'a major criticism of the NHS (National Health Service) has always been that it is a very large organization which decides for itself what is best for patients, and then develops its services accordingly. Patients are expected to be grateful for what they are offered, and to put up with delays or other inadequacies because we tell them we are short of resources'.

Indeed, while calls for a patient-centred approach to the delivery of physician services have been made for some time (see Pendleton and Hasler 1983), in the UK at least, the evidence of many years of complaints suggests that the idea of a customer focus is still anathema (BMA 1995).

In this chapter we will therefore examine a number of the structural reasons why this might be so, beginning with an overview of both the UK and US models of healthcare provision. We will then consider a number of ways in which providers could 'get closer' to their patients, and consider the role of service quality in enhancing overall customer satisfaction. This is now of great significance since attending to the important dimensions of service quality may be one of the few ways in which healthcare providers can in the future establish a truly sustainable form of competitive advantage.

The chapter will then conclude by considering the relevance of marketing to two key categories of healthcare provider, namely hospitals and those responsible for the delivery of primary healthcare, such as General Practitioners (GPs). A number of the key marketing issues faced by each category of organization will be discussed.

Healthcare Systems

It is important to begin this section of the text by defining exactly what we mean by the expression 'healthcare system'. The World Health Organization (WHO) defines health as 'a state of complete physical, mental and social well being and not merely the absence of disease or infirmity' (WHO 1986: 1). The system established by every member of the WHO should hence be capable of responding to a wide range of physical, chemical, infectious, psychological, and social problems. In short, the concept of healthcare is much wider than many people believe. Healthcare, as Edgren (1991) argues, should be viewed as much broader in scope than mere medical care. Healthcare systems thus need not only to give consideration to medical treatment but also to a range of social, cognitive, and emotional factors—societies must not only *be* clinically healthy, they should *feel* healthy too. Marketing thus has a key role to play in managing the expectations of customers and matching these as far as possible to the range of services provided. Marketing can also help in developing the quality of communications with various healthcare communities and in encouraging individuals to adopt healthier lifestyles, thus minimizing the use of resources. Importantly, however, marketing can also help improve the nature of healthcare relationships and gently prise some physicians away from a view of the world in which they offer daily consultations to a range of clinical complaints rather than the human beings who are suffering from them. As West (1994: 29) notes, the medical profession have always been effective in attempting to cure disease; regrettably, however, many physicians and indeed healthcare organizations have left patients with the impression 'that what matters least of all is the average human life . . . its comfort and its happiness.'

The root of the problem in some countries has been the manner in which the healthcare framework has developed. In the UK, for example, the National Health Service (NHS) has prided itself on its ability to be able to provide high-quality healthcare, free of charge to anyone who might require it. While, broadly speaking, it has proved successful in achieving this goal, its success has come at a price. Until recently patients had very few rights in respect of the treatment they received and from whom—it was necessary to take whatever was on offer. Individuals attended the family doctor that they had always attended and accepted any referrals that were recommended to whichever hospital happened to serve their locality. Since patient choice was not an issue, the medical institutions had a virtually captive audience for the services they provided. It was not surprising therefore that under such circumstances an inward looking product-oriented focus began to develop.

Interestingly, this manifested itself not only in declining levels of customer service, but also in wide variations in clinical care from one region of the country to another. The idea that one should both serve customer requirements and monitor the performance of 'competitors' to ensure that only the highest industry standards were maintained was anathema.

In an attempt to raise standards of service and to raise the performance of all healthcare organizations to that of the best, successive UK governments through the late 1990s and early 2000s have introduced changes into the way that UK healthcare is delivered and managed. The key changes introduced are as follows:

• Money now 'follows the patient'. Essentially NHS funds are now allocated to reflect the size of the population local to particular healthcare providers. Adjustments are made to account for different demographic patterns and patterns of need. A facility also exists for GPs to refer patients to a hospital of their choice, which may not necessarily be the local one. Under such circumstances funding will follow the patient to the hospital selected for treatment.

• Regulation of the market has been achieved through written contracts. Contracts are now drawn up between purchasers and providers which specify in detail the nature of the services to be provided, how many patients will benefit, and at what cost. Incidentally the term 'contract' is now rarely used by marketing practitioners in the sector—they prefer the term 'agreement'.

• Healthcare providers now have greater management autonomy. Providers are free to compete for service contracts and have the freedom to structure themselves in an appropriate manner in order to facilitate this process. Business units may, for example, be constructed around key competencies.

• Healthcare providers are now subject to medical audits to monitor the quality of healthcare provided and thus have greater accountability. The audit commission has also been given responsibility for conducting what might be termed 'value for money' audits as part of the new financial framework.

The changes in the UK have also switched the emphasis from cure to prevention, creating the need for the first time for GPs to actively encourage their patients to attend the surgery for a range of preventative treatments and healthcare advice. Moreover, GPs are now obliged to see their patients on a regular basis irrespective of whether or not they are sick. This monitoring system has compelled GPs to play a greater role in enhancing the overall health of the nation and for the first time many have had to consider researching the ongoing needs of those individuals comprising their local community. Marketing skills are therefore beginning to be sought for the first time and a number of larger practices now have a dedicated individual responsible for fulfilling such a role. Typically this might involve researching demand, promoting a range of health/wellness clinics, the attraction of new patients, and the general facilitation of healthier lifestyles in the local community.

In the USA both the need for and the application of marketing has historically been rather different. Under the US healthcare system, income-earning Americans are obliged to have their own healthcare insurance, in many cases provided as a benefit by their employer. Healthcare insurers then pay on their clients' behalf for any healthcare treatment that might prove necessary in hospitals associated with their scheme. As the system is a fee-paying one, Americans have traditionally had a much greater choice of where they will receive their medical treatment. In addition, individual doctors are remunerated not by the State but by fees reflecting the quality of their individual reputation. Marketing has therefore long played a role in communicating with the healthcare market, and the promotion of all forms of medical care is quite commonplace.

Only the very poorest members of American society are looked after by the State through the Medicaid and Medicare systems. The federal government pays over 60 per cent of the cost of Medicaid, with the balance being met from the finances of each individual US state. Tough decisions thus have to made at a local level both about the cut-off point at which Medicaid cover will be triggered and the range of services that will be provided. Often there is a trade-off between the two (Ranade 1994).

Thus the 'old style' NHS, before its recent reforms, and the US system could be viewed as being at opposite ends of a healthcare continuum reflecting substantial variations in the level of financial support volunteered by the State. The NHS reforms introduced in 1990 served to introduce quasi-markets into the UK system and thus established a 'halfway' house between these two extremes. Many other countries are now experimenting with similar systems, such as Sweden, Finland, New Zealand, and a number of the newly independent Eastern European states.

While the need for the application of the marketing concept at a philosophical level is universal, since all societies have the right to expect that their healthcare systems will reflect the needs and wants of their people, the need for its application at a functional level will differ substantially from country to country. In the USA, it is usual to encounter communication campaigns promoting practitioners in all branches of healthcare, whereas only the private institutions in the UK currently find it necessary to maintain such a heightened public profile. In the USA GPs openly advertise to attract patients, since they rely almost entirely on fees to survive. In the UK, however, where levels of income have at least until recently been guaranteed, advertising is all but non-existent. It is interesting to note, though, that British GPs are having to learn some new marketing communications skills as individual practices begin to face up to the need to encourage patients to attend a range of health and wellness clinics.

The Healthcare Marketing Challenge

Healthcare marketing is undoubtedly one of the most challenging of all the forms of nonprofit marketing. To begin with, the healthcare product is probably the most intangible of all the services previously described. The consumer has no real way of, for example, being able to assess the competence of a surgeon either before or after an operation has been completed. They have simply to put their faith in the skills of the medical profession and take everything on trust. Of course, patients can and do form opinions about the quality of the healthcare product, based on a whole series of surrogates, including their physical surroundings and the bedside manner of their physician. Ironically it is thus possible for a patient to leave a hospital dissatisfied with the service they have received, even if their operation was performed to the very highest of technical standards. Unfortunately the reverse is probably also true and physicians who are among the least competent of the whole profession can still attain very high levels of customer satisfaction by paying careful attention to other aspects of the service encounter! Putting aside the ethics of the latter approach to healthcare, it seems clear that marketing has much to offer professionals in allowing them to do justice to their image, by supporting the excellence achieved in clinical care with good-quality customer service.

Intangibility is, however, only one of the particular difficulties that healthcare marketers need to overcome. France and Grover (1992) list a number of other factors which serve to complicate the marketing task.

• *Mismatch between customer expectations and actual delivery*. While all service encounters offer a multitude of opportunities for the provider to fall short of the customer's expectations, this is perhaps a particular risk for healthcare providers. While a given individual may have set expectations about the outcome of a particular treatment, his physiology and psychology will in practice mitigate this substantially. In the former, no two individuals are alike and they will enter a programme of treatment suffering with various degrees of the ailment, have different demographic characteristics, and different levels of physical strength and recuperative power. All these individual characteristics are quite beyond the control of the physician and yet will impact substantially on the outcome achieved. Similarly, whatever the quality of the medical outcome, the psychology of the patient will determine how this is actually perceived. Moreover, psychology will also determine the emphasis that patients will place on the various components of the overall service. Thus some patients require a greater degree of hand-holding and/or information than others. Practitioners therefore have the difficult task of formulating a judgement about the degree of support required and acting accordingly.

● *The number of service providers.* In a healthcare setting, the individual patient will encounter a variety of different categories of personnel. During the course of attending a hospital for a routine operation, for example, patients will have to deal with administrative staff, nurses, anaesthetists, catering staff, hospital porters, a variety of physicians, and their own surgeon. Thus a variety of opportunities exist for the encounter to go awry.

● *Unpredictable demand.* It is almost impossible to predict with any degree of accuracy the demand for a healthcare service. Newly emerged strains of virus, serious accidents, natural disasters, and even armed conflicts make planning complex. Provision clearly has to be set at a level that will meet all foreseeable demands, but perishability can then become a problem. Under-utilization of a service can cause serious financial problems during a 'lean' period. Marketing can hence have an important role to play in attempting to even out demand as far as is practical.

● *Derived demand.* One of the major difficulties for healthcare marketers is that it can be difficult to know when to market and to whom. The key decision maker will often not be the patient, but rather their GP, a specialist, or a member of their immediate family. This is an issue for healthcare providers in the USA where considerable choice in respect of an appropriate provider can be exercised.

Of all these difficulties, the inherent intangibility is perhaps the most difficult for healthcare marketers to come to terms with. The increasingly competitive environment is making it essential for those working in this arena to clearly differentiate their provision from that available elsewhere in the market. The most obvious route to the achievement of this goal is to position an organization as providing excellence in clinical care. Since, however, the patient has no way of evaluating this aspect of the provision, the search for some form of competitive advantage is problematic. Moreover, many categories of healthcare provider (e.g. hospitals) provide such a wide range of clinical services that to position an institution as being 'a provider of excellent standards of clinical care' would be meaningless. Excellence in which field?

According to San Augustine et al. (1992) organizations which learn to deal with this complexity will in the future lead the field. Positioning, the authors argue, is set to become *the* key marketing strategy in achieving a sustainable competitive advantage in healthcare. Given the observations above, perhaps there are two primary dimensions of the healthcare service that could be used as the basis for a strong market positioning.

(1) Providers could aim to position themselves as 'the best in the world at . . .' (Quinn 1992). Hence the key clinical benefit of sending a patient to a particular institution would be clear to all healthcare purchasers. Indeed the portfolio of services could support the identified area of expertise, providing clinical service in related areas and building up appropriate resources accordingly.

(2) Where a wide portfolio of existing provision is already in evidence, however, the healthcare marketer may be better advised to seek elements of positioning which can have a direct benefit for the attraction of patients to every clinical service the organization can offer. There are comparatively few ways in which such a 'global' positioning might

be accomplished, and a reliance on some aspect of the overall service quality provided has hence become commonplace. If a particular organization can build a reputation in the marketplace for being a provider of a high-quality service, greater numbers of customers will be attracted. From the perspective of the provider, this means a concentration not only on clinical care, but also on the wider range of surrogates which patients use to build up their own perceptions of the quality of their experience.

Given the importance of service quality in healthcare, the next section will identify those 'ingredients' that have in the past been found to have the greatest impact on patient perceptions.

The Dimensions of Healthcare Service Quality

There is now a consensus emerging from the available research to suggest that patients actually define the quality of their healthcare provision as a function of three separate intangible factors. Bopp (1990) suggests that these can be viewed as:

- expressive caring
- expressive professionalism
- expressive competence.

Since the competence of staff is particularly intangible, the author argues that this is assessed using a number of other cues as surrogates. To determine what these might be, it is worth returning briefly to the service quality literature introduced in Chapter 7. Lytle and Mokwa (1992) adapt the SERVQUAL model for use in conceptualizing the overall healthcare experience. Their view of the healthcare 'product' is depicted in Figure 12.1.

Core Benefit

The core benefit is the outcome that the patient is seeking from the treatment she receives. This expectation will be shaped by conversations with family or friends, literature that the patient might have read in connection with her illness, and the advice and opinions of her physicians. Patients will clearly evaluate her experience according to the extent to which their expectations of its outcome have been met. Obviously they cannot assess the clinical skills of their physician, but they can assess the difference in how they feel after the healthcare intervention has taken place.

Intangible Benefits

The intangible benefits are received from the quality of the interaction which takes place between the patient and the physician and their staff. The four SERVQUAL dimensions of reliability, empathy, assurance, and responsiveness are each key areas for the healthcare provider to address as it is relatively easy for the patient to form an opinion on these.

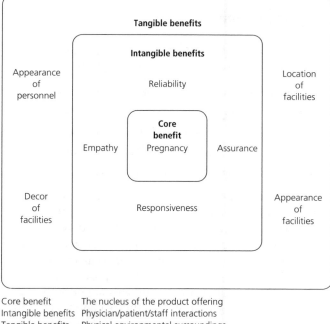

Core benefit	The nucleus of the product offering
Intangible benefits	Physician/patient/staff interactions
Tangible benefits	Physical environmental surroundings

Figure 12.1 Healthcare product bundle of benefits

Source: Reprinted with permission from *Journal of Healthcare Marketing*, Lytle and Mokwa (1992), Vol. 12, No. 1

In the case of comparatively minor interventions, where clinical benefits may be difficult to assess, these intangible elements will form the basis of the majority of the overall assessment of service quality.

Tangible Benefits

The expressive competence referred to earlier in the work of Bopp is difficult for a patient to assess. They have no way of being able to compare their surgeon's level of competence with that of another. They can, however, appraise the appearance of the facilities, the extent to which the latest technology appears to be being utilized, the comfort afforded by the physical surroundings, and the overall appearance of the personnel. These aspects, when combined, will allow the patient to form a perception of the overall competence of their healthcare provider.

While an attention to all these aspects of the healthcare encounter may be warranted, it is important for healthcare marketers to establish some sense of priority. Should priority be given to improving the quality of the physical environment, the interpersonal skills of staff, or reducing the length of time it is necessary to wait for treatment? From which of these areas would the patient be likely to draw the most value from potential improvements? These questions will be addressed below.

Enhancing Service Quality

The reader will recall from Chapter 7 that customer satisfaction can be modelled by looking at the five gaps proposed by Parasuraman et al. (1988).

- *Gap* 1—between consumer expectations and management perception
- *Gap* 2—between management perception and service quality specification
- *Gap* 3—between service quality specifications and service delivery
- *Gap* 4—between service quality and external communications
- *Gap* 5—between perceived service and expected service.

Of all the gaps, Gap 1 is undoubtedly the most important. Gap 5 cannot be managed directly, as it is merely the sum of all the others, and the size of Gaps 2 to 4 will largely be governed by the extent to which providers actually understand the expectations of their customers. Thus, for example, an attempt to address faulty service specifications without first acquiring a detailed understanding of what matters to the customer is likely to be both futile and costly. Any attempt to improve customer satisfaction with healthcare should hence commence with a thorough analysis of the nature of Gap 1.

In an interesting study of this gap in the healthcare context, O'Connor et al. (1994) concluded that clinical contact employees (such as nurses), physicians, and administrators consistently underestimate patient expectations for each of the five SERVQUAL dimensions. In particular, physicians were found to have the poorest understanding, and the dimensions of empathy and responsiveness were the least well understood.

To achieve meaningful improvements in perceived service quality, therefore, healthcare providers would be advised not to focus solely on the enhancement of tangible factors. The greatest impact will be obtained if physicians (and, to a lesser extent, clinical contact employees) are educated about the importance of good communication with customers, promptness, helpfulness, and the facilitation of easy access.

Indeed, there is much support for this view throughout the healthcare marketing literature and there has been considerable research conducted over the past thirty years to determine the components of medical care most likely to affect patients' perceptions of service quality. Ware et al. (1978), in a detailed review of the literature, identified eight satisfaction dimensions which they were subsequently able to reduce (through factor analysis) to four in the healthcare setting (i.e. physician conduct, availability of services, continuity/confidence and efficiency/outcomes of care). Brown and Swartz (1989) meanwhile identified physician interactions as being the most important in determining satisfaction. The authors also concluded that a fifth dimension of convenience/access should be added to those proposed earlier by Ware et al.

Allied to the factor 'ease of access' is the concept of waiting time which may also warrant consideration, particularly by primary physicians. A number of studies have confirmed that the time spent waiting for a doctor is inversely related to patient satisfaction (see LuAnn and Andersen 1980). When one considers that Maister (1985) found that anxiety can increase the perception of waiting time, this additional factor's relevance to the healthcare setting becomes readily apparent.

More recently Sage (1991) identified five key factors which may be used to measure the quality of healthcare outcomes: access, choice, information, redress, and representation. In the context of the primary healthcare practice, Gabbott and Hogg (1994) established that factors relating to the nature of the individual practice such as the range of services offered and the ease of access to them are important, as are the responsiveness and empathy of the physician.

The physical environment can also affect customers' perceptions of quality, and Lych and Schuler (1990) suggest that hospital patients in particular will evaluate the service quality received, in part by assessing their physical environment. Andrus and Buchheister (1985) found, not surprisingly, that pleasant and comfortable surroundings are important factors in determining patient satisfaction, in their case, with dental care.

In the USA a number of other studies are also of interest, each of which has examined patient satisfaction with medical services. These include Larsen and Rootman (1976), Hall and Dornan (1988) and Singh (1990). They broadly agree that the following factors all have the capacity to influence patient satisfaction:

- physician's manner
- quality of information
- professional and technical competence of physician
- interpersonal and relational skills of physician
- nature of the patient's medical problems
- demographic background of patient.

The reader will appreciate from the above that there has been considerable academic interest in this field. A variety of healthcare studies have shown that many different factors have the capacity to influence levels of patient satisfaction, and there is not always much agreement between authors on the specifics thereof. Health marketing professionals would hence be well advised to treat patient satisfaction as situation-specific and to conduct their own primary research before embarking on any form of service improvement programme.

Healthcare Information

While space here does not permit a detailed analysis of all the factors capable of influencing patient satisfaction, it is worth enlarging for a moment on the provision of healthcare information. Healthcare information has the capacity to influence satisfaction both directly and indirectly and in an age when consumers are increasingly expected to make their own decisions in respect of treatments and providers, the role of marketing in communicating effectively with customers will become increasingly crucial.

Healthcare communications can be either internal or external. With regard to the latter we have already established that the nature of expectations in respect of the core healthcare product can be shaped by the exposure of a particular individual to a variety of communications messages. These messages, which can now come from a plethora of different sources, help to inform patient perceptions of both their complaint and the likelihood of a successful outcome deriving from a medical intervention. A key task for healthcare marketers is thus to manage these flows of information to ensure that the patient's perceptions of the outcome of their treatment is as realistic as possible.

Most healthcare systems now actively encourage the development of consumer choice—the ability to select one's own physician and the ability to be able to discuss with him the relative merits of each course of action available. This dimension of the healthcare framework can only function adequately if physicians understand the range of information sources that are now available and understand the nature of their own role in relation to these.

The increased availability of good quality healthcare information has led to many individuals becoming what Berkowitz and Flexner (1980) refer to as 'activist health care consumers', a lifestyle category evidenced by rapidly increasing sales of home diagnostic equipment, greater involvement in decisions, and a general move (at least in the USA) towards increased 'doctor shopping'. This is a relatively new phenomenon since medical information, only a few years ago, used to be the preserve of the medical profession and be disseminated solely through scholarly journals and specialized conferences (Bunn 1993). Patients were ill informed and could hence exercise little judgement over the suitability of the treatment their physician was recommending. Today, the doctor is no longer even the primary source of medical information (Jenson 1987), with a wide range of communication channels now available for 'consultation', including:

- health magazines;
- medical textbooks;
- libraries;
- the Internet;
- pre-recorded health messages—such as those supplied by a number of food manufacturers;
- television/radio/general interest magazines;
- trusts/foundations—specializing in a particular medical complaint;
- other medical professionals.

One result of this explosion in healthcare information has been a move towards medical terminology finding its way into everyday language (Johnsson 1990) and the facilitation of a healthcare system in which consumers are encouraged to take a greater responsibility for their own health by adopting healthier lifestyles.

Healthcare information can also be viewed as flowing internally between the provider and the patient while they under the care of that institution. Patients need to be kept informed about the progress of their treatment and now have a right to expect healthcare providers to share the detail of the advantages and disadvantages of particular forms of treatment. This in turn has created a need for many staff to be re-trained to transform what used to be only a one-way exchange of information into a dialogue. There is hence a clear role for internal marketing within healthcare institutions to instil a mindset that makes staff aware of the importance of this process for both the well-being and the satisfaction of their patients.

Marketing Primary Healthcare

There are a range of marketing issues that primary healthcare practitioners (such as GPs) now need to address, including those listed below.

- *Identification of market needs*. A careful identification of the needs of those within their geographical catchment area is essential for every GP practice. An analysis of current and future healthcare needs will allow a practice to plan its portfolio of services. GP practices, for example, cited in an area with an increasingly elderly population may need to plan for the inclusion of chiropody or physiotherapy services at some stage in the foreseeable future. If demand is likely to be high, it may be more cost-effective for these to be provided within the confines of the practice rather than contracting other institutions to provide it. An analysis of need may also yield valuable information in respect of the range of preventative clinics that would best serve the community. Practice nursing staff may run a range of highly specialized clinics dealing with issues such as drug abuse, smoking, alcoholism, obesity, arthritis, asthma and, perhaps more commonly, motherhood.

- *Promotion of healthcare clinics*. Once a decision has been taken about the appropriateness of running a particular clinic, its existence will need to be carefully promoted among the patients of the surgery most likely to benefit. At a superficial level, this might require the staff to produce posters which could be displayed in the waiting room, local libraries, and community centres. More imaginative practices will use database records to promote the clinic specifically to those individuals they perceive would derive the greatest benefit.

- *Information/education*. GPs are increasingly recognizing the importance of good healthcare information to the well-being of their society. Recent meningitis scares and the emergence of a number of vicious strains of flu virus have placed the onus on GPs to supply up-to-date and timely information to those most at risk. It is no longer sufficient for practice staff to 'fire-fight' problems as they arise. A marketing perspective can help plan communications mechanisms that can easily be activated should the unthinkable occur. Moreover, as the society in which we live continues to age, it is likely that ever greater demands will be placed on the healthcare service. It will therefore be increasingly in GPs' interest to educate patients in the self-diagnosis of a range of minor ailments so that they can select their own treatments and avoid unnecessary consultations. Similarly, there can be few GPs who have not spent at least one sleepless night in the past attending to a range of relatively minor call-outs which could easily have waited until the following day for a routine appointment at the surgery. (Of course, today few GPs are willing to make home visits due to a lack of time.) Marketing can help educate patients to recognize how best to use the services that the GP can provide.

• *Enhancement of customer satisfaction.* Perhaps the greatest contribution that marketing can make to healthcare lies in its ability to be able to direct resources to those areas most likely to increase overall customer satisfaction. The preceding discussion has already highlighted the dimensions of the service encounter that could offer the greatest utility in this regard and it is a matter for individual practices to determine the factors of most relevance to their own circumstances. An understanding of how patients evaluate the quality of the healthcare they receive can allow those responsible for managing a GP practice to 'value engineer' the service they provide, concentrating resources in those areas most likely to enhance the overall experience of their clients. Similarly, cost savings could be made in those areas where little or no value is currently being perceived.

• *Motivation of practice staff.* If the marketing concept is adopted at a philosophical as well as a functional level, GPs will be encouraged to view their own practice staff as customers and treat them accordingly. There have been a number of instances reported of late where GPs have instructed their practice nurses to run a particular category of clinic and then failed to offer any additional support that might prove necessary. Internal marketing could hence have much to offer GPs to help them to consider the requirements of their staff for adequate training and support.

• *Attraction of patients.* The new healthcare framework rewards GPs, among other things, for the number of patients they are able to attract. While in most regions of the country a general shortage of doctors means there is no shortage of demand, those practices that do face direct competition will need to carefully assess its impact and plan their marketing strategy accordingly. Marketing skills can also be immensely valuable for new practices which are only just beginning to attract patients for the first time. In such cases, patients need to be given sufficient reason to switch from their existing practice and to register with a new GP. Marketing's role in such circumstances is to assist practice managers in overcoming consumer apathy and giving patients enough encouragement to ensure that sufficient numbers make the transition.

Marketing Hospital Services

The quality of hospital marketing varies considerably from country to country. In the USA it has long been recognized that marketing has a significant role to play in the attraction of patients, although there still remain some small pockets of resistance among hospital administrators (McDevitt and Shields 1985). Given that Wrenn (1994) determined that as little as a 10 per cent improvement in a hospital's marketing orientation could be associated with a $25 million increase in total net patient revenues and an 8 per cent increase in occupancy rates, it is no surprise that a change in perception is presently ongoing.

In the USA, over 79 per cent of individuals have a preferred hospital, although the strength of this bond does not appear to be particularly strong. Inguanzo and Harju (1985) found that fewer than 50 per cent of these individuals would characterize their preference as 'strong'. The strongest degrees of loyalty would appear to be exhibited by people living in the east of the country, in cities housing between 50 000 and 5 000 000 people, aged 55 or older and with household incomes of under $15 000. We may thus conclude that most segments of US society would be willing to change healthcare provider if given a sufficient reason to do so. Factors such as the level of new technology employed, the courtesy of staff, cost, and the recommendation of a primary physician have all been shown to influence switching behaviour. Healthcare marketers within a hospital thus have a key role to play in the development of future hospital business.

In the UK, however, the framework within which most hospitals work is rather different. Until recently, hospital income was guaranteed and as a consequence there was no requirement to view healthcare purchasers as customers. As hospitals now begin to face competitive pressures, a few are starting to recognize the need to market their services and to employ full-time marketers to assist them in this task. In particular, NHS hospital trusts require marketing skills to do the following.

- *Redefine their catchment areas.* Since hospitals are no longer restricted to treating patients within their immediate geographical area, there is a need to redefine the target market, concentrating on those areas which have the densest populations and hence the greatest demand for healthcare resources.

- *Define the competition.* In many regions of the country it may be possible to avoid damaging direct competition with neighbouring hospitals by emphasizing those aspects of the service that complement the other provision available locally. Even in cases where this proves not to be possible it will be necessary to monitor competitor activity and to benchmark hospital performance accordingly.

- *Network.* Despite the prevailing aura of competition it may well be in the interests of some hospitals to cooperate. Where service gaps exist, collaborative agreements could be developed to ensure that adequate coverage of all medical specialisms is provided within one geographical region.

- *Get close to customers.* Given that GPs now have the power to purchase hospital services from wherever they choose, it may be appropriate for a hospital to consider appointing a GP practice coordinator who will tour the local practices explaining the range of services available and the unique advantages of sending patients to their particular institution. Indeed since many NHS Trusts now have such an appointment, a hospital which fails to get close to its customers in this way may find itself at a significant disadvantage.

- *Identify the customers.* Hospitals need to identify those individuals who have the greatest capacity to influence the healthcare decision. In the USA, where patients arguably have greater choice, this is a key issue as the decision-making unit can often be complex. Moreover, the cultivation of customer loyalty becomes extremely important in retaining family business. Phillips (1980) found that the key to sustaining loyalty lies in the careful targeting of female patients. Women account for 70 per cent of all hospital admissions and have been shown to be responsible for over 70 per cent of their family's healthcare decisions—they therefore represent an important target market.

- *Involve customers in new service developments.* While it may be difficult to involve the end users of healthcare services in this way, there is no reason why intermediaries such as GPs should not be actively involved in the design of new hospital services. Having contributed actively to the birth of a new service, GPs are thereafter more likely to use it for the benefit of their patients. The process of service development is also likely to strengthen relationships between GPs and key management/clinical staff within the hospital.

• *Develop employees.* Given the key role of all hospital staff in delivering an appropriate level of service quality, hospital staff should be treated as internal customers of the organization and treated as the administration would have them treat external customers. Good internal communications and customer care training programmes should be initiated and the results monitored to ensure the achievement of the desired outcomes.

• *Conduct internal promotion.* There is still much resistance to marketing, particularly in UK hospitals. In order to win the hearts and minds of clinical staff, marketing staff need to promote their successes. Only when clinical staff understand the benefits that accrue to the hospital in increased patient throughput, job security, and enhancements to service quality, will marketing build a better reputation for itself. Marketing successes should hence be unashamedly promoted throughout the whole organization.

• *Incorporate three areas into institutional development: cost, quality, customer satisfaction.* Careful costing of all activities, together with a detailed analysis of service quality, should allow hospital marketers to engineer the value they deliver to their customers. This in turn should greatly enhance levels of customers satisfaction.

• *Not underestimate the impact of change.* The health services of most developed countries are currently in a state of flux. Ageing populations and a time of economic constraint are forcing governments to take a long hard look at the way in which healthcare is managed and delivered. Healthcare marketers therefore need to monitor their external environment particularly closely to ensure that they stay in touch with both proposed and actual change. Only by responding to environmental challenges ahead of the competition will the long-term stability of any healthcare organization be truly assured. (Source: adapted from Crowther (1995) and Petrochuk and Javalgi (1996)).

The Richmond case study below illustrates the role that marketing can play in respect of many of these issues.

CASE STUDY 12.1 RICHMOND COMMUNITY HEALTHCARE HAMLET

Background

Richmond has enjoyed the services of a local hospital for over 130 years. The Royal hospital in Kew Foot Road, Richmond on Thames has stood on its current site since 1868 when it was first opened by the Earl Russell. Interestingly the purchase of the original building was no more than a happy accident of fate. Following the marriage of HRH the Prince of Wales in 1863 the local community decided to celebrate the occasion by providing a very special dinner for the benefit of the local poor and children under the age of 7 years. Having successfully fundraised for the event and purchased the necessary foodstuffs, the organizing committee found themselves with the princely sum of £40, 6s and 2d remaining. Anxious to invest this sum in 'some charitable purpose of a more permanent character'

continues

the decision was taken to put the money aside as the nucleus of a fund for the creation of a local hospital—thus The Royal Hospital was born.

By 1869, 115 patients had been treated, with the average duration of each stay being 35 days. Interestingly, the average cost of each in-patient at the time was a mere £6 0s 10d—somewhat less than it would be today! In the years that followed, the hospital saw a gradual expansion of both its in- and out-patient provisions and a number of new ground-breaking clinics were added, including an ophthalmic wing in 1908. The hospital also looked after servicemen and local air-raid victims during the two World Wars and from 1939–45 a minimum of 45 beds were put aside for this specific purpose.

The National Health Service Act of 1946 brought the hospital into the new national healthcare system and by 1956 it had grown into a general hospital with 121 beds. Unfortunately, however, by the 1970s the buildings were becoming increasingly costly to maintain and much of the equipment was beginning to look dated. This, combined with improvements at other hospitals, compelled the district health authority to shut down the hospital in 1984. Aside from a brief spell as a homeless hostel, the buildings were hardly used from that time until 1988 when the earlier decision was revoked and provision started at the hospital once more. However, this reprieve was to be short-lived due to a serious fire which destroyed most of the building in 1992.

A New Healthcare Concept

With such a proud tradition of healthcare provision behind it, however, it was perhaps inevitable that this would not be the end of the Royal's story. The necessary monies were ultimately found to completely refurbish the buildings and only a few months after the fire the Richmond, Twickenham and Roehampton Healthcare NHS Trust (based at Queen Mary's University Hospital, Roehampton) was formed, following the national healthcare reforms of 1991. One of the primary aims of this new organization was to consider the situation of the Royal Hospital and to give it a new lease of life. The Trust thus decided that the site should form part of its 'Right Place' strategy—a radical new concept in healthcare provision. In essence the Royal was set to become a central health resource for the whole Richmond community. The new Richmond Community Healthcare Hamlet, as it was to become known, was formed to house a variety of medical services, including district nursing, health visiting, mental health services, a rehabilitation unit, and ultimately a general medical outpatients department.

In April 1996, the first wing was completed and the first medical services began to be installed in their new facility. The mental health service and community services (e.g. district nursing) were the first to take up residence, although in view of the size of the buildings, a decision was later taken to provide an outpatients department in an attempt to maximize the usage of the hospital. This move was also consistent with the desire of the Trust to outreach into its local community. Indeed, the primary motivation for all the provision at the site had always been the desire to take the services that were likely to be in most demand by the community and place them *in* that community. The creation of an ENT (Ear Nose and Throat) outpatients clinic, for example, would have been consistent with this goal, as some 20 per cent of patients attending at GP surgeries fall within the remit of this discipline and for this reason one of the local acute providers is currently in discussions to provide this clinic at the Hamlet.

In the new era of NHS competition, it was further realized that it was no longer appropriate for the Trust to expect patients to travel distances to consult their hospital specialist. While it may have been managerially optimal to see all outpatients at the Trust's primary facility (Queen Mary's), the Trust had now to actively seek patients, or face the possibility of losing them to Trusts based in other areas. Indeed, a number of NHS Trusts had already expressed an interest in 'poaching' business from the catchment areas of neighbouring organizations.

continues

Interestingly, this latter point has become less of an issue with the passage of time as Queen Mary's itself is now facing a de-merger. Historically Queen Mary's services were purchased by two health authorities—Kingston and Richmond, and Merton, Sutton, and Wandsworth, because the hospital was located on the boundary between the two. However, since each district health authority has its own general hospital the decision has been taken to move Queen Mary's services slowly out into these and to leave only outpatients clinics provided at a local level. With such a radical change in organization ongoing, concerns about the impact of competition on the Hamlet are therefore much less of an issue than improving the utilization of the assets on the site to ensure survival. With the outpatients facility only operating one day per week and the X-ray facility for only half a day, the unit costs of treatment are currently very high.

The Marketing Challenge

With this latter point in mind, the management of the Hamlet decided to encourage other health-care providers to use the facilities of the site. Consultants from other NHS Trusts form a key target market for this initiative. There was seen to be no reason why consultants from neighbouring health-care Trusts could not use the facilities of the Hamlet as long as the majority of the provision was seen to be complementary and to the overall benefit of the people of Richmond. Clinics will there-fore be operated at the Hamlet provided by a variety of different healthcare Trusts, each of whom will pay an agreed amount for the use of the facility. The initiative thus improves the amount of income accruing to the Hamlet and facilitates a greater degree of competition in the local area by allowing neighbouring Trusts to offer services to the local GPs. This will mean that patients will have access to specialist clinics and therefore a greater level of 'choice', thus ensuring that the existence of the healthcare Hamlet will improve the quality of the medical service provided to the people of Richmond.

Aside from encouraging other Trusts to utilize the facilities, Hamlet marketers are also considering the opportunities offered by the provision of private medical care. Richmond has traditionally been a very wealthy suburb of London where as a consequence the demand for private healthcare has always been strong. The establishment of a local clinic that specialists could use as their base for treating patients close to their own home is therefore likely to be attractive. Moreover, since the Hamlet buildings have been completely refurbished to the highest of standards, due to the existence of listing orders on some parts of the building, private patients attending the site for treatment would be unlikely to notice any significant difference in standards between those of the Hamlet and those of some private hospitals. Encouraging the provision of private healthcare at the site therefore also represents a possible growth opportunity.

Allied to this latter point, the Hamlet has recently been approached by providers of various forms of complementary medicine who also wish to make use of its facilities. Local demand for homeopathy, osteopathy, etc. is likely to be strong and the reputations of the various practition-ers would doubtless be enhanced by an association with their local community hospital. From the Hamlet's perspective, encouraging as wide a form of medical provision as possible would greatly enhance the degree of asset utilization and lead in future to a gradual expansion of the hours during which the site would be open for business. This latter point is a particular issue, since until access is expanded, the Hamlet is unlikely to be perceived by local people as a genuine community resource.

To assist in this, the decision was also taken to encourage associated voluntary organizations to utilize the building, and space was hence set aside for the local branch of the mental health charity, RABMIND, and the Kingston and Richmond Alcohol Counselling Services. Aside from deepening the

continues

already strong relationship between the healthcare and voluntary sectors, in the case of the Hamlet, the presence of these organizations would also ensure that rooms were used out of hours for additional patient support, counselling, self-help groups, etc.

The Launch

While the Hamlet has been open since April 1996 it has been a phased opening as each block of the building was completed. The Hamlet's portfolio is only now approaching that which was originally envisaged at the commencement of the project. For this reason the Hamlet's official opening did not take place until December 1997. The event was seen as being of considerable importance since it afforded Hamlet marketers their first real opportunity to genuinely promote the site to each of their three target markets.

The first of these is undoubtedly the general public. A key message on the day of the launch was that the 'Hamlet is here and open for business'. While there has been a hospital on the site for over a century, there were many individuals who simply did not know that the site has now re-opened and/or that it had been completely refurbished. For this reason, local press and radio-coverage was sought to help publicize the existence of the new community resource. On the day of the launch, the site was open to all visitors and the various healthcare providers erected displays detailing the nature of the services provided and, where appropriate, their benefits.

While this approach helped to raise public awareness, it was less effective at encouraging awareness specifically among members of the medical profession. Indeed, in the case of GPs in particular, a much greater degree of information must be imparted than simply 'we are open for business'. GPs need to understand the benefits that could accrue to their patients from the full range of provision and to experience something of the process that their 'customers' will encounter when they attend for a particular clinic or service. The problem, however, lies in persuading this target group to attend the site. They are particularly busy individuals with little time to simply walk around or be given some form of tour. Hamlet marketers have therefore encouraged the various providers that will be using the site to run CPD (Continuous Professional Development) workshops which GPs can attend to obtain credit towards their annual target of training hours. These workshops would hence have an educational function, in that they would serve to deepen GPs' understanding of some form of mainstream or even complementary medicine, but they would also bring individuals into the site where they can be informed of the full range of services provided.

The third target market for the launch is clearly the healthcare providers themselves. Individuals who might potentially use the facilities to operate their own clinics can be encouraged to attend to view for themselves the quality of the refurbishment and the accommodation available.

The Future

Clearly the official launch of the new facility will be only the first key role for marketing as a function to perform within the Hamlet. As the portfolio of services is extended, there may be many opportunities for the Hamlet as a whole to benefit from collective marketing activities such as contacts with GPs, other healthcare purchasers, or even local events hosted for the benefit of the Richmond community. The advantages of a united approach to marketing are likely to be considerable and hence marketing has been highlighted as one of the key issues that will be discussed at monthly meetings of the Hamlet's management committee. It is intended that these meetings will be attended by representatives from all the healthcare providers currently utilizing the Hamlet, so that all may have a say in its future.

■ **SUMMARY**

In this chapter we have reviewed the healthcare frameworks of both the USA and the UK. In the UK, substantial changes have recently been introduced in the manner in which the NHS is managed, through the creation of quasi markets in which healthcare purchasers now have a greater right to choose their provider. This structural change has created a need for marketing skills within the sector as institutions begin to respond for the first time to the threat of competition.

As in the education sector discussed earlier, positioning is likely to become the key marketing issue for healthcare marketers to address in the years ahead. Indeed this drive towards the attainment of some unique position in the market will undoubtedly compel healthcare institutions to give greater consideration to the needs of their patients and the quality of service they are afforded. This chapter has included a brief review of the available literature in this respect and concluded that service quality matters are best regarded as situation-specific, requiring the provider to conduct its own research to establish real priorities to improve them.

■ **DISCUSSION QUESTIONS**

1. In your role as the marketing director of a NHS Trust, prepare a briefing document for a newly recruited marketing colleague, explaining the changes that have recently taken place in the healthcare environment and the additional need for marketing that this has created.

2. In what ways might the marketing of a healthcare service differ from the marketing of other nonprofit services described in this text? Why should this be so?

3. What are the key service quality dimensions that should be addressed by hospital marketers in a bid to enhance overall customer satisfaction?

4. As the newly appointed marketing manager of a GP practice, what steps would you take to enhance patient satisfaction with the service provided?

5. Why is the provision of good quality information becoming an increasingly important issue for healthcare marketers to address?

6. With reference to your own healthcare organization, or one with which you are familiar, describe the issues that would need to be addressed under each of the headings of the 'typical' marketing plan introduced in Chapter 3.

■ **REFERENCES**

Andrus, D. and Bucheister, J. (1985) 'Major Factors Affecting Dental Consumer Satisfaction', *Healthcare Marketing and Consumer Behaviour*, Vol. 3, No. 1, 57–68.

Berkowitz, E.N. and Flexner, W. (1980) 'The Market for Health Services, Is there a Non-Traditional Consumer?' *Journal of Healthcare Marketing*, Vol. 1, No. 1, 25–34.

BMA (1995) 'Declining Standards in Community Care', as reported in *British Journal of Nursing* (Editorial), Vol. 4, No. 8, 425–6.

Bopp, K.D. (1990) 'How Patients Evaluate the Quality of Ambulatory Medical Encounters: A Marketing Perspective', *Journal of Healthcare Marketing*, Vol. 10, No. 2, 6–15.

Brown, S.W. and Swartz, T.A. (1989) 'A Gap Analysis of Professional Service Quality', *Journal of Marketing*, Vol. 53 (April), 92–8.

Bunn, M.D. (1993) 'Consumer Perceptions of Medical Information Sources: An Application of Multidimensional Scaling', *Health Marketing Quarterly*, Vol. 10, No. 3, 83–104.

Crowther, C. (1995) 'NHS Trust Marketing: A Survival Guide', *Journal of Marketing Practice: Applied Marketing Science*, Vol. 1, No. 2, 57–68.

Edgren, L. (1991) *Service Management Inm Svensk Halso-Och Sjukvard*, Lund, Sweden, Lund University Press.

France, K.R. and Grover, R. (1992) 'What is the Health Care Product?' *Journal of Health Care Marketing*, Vol. 12, No. 2, 31–8.

Gabbott, M. and Hogg, G. (1994) 'Care or Cure: Making Choices in Healthcare', *Unity in Diversity*, Proceedings of the MEG Conference, University of Ulster.

Hall, J.H. and Dornan, M.C. (1988) 'Meta Analysis of Satisfaction with Medical Care: Description of Research Domain and Analysis of Overall Satisfaction Levels', *Social Science and Medicine*, Vol. 27, No. 6, 637–44.

Inguanzo, J.M. and Harju, M. (1985) 'What Makes Consumers Select a Hospital?' *Hospitals*, Vol. 16 (March), 90–4.

Jenson, J. (1987) 'Most Physicians Believe Patients Obtain Health Care Information from Mass Media', *Modern Health Care*, Vol. 17, No. 19, 113–14.

Johnsson, B.C. (1990) 'Focus Group Positioning and Analysis: A Commentary on Adjuncts for Enhancing the Design of Health Care Research', *Health Education Quarterly*, Vol. 7, No. 1, 152–68.

Kotler, P. and Clarke, R.N. (1987) *Marketing For Health Care Organizations*, New Jersey, Prentice Hall.

Larsen, D.E. and Rootman, I. (1976) 'Physician Role Performance and Patient Satisfaction', *Social Science and Medicine*, Vol. 10, No. 1, 29–32.

LuAnn, A. and Andersen, R. (1980) *Healthcare in the USA*, Beverly Hills, Sage Publications.

Lych, J. and Schuler, D. (1990) 'Consumer Evaluation of the Quality of Hospital Services from an Economics Perspective', *Journal of Health Care Marketing*, Vol. 10 (June), 16–22.

Lytle, R.S. and Mokwa, M.P. (1992) 'Evaluating Health Care Quality: The Moderating Role of Outcomes', *Journal of Health Care Marketing*, Vol. 12, No. 1, 4–14.

MacStavic, R.S. (1975) *Marketing Health Care*, Gaithersburg, Aspen Publishers.

Maister, D.H. (1985) 'The Psychology of Waiting Lines', in Czepiel, J., Solomon, M.R. and Suprenant, C.F. (eds.) *The Service Encounter*, Lexington, Lexington Books.

McDevitt, P.K. and Shields, L.A. (1985) 'Tactical Hospital Marketing: A Survey of the State of the Art', *Journal of Health Care Marketing*, Vol. 5, No. 1, 9–16.

O'Connor, S.J., Shewchuk, R.M. and Carney, L.W. (1994) 'The Great Gap', *Journal of Health Care Marketing*, Vol. 14, No. 2, 32–9.

Parasuraman, A., Zeithaml, V. and Berry, L. (1988) 'SERVQUAL: A Multiple Item Scale for Measuring Consumer Perceptions of Service Quality', *Journal of Retailing*, Vol. 64, No. 1, 12–40.

Pendleton, D. and Hasler, J. (1983) *Doctor Patient Communication*, London, Academic Press.

Petrochuk, M.A. and Javalgi, R.G. (1996) 'Reforming the Health Care System: Implications for Health Care Marketers', *Health Marketing Quarterly*, Vol. 13, No. 3, 71–86.

Phillips, C.R. (1980) 'Single Room Maternity Care for Maximum Cost Efficiency', *Perinatology-Neonataology*, March/April, 21–31.

Quinn, J.B. (1992) *Intelligent Enterprise*, New York, The Free Press.

Ranade, W. (1994) *A Future for the NHS*, Harlow, Longman.

Sage, G.C. (1991) 'Customers and the NHS', *International Journal of Health Quality Assurance*, Vol. 4, No. 3, 23–34.

San Augustine, A., Long, W.J. and Pantzallis, J. (1992) 'Hospital Positioning: A Strategic Tool for the 1990s', *Journal of Health Care Marketing*, Vol. 12, No. 1, 16–23.

Singh, J. (1990) 'A Multifacet Typology of Patient Satisfaction with a Hospital', *Journal of Health Care Marketing*, Vol. 10 (Dec), 8–21.

Teasdale, K. (1992) *Managing the Changes in Health Care*, London, Wolfe.

Ware, J.E., Davies-Avery, A. and Stewart, A.L. (1978) 'The Measurement and Meaning of Patient Satisfaction', *Health and Medical Care Services Review*, Vol. 1 (Jan/Feb), 14–20.

West, P. (1994) 'In the Temple of Pain', *Harper's Magazine*, Dec, 29–30.

World Health Organization (1986) *Basic Documents, 36th Edition*, Geneva, Switzerland, World Health Organization.

Wrenn, B. (1994) 'Differences in Perceptions of Hospital Marketing Orientation Between Administrators and Marketing Officers', *Hospital and Health Services Administration*, Vol. 39, No. 3, 341–58.

Zaltman, G. and Vertinsky, I. (1971) 'Health Services Marketing: A Proposed Model', *Journal of Marketing*, Vol. 35 (July), 19–27.

13 Volunteer Support and Management

OBJECTIVES

By the end of this chapter you should be able to:

(1) understand the significance of volunteering to the nonprofit sector;

(2) describe current trends in volunteering;

(3) identify where volunteers may be recruited from;

(4) utilize knowledge of volunteer motivation in a recruitment campaign;

(5) develop a volunteer recruitment plan;

(6) utilize a range of research findings to develop a volunteer retention strategy.

Introduction

Recent years have seen many changes in the pattern of volunteering across the developed world. Changes in lifestyle, in the numbers of women entering the workforce, and in working patterns have impacted both on the nature of volunteer activity and on the demographic characteristics of typical volunteers. These observations aside, there are few truly global trends in volunteering since the propensity to volunteer and individual volunteer behaviour seem to be a function of the nature of the society in which this takes place. Volunteer numbers in the UK, for example, have dipped in recent years, down from 51 per cent of the adult population in 1991 to 48 per cent in 1997. In the USA the incidence of volunteering is not only increasing, but doing so markedly. From 2002 to 2003, the number of Americans who volunteered rose by 6 per cent to 63.8 million. It is interesting to note that the group exhibiting the largest growth rate was teenagers, with 29.5 per cent volunteering over the course of the year.

The reasons for the growth may be the establishment by the US Presidency of the USA Freedom Corps, which was charged in 2002 with the task of encouraging Americans to embrace a new 'culture of responsibility' and to commit 4000 hours over their lifetimes to serve their neighbours and country. It is equally possible, however, that the growth may be due to the increasing use of the Internet by volunteer centres and other nonprofit groups to publicize service opportunities.

Table 13.1 Bureau of Labor Statistics

Variable	September 2002			September 2003		
	Number	% of population	Median annual hours	Number	% of population	Median annual hours
TOTAL	59,783,000	27.4	52	63,791,000	28.8	52
Sex						
Men	24,706,000	23.6	52	26,805,000	25.1	52
Women	35,076,000	31.0	50	36,987,000	32.2	52
Age						
16–19 years old	4,276,000	26.9	40	4,758,000	29.5	40
20–24 years old	3,467,000	17.8	36	3,912,000	91.7	45
25–34 years old	9,574,000	24.8	33	10,337,000	26.5	36
35–44 years old	14,971,000	34.1	52	15,165,000	34.7	50
45–54 years old	12,477,000	31.3	52	13,302,000	32.7	52
55–64 years old	7,331,000	27.5	60	8,170,000	29.2	60
65 years and old	7,687,000	22.7	96	8,146,000	23.7	88
Race						
White	52,591,000	29.2	52	55,572,000	30.6	52
Black	4,896,000	19.1	52	5,145,000	20.0	52
Asian	n/a	n/a	n/a	1,735,000	18.7	40
Hispanic	4,059,000	15.5	40	4,364,000	15.7	40
Education						
Less than a high-school diploma	2,806,000	10.1	48	2,793,000	9.9	48
High-school graduate, no college	12,542,000	21.2	49	12,882,000	21.7	48
Less than a bachelor's degree	15,066,000	32.8	52	15,966,000	34.1	52
College graduate	21,627,000	43.3	60	23,481,000	45.6	60
Employment						
Total civilian labor force	42,773,000	29.3	48	45,499,000	30.9	48
Employment	40,742,000	29.5	48	43,138,000	31.2	48
Full-time	32,210,000	28.3	46	33,599,000	29.6	48
Part-time	8,532,000	35.4	52	9,539,000	38.4	52
Unemployed	2,031,000	25.1	50	2,361,000	26.7	48
Not in the labor force	17,010,000	23.7	72	18,293,000	24.6	66

Note: Data for Asians were not tabulated in 2002.
Source: © 2004 Bureau of Labor Statistics. Reproduced with kind permission.

Other key findings from a recent Bureau of Labor study in the USA included:

- The median amount of time Americans volunteered remained at 52 hours over the course of the year.
- Women continued to volunteer more than men, with 32.2 per cent of females saying they volunteered versus 25.1 per cent of males.

- Parents with children under 18 were more likely to assist a nonprofit group than people without children in that age range.
- Married people were more likely to volunteer than others.
- Churches account for the highest percentage of volunteering (34.6 per cent), followed by youth/education work (27.4 per cent), social/community service (11.8 per cent) and hospitals/health (8.2 per cent).

The demographic profile of volunteers, developed from the Bureau of Labor study, is reported in Table 13.1.

In the UK, the most recent national survey of volunteering was conducted in 1997 by the BMRB (British Market Research Bureau) on behalf of the Institute for Volunteering Research. Key findings include:

- The time volunteers donate increased from 2.7 hours per week in 1991 to 4 hours per week in 1997.
- A greater number of retired people are now volunteering, but participation has fallen among the young. When the young do volunteer they are significantly more likely to be motivated by a desire to learn new skills.
- Sports, education, and social welfare are the most common fields of volunteering with fundraising, organizing events, committee work, and providing transportation the most common activities.

It seems clear from the statistics on both sides of the Atlantic that the incidence of volunteering is generally high. Voluntary activity appears to touch the lives of a great many people as they seek to help others in their community. As we shall see, however, these figures belie a number of uncomfortable facts about the nature of volunteering and how organizations treat those individuals who elect to donate their time. Levels of volunteer attrition are high and levels of satisfaction with the work they undertake relatively low. Nonprofits have a long way to go to meet the needs of these individuals and in particular improve the way that they market themselves to such individuals, both before and after recruitment.

Recruiting Volunteers

Identifying the Need

The starting point for many organizations in the recruitment of volunteers lies in determining the tasks that volunteers might legitimately be able to perform. As a consequence organizations commonly begin by asking 'What can volunteers do around here?' This approach is overly simplistic and Jackson (2001) highlights three major weaknesses of adopting this perspective:

- An organization can screen out potential options based on staff's own beliefs about volunteer competence. Sadly, research has consistently shown that staff often undervalue volunteer input and perceive significantly lower levels of competence than is the case (Fisher and Cole 1993).

- An organization can run the risk of inventing work for volunteers to do, so that they have got something to give them, rather than because it genuinely requires such input.
- Volunteers can be used as a vehicle for offloading the most burdensome or mundane tasks the organization must carry out, resulting in poor motivation and a high post-recruitment attrition (or turnover) rate.

Instead the author recommends that the following process be adopted:

- Staff and volunteers should be asked to list the things they do in their job, or in a specific area of their job. It is important that this process be as precise as possible (i.e. answering the phone, filing, etc., rather than simply saying 'admin').
- Using this list as a backdrop, staff and volunteers should then be asked to indicate which of their tasks they like doing, which they dislike doing, and which they should be doing. They should also be asked why they hold these views.
- Staff and existing volunteers should then be asked to create a 'wish list' of things that they would ideally like to be able to achieve, and that they wish the nonprofit could achieve if it/they had the time, skills, money, etc.

Jackson argues that this data provides fertile ground in which to evaluate the need for volunteers and to ensure, where such new roles are created, that a genuinely meaningful post, with a number of potentially enjoyable tasks, can be developed. The involvement of existing volunteers in this process is key because it furnishes management with a detailed insight into what presently motivates volunteers and what might motivate them in the future. Using this data to define a potentially satisfying role lies at the heart of the concept of internal marketing, as discussed in Chapter 2.

Having identified the nature of the role to be created, a nonprofit will then be in a position to develop a job description. At a minimum such job descriptions typically comprise the following elements:

- *Title*. Organizations should avoid 'volunteer' and use the nature of the role as the basis for providing an appropriate job title.

- *Overall purpose*. The job description should explain what the purpose of the role will be, how it relates to other roles in the organization, and the contribution that it will make to the achievement of the mission.

- *Activities and key outputs*. This section of the job description maps out the tasks that the volunteer will fulfil and the measures of success that will be used to gauge their performance. Some organizations map out a range of suggested activities to achieve the outputs rather than being prescriptive. This allows the volunteer some flexibility and respects the fact that individuals can often bring a substantial amount of personal and subject expertise to their role.

- *Supervision*. It will also be important to specify the individual or individuals to whom the volunteer will report. In some cases this can be a supervisor in the functional part of the organization in which they are working, or it may be a specialized volunteer service coordinator (VSC). While the use of a VSC can assist in certain circumstances because such individuals have a good understanding of the nature of volunteering, it can often be better for volunteers to be supervised directly by the 'line supervisor' in whose department they are working. The reason for this is simply that the volunteer can then feel an integral part of the team rather than an outsider, donating their time.

- *Benefits*. The job description should outline the benefits that will accrue as a result of the individual volunteering their time. In the USA, these benefits can have considerable value, with volunteers being remunerated by vouchers (for use in local stores) or some form of allowance. In the UK, where the legal definition of a volunteer is a little different, direct remuneration is avoided as a contract of employment can thereby be created and conditions such as the national minimum wage would then apply. Formal benefits in the UK are rare and where they are available they are typically tied to the cause. Volunteers to a heritage charity, for example, may qualify for free or reduced entry to the site for themselves and members of their family.

- *Timeframe and site*. The job description will contain the details of where the volunteer will work, the hours it is expected that they will contribute, and for how long they will continue to work in this capacity. While some volunteer posts involve an open-ended commitment, many organizations are realizing that modern lifestyles no longer permit this level of commitment and that an open-ended need might dissuade volunteers. There may thus be circumstances where a specific timeframe is included in the job description so that both parties know from the outset how long the arrangement will last.

- *Arrangements for reimbursement of out of pocket expenses*. A good job description will also contain a summary of the categories of expenses that will be reimbursed (e.g. travel) and the typical length of time it will take the organization to reimburse the volunteer. This is considered good practice because a clear statement from the outset can prevent any future misunderstandings (Fisher and Cole 1993).

- *Equal opportunities statement*. Finally, every job description should contain an equal opportunities statement, which spells out the organization's stance on recruiting individuals with disabilities or from minority groups. It is important to note that this should be more than a simple statement of policy from the trustees of the organization; it should also be backed up with training to staff, to ensure that the reality of volunteer recruitment is grounded in this statement.

These are the basic components of a volunteer job description. From a marketing perspective, it is important to recognize that this document will play a critical role in persuading appropriate individuals to apply (or not!). The best job descriptions therefore move beyond these basics and are written in such a way as to reflect the marketing role many undoubtedly play. At its simplest level, this means that job descriptions should move beyond a simple list of uninspiring tasks. Jackson (2001) argues that job descriptions should explain how the tasks the volunteer must perform fit into the larger picture of what the organization does and in particular how the responsibilities of the post will assist in the achievement of the mission. He also advocates focusing on results rather than tasks, so that where appropriate the volunteer can have some flexibility over how his role is performed. A brief example is provided below.

Overall Purpose

To keep fundraising staff up-to-date on internal and external volunteering issues by producing a monthly newsletter, *Volunteering News*.

Key Result

Volunteering News will be a dynamic publication, promoting, networking, and allowing volunteer managers to share successes and learn from each other.

Suggested Activities

Undertake internal marketing of *Volunteering News* to ensure the readership is aware of the networking potential of the publication

Measures of Success

By (a certain date), a third of the internal news articles will be from volunteer managers other than the editor or volunteer development manager.

By (a certain date) a letters/networking section will be a regular feature.

(*Source*: Jackson 2001: 5–6)

Of course, the job description is only half of the recruitment equation. It is now common practice to develop a person specification which translates the role that will be performed into a series of skills and abilities that will be necessary to satisfactorily complete that role. Person specifications thus address the likely demographic profile of the volunteer, their skills and abilities, their availability, and any motivational needs they might have. As we shall see later in this chapter, volunteers can be motivated by a variety of perceived needs (e.g. to develop new skills, to acquire new social contacts) and the organization may have a preference, in a particular role, for someone who is motivated by a specific need. This should be specified and used to inform the recruitment process. Person specifications normally distinguish desirable characteristics from essential characteristics. As we shall see later, this distinction can be enormously helpful in performing an initial screen of completed applications.

Sources of Volunteers

All of the leading writers on volunteer management, such as Ellis (1994) or Wymer and Starnes (2001*a*) make the fundamental point that for volunteers to be attracted to an organization they have to be asked. While this might seem a little facile, some organizations either shy away from approaching likely volunteer prospects, or fail to utilize the network of contacts that the organization already has. The 1997 National Survey of Volunteering in England showed that 50 per cent of the people who did volunteer did so because they were asked, and similar percentages have been reported in the USA. All staff and existing volunteers may thus have a part to play in identifying appropriate individuals who might be able to assist the organization.

If utilising this network of contacts is impractical, or existing links have already been exhausted, Wymer and Starnes (2001*a*) argue that volunteer recruitment can then be achieved either directly or indirectly. Direct recruitment consists of a nonprofit reaching out *directly* to potential volunteers through activities such as advertising, direct marketing, publicity, events, and public speaking engagements.

Indirect recruitment occurs when other institutions are used as intermediaries to assist in the process of recruitment. Many communities now have volunteer referral centres which act as a focal point for individuals who are interested in giving up their time. These referral centres promote community volunteering and keep a wealth of up-to-date information about the opportunities available (Ellis 1989).

In the search for volunteers it is important that a nonprofit exploit all the opportunities that may exist for indirect recruitment through third parties. The rationale here is simply that scarce resources need not be wasted on an activity that can be better accomplished by another organization. Authors such as Ellis (1994) and Senior Corps (2000) cite the Retired and Senior Volunteer Program (RSVP) in the USA as one such example. It acts as a clearing-house for 'seniors' who are looking for opportunities to volunteer and are unsure of where they might apply and how their skills might be used. In the UK there is a network of volunteer bureaux that provide this function and Councils for Voluntary Service (CVS). There is also Timebank, a national charity that aims to get more people volunteering across the country. Timebank works with a number of partners to achieve this goal, including the BBC and 'Do-It' the national volunteering database, found online at **www.do-it.org.uk**. This is illustrated in Figure 13.1.

All these intermediaries specialize in fostering volunteering and have missions both to promote volunteering as an activity and to broker links between volunteers and potential beneficiary organizations. Equally, nonprofits can foster indirect recruitment by looking to other organizations with complementary missions whose members might have an interest in volunteering for the cause. Scouting groups, Lions Clubs and Rotary Clubs might all have a role to play here, and may prove to be fruitful sources of volunteers.

The Communication Process

Having defined the nature of the role and determined the volunteer characteristics that would be desirable to meet these needs, the organization can then turn its attention to recruiting the right individual(s). At this point it needs to decide whether it will attempt to recruit individuals directly, or whether it would be better to operate through intermediary groups or organizations, as outlined above. Irrespective of the approach adopted, the organization must be clear about what it has to offer and the volunteer needs it could meet. It must then translate this into a strong recruitment message, which in the case of direct recruitment would form the basis of a campaign and with indirect recruitment, the fundamental nature of the proposition that can be passed on through third parties.

To structure our discussion of the communication process we will employ the model depicted in Figure 13.2. Here the recruitment communication is generated by the nonprofit and directed at individuals most likely to have an interest in supporting the

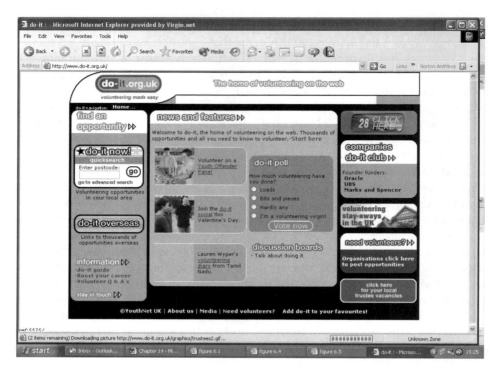

Figure 13.1 'Do-it' national volunteering database

Source: © 2004 Do-It. Reproduced with kind permission.

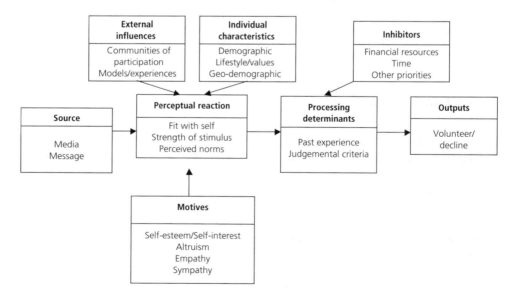

Figure 13.2 The communication process

organization. A good way of achieving this is to look at the profile of the existing volunteer base and to attempt to target others who appear to match the characteristics of existing volunteers. Organizations can also look back over the campaigns they have run in the past and refine both the quality of their targeting and the nature of communications they create.

Whatever form the ask might eventually take, there are a variety of variables which the literature suggests will tend to impact on a potential volunteer's perceptual reaction to the message being conveyed. The key variables here are the fit of the charity with a given donor's self-image, the existence of perceived norms of behaviour in their social group, and the strength of the stimulus the nonprofit is able to generate.

If the message survives this initial 'filter' and is perceived as being potentially relevant, a more cognitive decision-making process is entered into. Here, the literature suggests that two key categories of variable will impact on the manner in which the volunteering decision is processed: the individual's past experience with the nonprofit (if any), and the criteria that he might use to evaluate potential organizations for support. If the outcome from this cognitive process is favourable, the model concludes that the individual will elect to offer his support to the organization.

Of course, life isn't this neat! There are a number of personal and interpersonal influences that can either enhance a volunteer's motivation to respond or detract from it. Equally, an individual may be strongly motivated to offer her support but be constrained by a lack of time or pressure from other life priorities. The decision of whether and how to respond to a request to volunteer time is thus highly complex. In the next section we will employ the model shown in Figure 13.2 as a framework to consider the lessons from recent volunteer research.

Recruitment Communications

As the model indicates, there are two key facets to the communication for consideration. The first is the medium that will be employed, the second the nature of the message that will be imparted. Extant research has consistently shown that face-to-face requests to donate time are the most effective at engendering support. Other media lag way behind this in terms of effectiveness. Peer-to-peer 'asks' from staff, recruiters, and particularly other volunteers are thus a powerful way of expanding support.

In respect of the message that should be conveyed, Ellis (1994) suggests that designing an appropriate recruitment communication is a far from easy task. She argues that organizations can frequently sound 'desperate' to recruit the help that they need and that the very act of appearing so desperate may put off some individuals from offering their time.

Rather than conveying desperation, extant research suggests that recruitment messages should be upbeat and convey three distinct categories of information.

1. the importance of the cause;
2. the efficacy of the programme of work the organization undertakes;
3. the benefits that the post would offer the volunteer (e.g. feeling useful/productive, or the social interaction that would be afforded) (Wymer 1999; Okun 1994).

Volunteers needed for nonprofit chapter launch in Philly

On Your Feet Project (OYFP), a national 501(c)(3)-recognized nonprofit organization, is launching a chapter in Philadelphia. OYFP is entirely volunteer-run, and currently has chapters in New York and San Francisco. In these cities, OYFP builds partnerships with other nonprofit organizations and sponsors events on their behalf. These programs generate public awareness for the partner organizations, while also providing a way for young people to learn about the causes that partner organizations support and to get involved in the community. For example, in 2003, OYFP ran 17 events, including art and photography shows, concerts, film screenings, and comedy jams, benefiting nine nonprofit organizations, such as Direct Relief International, HELP USA, and the Urban Justice Center.

I am looking for people who would like to get involved with OYFP Philadelphia in any way, from being a part of the leadership of the organization, to helping to plan events, to just attending events. If you are interested in this exciting opportunity to make a difference in the community while meeting other like-minded individuals, please contact Jessica Merlin at jessica@onyourfeetproject.org. If you know of anyone else who might be interested in getting involved, feel free to forward this message. For further information about the organization, feel free to visit our website at **www.onyourfeetproject.org**.

For more information contact **Jessica Merlin at (215) 806-1888 or write to:**

On Your Feet Project
Center City
Philadelphia, PA 19103

Figure 13.3 Example volunteer recruitment communication

Source: © On Your Feet Project. Reproduced by kind permission.

An example of a volunteer recruitment communication is presented in Figure 13.3. Notice how each of these three themes are reflected in the content.

Perceptual Reaction

As we discussed above, whether the recruitment communication will be perceived as relevant to the potential volunteer will be a function of the fit of the nonprofit with a given individual's self-image, the existence of perceived norms of behaviour in their social group, and the strength of the stimulus the organization is able to generate.

In respect of the first variable, fit with desired self-image, Coliazzi et al. (1984) noted that individuals are more likely to help those who are perceived as being similar to themselves. They will thus tend to filter those messages from nonprofits existing to support disparate segments of society. The extremely wealthy, for example, tend to avoid causes involving the poor, such as homelessness, and are much more likely to support organizations that they, or members of their social class, can benefit from. Similarly, Millet and Orosz (2001) identified that people from ethnic minorities are significantly more likely to filter out messages from nonprofits not serving members of their community.

A factor closely related to the above is the issue of perceived norms. There is considerable evidence that volunteers will be motivated to filter messages on the basis of normative concerns (Morgan et al. 1979). People appear to pay considerable attention to what others contribute within their respective societal group and are thus significantly less likely to volunteer if they do not see others taking similar action. In an interesting study of volunteer behaviour, Fisher and Ackerman (1998) found that perceived norms were key in triggering volunteering behaviour where the voluntary action was perceived to be important to the group's welfare and where the volunteer was motivated by the potential for social recognition.

The strength of the stimulus can also be an issue. Clearly the stronger the stimulus generated by a particular nonprofit, the easier it will be for it to cut through competing messages from other organizations. To achieve this, a number of factors need to be considered. The first is the perceived urgency of the need. In general, high degrees of urgency would appear to engender high degrees of support (see, for example, Newman 1977; Pancer et al. 1979). It would also appear that approaches that build up the degree of personal responsibility are more effective at engendering a response (see Geer and Jermecky 1973). Clear and unambiguous requests for support are similarly more likely to engender compliance than those that are vague or general in nature (Clark and Word 1972).

Processing Determinants

The model suggests that potentially relevant messages will be subjected to a further and perhaps more cognitive decision-making process. Two key factors warrant consideration here: an individual's past experience with an organization, and the decision-making criteria they will apply.

In respect of the former, a variety of authors have argued that once a link is forged with a nonprofit, a given individual will be significantly more likely to help again in the future and to help in a variety of different ways (e.g. Kaehler and Sargeant 1998). A good source of 'new' volunteers can therefore be individuals who have volunteered in the past, or individuals who have been involved in campaigning/lobbying or even donating funds to the organization in the past. Of course this presupposes that the individual's experience will have been a happy one; if they were dissatisfied in some way, they are highly unlikely to wish to renew their association.

In respect of the conscious decision-making criteria that might be applied, there is a clear link here between the individual's motives for support (which we shall discuss below) and whether the individual believes these are likely to be met. Individuals might also evaluate potential recipient organizations on the basis of the extent to which they believe that the organization is doing good work and having the promised impact on the beneficiary group. There is evidence that the perceived efficiency of the organization (i.e. not 'squandering' resources on fundraising and administration) can also have a role to play in deciding whether support will be offered (Glaser 1994).

Motives

Economists have long argued that volunteers take decisions in respect of their support by reference to the degree of utility they will attain (Collard 1978). Under this view, volunteers will select charities to support on the basis of whether they have benefited in the past or believe that they will in the future (Frisch and Gerrard 1981). Individuals could, for example, volunteer for those organizations that will do them political good and/or serve to enhance their career, perhaps through the networking opportunities that will be accorded (Amos 1982). Volunteers may also evaluate potential recipient organizations against the extent to which their support will be visible, or noticeable by others within their social group, thereby enhancing the volunteer's standing (Cnaan and Goldberg-Glen 1991).

Sargeant and Jay (2004) argue that volunteers can also derive utility from

- the ability to make a difference;
- the ability to enhance their self-worth or self-esteem;
- the ability to obtain experiences that can be useful in paid employment;
- the ability to meet others—it is interesting to note that women appear to derive more social rewards from volunteering than men (Ricks and Pyke 1973);
- the ability to prepare for a volunteer 'career' after retirement;
- the ability to get inside institutions and organizations and ensure that they are doing what they profess to be doing.

Many of these themes are reported in the conclusions of other empirical work. In a study of the motives for volunteering for charity shops, for example, Horne and Broadbridge (1994) found that key motives included the opportunity to meet people and make friends. The researchers also found that this form of volunteering could follow as a consequence of previous retail experience.

A number of psychosocial motives for supporting organizations by volunteering time have also been reported. In particular, individuals are significantly more likely to volunteer if they can empathize with the recipient group (Eisenberg and Miller 1987; Mount and Quirion 1988) or have sympathy with them (Clary and Synder 1991; Schwartz 1977).

Clearly one or more of these motives can be specifically addressed in a recruitment campaign.

Individual Characteristics

In the introduction to this chapter the demographic profile of a typical volunteer was addressed in both the UK and the USA. Organizations can use either this generic profile, or (ideally) the profile of their existing volunteer base to ensure that messages are appropriately targeted. As the model suggests, the demographic profile of the recipients of a recruitment message will drive in no small measure the extent to which they perceive it as being relevant.

These general comments aside, Ellis (1994) suggests that the demographic variable 'lifestage' may have a particularly key role to play in volunteering. The author argues that as adults enter a new stage, they look for ways of giving meaning to their lives and enhancing their self-worth. Thus moving from a stage where they have children at home to the empty nest syndrome can prompt a re-evaluation, as can a move from paid employment into retirement.

Terminal

Comfortable Life
(a prosperous life)

An Exciting Life
(a stimulating, active life)

Sense of accomplishment
(lasting contribution)

World at peace
(free of war and conflict)

World of beauty
(beauty of nature and the arts)

Equality
(brotherhood, equal opportunity for all)

Family security
(taking care of loved ones)

Freedom
(independence, free choice)

Happiness
(contentedness)

Inner harmony
(freedom from inner conflict)

Mature love
(sexual and spiritual intimacy)

National security
(protection from attack)

Pleasure
(an enjoyable, leisurely life)

Salvation
(saved, eternal life)

Self-respect
(self-esteem)

Social recognition
(respect, admiration)

True friendship
(close companionship)

Wisdom
(a mature understanding of life)

Figure 13.4 Categorization of consumer values

Source: Rokeach (1973). Reproduced by kind permission.

A number of psychographic variables have also been highlighted as distinguishing volunteers from non-volunteers, with the topic of individual *values* receiving undoubtedly the most attention to date (Heidrich 1988; Williams 1987).

Values are beliefs about what is important in life. They

- are relatively few in number;
- serve as a guide for culturally appropriate behaviour;
- are enduring or difficult to change;
- are not tied to specific situations; and
- are widely accepted by the members of a society (Rokeach 1973).

They are thus broad beliefs that affect individual attitudes to other people, organizations, objects, or circumstances and in the context of volunteering would be likely to drive how a person might respond to a communication message.

One of the most widely cited categorizations of consumer values was developed by Rokeach (1973). It is depicted in Figure 13.4.

A number of authors have employed this categorization to distinguish between volunteers and non-volunteers and concluded that volunteers generally place a higher degree of importance on the pro-social values in this list (see, for example, McClintock and Allison 1989). Marketers may thus reflect these values in their recruitment communications, indicating how a given role might aid in the attainment or expression of a particular value.

In a further use of Rokeach's work, Wymer and Samu (2002: 983) studied differences in values between male and female volunteers. They conclude that

of the eight values for which there were significant differences (between the two groups), female volunteers weighted the values of a 'sense of accomplishment', 'world at peace', and 'mature love' more heavily. The values of 'a world of beauty', 'self-respect', 'social recognition', and 'true friendship' were weighted more heavily by male volunteers.

Their findings suggest that there may be a need to segment volunteer recruitment messages by gender and to appeal to a number of specific individual values in each communication. Of course, it is important to recognize that this reseach was conducted in the USA and that values are, by definition, culture-specific. The same results may therefore not be observed in Europe or indeed any other country.

External Influences

Individual behaviour can also be shaped by the events that an individual experiences during the course of their life, in particular their early life. In the context of volunteering, it is therefore likely that models and experiences from one's youth will shape future adult behaviour. Thus those who were helped by volunteers themselves or who grew up in a family with a strong tradition of volunteering are significantly more likely to exhibit such behaviours (Smith and Baldwin 1974).

In looking for external influences on behaviour, however, it is also necessary to look beyond the immediate family group. Wider communities of participation may be of relevance. These are defined as networks of formal and informal relationships entered into either by choice or by circumstance (e.g. schools, soup kitchens, soccer groups) that bring an individual into contact with need (Schervish 1993; 1997). Individuals will be predisposed to support causes connected in some way with these communities. Lohmann (1992), for example, found that helping behaviour was frequently related to personal membership of networks, societies, political groups, social movements, or religious, artistic, or scientific communities.

A recent Gallup survey concluded that above-average levels of volunteering were reported by those who had

- been active in student government
- gone door-to-door fundraising
- previously undertaken volunteer work
- always wanted to make a change in society

- belonged to a youth group or similar
- seen someone they admired (other than a family member) help others
- been helped by others themselves (Gallup 1992).

Writers such as Wymer (1996) have shown that individuals who have social contact with existing volunteers are significantly more likely to respond positively to a request to volunteer themselves. Data from Independent Sector (2000) confirms this, with 90 per cent of people being asked to serve by their peers accepting the role.

Of course it is not just contact with volunteers that can predispose individuals to agreeing to offer their own time. Emotional contact with the cause or issue itself can prompt volunteering behaviour. Wymer and Starnes (1999) found that a high proportion of hospice volunteers learned about opportunities to help when a friend or loved one had been terminally ill. In such circumstances, the need to volunteer can be a response to the death of someone they cared for.

Barriers

Even where an individual might otherwise be motivated to volunteer their time and respond to a recruitment solicitation, there are a number of barriers that can prevent them from agreeing to participate. The issue of time poverty is particularly critical here. Modern lifestyles are such that many individuals do not believe they have enough spare time to volunteer. Schindler-Rainman (1988) argues that typical volunteers of the future will be 'less willing to commit themselves to open-ended long-term volunteer assignments. Instead what they will seek out are volunteer roles that have a fixed end-date and a measurable outcome, and give evidence of making a real contribution to the problems facing society...'.

As a consequence, programmes need to include both short- and long-term places for volunteers, so that persons who cannot commit themselves for long periods will not be lost as a human resource for the programme.

There are also issues of distance and safety (Wymer and Starnes 2001*a*). Many volunteers otherwise willing to help may not be willing to travel far from their home. They may prefer instead to seek other opportunities to volunteer that do not require them to travel. Equally, in some contexts, individuals may be concerned with their own safety. Working with individuals with mental illness or substance abuse problems, for example, can be perceived as unsafe even if adequate safeguards exist, or where the risk is illusory. Both these issues have the capacity to block willingness to engage with an organization.

The Recruitment Process

The typical volunteer recruitment process is presented in Figure 13.5. Once a recruitment campaign has been conducted and completed application forms received, it will be necessary to subject the applications to an initial screening. This is typically done by comparing the person specification (described earlier) with the personal details supplied by the applicants. In the author's experience few, if any, applicants meet all of the

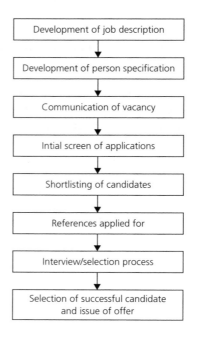

Figure 13.5 Volunteer recruitment process

desirable characteristics outlined in the person specification, but the organization should find a few that do meet all of the essential criteria they outlined and exhibit one or more of the desirable characteristics. References from these applicants may then be applied for (criminal record checks included if appropriate) and these can either be considered in advance of an interview, or alongside an interview. Those candidates deemed suitable at interview and who can provide satisfactory references will then be put through an induction/training programme and, if appropriate, placed on probation for a specific period of time after which their appointment can be confirmed.

Induction

Induction is a critical part of the recruitment process as it allows the organization to brief the volunteer on its history, mission, and the nature of the role they will perform. It is important as it serves to explain how the role the volunteer will perform forms part of the organization as a whole. It also provides the volunteer with all the information and initial skills they might need to satisfactorily carry out their role.

In the context of palliative care, for example, the National Council for Hospice and Specialist Palliative Care Services (NCHSPC) (1996) advocates the provision of an introduction to voluntary service work that ensures that the key principles of palliative care are properly understood, namely:

- focus on quality of life
- whole-person approach
- care encompasses both the dying person and those who matter to that person

- patient autonomy and choice
- emphasis on open and sensitive communication.

Such training leaves no-one in any doubt as to what is expected regarding (a) confidentiality, (b) professionalism, or (c) maintaining the organization's good image and reputation.

However, as Ratje (2003: 17), notes: 'nonprofit organizations often rely on volunteers as a vital component of their interaction with clients and potential donors. Yet selection, training and motivation for volunteers can be poor or non-existent.'

This will undoubtedly lead to poor performance and can give rise to a great deal of dissatisfaction on the part of the volunteer, who might ultimately decide to quit. A lack of formal training can also place the organization in breach of legal requirements since there may, for example, be a requirement for basic health and safety education.

From a marketing perspective, the failure to induct the volunteer presents further problems, one of which I have already alluded to above. To quote Ratje (2003: 17) once more: 'imagine a potential donor for a homeless shelter who walks in the door with a checkbook in hand, but then speaks with a volunteer who knows little about the mission, the tax deductability of the donation or just has a bad attitude.' The impact on the organization's brand image and ability to fundraise would obviously be profound, and yet successive studies have found that a lack of training or induction is one of the most cited problem areas by volunteers (Wymer and Starnes 2001*b*). It would thus appear that the nonprofit sector has much to do to improve these aspects of volunteer management. For a detailed consideration of induction/training issues, the reader is advised to consult a specialist text such as Fisher and Cole (1993) or Doyle (2002).

Retaining Volunteers

Many organizations struggle to retain volunteers. Turnover rates in excess of 100 per cent have been reported by some in the course of a typical year. To calculate the rate of turnover, the following formula is typically used. It was developed by the US Department of Labor for the purposes of measuring staff turnover rates in the private sector, but it is equally applicable to a nonprofit context (Mathis and Jackson 1982).

$$\frac{[\text{Number of volunteer separations during the year}]}{[\text{Total number of volunteers at midyear}]} \times 100$$

There are a number of reasons why a high turnover rate is problematic. First, the organization will be wasting resources on volunteer recruitment that it could otherwise be applying to the mission. Second, a high turnover rate is bad for the continuity of the relationship an organization has with its service users or clients. Most service users prefer to see a friendly face that they recognize and can develop a relationship with over time. The quality of service can also suffer. In circumstances where a high turnover rate exists, the organization may barely have had time to train its volunteers to deliver an acceptable standard of service before they quit the organization. As Fischer and Schaffer (1993: 93) note, high turnover rates are serious when 'there is a need for volunteers with special skills, intensive training is required, jobs require long-term commitments, when it can be disruptive for clients and there is a shortage of qualified volunteers.'

There are also more subtle problems created by high turnover rates. High turnover occurs for a reason and a high turnover can suggest that there is something wrong with the role the volunteer is being asked to perform or the circumstances in which it is being conducted. The environment could be over-challenging (or, at the other extreme, very dull) or it may be unfriendly or unsupportive. All these things can come back to haunt an organization as a dissatisfied volunteer will likely tell many of their friends about their poor experience. In short, a high turnover rate can impact negatively on an organization's brand or reputation.

Interestingly, research tells us that volunteers are most likely to quit after three months, six months, and twelve months of volunteering (Fischer and Schaffer 1993). The authors tell us that this occurs because volunteers begin their work in a honeymoon stage of euphoria, but regress to 'post-honeymoon blues' after gaining some experience. After longer periods of time, they are likely to quit because they were not able to accomplish what they had hoped or because the organization doesn't represent the values they thought it did on joining.

We also know that some categories of volunteers are more likely to experience turnover than others. Heidrich (1988) identified that fraternal service organizations, veterans' organizations, and cooperatives had a lower turnover than most groups, while youth-serving organizations had a higher turnover.

Sources of Dissatisfaction

We have already alluded to a number of sources of volunteer dissatisfaction, but it is worth elaborating for a moment on what the literature suggests are the key reasons volunteers quit working for nonprofit organizations. Wymer and Starnes (2001*b*) provide a helpful summary of the available research and suggest that the following factors are common causes of turnover.

- *Unreal expectations*. The volunteer may find that the work he has been asked to do does not meet his initial expectations. This could clearly be the fault of either the nonprofit or the individual himself. The individual could have approached the work with an overly optimistic view of what could be accomplished, or the nonprofit could have painted too glowing a picture of the time commitment, type of work, or probable impact on the cause.

- *Lack of appreciative feedback from clients and co-workers*. There is evidence that many volunteers feel undervalued by either the nonprofit or its clients.

- *Lack of appropriate training and supervision*. A number of volunteers quit because they feel unsupported by the organization or ill-equipped to perform the duties they have been requested to undertake. Problems can also arise with supervision since, as we noted earlier, organizations must make tough decisions about whether to supervise the volunteer as a volunteer, or whether to have them supervised by the line manager in the service department in which they are working. The balance of evidence is that volunteers prefer the latter, so that they can feel part of a team, but the real lesson from the literature is that 'it depends' and as a consequence the issue must be approached with some sensitivity.

- *Excessive demands on time*. Some volunteers find that longer hours are required than they had originally envisaged, or that the work they are undertaking encroaches on their home life and eats into the time available for other leisure pursuits.

- *Lack of personal accomplishment*. Equally, some volunteers discover that the post is not as personally rewarding as they had originally thought. Perhaps there is less opportunity to learn new skills, or they are simply unable to make the difference they had hoped for.

- *Burnout/emotional exhaustion*. Some volunteers find themselves physically and psychologically exhausted by their role. Others find that the role evokes excessive anxiety, which impacts on their home life. Volunteers working in human service environments, particularly those related to substance abuse programmes, the mentally ill, or the critically ill are significantly more likely to quit for this reason (Lafer 1991).

- *Fear of liability*. Kadlec (1998) identified that up to 10 per cent of volunteers are worried about liability issues. These include concerns about being held responsible for:

gross negligence, poor decisions involving the organization's funds, conflicts of interest to include taking advantage of a financial opportunity at the expense of the nonprofit or any kind of self-dealing without proper disclosure, not ensuring the organization is carrying out its mission as articulated to government agencies, spending donations for purposes other than what they were given for, damages in personal injury cases and not complying with rules and regulations set by federal, state and local governments, such as lobbying restrictions and building codes. (Wolf 1990: 52–3)

Such are the scales of these concerns that US Congress has now passed the Volunteer Protection Act to provide some immunity from these issues.

- *Stigmatization*. A number of volunteers will quite because they fear that long-term involvement will leave them stigmatized in their communities if they continue to work for what might be perceived as 'unpopular causes' (Kadlec 1998). Snyder et al. (1999) quote the examples of AIDS charities and those dealing with drug/substance abuse.

- *Feelings of second-class status with respect to full-time staff*. A common issue raised by dissatisfied volunteers is their relationship with paid staff. Many report being treated as in some sense inferior to paid staff, despite that fact that their time was being volunteered, rather than paid for.

This latter point warrants some elaboration. As Sargeant and Jay (2004) note, the interface between staff and volunteers can be a particular source of conflict. Staff are often critical of the attitude of volunteers, who can appear to be

- short-term members of the team and therefore not likely to assume responsibility for the long-term repercussions of their activity;

- insufficiently aware of the workings and ethics of the organization and thus likely to make mistakes when representing it;
- unwilling to take direction or guidance.

The attitude of management with regard to volunteers is thus absolutely critical. By setting an example, in the way that they treat volunteers, they can be key to the maintenance of good relations between paid and unpaid staff. The optimum attitude is to treat volunteers entirely straightforwardly and as much as possible like paid professional staff. This should encompass full training, opportunities for development and advancement, and the setting and monitoring of targets, benchmarks, and goals. This 'professionalization' of volunteering is challenging for nonprofits, and carries significant costs, but experienced organizations maintain that it brings results and greatly reduces turnover. 'The steady transformation of the volunteer from well-meaning amateur to trained, professional unpaid staff member is the most significant development in the nonprofit sector' (Drucker 1990).

Retention Strategies

Given the range of issues highlighted above, nonprofits need to give adequate consideration to the issues that might arise in all the volunteer roles they are creating and seek to minimize the opportunity for things to go wrong. As we have just noted, the role of management is key, but so too is the creation of processes that effectively integrate volunteers into the organization and into the systems that are often in place to assist paid staff in dealing with many of these issues.

While the following list is not exhaustive, the volunteer management literature suggests that the following points are worthy of consideration.

(1) *Screening*. The process of screening applicants for volunteer posts should be rigorous. Every effort must be taken to filter out individuals who are not physically or psychologically suited to the role that has been created. Individuals can also be screened out who have unrealistic expectations, or whose motivation seems unsuited to the role.

(2) *Matching*. Every effort must be taken to match volunteers with particular roles. As we noted earlier, every role should contain some pleasant tasks alongside the boring and mundane. Variety should be created, and this should be matched to the needs of specific individuals wherever possible.

(3) *Tenure*. This is a simple point, but surprisingly effective if actioned. Stittleburg (1994) notes that volunteers are significantly less likely to quit a project where a specific end-date has been supplied (i.e. they are significantly more likely to work out their contract). It appears that a fixed-term obligation is more likely to be honoured than an open-ended commitment.

(4) *Support*. Throughout this chapter the opportunities to provide greater support to volunteers have been highlighted. The literature suggests that the following points are among the most critical to address.

- *Communication.* Applebaum (1992) tells us that volunteers suffer from difficulty contacting staff, a lack of feedback from case workers, concerns about value of written reports, a misunderstanding of policies or procedures, and not being briefed properly by staff. It is essential that volunteers, irrespective of the hours that they work (which can often be why such problems occur—since they may not be on site when staff briefings take place), are party to the same internal communications as paid staff.

- *Inclusion in decision making.* Volunteers should be invited to participate in any staff consultations the organization may undertake—and be invited to offer suggestions for service improvements in the same way as paid staff.

- *Supervision.* Irrespective of the line approach adopted, supervision must be friendly, accessible, and supportive (Applebaum 1992).

- *Recognition programmes.* Nonprofits may either create a formal recognition system or deal with recognition on a more *ad hoc* basis as the need arises. Simple communications, such as notes of thanks, a mention in a newsletter or internal paper, or an expression of gratitude to a spouse or employer have all be found to be effective forms of recognition. Other nonprofits have nominated volunteers for external awards, displayed positive client comments on noticeboards, or created a graduated reward programme, such as providing passes to community parks and recreation areas and passing on coupons from local businesses. Also, certificates, pins, and recognition dinners form the backbone of volunteer recognition programmes in the USA.

- *Performance award systems.* In the USA some categories of volunteer receive formal rewards based on their results or level of commitment. Volunteer fire-fighters and paramedics, for example, can earn points which can either be redeemed for cash, or merchandise from local stores. Ellis (1989: 9) notes that 'such programmes allow people to "bank" credit for volunteering that they do and later "withdraw" their credit for some volunteer work by someone else on their behalf or for local "currency" '.

- *Performance evaluation or appraisal.* Volunteers should be subjected to the same internal programme of evaluation as paid staff. Most commonly, this may be a periodic appraisal of their performance, and ideally the organization's performance in assisting them to achieve their personal goals. An action plan for the coming period can be agreed upon and appropriate development opportunities actioned.

- *Watch the door.* Many nonprofits now conduct exit interviews of volunteers when they terminate their support. This can be an excellent way of identifying areas in which the organization might improve the quality of support and opportunities it offers to its volunteer base. While some turnover will be due to unavoidable factors, such as relocation, or a change in the individual's lifestyle, there will undoubtedly be some volunteer turnover that proves to be due to one or more of the factors we discussed earlier and on which the organization can take action to improve.

Recruiting Board Members

Before leaving the topic of volunteer management it is worth examining briefly the topic of board recruitment. In both the USA and the UK, volunteers are frequently required to comprise the board that will oversee the management of a nonprofit organization and ensure that its resources are appropriately directed towards the 'objects' it was set up to achieve. In the UK such boards have tended to comprise individuals with particular expertise in the cause, perhaps medical practitioners in the case of medical charities and conservationists in the case of wildlife organizations. In the USA, while there may indeed be individuals present with 'subject' expertise, the focus has been equally on individuals who may either make a substantial financial contribution to the cause, or who are acquainted with individuals who could make such a contribution.

In both countries, finding the right people to serve on the board and thus shape the future direction of an organization is a far from easy task, particularly for those organizations that lack a social profile. Nonprofits such as museums and galleries have a big advantage here, as there may be a high degree of prestige associated with becoming a board member of one of these institutions. A board role can be highly visible within a particular community and signal much about the individual(s) who have agreed to undertake this responsibility. Nonprofits without such a profile, or a tangible set of assets that may act as a recruitment mechanism in themselves, have a more difficult task in identifying and recruiting the right individuals.

As a starting point, Widmer (1985) suggests that four incentives apply to participation in nonprofit boards:

1. *material incentives*—tangible rewards in goods, services, or money for oneself or one's group;
2. *social incentives*—intangible rewards following from associating with others— friendship, status, and honours;
3. *development incentives*—learning new skills or assuming civic responsibilities;
4. *ideological incentives*—intangible rewards that come from helping achieve something greater than oneself.

Scanlan (2002) found that people willing to take on leadership roles have

- an interest in the big picture—the overall welfare and progress of the community;
- a social entrepreneur approach to the community, including a strong desire to solve problems through action and make it a better place (see also Dees and Economy 1991);
- limited ability to take on new commitments of time and energy, especially commitments that are longer term (heading campaigns for organizations with which they are not already associated, committee or board service with organizations with which they have previously been involved, etc.);
- unwillingness to take on vague or not clearly defined tasks that lack timeliness, goals, and specific outcomes;

- responsiveness to peers, colleagues, and close friends when asked by them to do something, especially if the something fits into some or all of the other categories above.

Clearly many of these factors can be reflected in the way that individuals are approached to volunteer in this capacity. It is important to recognize here the critical role that will be played in recruitment by the existing board. Research has shown that 43 per cent of board members first talked of volunteering with an existing board member. This stresses the high reliance in this context of organizations on personal networks and acquaintances. However, in some circumstances it may be appropriate to advertise for board members, particularly when specific expertise is required and where few personal contacts exist.

■ SUMMARY

In this chapter we have examined the contribution that volunteers make to the nonprofit sector. As we have seen, the percentage of UK and US populations that volunteer time to nonprofits each year is high. It is encouraging to note the growth in volunteering currently taking place in the USA and that, although volunteering is declining in some groups in the UK, support for the sector remains buoyant.

In this chapter we explored a range of issues in relation to volunteer recruitment and retention. While some readers may feel that many of the issues we have addressed fall in the domain of Human Resource Management (HRM) rather than marketing *per se*, I would argue that the attraction of appropriately qualified individuals and the matching of these individuals to tasks where they will make a genuine contribution is essentially a marketing task. I would also argue that the excessively high level of turnover faced by many organizations is testimony to a general lack of internal marketing currently taking place within the sector. It seems clear that a great number of volunteers continue not to be regarded either as internal customers or even stakeholders of an organization, and thus many of the tools and techniques of internal marketing may well have a real contribution to make to future development. A fundamental point, often repeated throughout this chapter, is the need to start the whole process of volunteer recruitment and management with a thorough and clear understanding of what requirements these individuals might have of the organization. Retention can then be greatly enhanced by ensuring that these requirements are met and even extended and developed over time.

■ DISCUSSION QUESTIONS

1. You have been approached by a local hospice for help in expanding their existing volunteer base from 20–35 carers. Outline a volunteer recruitment plan that could be used for this purpose.

2. As the head of community fundraising for a large national nonprofit, you have been asked to make a presentation to one of your local branches about how they might identify and recruit new volunteer fundraisers. Explain how a knowledge of volunteer motivation can be used to inform a recruitment strategy.

3. As the newly appointed Head of Volunteer Services for a national nonprofit, you have been concerned to discover that your organization presently has a 90 per cent annual attrition rate of volunteers. Develop a presentation to your Board of Trustees explaining why this should be addressed as a matter of urgency.

4. What are the primary reasons for volunteers terminating their support? What steps might an organization utilizing volunteer counsellors to assist young drug addicts take to ensure that its retention rate is as high as possible?.

■ REFERENCES

Amos, O.M. (1982) 'Empirical Analysis of Motives Underlying Contributions to Charity', *Atlantic Economic Journal*, Vol. 10, 45–52.

Applebaum, S. (1992) *Recruiting and Retaining Volunteers from Minority Communities: A Case Study*, Ann Arbor, MI, UMI Dissertation Services.

Clark, R.D. and Word, L.E. (1972) 'Why Don't Bystanders Help? Because of Ambiguity?' *Journal of Personality and Social Psychology*, Vol. 24, 392–400.

Clary, E.G. and Synder, M. (1991) 'A Functional Analysis of Altruism and Prosocial Behaviour: The Case of Volunteerism', in *Review of Personality and Social Psychology*, London, Sage, 119–48.

Cnaan, R.A. and Goldberg-Glen, R.S. (1991) 'Measuring Motivation to Volunteer in Human Services', *Journal of Applied Behavioural Sciences*, Vol. 27, No. 3, 269–84.

Coliazzi, A., Williams, K.J. and Kayson, W.A. (1984) 'When Will People Help? The Effects of Gender, Urgency and Location on Altruism', *Psychological Reports*, Vol. 55, 139–42.

Collard, D. (1978) *Altruism and Economy*, New York, Oxford University Press.

Dees, J. and Economy, P. (2001) 'Social Entrepreneurship', in Dees, J., Emerson, J. and Economy, P. (eds.) *Enterprising Nonprofits*, New York, John Wiley & Sons, 4.

Doyle, D. (2002) *Volunteers in Hospice and Palliative Care*, Oxford, Oxford University Press.

Drucker, P.F. (1990) *Managing the Non-Profit Organisation: Practices and Principles*, London, Harper Collins.

Eisenberg, N. and Miller, P.A. (1987) 'Empathy, Sympathy and Altruism: Empirical and Conceptual Links', in Eisenberg, N. and Strayer, J. (eds.) *Empathy and Its Development*, New York, Cambridge University Press, 292–316.

Ellis, S.J. (1994) *The Volunteer Recruitment Book*, Philadelphia, Energize.

Ellis, S.J. (1989) *Volunteer Centers: Gearing up for the 1990s*, Alexandria, VA, United Way of America.

Fischer, L.R. and Schaffer, K.B. (1993) *Older Volunteers: A Guide For Research and Practice*, Newbury Park, Sage Publications.

Fisher, J.C. and Cole, K.M. (1993) *Leadership and Management of Volunteer Programs*, San Francisco, Jossey Bass.

Fisher, R.J. and Ackerman, D. (1998) 'The Effects of Recognition and Group Need on Volunteerism: A Social Norm Perspective', *Journal of Consumer Research*, Vol. 25 (Dec), 262–75.

Frisch, M.B. and Gerrard, M. (1981) 'Natural Helping Systems: A Survey of Red Cross Volunteers', *American Journal of Community Psychology*, Vol. 9 (Oct), 567–79.

Gallup (1992) 'Volunteering in the UK', Gallup survey.

Geer, J.H. and Jermecky, L. (1973) 'The Effect of being Responsible for Reducing Others' Pain on Subjects' Response and Arousal', *Journal of Personality and Social Psychology*, Vol. 27, 100–108.

Glaser, J.S. (1994) *The United Way Scandal—An Insiders Account of What Went Wrong and Why*, New York, John Wiley & Sons.

Heidrich, K.W. (1988) *Lifestyles of Volunteers: A Marketing Segmentation Study*, PhD dissertation, University of Illinois at Urbana-Champaign.

Horne, S. and Broadbridge, A. (1994) 'The Charity Shop Volunteer in Scotland: Greatest Asset or Biggest Headache?' *Voluntas*, Vol. 5, No. 2, 205–18.

Independent Sector (2000) *Volunteering, Volunteering Levels and Number of Hours Recorded*. Available online at **www.indepsec.org/GrandV/s_keyf.htm**.

Jackson, R. (2001) 'How to Recruit and Retain the right Volunteers', Proceedings, *Recruiting, Retaining and Training Volunteers*, Henry Stewart Conferences, London, October.

Kadlec, D. (1998) *Pitch In, Get Sued*, Time, Vol. 151, No. 24, 79.

Kaehler, J. and Sargeant, A. (1998) Returns on Fund-Raising Expenditures in the Voluntary Sector, Working Paper 98/06, University of Exeter.

Lafer, B. (1991) 'The Attrition of Hospice Volunteers', *Omega*, Vol. 23, No. 3, 161–8.

Lohmann, R. (1992) 'The Commons: A Multidisciplinary Approach to Nonprofit Organization, Voluntary Action and Philanthropy', *Nonprofit and Voluntary Sector Quarterly*, Vol. 21, 309–24.

Mathis, R.L. and Jackson, J.H. (1982) *Personnel: Contemporary Perspectives and Applications*, 3rd edn, St Paul, West Publishing Company.

McClintock, C.G. and Allison, S.T. (1989) 'Social Value Orientation and Helping Behaviour', *Journal of Applied Psychology*, Vol. 19, No. 4, 353–62.

Millet, R. and Orosz, J. (2001) *Cultures of Caring: Philanthropy in Diverse American Communities*, The Kellogg Foundation.

Morgan, J.N., Dye, R.F. and Hybels, J.H. (1979) *Results From Two National Surveys of Philanthropic Activity*, Michigan, University of Michigan Press.

Mount, J. and Quirion, F.(1988) 'A Study of Donors to a University Campaign', *The Philanthropist*, Vol. 8, No. 1, 56–64.

National Council for Hospice and Specialist Palliative Care Services (1996) *Education In Palliative Care*, London, NCHSPC.

Newman, C.V. (1977) 'Relation Between Altruism and Dishonest Profiteering From Another's Misfortune', *Journal of Social Psychology*, Vol. 109: 43–8.

Okun, M.A. (1994) 'The Relation Between Motives for Organizational Volunteering and the Frequency of Volunteering by Elders', *Journal of Applied Gerontology*, Vol. 13, No. 2, 115–26.

Pancer, S.M., McCullen, L.M., Kabatoff, R.A., Johnson, K.G. and Pond, C.A. (1979) 'Conflict and Avoidance in the Helping Situation', *Journal of Personality and Social Psychology*, Vol. 37, No. 8, 1406–11.

Ratje, J.M. (2003) 'Well Prepared Volunteers Help the Brand Image', *Marketing News*, 14 April, 17.

Ricks, F.A. and Pyke, S.W. (1973) 'Women in Voluntary Social Organizations', *The Ontario Psychologist*, Vol. 5, No. 2, 48–55.

Rokeach, M. (1973) *The Nature of Human Values*, New York, The Free Press.

Sargeant, A. and Jay, E. (2004) *Fundraising Management*, London, Routledge.

Scanlan, E.A. (2002) Strategic Task Forces, *International Journal of Nonprofit and Voluntary Sector Marketing*, Vol. 7, No. 4, 334–42.

Schervish P.G. (1993) 'Philosophy as Moral Identity of Caritas', in Schervish, P.G., Benz, O., Dulaney, P., Murphy, T.B. and Salett, S. (eds.) *Taking Giving Seriously*, Center on Philanthropy, Indianapolis, Indiana University Press.

Schervish, P.G. (1997) 'Inclination, Obligation and Association: What we Know and What we Need to Learn about Donor Motivation', In Burlingame, D. (ed.) *Critical Issues in Fund Raising*, Hoboken, NJ, John Wiley & Sons.

Schindler-Rainman, E. (1988) 'Administration of Volunteer Programs', In Daniel, T. (ed.) *The Nonprofit Organization Handbook*, 2nd edn, New York, McGraw Hill.

Schwartz, S. (1977) 'Normative Influences on Altruism', In Berkowitz, L. (ed.) *Advances in Experimental Social Psychology*, New York, Academic Press, 221–79.

Senior Corps (2000) Part of the Corporation For National Services: RSVP Programs, available online at **www.seniorcorps.org** on 28 July 2000.

Smith, D.H. and Baldwin, B.R. (1974) 'Parental Socialization, Socio-Economic Status and Volunteer Organization Participation', *Journal of Voluntary Action Research*, Vol. 3, 59–66.

Snyder, M., Omoto, A.M. and Crain, A.L. (1999) 'Punished for their Good Deeds', *The American Behavioural Scientist*, Vol. 42, No. 7, 1175–92.

Stittleburg, P.C. (1994) 'Recruiting and Retaining Volunteers', *NFPA (National Fire Protection Association) Journal*, Vol. 88, No. 2, 20, 109.

Widmer, C. (1985) 'Why Board Members Participate', *Journal of Voluntary Action Research*, Vol. 14, No. 4, 9–23.

Williams, R.F. (1987) 'Receptivity to Persons with Mental Retardation: A Study of Volunteer Interest', *American Journal of Mental Retardation*, Vol. 92, No. 3, 299–303.

Wolf, T. (1990) *Managing A Nonprofit Organization*, New York, Simon and Schuster.

Wymer, W.W. (1996) *Formal Volunteering as a Function of Values, Self-Esteem, Empathy and Facilitation*, DBA dissertation, Indiana University.

Wymer, W.W. (1999) 'Understanding Volunteer Markets: The Case of Senior Volunteers', *Journal of Nonprofit and Public Sector Marketing*, Vol. 6, No. (2/3), 1–24.

Wymer, W.W. and Samu, S. (2002) 'Volunteer Service as Symbolic Consumption: Gender and Occupational Differences in Volunteering', *Journal of Marketing Management*, Vol. 18, 971–89.

Wymer, W.W. and Starnes, B.J. (1999) 'Segmenting Sub-Groups of Volunteers for Target Marketing: Differentiating Traditional Hospice Volunteers from other Volunteers', *Journal of Nonprofit and Public Sector Marketing*, Vol. 6, No. (2/3), 25–50.

Wymer, W.W. and Starnes, B.J. (2001a) 'Conceptual Foundations and Practical Guidelines for Recruiting Volunteers to Serve in Local Nonprofit Organizations: Part 1', *Journal of Nonprofit and Public Sector Marketing*, Vol. 9, No. 1, 63–96.

Wymer, W.W. and Starnes, B.J. (2001b) 'Conceptual Foundations and Practical Guidelines for Retaining Volunteers Who Serve in Local Nonprofit Organizations: Part 1', *Journal of Nonprofit and Public Sector Marketing*, Vol. 9, No. 1, 97–118.

14 | Public Sector Marketing

OBJECTIVES

By the end of this chapter you should be able to:

(1) describe recent changes in the scope and development of the UK public sector;

(2) determine appropriate boundaries for the application of a marketing approach;

(3) assess the quality of public sector services;

(4) understand the relevance of marketing to critical public sector issues such as CCT and public accountability;

(5) apply marketing tools and ideas to a variety of public sector contexts.

The Development of the Public Sector in the UK

Historic Overview

As we noted in the Introduction to this text, the term 'public sector' is typically used to refer to a set of institutions that a given society feels is necessary for the basic well-being of its members. The aims of these institutions are determined by the State and their budgets are typically derived from taxation, collected both locally and nationally. These resources are then divided between the institutions on the basis of a politically determined allocation, rather than market mechanisms or even by the likely take-up of services by citizens. It is argued that this approach ensures that a wide variety of needs are addressed by the State, rather than just those of the majority of individuals. In most Western countries the State now provides at least a proportion of key services such as healthcare, education, social services, defence, housing, policing, and transport.

In many countries there is now widespread acceptance that the State should take responsibility for providing a basic minimum of service in relation to each of these areas. There is also general acceptance that it is society itself, and in particular tax-payers, who should shoulder the responsibility for paying for this. This has, however, not always been the case. Looking back over the seventeenth, eighteenth, and even nineteenth centuries, the State was generally regarded as a source of forced tribute, either in the form of taxes or conscription to the armed forces. This was widely despised and state intervention in social life was viewed with great suspicion. It was not until the early part of the twentieth century that individuals began to recognize a wider role for the State in tackling a range of social issues and equally, began to recognize the legitimacy of the State seeking to fund these initiatives through general taxation.

While there had been a number of interventions by the State in social life throughout the late nineteenth and early twentieth centuries (such as the introduction of the state pension in 1908) it was not until the Second World War that the pace of change accelerated. During the war the government had been compelled to assume considerable responsibility for many facets of everyday life, including the rationing of food, clothing, electricity, etc. This created a climate where State involvement in social life was considered more acceptable, a feature of UK society that continued long after the cessation of hostilities.

In 1942 the Beveridge Report (the Report on Social Insurance and Allied Services) marked a landmark shift in government thinking and policy. Beveridge believed that a goal of full employment (or, rather, 95 per cent employment to allow for some mobility in the workforce) was achievable and that this in turn would lead to increasing consumption and a greater standard of living for all UK citizens. To achieve this 'full' employment he sought to tackle what he saw as the primary obstacles to its attainment, namely 'Want, Disease, Ignorance, Squalor and Idleness'. As a consequence he developed a number of policies designed to overcome these difficulties, with the concept of income security at their core. Initially his ideas met with only limited support from the wartime coalition government. It was not until after the 1945 election, which returned a Labour government, that many of his ideas were realized. Beveridge's vision and what ultimately became known as the 'welfare state' was created by a series of Acts of Parliament enacted between 1944 and 1949. These are briefly summarized below.

1944 Education Act

It was decided that greater opportunity would be afforded to all children, irrespective of their background, to realize an appropriate education. It was also decided that this should be funded and shaped by the State. The Act created a situation where an examination known as the '11+' would determine the aptitudes of children and decide whether these were practical, technological, or academic. On the basis of this test children were then streamed to attend secondary modern, technical, and grammar schools according to their needs (or rather what the government defined as their needs). It remained possible for wealthier parents to opt out of this process and send their children to a private school, but for all other parents the choice of school rested on the outcome of the 11+ examination. While to modern ears this may sound rather a draconian policy it should be remembered that the government's intent was to ensure an appropriate education for all members of society.

1945 Family Allowances Act

In a bid to assist families to avoid poverty, it was decided to pay an allowance to the parents of every child from birth until the age of 16. The size of this allowance was to be determined by HM Treasury and applied to all children in a given family except the first-born. It was not until 1977 that the first-born children in a family became eligible for this allowance.

1946 National Health Service Act

Under this Act healthcare was intended to be largely free at the point of delivery, although even in these early days there remained scope for some charges to be made. The Act also required local authorities to take on some responsibility for healthcare delivery and to take care of the disabled or long-term infirm in their area.

1946 National Insurance Act

This Act established a series of benefits that would assist citizens to cope financially with adverse circumstances such as maternity, sickness, retirement, unemployment, and the death of a spouse. Many of the original ideas proposed by Beveridge were brought into existence by this Act although, as the reader will imagine, the additional burden that this placed on tax-payers was immense.

1947 Town and Country Planning Act

The government had recognized the need to achieve a better balance in the geographical spread of the working population. It was felt that the best way of achieving this was to control the nature and location of the housing stock and/or business/industrial enterprise. Accordingly, this Act made it compulsory to apply for those seeking to build new developments or amend existing ones to seek planning permission to do so.

1948 National Assistance Act

This Act was significant in that it marked the end of the Poor Laws that had historically provided the responsibility in law for taking care of the poor and needy in society. It recognized that the State was now taking over that responsibility and would in future provide a specific minimum level of assistance which was deemed to be enough to allow the individual(s) to better their position.

1949 Housing Act

This Act sought to deal with the aftermath of the Second World War and to create housing to replace that which had been damaged or destroyed by the Luftwaffe. It also recognized that the birth rate was rising rapidly in the post-war era and as a consequence the need to build a lot of new housing, swiftly, was one of the most pressing problems facing the government.

The Period 1945–1979

The growth in the welfare state was coupled with a series of nationalizations. Civil aviation, transport, electricity, gas, iron, and steel were all nationalized in the immediate post-war period. The legislation to achieve this, together with the Acts listed above, greatly increased the number of civil servants that were required to manage these additional commitments. This gave rise to an increasing bureaucracy and the need for a systems approach to management to cope with the sheer scale of the State apparatus. While initially welcomed by the public, it was not long before the perception of the civil service became unfavourable; in particular it was seen as being impersonal and mechanistic.

The costs of managing this government bureaucracy over the next thirty years were considerable. In periods of high economic growth and low unemployment the financial burden presented by the welfare state was perhaps less of an issue due to the accompanying rise in income from taxation and falling demand for State benefits. In periods of higher unemployment, however, the demand for State benefits created a heavy burden on the tax-payer and when coupled with economic events such as the oil crisis of 1972–4 presented the Treasury with a real problem. It had to juggle rising needs on the one hand with the need to cap public spending on the other. It was against this backdrop that Margaret Thatcher was able to come to power in 1979 arguing the case that the State had become unwieldy and as a consequence should be cut back. She was also able to argue successfully that State control should be replaced by individual choice.

The Period 1979–2004

The period 1979–97 saw a succession of Conservative governments. Authors such as Thomson (1992) have argued that the early years in particular were characterized by a fervent desire to roll back the frontiers of the State and that as a consequence there was scarcely any area of the public domain that remained untouched. She argues that the central themes of these governments were efficiency, effectiveness, and economy as manifest by policies of privatization, delegation, competition, enterprise, deregulation, service quality, and the curtailment of trade union powers. This period is of considerable interest to the study of public sector marketing since, as we shall shortly see, many of the changes in policy instituted by these Conservative governments still have resonance in management practices today. Indeed the New Labour government that took office in 1997 has pursued many of these ideas, offering citizens a number of new rights in respect of the quality of services they receive and seeking to enhance user engagement in their planning and delivery.

Recent changes in public sector thinking and management are summarized below.

- *Commercialization.* Successive governments have sought efficiency gains, value for money in public services, and have encouraged or compelled the institution of market mechanisms (such as compulsory competitive tendering) to ensure the best value for tax-payers in the provision of services.
- *User involvement.* Recent governments have also encouraged user control of services, enhanced consultation with users, and/or made provision for formal redress should a poor quality of service be delivered.
- *Evaluation of performance.* To ensure that value for money is provided by government services, there has been a marked increase in formal measures of performance, together with regular inspections and audits.

- *Strategy.* Successive governments have encouraged the development of formal planning procedures, frequently borrowing ideas from the domain of strategic management as developed in the commercial sector.

- *Collaboration.* There has also been a move to foster and improve collaborative working across agencies whether between or within sectors, e.g. working with the voluntary sector or the collaboration of heath and social care.

The latter decades of the twentieth century have therefore seen considerable change in the manner in which successive governments have both viewed the public sector and sought to manage it for the wider benefit of society. In this chapter we will seek to explore the relevance of marketing to this domain, and address the critical marketing issues raised by recent changes to management practice in this context.

The Perception of Marketing

Since 1979, both Labour and Conservative governments have made efforts to introduce private sector management ideas, believing that improvements in the quality of service delivery and/or efficiency gains would result. This fascination with commercial management practices has led to an increasing interest in the topic of marketing, yet as Laing and McKee (2001) note, marketing has conventionally been viewed by public service professionals as antipathetic to the delivery of public services. Public services, it is argued, should be provided irrespective of demand and irrespective of the ability on the part of the user to pay the economic cost of providing that service. As a consequence, they argue, marketing is unnecessary.

While this may be a convincing philosophical argument, the policies of successive governments have created quasi-market mechanisms (particularly in relation to healthcare), competitive tendering procedures, greater public accountability, and a rapid growth in outsourcing the provision of government services through the integration of private sector suppliers into the wider public sector. In circumstances where organizations are forced to compete against each other for the right to provide services and where organizations are increasingly compelled to match the needs of service users with provision and to justify their priorities and expenditures in the public arena, the diversity of need for effective marketing practice becomes clear (Walsh 1994; Keaney 1999).

Despite the potential benefits of a marketing approach Buurma (2001) lists a number of objections to marketing typically raised by government officials or departments.

- *The government is a monopolist supplier* (van der Hart 1991). In such circumstances it is argued that there is no need for marketing, as there is no competition to beat. Since the customer has no choice there is no longer a need to market the one supplier they can use. Of course this argument is a little naïve since customers can, and frequently do, elect to substitute alternative services or to simply withdraw from the market altogether (as the case study below illustrates).

CASE STUDY 14.1

Hull School Dinners

A children's revolt recently foiled government attempts to introduce healthier menus for school lunches. A pioneering scheme to replace fry-ups and stodgy puddings with pastas and lighter options was rejected by pupils in 2004 and has led to a big fall in the number of children having school meals.

The most convincing evidence of the unpopularity of healthy menus was reported in Hull. There the school meals policy was launched by Stephen Twigg, the Schools Minister, in February 2004. The city which suffers from Britain's highest levels of obesity decided to cut back on traditional foods such as hot dogs, fish fingers and meatballs. Instead a meal plan devised by the council's own caterers was implemented and pupils were offered meals such as macaroni bake, chicken risotto, savoury cheese wedge, turkey curry, salad, and naan bread.

But four weeks after the healthy menus were introduced in 79 primary and nursery schools, the number of children on school meals fell by nearly a quarter. At one primary school take-up slumped from 50 per cent to 15 per cent. Even children entitled to free meals, whose parents were deemed too poor to feed them, preferred to go without.

- *The citizen is more than a customer.* While this is undoubtedly true, this argument does not preclude the use of marketing tools. Indeed, it strengthens the need for effective marketing. Aside from choosing to use a particular government service, citizens may also use their democratic vote to help shape policy and to achieve what they personally regard as the optimum allocation of government expenditure between the available options. Marketing tools can be used to help politicians to convey the desirability of particular options and/or portray the wider benefit that will accrue to society as a consequence of a particular option. Marketing can even be employed to encourage individuals to exercise their democratic rights to vote.

- *Collective goods (e.g. local government services such as recycling collections) are free goods.* This argument suggests that marketing is not necessary since there is no exchange between the supplier and the user. Users frequently do not pay the supplier directly for the services they receive. However, this neglects the fact that while the service may be provided free of charge the term 'free goods' merely reflects the compensation side and not the sacrifice that must be made by the user in using those collective goods. Thus, while a local authority may offer a recycling facility to the residents in a certain area, the fact that it is offered free of charge may not be enough in itself to stimulate use of the service. Inculcating a particular pattern of behaviour is often a key facet of achieving government objectives and cost alone may not be a determining factor, as the following case study demonstrates.

CASE STUDY 14.2

Municipal Recycling

The 1990s have been characterized as the decade of recycling. Goldstein (1997) reports that the national recycling rate in the USA climbed from 9 per cent in 1989 to 28 per cent in 1996, suggesting that civic environmentalism had entered the mainstream of behavioural norms. During this time, the nature of the recycling business also changed markedly, evolving from periodic paper drives by Scouts troops and volunteers into a challenging, complex, and expensive service that now competes with other local programmes for scarce resources (Folz 1999).

The data in Table 14.1 were collected by Folz (1999) from municipal recycling coordinators in 265 cities. The table indicates that for these cities recycling participation increased by 36 per cent over the period 1989–96. As one might expect, participation in mandatory programmes in both years was higher than that reported by voluntary programmes. However, the largest improvement in participation occurred in voluntary programmes, which average a 50 per cent increase over the period. The table also indicates that offering a kerb-side pick-up led to a much higher level of participation than leaving citizens to make their own way to local recycling centres with their materials.

Folz was able to use the statistical technique of regression to explore the relationship between the participation rates obtained by each city and a range of accompanying policies or factors. His results for both mandatory and compulsory schemes are summarized below.

- *Mandatory*. The most significant factor in increasing participation in mandatory schemes appears to be the timing of the kerb-side pick-up. Those cities that collected materials for recycling on the same day as other solid household waste experienced higher levels of participation. His data also revealed that the use of penalties or sanctions for improper recycling behaviour or a failure to recycle were associated with higher participation rates. It is interesting to note that the magnitude of the recycling goal set by the city did not appear to drive behaviour, suggesting that customers do not find the municipal targets to be of direct relevance to them when a mandatory recycling scheme is in existence.

- *Voluntary*. In voluntary schemes there appeared to be a link between these municipal targets and participation. The data suggests that the nearer the target year to achieve a particular level of recycling,

Table 14.1 Municipal recycling data 1989–1996

Indicator	1989	N	1996	N	Difference	% change
Mean participation rates (all cities)	53.53	149	72.80	139	+19.27	+35.99
Mandatory programmes	76.51	47	80.01	71	+ 3.50	+ 4.57
Voluntary programmes	43.02	101	65.27	68	+22.25	+51.22
Kerb-side pick-up	49.83	71	68.78	55	+18.95	+38.03
Drop-off only	26.96	30	50.39	13	+23.49	+87.32

Source: Folz (1999). Reproduced with kind permission.

continues

CASE STUDY 14.2 continued

the more motivated individuals were to recycle. Folz argues that a near-term goal may constitute a more salient appeal to citizen altruism. Of the other factors that were found to drive behaviour, the supply of free recycling bins was a highly significant factor, as was the appointment of neighbourhood 'block leaders' who were responsible for encouraging recycling among the households in their immediate vicinity.

It is interesting to note that across both categories of schemes, those cities that had introduced variable fees, or volume pricing for the collection of solid waste, had significantly higher levels of participation.

The case study illustrates that the simple provision of a service, even a free service, does not in itself ensure that citizens will participate. There is therefore a key role for marketing to play in understanding the real costs (perhaps opportunity costs in this recycling case) of participation in a scheme and the factors that could potentially motivate people to change their behaviour.

The Boundaries of Marketing

While we have argued above that marketing has considerable relevance to the public sector environment, it is important not to overstate the case and to recognize that there may be some aspects of government provision in which it would not be appropriate for marketing concepts or ideas to play a role.

The literature suggests that there are two ways of determining the relevance of marketing to specific public sector contexts. The first of these springs from a fundamental understanding of the nature of the exchange that is taking place. Readers will recall from Chapter 1 that *exchange* lies at the heart of the marketing concept. In the commercial context the nature of this exchange is easy to define, with something of value changing hands between both parties. In its simplest form, this would be the exchange of money for a product or service.

In the public sector context, however, authors such as Koster (1991) have argued that the exchange process is altogether more complex, with income from local and national taxation funding the supply of services that the tax-payer himself may derive no benefit from (e.g. the provision of a sports centre they don't use) or perhaps only indirectly benefit from (e.g. through effective policing preventing crime in their neighbourhood) (Pandya and Dholakia 1992).

Koster (1991) argues that for an exchange to be deemed a marketing exchange a number of criteria must be met. These are summarized below.

- There must be two or more parties involved. These parties must wish to achieve their objectives through an exchange with the other(s).

- The exchange must take place on a voluntary basis and both parties should have the freedom to enter into the exchange or not as they see fit.

- There must be a mutual exchange of value between both parties.

- The objects of this exchange should not be identical, i.e. both parties must exchange a different source of value to the other.
- The nature of the exchange should be characterized as a 'win-win'. To both parties the value received should represent more than the cost of the sacrifice.
- There should be communication between both parties.
- The nature of the relationship between the parties is viewed as legitimate by society and rests on good faith.
- The exchange involves both parties in rights and obligations that are mutual.
- Both parties have a mechanism to hold the other accountable for non-compliance.

Looking down through this list, it is apparent that the provision of many government services could legitimately (according to Koster) be regarded as marketing exchanges. The provision of some forms of healthcare, education, social care, leisure facilities, etc. would seem to meet the criteria for a marketing exchange and where as a consequence many of the ideas and tools we have elaborated on in previous chapters would be felt to apply.

Applying this framework to the full range of public sector exchanges, it is clear that exchanges such as the imposition of taxation or the internment of prisoners fall outside the domain of marketing.

In seeking to draw this distinction, other authors have preferred to focus on the nature of the services being delivered rather than the nature of the exchange. Authors such as van der Hart (1991), for example, elected to categorize services by the degree to which the user pays for the service and the degree to which the public have contact with the service. The extent to which marketing tools and ideas are of relevance is thus viewed as a function of where a particular service might sit within the matrix depicted in Figure 14.1.

Consider first the top left-hand corner of the matrix. Here we have a group of services that have a high degree of contact with the public, but where the payment for these services is made only indirectly through taxation. In these circumstances, van der Hart argues that marketing concepts are of little relevance since the relationship between

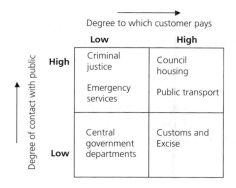

Figure 14.1 Categorization of public services

Source: Van der Hart (1991: 36). Reproduced with kind permission.

the funder and the service is primarily one of good citizenship. Of course, that is not to say that organizations such as the emergency services cannot use specific marketing tools (e.g. to persuade citizens only to call 999—the UK emergency number—in genuine emergencies), but such usage will be rare.

In the top right of the matrix are services that have a high degree of contact with the public and where users are generally expected to pay all, or a percentage of, the costs of providing that service. Here the relationship with users will be characterized by multiple interactions and the income derived from these services is directly related to discrete services to individual users. In such a context the relationship between the service provider and user can legitimately be regarded as one of customer—supplier and the full range of marketing tools and techniques will be of relevance.

In the bottom left quadrant are depicted services that have a low contact with members of the public and where individual users are not typically asked to pay for the service rendered. The majority of the services supplied by central government departments, such as defence, will typically fall into this category. Van der Hart argues that marketing has little or no relevance to this domain.

In the bottom right are services that have a low contact with the public, but where users are expected to pay. An example of an organization in this quadrant might be Customs and Excise or the agency enforcing the payment of the television licence. Here the opportunities to employ marketing concepts and ideas will be limited, except perhaps in respect of the promotion of rules/regulations and the publicizing of particular initiatives.

Laing (2003: 438) prefers to move away from a matrix-style approach in determining the extent to which marketing ideas and tools may be of relevance. Instead he proposes a spectrum of public services where the extent to which marketing may legitimately be applied will be a function of whether a service delivers private (i.e. consumer) or public benefits:

The relevance and applicability of current conceptualizations of marketing within public services can ultimately be viewed as being directly related to the balance between private and social benefit, together with the associated balance between consumer and producer judgement within such services. It is the distinction between the focus of benefit and judgement, rather than whether services are formally delivered in the public or private sectors (the balance of which is dynamic and is largely shaped by ideological considerations), that ultimately determines the extent to which marketing is relevant and the appropriateness of alternative conceptualizations of marketing to public services. (Laing 2003: 439)

Clearly there are few difficulties in applying marketing where private benefits predominate, but at the other end of the spectrum there are real problems in applying a set of consumer-focused management concepts to the delivery of such services. Laing concludes:

There is consequently a need for caution in extending the domain of marketing within the public sector to those areas where it is only of tangential relevance in order not to discredit the underlying concepts of marketing in those areas where they offer valid conceptual and practical tools to professionals in meeting the underlying objectives of public sector service provision. (Laing 2003: 440)

Characteristics of Public Services

The range of services provided by the public sector is very diverse; from criminal justice and social welfare on the one hand to social housing and public transport on the other. Lane (1995) argues that such services have little in common. Laing (2003), however, believes that there are three defining characteristics. These are detailed below.

(1) *Dominance of political objectives*. The provision of public sector services differs because the rationale for their existence and the shape of their provision is not framed in simple economic terms (Graham 1994). The nature of the services is shaped not by an ability to pay on the part of users, but on the basis of what is deemed as being right or good for a particular community. The benefit that accrues from these services is thus better expressed in terms of social profit (Bauer 1966) where, for example, levels of health, education, and housing, benefit not only users, but the community as a whole. Public services are thus targeted to particular groups, not on economic grounds, but on the basis of need and equity (van der Hart 1991).

(2) *Primacy of citizen rather than of the consumer*. Public services are targeted at citizens rather than consumers. Walsh (1994: 69) argues that the fundamental relationship between citizen and government 'is not one of simple exchange but one of mutual commitment and (thus) public services are not simply a reciprocation of taxes.'

The notion of citizens having a commitment to the community in which they live and its government is an important one. Schemes and services such as Neighbourhood Watch, recycling, and road safety are only possible with the active participation of citizens, frequently taking actions that are economically sub-optimal for them, but which are taken because of the need to benefit society as a whole. Historically there was a clear understanding of the need for a given individual to support the needs of others. In modern society there is an increasing tendency to define public services in terms of individual benefits (Laing and Hogg 2002), which some authors have argued could potentially be damaging to society as such a consumerist perspective could place increasing and inappropriate demands on public services (Buchanan et al. 1987).

(3) *Need to serve multidimensional customers*. Here Laing (2003) argues that public services differ because they are designed to both meet the needs of individuals and the wider society in which they live. In addition to this, the services provided by one component of the public sector may be provided to serve the need of additional stakeholders, such as community groups, interest groups, business/industry, politicians, or even the wider society of the country as a whole. There are clearly parallels here with the voluntary sector as discussed in Chapter 1.

Clearly all these differences must be taken account of in the design of an appropriate approach to the management of public sector marketing.

Quality in Public Services

Recent years have seen an increasing interest on the part of government in the quality of public service provision. Indeed, in the UK a succession of charters have sought to outline the rights that citizens have for a high standard of baseline service in a wide range of public services. These charters are a formal contract between public service providers and their customers or the wider community. The 1980s and 1990s, for example, have seen the introduction of the Citizens Charter, the Job Seekers Charter and the Parents Charter.

Accompanying these charters has been a rise in the measurement of delivered service quality. Frequently this has taken the form of measuring the outputs achieved by each service (e.g the number of people aided) or the time that it takes for particular actions to occur (e.g. the time spent on a hospital waiting list). More thoughtful public sector suppliers have also sought to measure the user 'experience' employing questionnaires based on the SERVQUAL or other such framework. While such models work well in the context of contact with individuals, they are perhaps less valuable in the context of institutional or organizational relationships. Since, as we noted earlier, many public sector services have institutional stakeholders or clients it is clearly important that the quality of service delivered here is similarly measured and appropriate action taken to enhance quality where weaknesses are identified.

The following case study highlights an innovative approach to the measurement of service quality in this context.

CASE STUDY 14.3

Social Housing

The Housing Act (1988) marked a change in direction in central government policy towards the provision of social housing within the UK. Whereas previously local authorities had been expected to provide and manage social housing, this was no longer to be the case. Housing associations became the new providers of this housing and local authorities were now mere enablers of its provision. Local authorities were thus required to work in partnership with housing associations to identify need in their area and to facilitate the housing associations in meeting that need. A body known as the housing corporation was to oversee the whole process of provision and provide capital finance and ongoing monitoring of performance to ensure value for money. In addition to the funding they might receive from the housing corporation, housing associations were also expected to seek private finance to support new social housing provision.

The interaction between these three bodies is depicted in Figure 14.2.

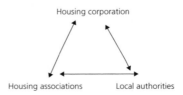

Figure 14.2 Key relationships in the provision of social housing

continues

Many of the measures of service quality alluded to in earlier chapters work best in the context of consumer to organization relationships. They are less well suited to the dyadic relationships represented in the figure (Rosen and Suprenant 1998). This occurs because these measures are highly focused on one point of view—i.e. the consumers'. Since in the context of Figure 14.2, each organization is in a sense a customer of the other, these forms of service quality measurement tend towards the meaningless.

Working with the South-East Region Housing Corporation to help them understand and improve their relationships in the process of social housing Williams et al. (1999) employed what they term a Service Template Process (Staughton and Williams 1994) to investigate the quality of the relationship between all the three parties alluded to in Figure 14.2. The process they developed is outlined in Figure 14.3.

The process begins with a series of meetings with representatives from each party to discuss each of the relationships under analysis. A separate meeting is held to consider each specific relationship (in this case, two for each institution) and each party to the relationship meets separately. As a first step, in the preparation phase of the process the service situation and the meanings of any terms outside the participant's normal experience (e.g. customer, or service) are clarified.

A brainstorming process of the characteristics of each relationship is then undertaken. The goal here is to develop a list of components that is continually refined until the group of participants as a whole are happy that the relationship has been fully and properly characterized and that a shared understanding of the meaning of the language employed has been fostered.

The next task is to plot the delivered service quality against these characteristics. To facilitate this, positive and negative descriptions of each characteristic are developed—e.g honest—misleading. Both the expected and delivered service quality is then plotted for each descriptor using a scoring system

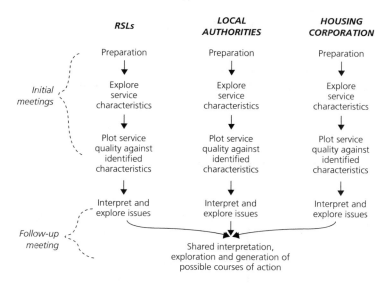

Figure 14.3 Service template process

Source: Williams et al. 1999. Reproduced with kind permission.

continues

CASE STUDY 14.3 continued

from 1–10 where 10 is regarded as excellent. Finally, each group must consider the importance they place on each aspect of the service by allocating 100 points between each of their dimensions.

An example of the resultant template is reported in Figure 14.4.

The next step of the process is a follow-up meeting to discuss and if necessary refine the template. Each group undertakes this separately. On the conclusion of this refinement each group meets with the other party to the relationship and discusses with them the differences and similarities between their two templates. This is undertaken in the spirit of enquiry rather than in an attempt to justify a particular template or view.

The outcomes from such a process can be reflected upon by both parties to the relationship and, where appropriate, corrective actions taken to improve facets of the service that are presently regarded as underperforming. This will be the case where this has occurred on dimensions of the relationship that are considered important by one or more parties.

Characteristic	Wt	+ve Extreme	10	9	8	7	6	5	4	3	2	1	–ve Extreme
Deliverability of programme	25	Effective	e	ep	p								Inadequate
Product (House, space, rent)	20	Superior	e		p								Interior
Strategy recognition by RSLs	15	Fulfilled		ep									Ignored
Partnerships–nature	15	Harmonious	e		p								Strained
Management–quality (to tenants)	15	Proactive	e			p							Infective
Communication–scope	10	All-embracing		e	p								Lacking
LA input to programme		Minimal		e		p							Intensive
Communication–nature		Open		e	p								Secretive
Strategy: purpose (LA)		Clear		ep	p								Confused
Common purpose		In empathy with		e	p								Disparate

Key: expectations e ep p perceptions

Figure 14.4 Specimen service template

Source: Williams et al. (1999). Reproduced by kind permission.

New Public Sector Management

Many governments in the 1970s and 1980s became committed to reducing the proportion of national income devoted to public expenditure and the range of functions undertaken by government. A neo-liberal agenda challenged the collectivist provision of social welfare by government arguing that it promoted a culture of dependency with morally damaging impacts upon citizens who demanded ever increasing services and bureaucrats who built ever larger empires to provide them (Humphrey et al. 1993). Competition, or the inculcation of market mechanisms, it was argued, was superior to monopoly situations which were typified by over-supply and excessive costs.

It is against this backdrop that what has become known as New Public Sector Management (NPSM) developed. NPSM is a generic label for a group of policy and administrative solutions characterized by competition, disaggregation, and incentivation. Instead of the State providing the full range of services it had previously identified as desirable for the welfare of society, many services are now put out to private tender and as a consequence pseudo-markets have developed. In effect, state policy-making and direction have been gradually divorced from service delivery.

Under NPSM, 'the state . . . becomes an enabling organization, responsible for ensuring that public services are delivered, rather than producing them directly itself. The delivery functions are entrusted to a variety of other agencies trading for profit or acting as voluntary bodies within a managed market, in which the concept of contract plays a key role' Rowley (1998: 1).

Managers have therefore been transformed from administrators and custodians of resources to accountable managers with greater delegated authority (Parker and Gould 1999). This notion of accountability is significant since managers are increasingly held accountable to the public. The notion of delegated authority is also important because it has afforded managers increasing opportunities to match service provision with the needs of 'customers' in their area. This new-found freedom and flexibility has required public sector managers to learn and practice a range of new marketing skills.

Compulsory Competitive Tendering

A key facet of the new public sector management has been the introduction of contracts for services previously delivered by government. Since 1979, for example, the Ministry of Defence has contracted out support and ancillary services that had traditionally been conducted in house (Uttley 1993). Services such as hospital, catering, domestic services, and laundry were all put out to Compulsory Competitive Tendering (CCT), where a range of private sector organizations, or an existing in-house team, could bid for the right to take over service provision.

Since 1979, successive central government legislation has pushed local government towards placing an ever-greater percentage of its delivery through CCT. In the 1980s local authority sports centres and leisure facilities, catering, street cleaning, and refuse services were all subjected to CCT. More recently CCT has been extended to include white-collar services, but unlike the manual services listed previously, it was determined that white-collar services should be only partially subjected to this process. This measure was designed to take into account the amount of work that could legitimately be 'parcelled up' for tender and to allow for adequate client-side management. It was also deemed necessary to preserve in the public sector those aspects of infrastructure that provided for core democratic processes (Walsh 1995). At the time of writing, the percentage of each local authority service that may be contracted is shown in Table 14.2.

The introduction of CCT has had a number of marketing implications. First, government departments must ensure that appropriate suppliers are identified and encouraged

Table 14.2 Percentage of services subjected to CCT

Service	%
Legal services	45
Financial services	35
Personnel services	35
Construction and property services	65
Information technology services	70
Housing management	95

to bid for the services being tendered. The pseudo-market created by the bidding process must then be managed and the full implications of the approach outlined in each bid explored for the users of the service in question; only then can decisions in respect of the best supplier be taken. Clearly, a range of the skills we have outlined in previous chapters will have a relevance here. There will also be a need for the government department to develop internal marketing ideas and concepts to manage the relationships it develops with each selected supplier. It must not be forgotten that from the public's perspective it will still be the government department that is providing the service. The fact that they have contracted out provision to a third party is, from the public's standpoint, an irrelevance. They are still responsible for the service and the perception of the department by the public will be determined in no small measure by the way in which the contractor fulfils their role. As a consequence internal marketing tools are essential to ensure that the relationship with the supplier works well and that the government department is represented on the ground, by this organization, in the way it would wish.

Accountability

As we noted above, NPSM has provided an impetus to greater accountability on the part of public sector managers (Pendlebury et al. 1994). At the senior management level, Sinclair (1995) has identified five forms of accountability operating.

1. *Political*. Senior public sector managers are primarily accountable to government ministers.
2. *Public*. Managers are increasingly accountable to the public, lobby groups, community groups, and individuals.
3. *Managerial (financial)*. Managers must now show that not only are their processes working as they should, but that the inputs and outputs to their departments are appropriate and represent value for money.
4. *Professional*. Many managers are members of a professional association to which they will also be accountable for their actions.

5. *Personal*. Managers will also wish to retain fidelity to internalized moral and ethical values. The power of this personal accountability should not be underestimated, as a number of high-profile incidents where senior civil servants have acted as 'whistle blowers' will attest.

The ways in which senior public sector managers are in some sense accountable gives rise to a number of potential tensions. Often the needs of these diverse groups are conflicting, or the accountability in question takes a variety of different and not necessarily complementary forms. Perhaps the most notable of these potential conflicts arises in practice between the needs of ministers on the one hand and the public on the other. As Plowden (1994: 308) notes: 'Telling managers that they must pay attention to the views of their customers does not absolve them from responding to politicians. It does not simplify their task. If anything, it complicates it, because they now have to take account both of the modified points of view that filter through the political process and of the direct undiluted force of service users'.

Sadly, marketing cannot claim as a discipline to simplify this process, but again, many of the ideas expressed in previous chapters and in particular the notion of a customer orientation and the tools and techniques of marketing research can at least aid managers to develop a clear picture of the needs of both groups. While achieving a balance in terms of the actions taken will still not be easy, it will be facilitated by the use of the best available data.

Conclusions

Throughout this chapter we have examined the marketing implications of a number of changes in government policy and approach. No chapter on public sector marketing would be complete, however, without a brief summary of those facets of marketing that *are* being adopted and *have* met with success.

Buurma (2001) argues that public sector organizations employ four categories of marketing activity:

1. *Marketization*. Marketing is employed to expose services to competitive forces with the policy objectives of bringing down the price level of a given service while matching delivered quality with customer expectations.

2. *Promoting self-interest*. Many government departments employ marketing to secure their future, by seeking support from society for their activities (see, for example Burton 1999).

3. *Promoting an area of responsibility*. Many public sector marketers have responsibility for promoting specific services. Kriekaard (1994) cites the now common practice of city marketing, where particular places are marketed to both potential tourists and businesses that might be persuaded to relocate to the area.

4. *Marketing to achieve political or social objectives*. Public sector marketers may also employ marketing to achieve specific political or social objectives such as a reduction

in drink driving, smoking, obesity, or disease. They may also promote healthy living, exercise, vaccination, and a range of other actions that are deemed socially desirable.

A number of these forms of public sector marketing and their interaction are well illustrated by the following case study.

CASE STUDY 14.4

Électricité de France (EDF)

For a number of years EDF has conducted surveys of its residential customers facing payment difficulties. The aim has been to develop a deeper and fuller understanding of how EDF might work with these customers to avoid them entering into payment difficulties. An analysis of their data conducted by Wodon (2000) suggested four segments of customers who typically faced difficulties.

(1) *Default*. These are low income households who normally succeed in paying their energy bills. Despite their limited financial resources they demonstrate a remarkable capacity to control their budget. This does not mean that they are shielded from disconnection or that they should not be helped even without the threat of disconnection. Helping these households would lighten the toll of their energy bills. For example, advantageous social tariffs would ease the strain on their lives. In an emergency situation when these households suffer larger than usual payment difficulties, debt forgiveness is welcome.

(2) *Extreme poverty*. These households suffer from an accumulation of handicaps. Besides a lack of income they may also lack a decent education or training. They may be poor in health and unemployed (often for a long while). They may have lost hope of finding declared (formal) employment and survive thanks to social security allowances and casual (informal) work. Due to their extreme level of poverty, their inability to pay their energy bills is chronic. To help these households, it is necessary not only to provide short-term access to energy (for example, by providing service limiters instead of disconnecting) but also to invest in their social and human capital so that they may emerge from their state of deprivation in the long run.

(3) *Miscalculation*. These are households who, despite medium or high incomes, are unable to pay their bills as a result of a temporary debt problem due to negligence, an accident, or simply miscalculation. Given the temporary nature of the problem, these households are the easiest to assist. A payment plan generally resolves the problem, avoiding the need to modify the base tariff or to write off part of the debt.

(4) *Debt overload*. These are households who, despite medium to high incomes, suffer acute difficulties in paying their bills due to the burden of paying interest and capital on a large amount of loans taken out for other goods. Civil bankruptcy, which is similar to reorganization plans used by companies, may prove necessary in order to help these households get back on their feet. Energy distributors would be on equal terms with other creditors which, according to each case, would allow them to find more or less advantageous terms (Wodon 2000: 230).

In employing marketing tools to deal with the sensitive issue of disconnection, EDF recognizes that it is politically unacceptable for it to be seen as disconnecting substantial numbers of customers without first giving them every opportunity to resolve their problems. Failure to deal with this adequately would likely result in increased political interference in the industry on the part of central government,

continues

a hostile consumer backlash, and/or a knowledge on the part of managers that they were contributing to France's social problems.

EDF has thus expended much effort in modelling consumer behaviour and attempting to identify those individuals likely to default on payment early in that process. They then take steps to manage the difficulty by offering advice on usage and appropriate adjustments to tariffs. EDF has committed itself to a personalized dialogue with each customer in difficulties, with disconnection viewed only as the last resort.

The introduction of the service limiter described above has also proved important. It has the obvious impact of forcing individuals to make sensible use of their electricity resource and to, in effect, learn to live within their means. Since the use of a limiter could hardly be viewed as a desirable development, the threat of its imposition can also persuade those who do have the ability to pay to do so, and avoid compulsory changes in their consumption.

In addition to the measures that can be taken with individual customers EDF has also attempted to fight poverty in partnership with social welfare agencies. Each local EDF service centre has a 'solidarity officer' who liases with public and private partners. It also provides finance to local conventions on poverty that allocate financial assistance to households in need.

Of the concepts and tools discussed in this text, the notion of a customer orientation has a clear relevance to public services (see, for example, Rosenthal 1995; Chapman and Cowdell 1998). Marketing research techniques have also been used to good effect in assessing need (Severijnen and Braak 1992) and internal marketing can be used to foster and develop relationships with 'external' suppliers now providing government services (Ewing and Caruana 1999).

Of the specific marketing tools that may be adopted Buurma (2001) suggests that the following ideas offer the most relevance to the public sector context.

- Marketing can be employed to develop a clear differentiation of stakeholders and their interests.
- The marketing mix can be employed to match and manage quality levels (see also Foxall 1988).
- Marketing can identify need and demand patterns as the basis for a matching process.
- Market segmentation can be used to bundle and anticipate user/customer needs.
- Relationship marketing can be fostered with particular groups of users/customers.
- The principles of marketing organization and strategic marketing planning also apply in the context of public sector service provision, although the legitimate boundaries of marketing alluded to earlier must be considered here in determining what is truly appropriate.

As we discussed earlier, NPSM has introduced a variety of changes into the way that public sector organizations are managed. In particular, it has revolutionized the approach to service provision and the manner in which service users are now viewed by the organizations that support them. It is clear from the above that marketing can and does have much to offer the public sector, and looks set to play an increasing role in the future.

▓ DISCUSSION QUESTIONS

1. To what extent can marketing be applied to all public sector service provision? Are there specific services where marketing would appear to have no relevance? Justify your answer by reference to the frameworks presented in this chapter.

2. What is New Public Sector Management? What role has this played in the development of marketing in the public sector? Why?

3. As a senior manager in a National Health Service hospital, explain to your board how the quality of service your organization provides to both patients and their GPs might be assessed.

4. Look back to the Hull School Dinner Case. How might marketing tools have been employed to ensure a higher rate of take-up of the new school dinner menus?

5. Plowden (1994) argues that if managers of public sector services simply pursue the best interests of their own organization in a marketized environment, they do not automatically serve the public welfare or the community's best interests. Where do you stand on this issue? How might you counter this argument?

▓ REFERENCES

Bauer, R.A. (1966) (ed.) *Social Indicators*, Cambridge, MIT Press.

Buchanan, W.W., Self, D.R. and Ingram, J.J. (1987) 'Non-Profit Services: Adoption or Adaptation of Marketing', *Journal of Professional Services Marketing*, Vol. 2, No. 4, 83–95.

Buurma, H. (2001) 'Public Policy Marketing: Marketing Exchange in the Public Sector', *European Journal of Marketing*, Vol. 35, No. (11/12), 1287–1300.

Burton, S. (1999) 'Marketing for Public Organizations: New Ways, New Methods', *Public Management*, Vol. 1, No. 3, 373–85.

Chapman, D. and Cowdell, T. (1998) *New Public Sector Marketing*, Financial Times/Pitman, London.

Ewing, M.T. and Caruana, A. (1999) 'An Internal Marketing Approach to Public Sector Management: The Marketing and Human Resources Interface', *International Journal of Public Sector Management*, Vol. 12, No. 1, 17–26.

Folz, D.H. (1999) 'Municipal Recycling Performance: A Public Sector Environmental Success Story', *Public Administration Review*, Vol. 59, No. 4, 336–45.

Foxall, G.R. (1988) 'Marketings Domain', *European Journal of Marketing*, Vol. 23, No. 8, 7–22.

Goldstein, N. (1997) 'Biocycle Nationwide Survey: The State of Garbage', *Biocycle*, April, 60–7.

Graham, P. (1994) 'Marketing in the Public Sector: Inappropriate or Merely Difficult?' *Journal of Marketing Management*, Vol. 10, 361–75.

Humphrey, C., Miller, P. and Scapens, R. (1993) 'Accountability and Accountable Management in the UK Public Sector', *Accounting Auditing and Accountability Journal*, Vol. 6, No. 3, 7–29.

Keaney, M. (1999) 'Are Patients Really Consumers?' *International Journal of Social Economics*, Vol. 26, No. 5, 695–706.

Koster, J.M.D. (1991) *Grondslagen van de Marketingwetenschap*, dissertation, Erasmus University, Rotterdam.

Kriekaard, J.A. (1994) *Het Domein Van City Marketing: Een Bijdrage Aan Theorieontwikkeling*, Report No. R 9407/M, Rotterdam Institut voor Bedrijfseconomische Studies, Erasmus University, Rotterdam.

Laing, A. (2003) 'Marketing in the Public Sector: Towards A Typology of Public Services', *Marketing Theory*, Vol. 3, No. 4, 427–45.

Laing, A. and Hogg, G. (2002) 'Political Exhortation, Patient Expectation and Professional Execution: Perspectives on the Consumerization of Health Care', *British Journal of Management*, Vol. 13, No. 2, 173–88.

Laing, A. and McKee. J (2001) 'Willing Volunteers or Unwilling Conscripts? Professionals and Marketing Service Organizations', *Journal of Marketing Management*, Vol. 17, No. (5–6), 556–76.

Lane, J.E. (1995) *The Public Sector: Concepts, Models and Approaches*, London, Sage.

Pandya, A. and Dholakia, A. (1992) 'An Institutional Theory of Exchange in Marketing', *European Journal of Marketing*, Vol. 26, No. 12, 9–41.

Parker, L. and Gould, G. (1999) 'Changing Public Sector Accountability: Critiquing New Directions', *Accounting Forum*, Vol. 23, No. 2, 109–35.

Pendlebury, B., Jones, R. and Karbhari, Y. (1994) 'Developments in the Accountability and Financial Reporting Practices of Executive Agencies', *Financial Accountability and Management*, Vol. 10, No. 1, 33–46.

Plowden, W. (1994) 'Public Interests the Public Services Serve, Efficiency and Other Values', *Australian Journal of Public Administration*, Vol. 53, No. 3, 304–12.

Rosen, D.E. and Suprenant, C. (1998) 'Evaluating Relationships: Are Satisfaction and Quality Enough?' *International Journal of Service Industry Management*, Vol. 9, No. 2, 103–25.

Rosenthal, U. (1995) 'Publiek Partnerschap', *Bestuurskunde*, Vol. 4, No. 3, 15–21.

Rowley, J. (1998) 'Quality Measurement in the Public Sector: Some Perspectives From The Service Quality Literature', *Total Quality Management*, Vol. 9, No. (2/3), 321–34.

Severijnen, P.C.A. and Braak, H.J.M. (1992) 'Marktonderzoek Bij Beleidsvoorbereiding En Beleidsbepaling', *Management in Overheidsorganisaties*, 22 Aug, A412–51.

Sinclair, A. (1995) 'The Chameleon of Accountability: Forms and Discourses', *Accounting Organizations and Society*, Vol. 20, No. (2/3), 219–37.

Staughton, R.V.W. and Williams, C.S. (1994) 'Towards a Simple Visual Representation of fit in Service Organizations: The Contribution of the Service Template', *International Journal of Operations and Production Management*, Vol. 14, No. 5, 76–85.

Thomson, P. (1992) 'Public Sector Management in a Period of Radical Change, 1979–1992', *Public Money and Management*, Summer, 33–41.

Uttley, M. (1993) 'Citizens and Consumers: Marketing and Public Sector Management', *Public Money and Management*, Summer, 9–15.

van der Hart H.W.C. (1991) 'Government Organizations and their Customers in the Netherlands: Strategy, Tactics and Operations', *European Journal of Marketing*, Vol. 24, No. 7, 31–42.

Walsh, K. (1994) 'Marketing and Public Sector Management', *European Journal of Marketing*, Vol. 28, No. 3, 63–71.

Walsh, K. (1995) 'Competition for White Collar Services in Local Government', *Public Money and Management*, April–June, 11–18.

Williams, C.S., Saunders, M.N.K. and Staughton, R.V.W. (1999) 'Understanding Service Quality in the new Public Sector: An Exploration of Relationships in the Process of Funding Social Housing', *International Journal of Public Sector Management*, Vol. 12, No. 4, 366–79.

Wodon, Q.T. (2000) 'Public Utilities and Low Income Customers: A Marketing Approach', *International Journal of Public Sector Management*, Vol. 13, No. 3, 222–40.

INDEX

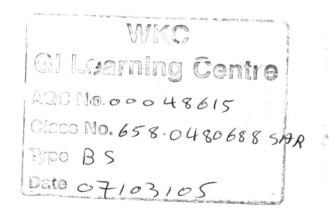